Lady Caroline Lamb

A Biography

By Paul Douglass

palgrave
macmillan

Genealogy

Broken lines indicate extramarital affairs.

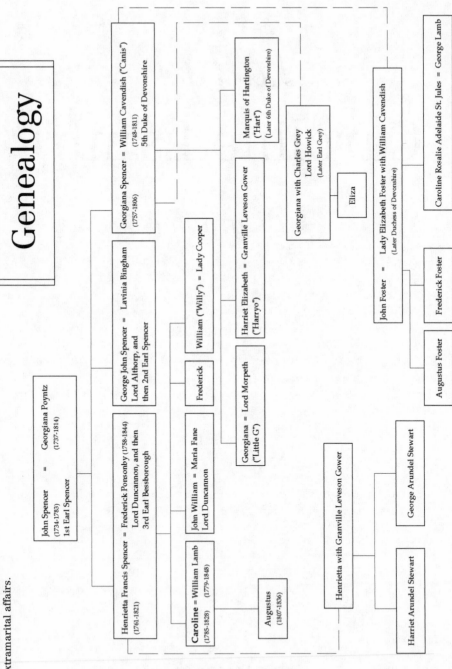

For Charlene

LADY CAROLINE LAMB: A BIOGRAPHY
Copyright © Paul Douglass, 2004.

First published 2004 by
PALGRAVE MACMILLAN™
175 Fifth Avenue, New York, N.Y. 10010 and
Houndmills, Basingstoke, Hampshire, England RG21 6XS.
Companies and representatives throughout the world.

PALGRAVE MACMILLAN IS THE GLOBAL ACADEMIC IMPRINT OF THE
PALGRAVE MACMILLAN
division of St. Martin's Press, LLC and of Palgrave Macmillan Ltd. Mac-
millan® is a registered trademark in the United States, United Kingdom and
other countries. Palgrave is a registered trademark in the European Union
and other countries.

ISBN 1-4039-6605-2 hardback

Library of Congress Cataloging-in-Publication Data
Douglass, Paul, 1951-
    Lady Caroline Lamb / Paul Douglass.
        p. cm.
    Includes bibliographical references and index.
    ISBN 1-4039-6605-2
    1. Lamb, Caroline, Lady, 1785-1828. 2. Novelists, English--19th century-
-Biography. 3. Politicians' spouses--Great Britain--Biography. 4. Women
and literature--England--History--19th century. 5. Byron, George Gordon
Byron, baron, 1788-1824--Relations with women. 6. Melbourne, William
Lamb, Viscount, 1779-1848--Marriage. I. Title.

PR4859.L9D68 2004
823'.7--dc22
[B]
2004045620

A catalogue record for this book is available from the British Library.

Design by planettheo.com

9 8 7 6 5 4 3 2

Printed in the United States of America

Contents

List of Illustrations

Much madness is divinest sense
To a discerning eye;
Much sense the starkest madness.
'Tis the majority
In this, as all, prevails.
Assent, and you are sane;
Demur,—you're straightway dangerous
And handled with a chain.

—Emily Dickinson

Acknowledgements

T he life of Lady Caroline Lamb has been documented by so many biographers, memoirists, and critics that simply reading and evaluating partial accounts and sifting through letters and documents relating to her marriage and extended family has been an immense task. I could never have done it alone.

Margot Strickland generously gave me access to her research, including microfilms she had gathered; she corresponded with me over a period of several years, and I am deeply grateful. John Clubbe also encouraged me and shared his research. Frederick Burwick's *Poetic Madness and the Romantic Imagination* influenced my approach to my subject, and more important, his brilliant mind and generous heart have challenged and sustained me throughout our long friendship. Peter Cochran corresponded with me and corrected errors in the manuscript with a wit that rivals those of Lady Caroline's extremely witty contemporaries. Eve Culver, a graduate assistant at San Jose State University, spent many hours combing libraries and transcribing letters for me. Her sharp eye and quick understanding were invaluable. Those who have read Peter Graham's *Don Juan and Regency England* will recognize that the fourth chapter of that book eloquently states main themes of my own work. I am indebted to him and to Graham Pont, who pointed out to me that Isaac Nathan was a major character in the drama of Lady Caroline's life. Similarly, I am grateful to Frances Wilson, who edited the Everyman reissue of Lady Caroline's *Glenarvon* and defended Lady Caroline against moralizers and melodramatists in her *Byromania,* and to Jonathan Gross for his fine edition of Lady Melbourne's letters.

Without doubt the turning point in this project came on a hot August night in 2001 in Battery Park when Marilyn Gaull of NYU told me she believed in my book and would bring it to Palgrave and see it through the press. Thank you Marilyn, for all your advice and hard work to make this book as good as it could be.

My colleagues at San Jose State University, Marianina Olcott and Dominique Van Hoof, read Greek and French for me and saved me from many mistakes. As I struggled to finish this book while chairing the English Department of a large state university, my friend, coworker, and fellow writer Mark Bussmann, helped me find time to write and gave me invaluable feedback.

I must here gratefully acknowledge the generosity of Gerald Burdon in permitting me to reproduce the two remarkable watercolors that Lady Caroline did in 1812 for Byron's *Childe Harold's Pilgrimage.* Acknowledgements for permissions to reprint other pictures may be found in the List of Illustrations.

The staffs of the Hertfordshire Records Office, the British Library, the Victoria and Albert Museum, and the Bodleian Library at the University of Oxford were extremely helpful. Diane Naylor, of the Devonshire Manuscripts in the Chatsworth Archive, was marvelously kind and efficient. How sweet were the hours spent working in these facilities! Sweetest of all, though, was time spent in the John Murray Archive receiving Virginia Murray's indispensible help. Quotations from manuscript sources are by permission of Hertfordshire Archives and Local Studies; the Bodleian Library; the Devonshire Manuscripts Archive in Chatsworth (United Kingdom); the Trustees of the Victoria & Albert Museum; the John Murray Archive; the Carl Pforzheimer Collection of Shelley and His Circle of the New York Public Library (Astor, Lenox and Tilden Foundations); the James Marshall and Marie-Louise Osborn Collection, Beinecke Rare Book and Manuscript Library, Yale University; the Houghton Library, Harvard University; and the Clifton Waller Barrett Library, Special Collections, University of Virginia Library. Extracts from the Lovelace/Byron Papers are reproduced by permission of Pollinger Limited and the Lovelace Papers on deposit in the Bodleian Library.

My partner in marriage, Charlene Keller Douglass, spent many hours finding materials that enriched my work. When the chance came for us to go to England together, she accompanied me and did much research. She helped me to edit the final manuscript's footnotes. I cannot thank her enough.

Our children, Jeremy and Regan, were not yet in college when I started writing. Now, they have both graduated. I am thankful that my family understood my need to finish this task, which so long preoccupied me. I am further blessed in that they seem to appreciate my work, just as I love and appreciate them without end.

Preface

In 1785, Caroline Ponsonby—the future Lady Caroline Lamb—was born into a distinguished family. Her mother, Lady Bessborough, was one of the two or three most politically influential women of the era. Caroline's Aunt Georgiana was the accomplished Duchess of Devonshire. Marie Antoinette was a family friend. Edward Gibbon, author of *The Decline and Fall of the Roman Empire,* once bounced six-year-old Caroline on his knee in Lausanne. She had already gained a reputation as a brat, and she infuriated her aunt by telling Gibbon that his face was so ugly it had frightened her puppy. She became such a difficult teenager that her mother considered sending her away to a caretaker in the country.

Lady Caroline lived through the Napoleonic wars and the "Regency," named for the period during which the Prince of Wales exercised the King's powers. She knew the Prince—the family called him "Prinny"—and his wife, whose liberal politics Lady Caroline supported. Lady Caroline's social, political, and literary activities brought her the acquaintance of such notables of the era as Charles James Fox, Richard Brinsley Sheridan, the social philosopher and novelist William Godwin, and also literary figures like Walter Scott, William Blake, Thomas Moore, Samuel Rogers, Ugo Foscolo, Letitia Elizabeth Landon, Edward Bulwer-Lytton, and Samuel Taylor Coleridge. Indeed she knew most of the politicians, powerbrokers, and literati of the day, and they knew her as the petite redhead described by Byron as "the cleverest most agreeable, absurd, amiable, perplexing, dangerous fascinating little being that lives now or ought to have lived 2000 years ago."[1] As it turned out, Lady Caroline played a role in changing the possibilities for women of the nineteenth century. Her role would, however, not be an enviable one, for she sought her own independence, and so was reviled for breaking the rules by which women generally exercised power and influence.

When Lady Caroline married William Lamb in 1805, they expected he would soon inherit a substantial estate from his aging father, Lord Melbourne, and that they would emerge on the stage of English society as ranking members of the elite. When Caroline died in 1828, however, William had still not received his father's title or his riches, because his father had simply outlived her. Throughout her life Caroline lived in a wealthy world without really possessing any of it herself. Her father and mother had financial troubles, and her husband received a relatively small allowance. Caroline never became the mistress of a household or the arbiter of the social scene in the way of her Aunt Georgiana or mother-in-law Lady Melbourne. Slowly, painfully, she fell from great expectations to a crippled marriage and collapsing health. A frequently cited cause of that fall has been William's overindulgence of his wife, who is generally described as "spoilt" and "vain," and "at heart a frustrated actor with a weakness for melodrama."[2] William, however, remained devoted to Caroline despite her tantrums and extramarital affairs, and Caroline loved William. Their partnership endured—despite the very public liaison she had with Lord Byron in the spring and summer of 1812, and despite his own family's campaign to separate them—until she drew her last breath.

When Byron broke off the affair, Caroline suffered a breakdown. The psychiatry of the time called it "erotomania"—dementia caused by obsession for a man. It was a malady she shared with hundreds of other Byron fans, except that she actually became Byron's lover during the first great flush of his success. The experience made it somehow impossible for her to lead a normal life. Gossip soon made the affair and its aftermath into a sexual melodrama, and even sympathetic portrayals of Lady Caroline convey the image of an adulteress whose obsession with Byron drove him wild and her crazy. While Caroline was certainly Byron's lover in the flesh, her pursuit of him was literary as much as libidinous.

It was not a one-sided or narrow liaison, for she had talent and an education augmented by the study of Greek and Latin. Caroline was Byron's equal in verbal wit at the time they met, when she was twenty-six and he had just turned twenty-four. They shared a love for dogs, horses, and music. Byron could sing, and Caroline played the harp and harpsichord and wrote songs. She made drawings and watercolors, and canvassed for elections. Byron also admired her for raising Augustus, her mentally retarded, epileptic son, at home instead of placing him with caretakers.

By 1812, when she met Byron, Lady Caroline had developed a contempt for the low morals and superficiality of Whig culture. Byron shared her contempt and admired her outrageousness. At first. But once he saw that she stood ready for any consequence—even exile from England—he pulled back, unprepared to burn his bridges. Wounded, Caroline wanted him to admit that he had been deeply affected by their relationship. To his annoyance, he found it impossible to drop her cold. He turned distant. She grew hysterical. She became for him a ghost whose skeletal features preyed on his imagination, for she simply did not know how to crawl away and suffer silently as married women did when their lovers jilted them.

Most biographers have shared Byron's frustration at Lady Caroline's failure to conform to the feminine role of her era. They have not hesitated to prescribe a "sharp slap judiciously administered,"[3] or even an out-and-out beating.[4] Criticism, too, has administered body blows to the modest corpus of her literary work, starting with the publication of *Glenarvon,* her first novel, in 1816. She found herself wondering why "everybody wishes to run down and suppress the vital spark of genius I have, and in truth, it is but small (about what one sees a maid gets by excessive beating on a tinder-box). I am not vain, believe me, nor selfish, nor in love with my authorship; but I am independent, as far as a mite and bit of dust can be."[5] The overreaction of criticism to Caroline's literary offenses seems itself mildly hysterical, like her biographers' obsession with her outrageous entrances, temper tantrums and crockery-smashing. Those who have judged her novels and poetry have treated them as an extension of her personality: at best the production of a neurotic mind, and at worst a devious attempt to hurt Byron. This does no justice to her as a writer or human being.

That is not to deny that the collapse Lady Caroline suffered when Byron ended their affair was serious. In certain periods Caroline was threatened with a straitjacket by two stout nurses she called "The Women." After Byron left England, however, her life did not become a continuous round of whining and histrionics. She published three novels, two accomplished parodies of Byron's poetry, several poems in literary journals, and a number of songs—besides having worked up three other novel manuscripts and a book on "domestic economy" that she printed in England and sought to publish in Ireland. This is not to say she did not fret. She did—and she overdramatized. But she also described herself and her world in memorable language. Her fiction shows a full awareness of her political and cultural milieu.

With the completion of this volume, I have given Lady Caroline what I think she most desired from the time she was a little girl: undivided attention. She also receives herewith my sympathy, my laughter and astonishment, my pity, and, in the end, my admiration—though she long ago passed beyond anyone's power to reassure.

A Child of the Mist

1785–1791

$\mathcal{L}$ ady Caroline Lamb was born Caroline Ponsonby on a cold and foggy Sunday, the thirteenth of November, 1785. Her mother Harriet's labor had been blessedly free of complications, and her grandmother Lady Spencer wrote that the baby was "a lovely little girl—who seems very lively & in perfect health."[1] "Lively" would turn out to be quite an understatement. Caroline would grow up to become a "little volcano," as Byron put it,[2] whose antics, affairs, and eccentric novels astonished, enraged, and finally exhausted her family and friends. This little girl, who rested comfortably on her mother's breast, had been blessed with charisma, intelligence, and a sharp wit, but also an unrelenting character that would lead her incessantly into harm's way.

Caroline's grandmother stayed with her daughter and the newborn, and she was truly needed, for on the third day Caroline would neither sleep nor eat until Lady Spencer took her into her own bed and quieted her.[3] After ten days, when she was satisfied that mother and child were "vastly well," Lady Spencer departed for Holywell House near St. Albans, Hertfordshire, her home. She was never long apart from her grandchildren, however. She visited Caroline's older brothers John and Frederick often, and when Caroline was just six months old, her grandmother nursed her through her first cold at Holywell House. Lady Spencer's sentiments were clear: "I shall be delighted to be entrusted with Caroline."[4]

Caroline acquired a love of the Bible from her grandmother, whom she soon enshrined as a demigoddess among whispering divinities. Caroline wrote this poem for her:

> May no sad dreams disturb thy rest,
> No anxious care thy peace molest,
> But angels' whisper'd blessings shed,
> For tho' so glorious high their state,
> Proud they will be to guard that head
> Where all is noble, good & great.[5]

Indeed Lady Spencer sometimes exhibited the arrogance of a goddess. She insisted that Harriet should trim her daughter's hair *daily,* "not so much to shorten as to thin it."[6]

At her mother's and grandmother's hands, Caroline received a very good early education. Harriet was a natural teacher, and Lady Spencer, though not intuitive, was a conscientious instructor. The two women's efforts were not wasted on the precociously literate and musical Caroline, who at age four and a half stood only three feet three inches tall.[7] Her hair was reddish-blond. She had delicate features, excellent teeth, and freckles across her cheeks and nose. She could draw a map of England freehand and had begun to read. At five she spoke some French and Italian, and at six she began to study music. At six and a half Caroline could speak French "very tolerably" (according to her father) and play a tune on the harpsichord. By the time she was seven she had begun to read French and Italian.[8] She was lithe, well-coordinated, and even athletic. Yet, despite her accomplishments, Caroline seemed infantile and elfin. She lisped, and her pronunciation was influenced by the private dialect of her Aunt Georgiana's household—a nasal drawl seasoned with baby talk. If she had been born two centuries later, she would have been sent to speech therapy.

Caroline received formal instruction from tutors, including her governess Selina Trimmer, the daughter of Sarah Trimmer, an author of textbooks and moral tales for youth. Selina brought an amiable touch to her relations with John, Frederick, and Caroline Ponsonby, though she exhibited a plain and cowed personality and rarely won a fight with a determined child.[9] Caroline's formal schooling was inconsistent mainly because she and her brothers were constantly on the move. Mixed together with their cousins and with children who had been adopted into the household—sometimes out of charity, sometimes to cover up the adulterous affairs of relatives—Caroline, John, Frederick, and their new little brother Willy (Caroline's favorite) trailed after their mother and their Aunt Georgiana, the Duchess of Devonshire, in an endless round of visiting. They migrated between the principal city residences of the Duncannons and Devonshires, to the Spencer property in Northamptonshire, and to the Devonshire estate at Chatsworth in Derbyshire. They visited Brocket Hall, the country residence of Lord and Lady Melbourne—and of course the homes of friends in Belgium, Italy, France, Switzerland, and Germany. The uncertain parentages of some of the children and the intricacy of the domestic arrangements gave the Duncannon-Devonshire group a famous mystique. As one observer later wrote: "There [were] such countless illegitimates among them, such a tribe of Children of the Mist."[10]

Yet, despite its wide scope and misty boundaries, the world of Caroline's childhood was inhabited by a fairly short list of characters, most of them related by blood. Indeed, it is hard to overstate the closeness of this family. Harriet and her sister Georgiana had married men who were first cousins. In London, Georgiana occupied Devonshire House at the south end of Piccadilly, while Harriet lived nearby in her father-in-law's residence at number 2 Cavendish Square, behind Oxford Street. The Duncannon country villa at Roehampton, called "Manresa," with its grounds sloping down into Richmond Park, stood not far from Chiswick House, another of the London residences of the Duke and Duchess of Devonshire. These opulent estates were the backdrops to Caroline's early years, and it is unsurprising that a child growing up in such settings might become imperious and self-centered.

The level of Caroline's privilege has, however, been exaggerated as the result of stories she herself told. For example, she informed her friend Lady Morgan that from age three to nine she was allowed to run wild. She claimed to remember being served breakfast on silver plate, but that she had to carry her own dishes because the household staff were inattentive. She also said she believed that horses ate beef, that bread and butter grew in loaves and pats, and that everyone in the world was either a duke or a beggar.[11] These fabrications—offered perhaps in a spirit of whimsy, or even to bait her listener—have acquired a life of their own.[12] In truth, the children were not permitted absolute license. They were disciplined—sometimes severely, if the tutors had their way. Despite her privilege, Caroline developed a typical child's hatred of injustice to others. She treated laborers with respect and loved animals, especially dogs and horses, whom she viewed as fellow humans.

Above all, Caroline adored and admired her mother, and it is easy to understand why. Among the politically liberal Whig women of the era, Harriet was famed for her beauty and political savvy. She had a soft, generous, and loving personality. Caroline's father, Frederick Ponsonby, was more distant, but he too formed a strong bond with his daughter, so that later in life she possessed (as her brothers recognized) a unique ability to comfort and support him. Frederick held the title of Viscount Duncannon, which indicated his expectation of inheriting the estate of his father, the second Earl Bessborough. The Bessborough estates were already mortgaged, but this had not inhibited the lifestyle of other aristocrats. That lifestyle had its pitfalls, of course. Frederick had a temper which Harriet provoked with frequent, flagrant flirtations, particularly with Richard Brinsley Sheridan, the playwright and politician.

Naturally, Caroline found her Aunt Georgiana, the Duchess of Devonshire, an imposing figure, for she possessed stunning looks, a vivacious personality, and an astuteness that riveted the attention of male and female admirers. Georgiana had married the wealthiest aristocrat of the realm, William Cavendish, 5th Duke of Devonshire, who was nicknamed "Canis," perhaps because of his doglike personality. When she was old enough, Caroline observed her mother and aunt's parties, which they attended in fancy dresses with circumferences exceeding thirty feet and powdered hair trained to a height of twenty inches—to which Georgiana added curling ostrich plumes. Georgiana and Harriet sat for most of the significant portrait artists of their era, including Thomas Gainsborough, Joshua Reynolds, Thomas Philips, John Hoppner, and Maria Cosway. They also appeared in the newspapers as subjects of gossip or as caricatures by sketch artists like Thomas Rowlandson.

Behind these powerful women stood Caroline's grandmother, a guardian angel who knew well that women must play by different rules.[13] Lady Spencer was a woman of remarkable authority and a fierce leader of her clan. She had high standards, and she applied them in no uncertain terms. Not three weeks after Caroline's birth, she wrote to Harriet, "as soon as you are dressed and disencumbered of your Child you will call for a table—(mind what I say) some fresh ink & a New pen, & then sit down & write *distinctly* as I have done this whole page, making the tops & bottoms of your letters quite even." Promising to be "an incessant plague & torment," Lady Spencer vowed, "if my reproofs keep pace with my affections, I shall be a very troublesome animal." She expected her family to understand that, "the more I scold, the more I love you."[14] She was true to her creed. When Harriet reached forty-five years of age, her mother was still determined to teach her better penmanship. Lady Spencer often complained there were "literally not above four words in five of your whole letter I can make out, & not one of the names or places are legible."[15]

In this, Lady Spencer was the polar opposite of her daughters, for they saw writing as self-expression, not scribe-work. Georgiana wrote these verses for Caroline one Christmas:

To Lady Caroline Ponsonby With a New Year's gift of a pencil:

Fairy, sprite, whatever thou art
Magic genius waits on thee
And thou claimst each willing heart
Whilst thy airy form we see

Take the gift, the early year
Shall for thee in Splendor shine.
Genius gives it. Do not fear
Boldly mould, invent, design.[16]

Such encouragement made Caroline desire to sketch and write, and to fulfill her image as the vivacious "sprite" of the household. Her family took to calling her, simply, "Caro," as if she were an embodiment of love itself.

Though she hardly believed the world was divided into dukes and beggars, young Caroline must have thought that there was hardly anyone of any significance to whom she was not related. Indeed, she had more family relationships than she could comprehend, for intermarriages had been complicated by extramarital affairs. Many events that conditioned her childhood took place before her birth or when she was too young to know of them.

The most obvious example is the ménage a trois that had begun three years before she was born. Newly separated from her husband, Lady Elizabeth Foster met the Duke and Duchess of Devonshire in Bath, where they had gone to take the cure for his gout and her "infertility." Georgiana was worried that she might not be able to produce an heir.[17] The tale of Lady Elizabeth's unfortunate marriage moved the Duke and Duchess, and her charm and good looks won their hearts. Soon, Georgiana began to call her "sister" and "Bess."[18] She came to live with them and became the Duke's mistress, though also remaining Georgiana's dearest friend. Not long after meeting Bess, Georgiana discovered she was pregnant and delivered a girl, Georgiana, nicknamed "Little G." It was a good sign, but without a male child, Little G would lose the wealth of the Devonshires when her father died, for the riches would follow the lines of male descent to another part of the family.

Soon, Bess and Georgiana *both* became pregnant by the Duke. In August 1785, just two months before Lady Caroline was born, the Duchess of Devonshire presented the Duke with another little girl, whom she named Harriet Elizabeth, in honor of her sister and Bess. Harriet Elizabeth quickly acquired the nickname "Harryo."[19] In the meantime, in a village in Italy, Bess Foster gave birth to a little girl whom she named Caroline Rosalie Adelaide.[20] Thus, Lady Caroline had a doppelgänger, an illegitimate cousin exactly her age also named Caroline (no surname), whose existence would affect her entire life. Lady Caroline's obsession with doubles—so evident in her fiction, in which characters multiply and adopt dual identities—stems from her early awareness of a shadow world.

Harriet Ponsonby must have been considered a doting parent, for she spent more time with her children than was customary. Supportive and loving, she suffered the typical parental terrors of tuberculosis, smallpox, and mad dogs. Yet, while Harriet paid more attention to her children than many women of her station, her children grew up observing a riotous life of drinking, card-playing, balls, plays, and musical concerts. Devonshire House was a breeding-ground for vice, providing ample time and space for adulterous connections and the machinations of corrupt card-dealers.[21] Gambling was as universal an addiction as drinking among the Whig aristocracy, and anyone who expected an inheritance found himself pressed to take ready cash from scheming lenders. Huge legacies were thus squandered before they were ever received. Politician Charles James Fox and his elder brother Stephen once lost £32,000 in three nights (the equivalent today of perhaps five million dollars). Charles lost large sums regularly at Devonshire House parties. On many mornings-after, he kept creditors waiting in a special room called the "Jerusalem Chamber."[22]

While men gambled, drank, and had affairs at Devonshire House, their wives and lovers controlled the scene. Harriet, Georgiana, and Bess formed a bond so tight that Harriet would later say they "made it a rule never to conceal anything great or small from each other that concerned ourselves, and never to impart anything that concerned our respective friends unless by their desire or consent."[23] These women formed a confederacy of feminine freedom—a freedom they vigorously exercised. This sometimes led to trouble. When Caroline was three, Harriet's gambling and her affair with Charles Wyndham, one of the Prince of Wales's friends, made Lord Duncannon so angry that he gave his wife sedatives to control her. The servants noticed his stealth and thought he was trying to poison Harriet. When she suffered a collapse that required the doctor, a chastened Lord Duncannon stopped the drugging, but the incident made even Canis (the Duke) suspicious of his intentions.[24]

Lady Spencer feared that her granddaughter Caroline might inherit Harriet's weakness for gambling. She therefore asserted her influence over her granddaughter from the beginning. She told Harriet, Caroline has "grown very fond of me & is delighted with sleeping in my room." She liked to have Caroline exclusively to herself: "I had rather have her when I am alone than when the other children are with me, if it can be managed."[25] Lady Spencer had been a gambler herself, sometimes playing all night. A widow at forty-six, she had retired to Holywell House and engaged in charitable work, turning a critical eye on the behavior of her daughters.[26] With her piety renewed, her living secure, and her fears stirred, Lady Spencer tried to inculcate in Georgiana and Harriet a patience she had never shown at cards: "Consider how much better it is in general," she wrote Harriet, "that things should not go exactly our own way, but that we should occasionally bend our dispositions to the circumstances around us, & accustom ourselves to make the best of every thing."[27] But though Lady Spencer had renounced the life of gambling and dissolution, her daughters proved intractable. She advised them incessantly to practice restraint, but this did no good. Despite immense wealth, Harriet and Georgiana had constant money worries, for their gambling debts rose into the tens of thousands of pounds. The sisters sometimes left London to avoid creditors.

Occasionally it appeared that Lady Spencer was making headway in her battle to reform her daughters. Harriet toyed with the idea of setting up a school for poor children, and eventually started a hostel for pregnant single girls. But she never seriously tried to exchange the life of cotillions and claret for that of philanthropy and the pew. Nor did Georgiana, who was such an avid gambler that poet and playwright Horace Walpole commented after the birth of Little G: "She will stuff the poor babe in her knotting [knitting] bag when she wants to play *Macao*."[28] Though this jibe seems cruel, it mirrored the worries of Lady Spencer: "What are you about my Dearest Harriet—not playing at Faro or Macao I hope."[29]

Harriet loved politics as much as gambling and drinking, and this affected Caroline's development profoundly. It would make her an activist within the sharply circumscribed realm conceded to female political engagement. Harriet and Georgiana were longtime supporters of Richard Brinsley Sheridan, the Whig orator and dramatist who had achieved success as the author of *School for Scandal* (1777) and *The Critic* (1779). Sheridan's speeches on social democracy attracted large audiences in the public gallery of the House of Commons. But Lady Spencer did not like Sheridan, despite his attempts to placate her.[30] As a former woman of the world, she understood perfectly that he lusted after her daughter, and it galled her to watch Harriet flirt back. The affair had started at least five years before Caroline was born, when Sheridan had caught Harriet alone, grabbed her by the hair, and practically raped her—at least, this was the story told by Harriet herself. It was widely understood as a subterfuge.

In March 1789, when little Caro was just three and a half, a crisis had erupted when Sheridan and Harriet were caught together. "The accusations against me quite bad, told Ca[nis]," she wrote in her diary.[31] She promised not to see Sheridan any more—but she lied. Her diary shows that she saw him on seven subsequent occasions in March and April.[32] Sheridan wrote to her after one of their encounters, mimicking the Devonshire House baby talk: "I must bid oo good Night for by the Light passing to and fro near your room I hope you are going to bed." While Sheridan described Harriet's rest as the "sleep of purity," he could not resist a jealous warning, "Beware!! Milton will tell you that even in Paradise Serpents found their way to the ear of slumbering innocence."[33] In May or June, someone (probably Sheridan's own sister, Betsy) tipped off Lord Duncannon, who began divorce proceedings.[34]

Given the "mist" surrounding the origins of some of Caroline's cousins, one must wonder whether Sheridan might not have been Caroline's father. While the argument for this theory remains weak, it has never been entirely demolished. Harriet's affair with Sheridan was of a remarkable intensity, and Caroline later referred to herself as "The She Sheridan."[35] Sheridan's amazingly facile tongue, moodiness, and tendency toward self-destructive behavior all find echoes in Lady Caroline's personality, though it is unlikely they were related by blood.

The debacle of Sheridan and Harriet's liaison occurred at the same time that Canis, Bess, and Georgiana had left England to partake of the waters at the little Belgian town of Spa in hopes that Georgiana would conceive a male child. They departed in June for Calais, then went to Paris. Despite some small indications of future trouble (like the storming of the Bastille), they visited Louis XVI and Marie Antoinette at Versailles. Georgiana found the Queen "sadly alter'd, her belly quite big, and no hair at all."[36] By late September they were settled in Brussels, and Georgiana believed she was pregnant. When it appeared she was well along, Canis returned to England to stop the divorce. He argued that Lord Duncannon's own father opposed it because it would damage the family's prestige and finances. These arguments won the day, but rumors circulated that Frederick was simply waiting until his father died to divorce Harriet.[37]

Harriet and Frederick returned with Canis to Brussels, leaving four-year-old Caroline behind, but local authorities, who suspected them (rightly) of passing information about the French revolution back to England, ordered them to leave. The household, which consisted of several children and a hundred adults, piled into the carriages and lurched over the road to Paris without a clue where to stay. En route, they met a fleeing French nobleman who offered them his house at Passy. There, on 21 May 1790, the Duchess gave birth to a little boy, the future 6th Duke of Devonshire, whose honorific title was "Marquis of Hartington." To scotch rumors that a switch of babies had been planned if the Duchess bore a girl, the family sought high-born witnesses, one of whom arrived just in time to verify the birth for Dr. Richard Croft.[38] Georgiana's delivery proved hard, and her recovery difficult, but by August the whole party had returned to England.

That winter, after Caroline turned five, the family fortunes darkened when a private share syndicate of the stock exchange collapsed. Georgiana and Harriet suffered huge losses, perhaps as high as £50,000.[39] Caroline would have been unaware that anything had gone wrong, except that her mother suffered what appeared to be a stroke and began to cough up blood. Since Harriet was only thirty years of age at the time and not obviously consumptive, the diagnosis remains mysterious. Some said that she had tried to poison herself after having been caught with Sheridan two years earlier and that this was the lingering consequence. Georgiana's biographer Amanda Foreman speculates that Harriet may have attempted suicide after the news from the exchange, perhaps had an abortion that went awry, or even that her husband beat her. Harriet and Frederick might well have quarreled—especially since Sheridan had convinced her to invest in the shares that collapsed. From this point, Georgiana carried Harriet's principal gambling debts, "as indeed I ought," she later wrote, "its having been my example and folly that had drawn her in."[40]

Little Caroline was terrified by her mother's collapse. Harriet developed bronchial pneumonia and was virtually given up for dead, then rallied. Canis responded generously by accompanying her, Frederick, and Georgiana to Bath, where she slowly recuperated. Caroline and the other children of the mist, including Caroline Rosalie (still surnameless), went with them. So also did youthful Lord Charles Grey, now famous for Earl Grey Tea. He had been an admirer of Georgiana's since 1787, when he had entered the Devonshire House circle after having made his first speech as a Member of Parliament. He had pursued her relentlessly, and she had eventually succumbed. After the Duke left Bath, Grey was with the Duchess of Devonshire constantly. Her friends admonished her. She paid no attention. She got pregnant.

It so happened that novelist Fanny Burney was also taking the waters in August of 1791. Burney's political allegiance was solidly with the crown, and she condemned the unhappy Georgiana, adulterous Harriet, and infamous Bess. But the whole *ménage,* including a little French refugee, Corisande de Grammont, and Caroline Ponsonby and her doppelgänger, aroused her curiosity, and so she arrived at 6:00 P.M., as invited, at the house the Devonshires and Duncannons had taken in Gay Street for a party in honor of Harryo's sixth birthday. Caroline and Caroline Rosalie were helping Harryo put together a "play-town" when Harriet arrived, still half-paralyzed by the stroke brought on (so Fanny Burney believed) by her suicide attempt. Lord Duncannon then entered, showing affection and concern for his spouse. Burney's reaction softened as she watched Lady Spencer hold a lottery for party prizes for the children.[41]

At this moment, Bess came in, and Mrs. Burney's mood chilled at being trapped in the room with the Duke's concubine. Caroline, whose own sixth birthday was just two months off, flew to Bess's side to show her the prize she had won in the lottery, and "cast herself into a thousand affected attitudes" telling Bess that it was *"precisément ce qu'elle avoit la plus souhaité"* (precisely what she had wished for the most). Bess kissed Caroline affectionately, and Mrs. Burney's gorge rose at the innocent child's intimacy with a fallen woman. Burney rebuffed Bess's advances, speaking in monosyllables. Yet Mrs. Burney was forced to admit that Bess was alluring. She visited once more in September and ended up thinking Georgiana a "sensible" person, and that "not the most rigid critic could deny the justice of her personal celebrity." She also convinced herself that the rumors of Harriet's infidelity were false. After all, how could someone with "so interesting a softness" be wicked?[42]

Had Burney but known! By October, it had become impossible to keep Georgiana's pregnancy a secret, so they prepared to go to Cornwall on the quite believable pretext that Harriet's convalescence required an escape from the worst of the English winter. The Duke was tipped off, however, and made a surprise visit. After much screaming and crying, he pronounced his verdict. The Duchess must go away directly from Bath. She would not be permitted to take her children—not even little Hart, who was just a year and a half old. Bess would have to go, too. Misery prevailed in the Bath apartments shared by Caroline, her cousins, mother, and aunt: "Vexation and unhappiness surround me," Harriet wrote to her friend Lady Melbourne. "I almost wish myself at the bottom of the sea."[43] Dependent as she was upon Georgiana's resources, Harriet faced the prospect of being left with no money.

Would Georgiana's banishment be to Cornwall or the Continent? After some deliberation the Duke decided that Georgiana must leave England and promise to drop Grey completely, giving the baby up for adoption. Otherwise the Duke would divorce her. Canis appealed directly to Harriet to help save Georgiana's reputation and their marriage—not to mention his chances of seeing Bess again—

by maintaining the cover of Harriet's precarious health as a motive for travel.[44] Sorrowfully, Harriet and Georgiana agreed. When young Grey heard, he lashed out, selfishly blaming Georgiana for his own pain.

Perhaps six-year-old Caroline was precocious enough to recognize her first lesson that feminine impulses would be indulged in her world only so long as appearances—especially those necessary to the conservation of wealth through primogeniture—were preserved. Even more than her mother and aunt, Caroline would find it difficult to keep up appearances.

Growing Pains

1792–1798

S ince Harriet and Frederick's financial security depended upon Georgiana's return, Caroline's father went along with his wife. They were accompanied by Harriet's personal physician, Dr. Samuel Drew, who would also serve as a tutor for Caroline. Lady Spencer, Georgiana, Bess, Caroline, and Caroline Rosalie followed, with the servants behind. Selina Trimmer would remain in England to care for Caroline's little brother Willy and the Marquis of Hartington, now a toddler.[1] The weather was terrible, and the vessel tossed its passengers around like toys. Caroline fell violently sick.

Indeed, no one felt well on this journey. Georgiana was in the last stages of her pregnancy. Harriet suffered intermittent paralysis of her leg and arm, and dizzy spells, as their journey took them through Paris and Aiguesmortes to Montpellier. She could only walk with the aid of crutches. Most of the contingent now went on, leaving Bess with her daughter, Caroline Rosalie, to see Georgiana through her labor. By now, the children in the party knew that Georgiana was giving birth to an illegitimate child, and that dire consequences might follow. Nor did Georgiana try to conceal the truth from her own children back in England, to whom she wrote abject, penitential letters.[2] At Toulon, Caroline and her family spent a freezing night in the garret of an inn overcrowded with refugees from the revolution. They pressed on, finally arriving in Nice.

In Montpellier, in late February 1792, Georgiana gave birth to a daughter, who was named Eliza. She was given to a wet nurse, who took the infant to live with Charles Grey's parents. Once again, Bess had done her duty, and Georgiana thanked her by going with her to see the Comte St. Jules to persuade him to lend his surname to little Caroline Rosalie. For reasons that remain mysterious, the Comte performed this act of generosity just before he died. In Nice, the main party found itself safe from the highwaymen and gangs of roaming rebels that had threatened them along the way, but they were not a happy lot. Lady Spencer fumed over Bess's influence on Georgiana. Lord Duncannon quarreled with Lady Duncannon because he wished to go home, now that Georgiana had delivered the baby. He wished to become reconciled with his ailing father, but Harriet quite reasonably refused to travel.[3] On top of all this, a sickly little seven-year-old boy died under Dr. Drew's hands after much suffering and was autopsied to rule out a contagious illness. Frederick insisted that these events were incomprehensible to Caroline, whom he described as "very well," despite the ominous death of a child scarcely a year older than she.[4] Frederick finally left, disgusted at his wife's intransigence, though she really was in no condition to travel.

Georgiana, Bess, and Harriet now mounted an attack on Canis, complaining of his "persecution" and calling him "a brute and a beast."[5] These efforts did not work. In April Lady Spencer received a letter from the Duke asserting that the Duchess "had better remain with Lady Duncannon whether she comes to England or stays abroad." He would visit in the summer, if they remained in Europe.[6] Discouraged, the entire party headed for Switzerland to spend the summer in Lausanne, where they would be the temporary guests of Edward Gibbon.

Overweight, with failing sight, Gibbon nonetheless fascinated Caroline. He talked to her as she played on his knees, and she even danced for him—much to the disapproval of her grandmother. He had retired to Lake Geneva after publishing the final volumes of *The Decline and Fall of the Roman Empire,* and he was fond of taking walks in the garden and wearing a green jockey cap to keep the light out of his sensitive eyes. Caroline would demand to have the cap, then twist it about and request knee-bouncing from the footmen, whom she also requested to bounce rotund Mr. Gibbon. They visited Val d'Aosta, where Caroline was appalled but enthralled by the fact that (as she thought) practically everyone she met had a goiter.[7]

Shortly before Caroline's seventh birthday Georgiana wrote, "[S]he is very naughty and says anything that comes into her head," confessing that she wanted to slap Caroline for rude remarks to Harriet and others, including Gibbon, whose face had supposedly frightened Caroline's puppy.[8] Caroline also began to annoy her grandmother by pestering her with questions to which there seemed no satisfactory answers.

The family had rented two houses on Lake Geneva across from the castle of Chillon, hoping the Duke would come, but in August Canis wrote to say that his plans were uncertain. They could continue to wait in Lausanne, or else they could go on to Italy for the winter.[9] Georgiana and Harriet decided it would be better to go to Italy. In January, Lord Duncannon rejoined the party as they reached Pisa. His eighty-nine-year-old father, though ill, was very much alive. As they traveled on to Florence and then Siena, San Lorenzo, and Viterbo on their way to Rome, they received the news that Louis XVI had been guillotined.

As if in counterpoint, in late March 1793 the message came that the 2nd Lord Bessborough had died. Frederick, now thirty-five years old, at long last became the 3rd Earl. The Duncannon title passed to his eldest son, John, and Caroline now received the honorary title of "Lady." She had progressed rapidly with her languages and now spoke fluent French and a little Italian—actually preferring French to English. Her favorite activity was drawing. She sat for hours sketching little figures in charcoal or pencil: elves, dogs, faces, and often the little cherub-like infants she saw in Italian churches called *putti.*[10]

While her father rode off on another arduous journey home (it would take him two months to arrive in London), Caroline and her mother, now Lady Bessborough, headed for Naples, accompanied by Georgiana. There, in May, they received word that Canis would permit his wife to return home after all. Caroline's father had lobbied him to do so, but perhaps it was the deterioration of the Duke's own health that finally caused him to relent. He drank heavily, suffered from gout, and was spitting blood. The London fogs, polluted with soot and animal waste, certainly did him no good.[11]

Everyone packed for England, but Harriet immediately suffered a relapse. The new Lord Bessborough wrote sadly of his disappointment: "[I]t is a pity you had not staid in Naples as you were so well there."[12] Still, they pressed on, reached Florence, and prepared to go further north, but Harriet was unable to continue. Georgiana felt so anxious to see her children that she determined to leave Harriet behind, and when she and Bess finally departed, Harriet cried violently. During her paroxysms, she was comforted by seven-year-old Caroline.[13]

Dangers of travel and fears for her mother had made Caroline insecure. She was an animal lover at heart, and emotional desperation increased her passion for pets. In Florence that July she had adopted a fox cub: "Your sister complains bitterly of being made to lie down & go to bed in broad sunshine," Lady Bessborough wrote her sons, "but luckily it does not disagree with her. She is growing quite a little Italian. I have drawn you the picture of her little fox which she is very fond of & hopes one day to show you."[14] Caroline had a tan from exposure to the sun, despite her mother's express orders. Whenever she could get away, she roamed, perhaps staying out the longer in order to avoid her tutor Dr. Drew. It was on such a ramble that she had found the abandoned fox cub, brought it home, and nursed it to health.

The weather was cruelly hot. They visited Pistoja and Bagni di Lucca, but Harriet continued to experience "hysterical choking" fits and spasms in her side.[15] Her poor health made it painful even to write or read. "This is a sad loss to me," said Harriet, "especially as [Caroline] is so young that tho' she reads both French, Italian & English very tollerably, yet she requires a great deal of attention & correcting."[16] The lessons Harriet could not give her daughter now became the exclusive responsibility of the tutors, who were unimpressed with Caroline's writing. She began a letter to her eldest brother John, Lord Duncannon, that her mother said "will be a curious one, for I shall certainly let her write it exactly her own way & she makes so odd a language between French, English & Italian that it is difficult to understand."[17]

Lady Spencer continued to worry about Caroline, for her granddaughter exhibited a personality prone to extremes. For example, she intensely disliked her sly and obsequious Aunt Lavinia (the wife of her uncle, the new Lord Spencer).[18] Caroline also threw tantrums, leaped coltishly over furniture, and talked familiarly with the servants. In Bagni di Lucca, she had open conflicts with her tutors. Children under duress sometimes learn that they can control adults by asking incessant questions. She had shown signs of this tendency six months earlier, when Lady Spencer had expressed hope that she had "finally got the better of asking those foolish questions."[19] Now the habit became entrenched. She would ask a question and then return obsessively to it, no matter how many distractions were put in her way, anxious to obtain yet another affirmation that she had been heard and noticed. Lady Spencer gave a detailed account of one such conversation to Selina Trimmer: "She asked me the other day if her doll did not look very droll today, to which for the sake of peace I answered Yes & then changed the Conversation to something that I thought would interest her. I took her out & walking we called upon some little Girls she likes to play with, we read together, I told her one or two stories, but at the end of every occupation & every change of place, she asked me with a fretful tone, "Why won't you answer me Grandmama, I say my Doll looks very droll today."[20]

According to her grandmother's journal, on Tuesday, 23 July, Caroline "fretted" Harriet so much with her questions that she sent her to Lady Spencer's room. "I was obliged to whip her severely," Lady Spencer wrote in her journal, "by which I mean three smart strokes with my hand, for more than that can never I think be necessary." Caroline was forced to take her soup and bread in her grandmother's room. Afterward, they took a walk together on a path near the village. On Wednesday, Caroline was again "very naughty" but attained better humor and was allowed to take a walk with her grandmother. On Thursday once again, Caroline was "so excessively naughty all day as to make both Harriet & me uneasy from the fear she was not well." Again, Caroline improved toward evening, when she was able to take a walk with her grandmother to get a glass of fresh milk. This pattern was repeated on Friday, with Caroline "outrageously Naughty" but toward evening "quite good & sorry she had been so much otherwise."[21]

As if her mother's blood-spitting and side spasms were not enough, at exactly this time Lady Spencer's dog, Roma, ran off and died. When its body was found, Dr. Drew dissected it in a vain attempt to rule out hydrophobia.[22]

Caroline's problems continued in August, as her grandmother again recorded in her journal:

> We had a sad day again with Caroline. The Irritation of this Dear Child's temper must be from illness—doctor Drew persists in it that it is only Obstinacy & that harsh means must be used—but from all I can observe they only irritate & make her more obstinate while the perpetual Crying they occasion shakes her delicate frame & makes her pale as Death—at least while this extreme hot weather continues—which I am sure disagrees with her, I must try what encouragement & indulgence will do but her perverseness is beyond what can be described or conceived.[23]

And so it went, with Caroline "tollerably good" one moment and "excessively obstinate perverse & ungovernable" the next. Lady Spencer preferred to believe that "it is the hot weather that makes the poor little thing so very fractious."[24] She bought a didactic book called "The Happy Family" to teach Caroline that rewards came to the well-behaved. The only punishment that seemed to have any immediate impact, however, was to give Caroline the silent treatment and lock her out of her grandmother's room. Lady Spencer saw that it was as if Caroline "frets *herself* till she is so nervous that it is quite Vexatious."[25] These self-induced periods of frenetic activity and constant question-asking seemed to have no obvious cause to Lady Spencer, though it appears clear enough that the young girl wanted someone's undivided attention and was upset to the point of panic by Harriet's regular bleeding and gagging fits. Lady Spencer acknowledged to

Selina Trimmer that if she or Harriet "give up our whole day to her, she is well contented, but if she sees us employed or in Conversation, it is then she begins," and that Caroline simply wanted to be "the person always attended to."[26]

Lady Spencer now became caught in a battle of wills between Dr. Drew and her tiny but ungovernable granddaughter, whose neediness was driving everyone mad. "Caroline was very good all Morning," she noted on 14 August, "but naughtier than ever at dinner & Doct. Drew insisted upon her being carried out & suffered to scream & cry as long as she would." Drew and Nandini (the Italian master) treated Caroline's offenses with severity. Perhaps this is the source of Lady Caroline's later observation in *Ada Reis* that "it is a common practice to condemn children to the society of those with whom parents cannot endure even for a moment to associate."[27] Certainly it must be the origin of her vision of hell in which adults are dressed up as infants and forced to endure "the various entertainments, lessons, or punishments inflicted upon children," to "translate and analyze dark passages in difficult dialects," and to be "exposed to every temptation [and] permitted to transgress every hour" until "on a sudden, at the convenience or pleasure of that sedate little urchin, they are to be beaten for the detection of the same errors when *found out,* as it is called, which, until they are found out, they are daily allowed to practise."[28] The conflict escalated, with Caroline cast as the aggressor. Much later, she told her friend Lady Morgan, "My mother, having boys, wished ardently for a girl, and I, who evidently ought to have been a soldier, was found a naughty girl—forward, talking like Richard the Third."[29]

Lady Spencer and Harriet struggled to counteract what they felt was the overly strict regimen of Drew and Nandini. They were lenient and understanding, giving Caroline "Indulgence, Encouragement, & Security," while the tutors administered scolding, incarceration, and corporal punishment. The inconsistency with which Caroline's behavior was treated exacerbated and prolonged it. Worst of all, she had become a drag on her mother's recovery, and she knew it: "Car[oline] was in one of her violent ways this Morning," Lady Spencer recorded, "& Ly B was so fretted with it that it gave her a slight spasm & made her unwell the whole day."[30] Added to Caroline's other problems, then, was the guilt of making her mother worse. The seeds of her later tempers and eccentricities were planted in Italy, though of course there could be physiological causes of these patterns.

Whatever the origins of her agitation, Caroline was clearly terrified by her dawning awareness of mortality. Lady Spencer recorded an incident in September 1793 when she sat down to have a cup of tea with her granddaughter, who continued to be "the pleasantest Child in the world" so long as she had her grandmother's exclusive attention. Lady Spencer spoke to her granddaughter of losing her teeth. This upset Caroline. Lady Spencer assured her that "it was among those infirmities of Old Age that must be borne with patience & chearfulness & I added that blindness deafness & several other infirmities would probably come on if I lived long enough."[31] Caroline's distress increased: "The poor little soul tried to assure me that I did not look old, but while she was speaking she turned her head aside lest I should see the tears that were running down her cheeks."[32] This satisfied Caroline's grandmother that there was still hope for the wayward child. Perhaps Lady Spencer would have been less pleased at the emotion she had extorted had she recognized its whipsaw effect upon this little girl, already terrified of losing her mother.

Gradually, Harriet improved, but she was in no condition to return to the climate of England, and so she, Lady Spencer, and Caroline awaited the return of Frederick, who would bring little Willy with him. The new Lord Bessborough had been unpleasantly surprised when wrapping up his father's affairs, which he knew were not in the best of order, to discover that his income was even less than what he had expected. Worse, Harriet had run up a sizable debt for a firm that had recently failed. "I hear you owe them £1,100, which I wish you had told me of," he wrote in annoyance. As usual, these figures did not tell the whole story. Harriet was eventually forced to confess that her debts totaled almost three times the original sum. She was forgiven, so long as she promised that from this point on she would "be firm" and resist temptation.[33] Frederick was kept very busy tidying up his wife's and sister-in-law's finances while also traveling to Ireland to visit the family estate, which he had—in a way characteristic of English absentee landlords—never visited.

On 18 September 1793, Frederick arrived with Willy. Overexcited, Caroline caught a cold, and while Harriet stayed with her in Naples Lord Bessborough visited Rome and other places of interest, taking Willy with him. In Naples, Caroline met the Queen of Spain, Maria Carolina, the sister of Marie Antoinette, shortly before the news came that the Queen of France had been guillotined in October.

No one who lived through this period—especially not precocious young girls whose mothers are personal friends of executed monarchs—can fail to have been profoundly affected by the collapse of the French aristocracy. In Caroline's case, the impact was both immediate and delayed. In the short run, she found another source of anxiety about her mother's fate. In the long, she discovered an ambivalence about her social position which would eventually ripen into an informed, if inconsistent, feminist politics. Rebelliously, Caroline now demanded to be allowed to climb Mt. Vesuvius, but Harriet wouldn't have it. The unpredictable volcano spat large hot rocks randomly around the landscape, nearly killing Lord Bessborough's footman and a visiting count who had foolishly ascended to the crater's edge, only to be driven off by "a great volley of stones."[34]

At this tender moment, another misfortune befell Caroline. Her mother met twenty-one-year old Granville Leveson-Gower. Having recuperated, Harriet was beginning to look more like her attractive self, and he fell for her on sight. For a long time she put him off. Twelve years his senior and still suffering from paralysis, she expected to play only the role of elder confidante. This apparently inflamed Granville, who pressed harder. It seems hard to believe, but biographer Dorothy Howell-Thomas argues fairly convincingly that it was perhaps as long as two years before Harriet's affair with Granville was consummated. Whether it was then or later, Granville became the center of Harriet's emotional and intellectual life from that moment on.[35] Already jealous of her mother's affection, Caroline had suddenly to compete with yet another person for attention.

As if Death had been waiting for the right moment to inscribe fear indelibly in the little girl's consciousness, Caroline now developed a life-threatening illness. It began on 12 November, the eve of her eighth birthday, with fever and headache. She had passed a worm in her stool two weeks before but had seemed fine since. Now, more worms appeared. She developed a fever that fluctuated but never went away, and she could keep no food down. Dr. Drew called in another English physician. Neither of them could find an effective treatment. On the fifth day Caroline became delirious for a period of eight hours, then, after a respite, her fever spiked and her pulse raced. Lady Spencer refused to leave her side even when the Queen of Spain sent her a personal note requesting a visit. The night passed, and the fever broke long enough for her to eat some bread sopped in tea and take two doses of analgesic powder.

Thereafter, Caroline gradually improved, though it was an agonizing recovery. A month later, she was still coughing, and when she developed a pain in her side like her mother's, Lady Spencer thought it a fatal decline: "I feel a thousand fears," she wrote of Caroline's skeletal appearance. On New Year's Eve, Lady Spencer sat up all night to be sure her granddaughter received medicinal bark on the proper schedule.[36] Over the next weeks, Caroline's illness gradually departed, though on 18 January her grandmother still described her as "ghostlike," and in February Caroline was afflicted with an attack of ague.[37] After spending the spring in Naples and Pisa, Harriet and Caroline seemed ready to begin the journey home. Lady Spencer traveled ahead, planning to meet them in Germany.

Caroline was heartbroken to learn that she would not be able to bring her prize fox back to show John and Frederick. In Milan, Caroline finished a letter in French to her eldest brother John. It is the earliest known letter of Caroline's—evidence that she still preferred French to English.[38] Lady Spencer wanted to take a summer house in Munich to avoid further travel, for the French had come within ten miles of Brussels and overrun the countryside. The one large drawback with living in Germany was that none of them spoke the language, though little Willy was convinced he could, much to Lady Bessborough's amusement: "[H]e runs about saying *yaw yaw, nein nein,* & fancies he is of great use."[39] In the end, no house was leased, and Caroline and her family struggled back to England, arriving in August 1794.[40]

Caroline returned from this journey quite altered. Having lived among expatriates who feared that revolution in France would blow across the English Channel, she had also acquired a nervous horror of death that ran as a rich vein through her emotional dependence upon her mother. She had also gained a reputation within the family. When her father had become exasperated while traveling with Willy, he had written that the boy seemed "perfectly well, but we have had some sad quarrels, a little in the stile of Caro's, when he grows tired."[41]

Caroline's life upon her return was as unsettled as ever. She found her cousins Harryo and Little G quite changed, and much less susceptible to her will, though Hart (who had just turned four) worshipped her. Harriet's health remained precarious, and so Lord Bessborough arranged for the family to go to Teignmouth in South Devon, where they planned to spend the winter in a residence called "Stonehouse."[42] Lord Granville was stationed near Plymouth, Saltram. He had been slipping into London to see Harriet, and he continued to visit her in Teignmouth. While they were staying there, Caroline's Aunt Georgiana, the Duchess of Devonshire, received the depressing news that her ex-lover Charles Grey had married. Not long after, she suffered a recurrence of headache and eye pain that had plagued her years before.[43]

The political situation—usually the source of much lively debate and fun—offered no relief from anxiety. Tension continued to build between France and England. An invasion was anticipated at any time. It thus seems incredible that Harriet should choose this moment, in May 1795, to travel by ship from Teignmouth—very near the naval arsenals of Plymouth and Torquay—to Harwich, sailing the whole length of the southern coast. On passing the Isle of Wight, they were forced to heave to by a shot across the bows from the *Spitfire,* and only upon signaling that the sister of the First Lord of the Admiralty (Harriet's brother) was aboard did they gain permission to proceed.[44] Caroline had been furnished with another example, if she needed it, that the world centered upon the Devonshires and Ponsonbys and that everything would come right in the end, no matter how risky their behavior.

Caroline now spoke English seasoned with Italian and French, and she had become an avid equestrian. Although her mother's friends remonstrated, she insisted on riding astride her mounts—not sidesaddle as was recommended to avoid "spoiling her figure." She saddled and bridled her own horses and even broke in some colts at Roehampton, where the family now settled for the summer. Her love of horseback riding, which lasted her lifetime, was part of her general hunger for outdoor activity. As a good squire-in-training, Lady Caroline continued to be very fond of dogs. If she found strays, she took them in and taught them. She made sketches of her canine companions and wrote a poem to one titled "To a Lanky Cur I Lov'd":

> To the greenwood I'll repair
> There unbind my yellow hair.
> Breathing in my native air
> Come follow me dog rover.[45]

Lady Caroline's tomboy tendencies may perhaps have spurred her mother to enroll her in school once they returned to London in October 1795.

The dame school at 22 Hans Place in nearby Knightsbridge was run by Frances Rowden, a former governess in the Bessborough household. It had numbered among its pupils Jane and Cassandra Austen. The pupils were taught cursive writing and required to wear uniforms of white muslin gowns and black sateen aprons. French and Italian comprised important parts of the curriculum, but students also received dance instruction, and twice a week the Knightsbridge barracks furnished them a drill sergeant who marched them up and down to improve their deportment, for which the girls also lay on their backs on boards for half an hour each day after lunch. Plays were not commonly produced at such schools, but Lady Caroline apparently instigated one at Hans Place.

Lord Granville's attentions to Caroline's mother continued. Though he could not often be together with Harriet, they wrote a stream of letters and spent huge mental and emotional energies on each other. She was not so distracted, however, as to fail to notice that her daughter was becoming more imperious than ever. By April 1796, it seemed that everyone had noticed. Her cousin Little G wrote to Selina Trimmer, "I am grieved more than I can tell you my D[ea]r Selina at Caro's having been naughty," and enclosed a paper magic trick intended to divert the misbehaving child.[46] Caroline had become such a problem that the Devonshires tried to time the visits of friends and relatives so that she would be elsewhere.[47] For this reason, Selina Trimmer was sometimes given exclusive charge of Caroline for an extended period of "quiet time." Caroline continued to be pacified by drawing images of *putti* and of her favorite animals. Selina told Lady Spencer,

> I find it of great use letting her garden & leave her to work in it by the hours together . . . & when I think she must be nearly tired I go down & put her into the swing & then bring her to the house where she reads or works or amuses herself with drawing—this is I am sure the kind of life most likely to set her up but the only difficulty is to know how she can lead it & where & with whom—for the present I shall have her here when I can be with her & when I cannot will have her with my mother.[48]

Lady Bessborough and Lady Spencer had hired a governess named Mary whose iron will they hoped would keep Caroline on the right path. At age ten she was approaching the time when eccentricities could blight her hopes of a good marriage. In war counsels, Selina, Lady Spencer, and Harriet agreed they wanted someone to act not as a nurse or governess "but as something that is neither & yet will supply the place of both." They considered a local school mistress as a possible stopgap to "take charge of [Lady Caroline] till somebody else can be found," and they planned to put her into quiet lodgings in Sutton Court, not far from the Devonshires' residence in Chiswick, and hope for the best.[49]

Lady Caroline had no idea that she was about to be placed in the custody of a caretaker. Her grandmother hesitated entirely to support such a decision, but she endorsed Miss Trimmer's plan to take the rooms in Sutton Court because Caroline was not improving. On 3 June she wrote to Selina that Caroline had gotten through that Friday morning "delightfully," but that the evening brought

> questioning so much & of such a kind (upon Religious subjects which is what I most dread) that I was forced to put her into Mary's hands—I set myself down immediately at the Closet door & could hear no other violence on the part of Mary than saying she would be minded, & that Caroline who intreated she might return to me should not stir till she [Mary] pleased, she soon after got her into good humour & they played at different things but it left the Child's mind in a state of Irritation that continued the whole evening—I gave her 4 drops of laudanum disguised with four of lavender drops—& tho' she did not sleep well she was perfectly calm & good humoured whenever she awoke.[50]

They used liquid opium to control Caroline's behavior more frequently now, in addition to a "Physick" that she took regularly, though she hated "anything that has a smell," like the *asafetida* she was given as a sedative for her hysterical episodes and nervous irritability.

Lady Spencer asked Selina to check with Dr. Warren about the advisability of the laudanum, also admitting that every time she turned Caroline over to Mary there was a physical struggle—this explains her remark that there had been "no *other* violence on the part of Mary." The struggles wore Caroline down, agitating "her weak frame so much and so long that I sometimes think it must soon destroy her poor little delicate texture." Lady Spencer added: "I think she has at times more involuntary Motions than she used to have." To the twenty-first century reader, Caroline sounds very much the hyperactive child.

Georgiana and Harriet became afraid to leave their mother alone with Caroline because it exhausted and depressed the older woman, who admitted that "despondency" had overtaken her: "I feel incapable of doing anything with the Dear Child, the little attempt I made at opposing the questions today has quite discouraged me."[51] Sadly, Georgiana's own health worsened that summer. It may have been a thyroid disorder that caused the eye, eyelids, and cheek to swell to the size of a fist, protruding from her face. If it burst, it might cause the eye to collapse in its socket.[52] Harriet's health was not much better: "I have passed three hours in dreadful spasms; but Laudanum has still'd them," she wrote to Lord Granville. They operated on Georgiana then and again that fall, followed a month later by the application of a "blister" to the back of her neck for four hours.[53] Lady Bessborough again suffered a return of her muscle spasms after her sister's dreadful treatment.

While Georgiana was convalescing, Lady Caroline's problems returned to Harriet's and Lady Spencer's attention. By shuttling Caroline to Roehampton when others were around, they had managed to keep her environment calm during the summer. Together with another servant named Julia, Selina seemed to be able to stymie Caroline's questions without resorting to the brute force of Mary. Observing the way Caroline struggled to resist "any little perverseness that comes across her," Selina found tears in her eyes. "God grant her a perfect & permanent recovery!" she wrote to Lady Spencer. To ensure that recovery, Lady Spencer consulted with Georgiana's physician, Dr. Warren, who continued to visit the Duchess of Devonshire regularly to monitor her eye. Warren thought that the regimen of quietude was working for Caroline, but he agreed that Mary should be kept on hand.[54]

Here lies the origin of an odd story Lady Caroline later passed to Lady Morgan: "I was ordered by the late Dr. Warre[n] neither to learn anything nor see any one, for fear of violent passions and strange whims they found in me should lead to madness; of which, however, he assured everyone there were no symptoms. I differ, but the end was, that until fifteen I learned nothing."[55] Obviously, this last assertion is false. But the worry over Caroline's mental stability was quite real. The 6th Lord Bessborough has written that "Lady Spencer was on no occasion so alarmed at her eccentricities that she consulted a doctor about her [Caroline's] medical condition."[56] True, Lady Spencer merely asked Doctor Warren if they were doing the right thing. However, there is no doubt that Caroline's grandmother *was* alarmed about her granddaughter's problems and considered them medical in origin.

Harriet and Georgiana's financial situation was also unstable. In 1797 a run on the banks occurred when a French invasion force of two thousand troops was intercepted in Bantry Bay off Southern Ireland. Reports of an impending civil uprising posed another grave danger to the economic well-being of Caroline's family circle, for the Ponsonbys and Cavendishes depended heavily on the proceeds from their Irish estates. A revolution would drastically curtail their income.[57]

As for Caroline at this time, more than anything she wanted a dog. But in her desire to prevent strong emotions, Lady Spencer strenuously argued against a puppy because, she said, Caroline had "too much anxiety about what she loves."[58] In this we can hear the echo of Caroline's anxiety attacks from 1793, when her mother had been gravely ill and a fox cub her delight. The paroxysms of grief into which Caroline had fallen when told she could not bring the fox back with her—and perhaps a memory of the dog Roma's death in Italy and how it had affected Caroline—made Lady Spencer adamant that no pets should be given her granddaughter in February of 1797.

On her best behavior, Caroline was included in the family's round of visits to Bognor, Chatsworth, Holywell, Hardwick, Wentworth, and Woburn. Finally the Bessboroughs arrived back in Roehampton in late fall—not that there was much rest. While Lord Bessborough entertained himself and his elder sons with shooting at Wimbledon, Lady Bessborough kept the household busy with preparations for a stream of visitors planned after New Year's. Caroline was gradually being reintegrated in the family circle. Inconveniently, she came down with the chicken pox in January 1798. Her case was not life-threatening, but Harriet felt extremely anxious that Caroline not be left with a scarred and pitted face.[59] No sooner had Caroline begun to recover than Willy caught the illness, and Caroline helped care for him, giving her mother a much-needed rest: "I have never seen anything so pretty as Caroline Nursing him," she wrote to Granville.[60] Not long afterward, Harriet herself came down with the chicken pox, but the case seems to have been mild, and she recovered rapidly.

When everyone seemed well enough, they moved back to London. In Cavendish Square, Harriet negligently allowed herself to be caught by Caroline with Granville in her dressing room. He left quickly, without saying a word, and Caroline concluded it was because she was unattractive: "I suppose Lord Granville would not deign to look at me if I am all pitted with chicken pox." When Harriet asked Caroline why she thought this, Caroline replied "he seems too fine a gentleman to like ugly people," and then added with characteristic bravado, "but I can assure him I would not give sixpence for any body who would not like me as well with a rough face as a smooth one." Harriet communicated all this to Granville himself, adding coyly that she had no idea "why Caroline supposes you are so govern'd by looks."[61]

Caroline's insecurity continued to cause wildness of temper and sometimes flight—but it appeared to be a wildness she could control if she chose, and sometimes she simply aped her own "craziness." We find evidence of this in a typical letter of this period in early 1798, written to Little G as part of a joint effort with Harryo. She began by forging Harryo's writing: "Haryo is *so so so* naughty not to write to *'oo* my love. Have I not imitated her well?" Caroline then continued in her own handwriting: "Haryo forces me to write tho' I have no time, no interest, no anything and in a great passion, so goodbye."[62]

In March 1798, Georgiana was back under the knife. Her appearance had deteriorated: "Her figure is corpulent, her complexion coarse, one eye gone, and her neck immense," reported Lady Holland with relish. Georgiana continued to be grateful for Bess's support, in whatever form, and now anticipated that Bess might be her *main* support, should she become totally blind.[63] Harriet downplayed these prospects to Caroline, whose mistrust was exacerbated by the lies Harriet told about her own condition, which she referred to as the "hooping cough."[64] Caroline simply observed how exhausted and sallow her mother had become. Additionally, she became aware of Sheridan.

Jealous of Granville, Sheridan became enraged and, in revenge, married his second wife, a woman twenty five years his junior whom he had met at Devonshire House—Esther Jane Ogle, nicknamed "Hecca," just eighteen and the daughter of a political radical.[65] Now, with Granville in France as a member of the peace mission, Sheridan returned to visit with "the Majesty of grief," as he sardonically described Harriet. Rebuffed, he returned three days later. "I was vex'd and received him crossly," she wrote to Granville, "but Demon like, he was so abominably entertaining that I ended by being glad he came, and letting him stay till almost dinner time."[66] Sheridan was still intensely jealous: "When he found I did not come to town, he imagin'd that you interdicted my coming till your return, and he is always asking me whether what I am doing is allow'd."[67] In August 1798, Sheridan invited himself to dine with Harriet alone at Cavendish Square, lamenting that she hardly noticed him and that she obviously wished he was "Ld. Levison [sic]."[68] Not long after, Sheridan intruded again, "chattering away at such a rate" that Harriet could concentrate on nothing.[69]

Sheridan had returned as Caroline teetered on the brink of adulthood. She had become a young lady of volatile tempers, precocious talents, and profound insecurities. Her nicknames included Ariel, Sprite, Squirrel, and perhaps more appropriately, Young Savage.[70] Self-aware and highly articulate, Caroline began to show a gift for self-analysis. After a violent tantrum she wrote a poem titled "Car Ponsonby in a Passion to Caroline de St. Jules." The poem is illustrated with the seated figure of a grinning satyr:

> There is a string when touched that wakes my ire
> Boils up my blood and sets my soul on fire.
> Pride is the ruling passion of that soul.
> No chain can bind it and no power control.
> It snaps each tie to feeling hearts allied
> And even affection must give way to pride.[71]

Caroline was quite aware that such paroxysms now defined her character for everyone, especially Harryo, who distrusted Caroline's unpredictability and disliked her bossiness.

Caroline continued to take "Physick" and sedatives, including laudanum, nicknamed the "black drop." She wrote about this treatment and later labeled it "the first poem I ever wrote":

> Oh balm of nature to the mind opprest,
> Descend and calm the tumult of my breast.
> Bind with oblivious veil those wakeful eyes,
> And still the varying passions as they rise.
> While dreams of love and fairy fictions light
> Sport with the gloomy darkness of the night;
> While cherub angels borne on silver wings
> To heaven's high arch their songs of triumph sing.
> Oh sleep, descend and on Thy downy breast
> Lull with thy poppy wreath my soul to rest.[72]

Aside from the dangers of drugs to which she was becoming habituated, these poems testify to the war between imagination and existence taking shape in Caroline.

Caroline had not been educated—as she had not been bred—to accommodate to others' expectations. Rather, she had learned to respond to pressures toward conformity with verbal, and even physical, intimidation. There were few who could withstand her when she was blowing at a full gale—then, even the strong and taciturn Mary found her hands full. As an escape and a form of meditation, Caroline formed the habit of turning her intense experiences into poetry and sketches, and these outlets, combined with music, might have become a career, even though she had been born a woman. But she had not been born or raised the right kind of woman to be satisfied with the creative outlets that harmonized with drawing room entertainments: *tableaux vivants,* light fiction, miniature portraits, the harp and harpsichord.

Of all her family, Hartington was most fond of Caroline. She, in turn, spared him her tantrums. Hart's health had always been poor. He had a congenital hearing loss that was gradually worsening, and Lady Spencer described him in December 1797 (he was six) as "very deaf, very thin, & very nervous."[73] Caroline apparently returned Hart's affection and sought to protect the vulnerable child. She loved him in the way she loved her little brother Willy and her "lanky curs"— artlessly. Hart told Lady Caroline that he would marry her some day.

For Lady Bessborough's health, the family spent the autumn of 1798 at Margate in a large furnished house with a panoramic view of the sea where Harriet delighted in giving dinner parties and Caroline in riding and roving. There they celebrated Caroline's thirteenth birthday before they returned to Roehampton.

By now, young Caroline's apprehension about abandonment was accompanied by real courage. One evening, she was riding home with her mother and father in a "curricle," a two-wheeled chaise drawn by two horses. The night was moonless and Lord Bessborough lost his way, and, in the great tradition of male pigheadedness, became angry when this was pointed out. The horses began to rear and kick, and Lord Bessborough's embarrassment increased when he saw that his wife and daughter were becoming frightened. Unable to keep the horses from backing, he was forced to hand the reins to his wife and alight to take control of the animals. Pulling back on the reins with one hand, Lady Bessborough gave a boost to her daughter with the other, and Caroline crawled out over the back of the curricle. It turned out that they had driven right to the edge of a deep chalk pit, in a position that did not permit withdrawal without risk of plunging over the precipice.

Caroline ran all the way home in the pitch darkness and fetched the servants.[74]

Coming Out

1799–1805

$\mathcal{C}$aroline shared Harryo's dislike for Lady Elizabeth, who had captured the Duke's affections. Harryo scathingly described how Bess fussed over her little dog Sidney, debating what style shawl to make for him. The "silly affected" dog and its "silly affected" owner were, to Harryo, "both unwell, both whining and both finally as agreeable as you know I always think them."[1] Bess made efforts to ameliorate the hostility of Hart, Caroline, Harryo, and Lady Spencer, but could achieve very little while her opposition maintained its solidarity.

Lady Spencer's determination not to negotiate was undergirded by intelligence from Selina Trimmer, who continued to play the role of mediator and spy in the thickets of the Devonshire/Bessborough circle, informing Lady Spencer, for example, that Bess was expecting a proposal of marriage. Caroline later described Miss Trimmer in verse:

The cowslip & the lemon pale
with Selly's cheeks might vie;
But never maid that was not frail
had such a jet-black eye.

. . . . .

Like a fair fruit Peach that never has been tasted

its sap its bloom & all its flavour wasted,

droops our Selina on her virgin Tree

unloved unloving any living he.[2]

Unkind as it may seem, the verses captured the children's distaste for Selina's simpering personality. To be fair, when the older boys—Bess's two sons and John, Frederick, and William Ponsonby—came home from school, Devonshire House must have been beyond the control of any governess, servant, mistress, or even drill instructor—no matter how sharp his or her looks. Miss Trimmer was caught in an untenable position; she needed to protect Bess from the ill will of the children, for the Duke and Duchess wished it, yet she spied for Lady Spencer, who did not. Caroline ignored Selina's admonitions and continued mocking Lady Elizabeth's superfeminine voice. She also continued tormenting Selina—once, by loudly proclaiming that Bess was secretly married, just so that she would report this false intelligence to Lady Spencer.[3]

In May 1799, Caroline attended her first communion in Westminster Abbey, where she was confirmed, along with Harryo and Caroline St. Jules. The girls wore white gloves and headbands and conveyed the very soul of seriousness.[4]

William Lamb, the second son of the Viscount and Viscountess Melbourne, dined several times that season with Lady Bessborough at Cavendish Square and Roehampton, in company with other devotees like Sheridan and Lord Holland. William, who seemed to have little drive and ambition, but who was thoroughly handsome and charming, had fallen a little under Harriet's spell, for even at thirty-eight, and gaining weight, she was still an enchanting hostess. He had even dined with Harriet just as Georgiana was about to undergo her third eye operation.[5] Perhaps Harriet was flattered, but she soon had other problems. Early in 1800, she realized she was pregnant by Granville. She hid herself at Manresa House in Roehampton and completely missed the excitement generated in May by an attempt upon George III's life while he sat in the Royal Box of Drury Lane Theater. She was forced to skip Little G's coming-out ball on her seventeenth birthday in July. She was also driven nearly frantic when she heard that her little Willy was taken aboard ship to give him a chance of "seeing service," an idea that appalled her.[6] But she couldn't chance being seen in such an advanced state of ripeness. She arranged, however, to take a mysterious fall in late August, while her husband and children were away on holiday. Although Roehampton is just a few miles from London, no doctors were called, nor was anyone else immediately informed. However, the Duchess of Devonshire traveled every day from Chiswick House with baskets of fruit.

The new baby was named Harriette Arundel Stewart, using the surname of Lord Granville's mother's family. This child was taken to a nearby hostel for fallen women awaiting their babies' births, a charity that Harriet herself had set up two years before as a down payment on a more pious life.[7] Harriet then staged a dramatic return to Cavendish Square in early September, complaining of her fall. Five doctors were called. They shaved part of her head and pondered an operation—then declared it unnecessary. These subterfuges worked. Harriet stayed in touch with her love child mainly by correspondence.

In the meantime, Caroline continued to stay with her grandmother at Holywell. She was there for a month after Christmas, ostensibly because of Lady Bessborough's rheumatism and other complaints, although it is likely that Harriet and Granville wanted the fifteen-year-old girl to have no direct knowledge of their ongoing affair. Thus, after a brief hiatus, Caroline was back with her grandmother in February 1801. She brought a dog, which she had taught to do tricks, and in a burst of generosity she offered to make a present of it. Her grandmother found Caroline "uniformly affectionate and kind," and "without any hurry or fidget," though she expressed concern over the girl's lackadaisical attention to personal hygiene—a probable allusion to Caroline's lack of interest in dresses and coiffure. Lady Spencer suggested it might be time to hire a personal maid for her as she prepared for her coming-out ball, which was planned for Devonshire House in May. As if to underscore the momentousness of such rites of passage, her elder cousin Little G, whose coming-out had taken place less than two years before, was married (at age seventeen) on 21 March to Lord Morpeth, eldest son of the 5th Earl of Carlisle. The party took place, but the marriage seems not to have made a large impression on anyone. Caroline was shipped back to Holywell and her grandmother for most of the ensuing month, where Lady Spencer fretted about a potential French invasion. They soothed their fears with reading and conversation. Caroline had become fluent in French and near-fluent in Italian, and now started to learn German.[8]

Christmas of 1801, spent at Chatsworth, was one of Caroline's happiest. The weather was cold, just as she liked it, and the snow thick. She skated and sledded to her heart's content. That December and January were also happy for Lady Bessborough. A very large party was thrown, and visitors lingered. Lord Bessborough suffered an attack of gout after his eldest son (John William) pushed his chair too hard on the ice and dumped him out. Harriet nursed her husband during the day, then welcomed Granville into her arms at night.[9] Caroline's cousin Hart had been sent to Harrow, and Willy was in school, so now it was only the unmarried females—Harryo, Lady Caroline, and Caroline St. Jules—who continued under the doleful eye of Selina Trimmer.

In March 1802 a peace treaty between France and Britain was finally signed at Amiens. Sheridan spoke to the House of Commons on the occasion. Signaling the singular discomfort that Napoleon created for the Whigs, he described it as "a peace of which every man is glad and no man is proud."[10] Lady Caroline and her mother attended the opera and the theater and witnessed the nationalistic celebrations taking place in London. A stream of French émigrés visited the Bessboroughs at Roehampton that summer. The upper class flowed back to Paris. Georgiana and Harriet prepared to take their retinue on the same journey, but first they would spend more time at Margate intriguing over a potential match between Harriet's eldest son and Lady Elizabeth Villiers. Shortly before they were to leave, Harriet returned from dining with the Melbournes and sat up late writing yet another letter to her darling Granville, full of the news of the day. Just as she was sorrowing over the fact that Granville's carriage was not to arrive that night, nor would she hear his knock on the door, she heard a rapping. Then she heard Sheridan's voice.

Claiming later that she did not know why, Harriet recoiled from meeting him. She sent Sally, her maid, to say she was not at home, but Sheridan remonstrated that he had already called twice and been rebuffed. He then promised to haunt the doorway in Cavendish Square until he was received. The door closed. He knocked again, and Harriet sent down word that she was unwell. As she told Granville later, "I am not in a humour to be flatter'd or abus'd, frighten'd or complimented, and he is in one . . . to torment me instead of amusing me." The next morning, Sheridan reappeared, but Lady Bessborough ignored him—or at least that is what she told Granville. She also told him that she believed Sheridan feared her, and yet she admitted, "there was a time when I was not afraid of him . . . but now I feel the justice of some of his attacks."[11]

That summer the families moved to a coastal resort area at Ramsgate, and Harriet wrote Granville more happily of the cacophony of the Devonshire and Bessborough households: "on one side I have a boarding school, where various instruments and Voices are playing and solfegeing so loud that it makes perfect discord; on the other side [Harryo] is practicing the harp with Mdle Menel, Corisande on the piano forte, Caroline St. Jules on the Guitar, and my Caro upstairs on the Piano forte—all different music, all loud, and all discordant."[12] In August 1802 everyone went to Brocket Hall, the country estate of the Melbournes, some twenty-five miles north of London. Lady Caroline went along with her aunt, mother, and cousins to see familiar faces, for they had just visited the Melbournes' residence in Whitehall. At Brocket Caroline attracted the attention of William Lamb, now a young man of twenty who was completing his education at Trinity College, Cambridge.

Lady Caroline, whom he had scarcely noticed before, had suddenly matured. Slight in figure, with large eyes, a fair, if freckled, complexion, and excellent teeth, Caroline was attractive without being a beauty.[13] But her vivacity and voice set her apart. Her soft, low, caressing voice "was at once a beauty and a charm, and worked much of that fascination that was peculiarly hers," as Caroline's friend Lady Morgan later noted.[14] Caroline's accent was certainly music to William, and her capriciousness in mood and subject charmed him. She seemed to him both infantile and droll, gushing and reticent. William was mesmerized, as if watching light glance off a faceted mirror. Everyone noticed. "There was an estraordinary flirtation between William Lamb and Caro Ponsonby," wrote Harryo, "and they seem, I hear, mutually captivated. When the rest were at games etc., William was in a corner, reading and explaining Poetry to Car., and in the morning, reading tales of wonder together on the *tithertother*. When she played at Hunt the squirrel, Hunt the Slipper etc., he did; always sat by her etc."[15] William completely preoccupied Caroline, though he "did not captivate anyone else," continued Harryo, who was much more taken with Caroline's brother John. Harryo and Corisande de Grammont considered the Lambs ill-bred, for they laughed raucously and snored in afternoon naps on the couch. But William made his impact on Caroline, as he read aloud to her from his cousin M. G. "Monk" Lewis's *Tales of Wonder,* and she lisped about her love of poetry and music. He is supposed to have said afterwards, "Of all the Devonshire House girls, that is the one for me."[16]

The gardens at Brocket were superbly maintained, and the orchards and forest well groomed. The food was good as well; but Caroline seems to have noticed only this large, serious young man with dark hair and blue eyes who had published a few poems and whose literary aspirations were being encouraged by Sheridan. William was accomplished—he won the declamation prize at Trinity, Cambridge that year—and though Harryo dismissed him now, she would come later to appreciate his "zeal & open curiosity" and the small "scornful smile" he would wear "when he does not believe or approve."[17] Caroline found William endearingly shy. Years later, Lady Caroline would tell the philosopher William Godwin that her husband was "certainly not a person who lets himself out kindly he is really shy—very very shy an odd thing for a man who has liv'd as he has much in the World."[18]

When Lady Melbourne became aware that her son William had shifted his interest from Harriet to young Caroline, she calculated that he had a chance, despite his lack of prospects. But he must, when it came time to declare himself, persuade Caroline's mother and the family matriarch, Lady Spencer. Such a match, while not perfect from the Melbourne view, had considerable advantages. Caroline was, of course, near the pinnacle of British aristocracy.

By comparison with the Cavendishes and Ponsonbys, the Lambs were *nouveau riche,* and it showed. William's grandfather Matthew, son of a trades-man, had inherited a small fortune that he increased dramatically by practicing law—some said unscrupulously. He thereby gained the means to purchase Brocket Hall in 1746, received a baronetcy in 1755, and shortly thereafter an Irish barony. When he died in 1768, his son, Peniston, inherited a fortune valued at over £1,000,000 (what would amount to at least $160 million today). Peniston Lamb was no sharper than the dullest aristocrat, but he purchased an expensive home near Westminster Palace from Lord Holland and then fell into the web of the dynamic, crafty, and indefatigable Elizabeth Milbanke. Elizabeth would give him six children, five of whom survived to adulthood, though only the first, Peniston Jr., sprang from the seed of her lawful husband.

Elizabeth Lamb practiced the philosophy that matrimony serves patrimony best when it is not too scrupulously chaste. Having fulfilled her duty as a wife to provide her husband with a son and heir, she now used her personal charms to further her family's interests, while Peniston Senior began a long journey into alcoholism. For her next child—William—Elizabeth chose the Earl of Egremont for paternal honors, and he apparently took pride in his son, whose picture he hung at Petworth. William's sister, Emily, was born next, reputed to be the daughter of Earl Fitzwilliam, although in appearance she was remarkably similar to William, with black hair, dark brows, and grayish-blue eyes.[19] William's younger brother, George, was sired by an even more illustrious personage: the Prince of Wales. Lady Melbourne's skill at bestowing the favor of herself paid off. In honor of the birth of George Lamb, Peniston Senior was named Viscount Melbourne and took a seat in the House of Lords.

Though Caroline and William were obviously smitten, the likelihood of a match stood low. William had no prospects, and, in any case, the déclassé Lambs made the Bessboroughs and Devonshires wrinkle their noses. Four days of the Lambs' wisecracks and rude noises was, according to Harryo, a surfeit. The vigilant Selina Trimmer had not failed to notice Caroline's attention to William, and she reported it to Lady Spencer, who unwisely remarked upon it to her daughters, unwittingly revealing the source of her information. This provoked a sharp response from Georgiana, who threatened to dismiss Selina if such intelligence-gathering did not cease.[20] Not that Georgiana thought William stood a chance with Caroline. He was a second son who would have to enter a profession, and money was a very important consideration, especially now that Harriet and her husband were financially embarrassed, due to previous mortgages on the Bessborough estate, their gambling debts, and his weakness for purchasing absurdly expensive prints. But neither Georgiana nor Harriet felt easy at the prospect that handsome, penniless William Lamb had fanned an ember in Caroline's heart.

In December, the Devonshires and Bessboroughs embarked for France, and Harriet turned her attention to bringing out her daughter for the Anglo-French *ton* in the most prominent way possible—despite the fact that Lady Spencer feared French "indecency" would tarnish her granddaughter's character.[21] This would be Caroline's true coming-out, and she recorded her metamorphosis under the hands of Parisian couturiers with ironic glibness:

> Farewell to England and farewell to frocks.
> Now France I hail thee with a sweeping train.
> Subdued I'll bend my stubborn locks
> And enter on a life of art and pain.
>
> Farewell to childhood and perhaps to peace
> Now life I sail upon thy dangerous stream.
> And oh may wisdom with each year encrease
> And prove my follies but an infant's dream.[22]

Though she cannot really have been much aware of the "art and pain" practiced and suffered by the denizens of the *beau monde,* Lady Caroline felt no haste to debut at the Duchess of Gordon's ball on December 22. Nevertheless, she appeared, dressed in a white gown with rows of blue-ribbon bows, shoulder-length white doeskin gloves, and white satin slippers. Her hair had been given the Whig bouffant and decorated with pearls and a diamond diadem. Pearls and diamonds adorned her neck. She was the image of a fairy-princess, a vision the more astonishing to those in attendance who had known her as a tomboy. This party, thrown by a skilled matchmaker whose daughters had all married dukes, lasted until dawn.[23]

The Duchess of Gordon's was only the first of several at which Caroline played a role. Others were given by the Duchess de Luynes and the Princess Dolgorouk. She attended a banquet given by Talleyrand in December 1802.[24] She also met William and Frederick Lamb at a party given by Lady Melbourne on January 13, 1803, at which the two men got drunk and William lectured Harryo in a loud voice about "the danger of a *young woman* believing in *weligion* and *pwacticing mowality.*"[25]

If any family of French nobility entertained thoughts of Caroline's marrying one of their number, they were to be disappointed. She wrote the following poem to accompany a sketch of an English girl scolding her dapper interlocutor:

Frenchman, smile not thus on me;
I hate your race, I hate your nation.
In vain you bend your supple knee,
I care not for your adulation.
I love a man of English race
Who never learned to fawn or dance.
He has an English heart and face.
Oh there is no such man in France.[26]

Caroline's dislike of the effeminate males she met at balls and parties was reinforced by her mother's disdain. The days were gone in which French officers had to prove they came from three generations of nobility. Napoleon Bonaparte had changed that policy and destroyed what was left of the pretensions of the old regime. Lady Bessborough objected to being presented to the Empress Josephine, saying that her lineage was doubtful, though she mainly wished to honor the memory of her friend, Marie Antoinette. She was also upset at being seated next to "common people" in the theater. Though a supporter of universal suffrage who learned with horror that eighteen "poor blacks" were to be guillotined before Christmas, Lady Bessborough drew the line at sitting with the rabble in the theater.[27] Caroline and her mother watched a military parade on January 5, 1803, honoring Napoleon, but Lady Bessborough still avoided being introduced. Bonaparte may have begun to resent the aloofness of the Bessboroughs, whom he suspected (rightly) of discouraging other English gentlemen and ladies from being presented to him.[28]

Caroline followed her mother's lead in rejecting the French men she encountered. But in Paris she discovered some shining examples of feminine accomplishment. One was Germaine de Staël, recently divorced from the Baron Staël-Holstein. Madame de Staël's independence and liberalism, expressed not only through her divorce, but also through criticism and novels, had caused Napoleon to exile her on more than one occasion. Her feminist novel, *Delphine,* had just been published, and many discussions centered on it and on her *De la littérature* (1800), which applied the theories of Montesquieu to literary works, concluding that only in a free society would French literature progress and develop. Lady Bessborough and her daughter admired *Delphine,* despite the fact that "some people [think] it has an immoral tendency." Lady Bessborough found the novel so moving that she wrote Granville: "My eyes are swell'd out of my head with crying over Delphine, and I have but just got through the first Vol. Pray read it if you have time and *mark*."[29]

Another figure even more attractive and inspiring to Caroline at this time was that of Juliette Récamier, the wife of a banker. Like de Staël, Récamier held court in her home, "beautiful white Shoulders expos'd perfectly uncover'd to view—in short completely undress'd and in bed."[30] The thrill of Récamier's daring undress stayed in Lady Caroline's imagination when they departed on 15 February, and Lady Bessborough left invitations for both de Staël and Récamier to visit in England. Upon their return, however, Lady Caroline was once more sent to stay with her grandmother at Holywell, ostensibly to "rest" after the arduous party season in Paris.

Madame Récamier was the first to avail herself of the Bessboroughs' proffered hospitality. She arrived in April 1803, making a stir by strolling through Kensington Gardens dressed in flowing white lace. According to biographer and scholar Margot Strickland, Caroline was so impressed by the utter self-possession and seeming self-sufficiency of Récamier that she decided to wear a similar lacy white robe and learned to recline on a sofa made specially for her, a copy of Marie Antoinette's. This theatrical get-up was made complete with the addition of a small pug dog. She also memorized Sappho's "Ode to Aphrodite":

Undying Aphrodite, on your caparisoned throne,
Daughter of Zeus and weaver of ruses—
Now I address you . . .

Her favorite costumes for masquerades included Ariel (one of her nicknames) from *The Tempest* and Titania, Queen of the Fairies in *A Midsummer Night's Dream*.[31]

These roles, with their trappings of superfemininity, formed part of Lady Caroline's exploration of gender, which included male as well as female dress. She found herself impressed and titillated by women playing breeches parts on the stage, like Viola in Shakespeare's *Twelfth Night* and Jacintha in the Hoadley brothers' *The Suspicious Husband*. She still liked to ride beside the carriage driver when she went places, leaping down like the tomboy of old when she arrived. Though she had now already "come out" in society, she continued to ride horseback and ramble in the woods around Roehampton with canine companions. She professed to see and befriend fairies. One particular fairy acquaintance, she claimed, had given her a necklace that consisted of a little heart bound with chains to a diamond. She drew a picture of this fairy as it descended on her dog's back.[32] She had the knack of belief, causing moments of real discomfort for her more earthbound listeners. Yet such visions characterize certain powerful imaginations of her era. William Blake also saw fairies, and Caroline's drawings bear a resemblance to some of Blake's engravings and watercolors.

Naturally, Caroline's family sought to "round off" these rough edges. The impulse to domesticate Caroline is reflected in her portraits, for example Sir Joshua Reynolds' watercolor sketch showing Lady Caroline on horseback, carefully coifed, riding sidesaddle and wearing a full-length black dress and plumed hat. It may be an accurate portrayal. A more likely picture, however, would have been a hatless Caroline in breeches astride her horse, holding a riding crop, hell-bent for the hedgerows with "Rover" in pursuit.

That summer, Harriet's attention was not on her daughter, but on Granville and Sheridan. A strange article had appeared in the *Morning Post* in late April 1803 describing a ball Harriet had attended. The article embarrassingly described her "elegance of person" and "dazzling beauty." It betrayed, in short, that the author was an admirer.[33] Harriet began again to correspond regularly with Sheridan. Whether this was the cause or effect of the marital dissension Sheridan was then experiencing is unclear. Harriet wrote to Lord Holland that she knew Sheridan and Hecca were fighting and had even separated for a while. "[T]hey live in the same house, but [are] not very good friends." she said with a certain satisfaction. Sheridan was drinking heavily. He left the debates in the House on more than one occasion in June partly or wholly inebriated in order to write cloying, annoying, entirely fascinating letters to Harriet.[34]

By August 1803, Sheridan's behavior had disgusted both Charles Fox and the Duchess of Devonshire. Sheridan's jealousy then took an explicitly political avenue. He told the Prince that Harriet and Georgiana had betrayed his interests and were untrustworthy. He also tried to damage Granville's image with the Prince, and charged that even Little G's husband, Lord Morpeth, was talking about him behind his back.[35] This necessitated some repair work, which Harriet undertook because Georgiana was simply not up to it.

The Duchess of Devonshire's health had continued to deteriorate, and Georgiana suffered a severe attack of kidney stones in September 1803. Harriet and Lady Spencer took turns sitting up with the patient.[36] As she gradually recovered, she realized that, had she died, she would have done so without having put her affairs in order. She asked Lady Elizabeth to undertake the ordering of her private papers in the event of her death, and the bond between the two women was yet more closely cemented.[37] Bess had given up completely on the Duke of Richmond and now spent all her time with her friend and protector, Georgiana.

William Lamb and Lady Caroline met on and off during 1803 and 1804, but she was being courted by others—among them her cousin Lord Althorp, heir to the Spencer estate. Nor had Hart given up the idea that he was destined to wed Caroline. William faced the facts, and after deciding not to join the clergy, sought to practice law, while not foregoing the pleasure of composing a few verses and prologues for private theatricals.[38]

That fall of 1804, Lady Bessborough gave birth to another child by her beloved Granville, a boy named George Arundel Stewart. Harryo's biographer, Betty Askwith, conjectures November as the month of his birth, and strong clues reinforce this as the probable time.[39] Lady Bessborough refers on 6 December to having caught "a terrible cold, and no wonder with going out for the first time after my long confinement . . . to a hot, crowded play house."[40] The play she had attended was *Lover's Vows,* adapted from August von Kotzebue's popular *Das Kind der Liebe*. This melodrama—which Jane Austen would incorporate into *Mansfield Park* (1814)—focuses on a Baron who has seduced and abandoned a young woman, then married another. The "love-child" becomes aware of his origins and decides to assist his destitute mother by begging. He is tempted into robbing a gentleman who turns out to be his own father. Lady Bessborough told Granville simply: "I cried my eyes out. The detail of all ye disadvantages a natural child must suffer would alone have affected me, but it is impossible to give you an Idea of what this creature is—his tenderness to his Mother, his perfect freedom from all affectation and whining . . . it is impossible to conceive greater perfection."[41] Harriet's emotionality must have been apparent to Caroline, if she had any opportunity to observe it.

Fate now intervened on behalf of William Lamb. His brother Peniston was dying of consumption, and in that event William would stand to inherit the Melbourne estate. This prompted him to propose to Caroline, knowing that other suitors might prevail before his brother's death. Lady Bessborough had her eye on the Prince of Wales himself, but William believed that Caroline would prefer his proposal, and he had good reason, according to one observer, who remarked disapprovingly that Caroline had already "acted the gentleman's part and told him of her passion."[42] Whatever the case, William made his intentions known, and he almost succeeded. He was an attractive man who had exhibited a spirit of independence in his opinions, and he had chosen Whig leaders like Charles Fox, who expressed love of liberty, as his heroes. The fact that he felt no attraction to the dissipated life of the professional aristocrat only raised him higher in Caroline's estimation. She probably endeared herself to him the more by suggesting half-seriously that if they married she would have to dress up as a clerk in order to accompany him on the circuit.[43] No doubt the piquancy of her playing a breeches role in real life attracted them both. And yet, she had misgivings. She knew marriage would not be easy. She had other admirers. She turned him down.

Someone with jealous feelings must have been aware of William's suit, for a very unpleasant letter was received by Lady Caroline immediately after the New Year. Harriet wrote to Granville in Russia on 3 January 1805:

> If you were here I know you would feel almost as indignant as I do, and as much puzzled at something that has happen'd to me, or rather to my Caro. Think of her receiving a letter fill'd with every gross, disgusting indecency that the most deprav'd imagination could suggest—worse, indeed, than any thing I ever heard, saw, read, or could imagine among the lowest Class of the most abandon'd wretches. It is what I am quite convinc'd you could not believe possible, even supposing it addressed to some of the women in the street: think, then, of writing thus to a Girl! She luckily only read the first few lines, when she was so shock'd that she flew to me and gave me the horrid letter, which the writer (lest the coarseness of his language should prevent her understanding) had taken care to add explanations to. What adds to our perplexity is, that what is not too *nasty* and disgusting to look at, is very well written and alludes to conversation and jokes that pass'd at my Sister's a very few days ago.[44]

The letter had been posted in the name of a Mr. Hill, about whom Caroline had heard, for he had touted her as "the cleverest and prettiest Girl in London." When told of this compliment she had replied thoughtfully, "Dear Mr. Hill, I shall set about admiring him whenever I meet him."

Mr. Hill was not, of course, the actual correspondent. But who was? It had to be someone who was familiar with the intimate conversations of the ladies of the Devonshire and Bessborough circle. The letter was well-written, witty. It went into the fire, leaving Harriet with the uneasy conviction that, since no one could wish ill of such an innocent thing as Caroline, "therefore it must be because she has a Mother unworthy of her." Harriet's recent pregnancy and her career as a reforming gamester left her open to such attacks.[45] But who among their acquaintances would know all that this correspondent did, and who would be motivated to hurt her?

Of course it was Sheridan. He had sunk into "a fit of low Spirits," and he and his wife Hecca had convinced themselves they were both about to die. The letters were part of a break-down, in which Sheridan's sexual Puritanism—a reaction against his upbringing in the theater—created self-revulsion at the debauchery that had characterized his adult life. It seemed almost as if he had turned into one of his own characters, the hypocrite Snake, from *School for Scandal,* as historian Fintan O'Toole has pointed out.[46] Two days later, another "infamous letter" arrived, this time addressed to Harriet herself. Some paragraphs had also been published in the *Morning Post* and the *Courier* that were unflattering in the extreme to Lady Bessborough, Harryo, and Caroline's eldest brother Duncannon.[47] The perpetrator of these attacks now sought fresh targets. Lewd prints were sent to Caroline St. Jules and Harryo with another letter, this time under the signature of a "Mr. Ward." Even Lady Elizabeth Foster received a letter. Sheridan's further attempts to publish personal attacks in the newspapers had been temporarily scotched, however, by Lord Bessborough's intervention with the editors. The manager of the *Morning Post,* Dr. Fleming, stopped by on 21 January to show Harriet the manuscripts of poison-pen letters he was receiving daily. Harriet's suspicions were confirmed: "The hand is dreadfully like one I know very well," she told Granville. Although abuse had been thrown at Lady Caroline, Caroline St. Jules, the Duchess, and Harryo, among others, it now seemed plain to Harriet that it was "a plan to hurt me."[48]

While this unpleasant business went on, William Lamb and his family prepared for Peniston's death. Lady Melbourne risked social disgrace by inviting her eldest son's mistress, Mrs. Dick Musters, to live at Melbourne House in order to provide comfort in his last days.[49] Things went quickly, and he died 24 January 1805. William now stood to inherit the Melbourne estate. It was a mixed blessing, for he had no relish for the role of a future peer, acting as a cog in the machinery of English political life. He would need to stand for election to the House of Commons as soon as possible. The leisure he so much prized would be scarce or nonexistent. Yet now he had a social and financial standing that would permit him to try again for Lady Caroline's hand in marriage.

Yet there was a difficulty. Peniston's death caused an earthquake in the fault-ridden geology of Melbourne House. Lady Melbourne was devastated, her husband more so. Lord Melbourne had lost his only legitimate child, and he responded with rage, refusing William the allowance of £5,000 per annum that he had previously settled on his eldest son. He was so adamant that even the indomitable Lady Melbourne resorted to asking a friend to intervene on William's behalf. In the end, William was allowed only £1,800 a year. It was an insulting reminder of his illegitimacy, over which William brooded his whole life. But it was good enough for his current purpose to wed, until the day came when the elder Melbourne departed this earth himself.

In the meantime, the poison-pen letters continued *de plus belle*. The writer struck a note of whimsy when he sent one to Mr. Hill himself in early February, under the signature of Lady Bessborough. She had received several, under various signatures, and the most recent, she wrote to Lord Granville, began "as usual with verses," and with innuendo about Lord Granville himself. It was "very abusive of us all . . . but chiefly again attacking me, saying my Sister had forbearance enough to stop short of danger and only took money from her lovers but that I— . . . ."[50] What worse pecuniary sins were supposedly hers, she did not disclose. The "news paper persecution" continued, and some editors succumbed to the temptation to print the scurrilous but eloquent material despite the objections of the families. In mid-February, Harriet and her sister—who was now ailing with an attack of gallstones—enlisted Bess in drafting a stanza to be sent to the *Morning Post* in hope that it would shame or frighten Sheridan into silence:

> Shame to the pen whose coward poisons flow
> In secret streams with baneful malice fraught,
> That emulates th' assassin's Midnight blow,
> By hate directed and by Vengeance wrought.
> Yet generous Minds the name will ne'er reveal,
> Tho' known! nor deign a stigma to impart,
> But leave the dastard miscreant to feel
> The conscious pangs of a corrupted heart.[51]

Harriet only regretted the choice of the word "vengeance," which implied some justification for the attacks. Her ambivalence suggests that she felt they did indeed stem from some wound she had inflicted on Sheridan. The reproachful verse, whether it was printed or simply posted to Sheridan directly, seems to have had its effect, or else an unrecorded interview may have taken place between Lady Bessborough and Sheridan. There is only one further mention (on 27 February 1805) of letters containing indecencies.[52] Sheridan left London and spent most of the rest of the year away from the city. He made only one speech in Parliament during 1805.[53] His party missed him when the bill to abolish the slave trade was defeated. As rumors of infidelity swirled around the Princess of Wales, a financial scandal threatened to drag down Pitt, seriously weakening the government.

William renewed his suit for Caroline's hand, allowing for no half-measures: "I have loved you," he wrote on 1 May, "for four years, loved you deeply, dearly, faithfully—so faithfully that my love has withstood my firm determination to conquer it when honour forbade my declaring myself—has withstood all that absence, variety of objects, my own endeavours to seek and like others, or to occupy my mind with fix'd attention to my profession, could do to shake it."[54]

The arrow hit the mark. Caroline brought this letter to her mother immediately, threw her arms round Harriet's neck and told her she loved William better than anything in the world, except, of course, her own mother. Caught off guard, Lady Bessborough played for time. A letter from her brother, Earl Spencer, had also arrived, suggesting that a marriage to his son Lord Althorp was indeed desirable and might be encouraged through bringing the two young people into closer proximity.[55] She was in an awkward position.

Because she wanted to make her daughter happy, Lady Bessborough worked herself around to accepting William. "I have long foreseen and endeavoured to avoid what has just happened—Wm Lamb's proposing to her," she wrote to Granville, on 2 May 1805,

> but she likes him too much for me to do more than entreat a little further acquaintance on both sides, and not having this declared immediately, which precludes all possibility of retreat. In some things I like it. He has a thousand good qualities, is very clever, which is absolutely necessary for her; and above all she has preferred him from childhood, and is now so much in love with him that before his speaking, I dreaded its affecting her health. But on the other hand, I dislike the connection extremely. I dislike his manners, and still more his principles and his creed, or rather no creed. Yet to her his behaviour has been honourable and his letter is beautiful.[56]

Lady Bessborough had stated her reservations delicately. She and her sister and mother all saw William as a hedonistic man who lacked "seriousness." His promises to reform now and to be guided by his mother-in-law's advice were not entirely convincing. Unable to say yes or no to his suit, Lady Bessborough fell into a nervous prostration. "In short, my poor sister is more dead than alive," wrote Georgiana to Lady Spencer, although she may have been dramatizing in order to persuade her mother to approve the marriage. Harriet took counsel with Georgiana, and they both agreed to support the match. Harriet now told Lady Spencer that William's proposal had evoked from Caroline "such evidence of the most boundless attachment, that I really believe—so does the Duke, that any check would be productive of madness or death."[57] Perhaps Harriet did not exaggerate, for William later described his own state of mind to Queen Victoria as similar: "I do believe if I had been refused, I should have died of it; it would have killed me; I was so very vain."[58]

By 6 May the marriage was "settled and declared," though it had been a messy business.[59] Caroline wanted to conclude matters without having William come to the house, so William had been invited to a performance of *Hamlet* at Drury Lane Theatre, starring the young prodigy William Henry West Betty. There, spurred on by Caroline's presence, he used all his powers of persuasion on Lady Bessborough, waxing, as she said, so "warm and animated" that he "soon succeeded in obtaining every promise he wished."[60] A flustered Lady Bessborough stopped short of a flat yes, however, repeating that she and her husband would accept Caroline's decision in the matter, whereupon William, sure of his prize at last, threw his arms around Harriet, declaring, "And that decision is in my favour, thank Heaven!"

At that moment, Harriet looked up and saw two observers, including the politician George Canning. From his expression, she knew that Canning had conjectured she was having an affair with William. Lady Bessborough had known Canning for some time, and William was his rival in the party. There was nothing for Harriet to do but disclose the secret that Caroline was engaged. Canning's response was so kind that Harriet impulsively kissed his hand—yet another faux pas of the type that drove Lady Spencer wild. Just the previous February, Lord Bessborough had been very unpleasantly surprised upon returning home in the wee hours of the morning to find Canning on his way out the door.[61] Having narrowly avoided further embarrassment now with Canning, Harriet felt that the evening seemed to have ended well after all.

Well enough, that is, until they went on to Devonshire House, where Hartington was stunned to learn that he had lost all hope of marrying Caroline. He went into hysterics, reproaching her and everyone else. What Caroline felt on this occasion goes unrecorded, but she must have pitied Hart, for he became so distraught that Georgiana's physician Walter Farquhar had to be called in to sedate him.[62] Hart would live into his late sixties, but he never married.

Having accepted her son-in-law-to-be and survived Hart's tantrum, Harriet now expressed the hope that marriage would transform her daughter: "I believe all her ill health, all the little oddities of manner and *sauvagerie* that us'd to vex me, arose from the unhappiness that was preying upon her."[63] Lady Bessborough simply expressed the common wisdom that marriage to the right man would improve a disordered female personality, just as frustrating the marriage would doom her to the derangement of erotomania—mental collapse through disappointment of her desire. "[H]er poor little mind would not bear it," agreed Georgiana.[64]

There could be no turning back now. William appeared in Cavendish Square the next morning to make a formal request of Lord Bessborough for Lady

Caroline's hand. It was freely given. William knew, however, that Caroline would be miserable if she could not obtain the blessing of the Spencer matriarch: "I listen for the postman's knock with cold hands, and indescribable anxiety. Your peace of mind is I know so connected with yr. dear g[ran]dmama's happiness."[65]

Lady Caroline and her relations worked hard to gain Lady Spencer's approval. Her brother John, her uncle, Lord Spencer, and Little G's new husband Lord Morpeth all wrote or made visits to press Lady Spencer to assent. "They are all wonderfully afraid of my sentiments," she noted with pleasure in a letter to Selina Trimmer. Caroline came to her accompanied by Hart and letters from Georgiana and Lord Duncannon entreating her not to oppose what could not be prevented. Afraid to give the letters to her grandmother, Caroline held on to them overnight, then read them aloud to her. "The D[ea]r child was on her knees," said Lady Spencer, "the tears streaming from her eyes & repeating that she w[oul]d not marry without my consent." Caroline's histrionics were sincere, but they did not sway her grandmother, who told her plainly it was "a match I would not approve—that talking of my Consent was Childish as from all I saw everything was settled." Caroline then produced "a most extravagant letter" from William promising that "his whole life shd be passed in trying to make [Caroline] happy." This still did not produce the desired result, however. The dowager Lady Spencer instead wrote a formal reply to William, noting that she was not "in the least acquainted with him," but promising that if he made Caroline happy, she would receive him as a Gr[and] Son & give him as much of her esteem & affection as she thinks it worth his while to require."[66] Sobered by this display of steely reserve in her honored grandmother, Caroline decided to declare victory and move on.

News of the engagement traveled swiftly, and the general reaction was one of incredulity, for most family acquaintances thought Caroline was staggeringly immature.[67] The Queen was pleased, however, and complimented Caro at court in the presence of her aunt.[68] The Prince of Wales seemed ecstatic at the news, and told William "I *am* so happy, oh! but so very happy!" William left the party on that night to visit Lady Bessborough, with whom he talked about Caroline and his prospects until two in the morning.[69]

The wedding was scarcely three weeks off. A special license had to be gotten from the Archbishop of Canterbury, and the preparations wore everyone to a frazzle, especially Harriet. The only real reason for all this rush was the threat of another invasion by the French army under Bonaparte. False reports of landings in Ireland kept anxiety high in the Bessborough household.[70] Caroline stayed with her grandmother at Holywell House during May. Brocket Hall was just one half hour's ride away, and William came to see her frequently. On 22 May, their marriage settlement was executed there. It was the most important document she signed in her life, and would in spirit outlast even the separation agreement that was yet to come.

Marriage

1805–1806

$\mathbb{C}$ aroline and William's wedding was preceded by arrangements for what would follow, including the all-important question of livelihood. Lord Melbourne still smoldered at the loss of his only biological child, and he refused his newly married son any additional allowance. Indeed, when he got wind that William was courting Caroline, he told his wife that he strongly advised his son "to marry a fortune."[1] Though he relented on this point and eventually promised Caroline her own "pin money," the newlyweds would still have to live at Melbourne House. The phrase "pin money" refers to a Lady's allowance for her personal expenditure. Caroline would receive £400 per annum.

Lady Melbourne compensated by giving William and his betrothed the magnificent first-floor apartments, which had a view of St. James's Park. She would retain the less attractive but more practical ground-floor apartments for herself. Charming and generous as she could appear, Lady Melbourne never let her eye wander far from business. When her housekeeper of many years, Mrs. Guidon, died, she called it a "happy release" and hired a replacement the same day.[2] She had earned the nickname of "The Thorn" for her wicked wit, but it was her pragmatism that Sheridan had in mind when he told her, "You are an admirable *prose* woman, but God denied you a poetic mind. You are fit only to pick out the eyes of potatoes by the dozen."[3] Lady Melbourne's passion for her children ran deep, however, especially for William. Supremely skilled in sexual politics, she disliked hearing that William had once been numbered among Lady Bessborough's admirers. Now, as William showed open affection toward his future mother-in-law, Lady Melbourne felt the prickings of jealousy. After the betrothal, she wounded Harriet by hoping out loud that the *daughter* would turn out better than the *mother*. Lady Bessborough turned aside this cut by replying mildly that she trusted that Lady Melbourne's advice—if not her *example,* she was tempted to add—would guide her daughter's behavior.[4]

Wedding preparations soon distracted Harriet from such skirmishes. "I have scarce a moment to write," she told Granville. "My whole day passes in seeing milliners and Mantua Makers for Caroline's marriage." Canis presented Caroline with a wedding gown made with long sleeves of extra fine lace and the very finest muslin to be had, and the Duchess gave her a lace veil.[5] In addition to preparing her trousseau, Lady Caroline began decorating her new apartments, which she adorned with *putti,* the cherubs she had loved during her time in Italy. She had sketched them often, and now she would have these androgynous creatures around her in stone, marble, and paint. Hartington seemed to have recovered from his disappointment, and they danced together at a ball in Caroline's honor.[6]

The Sunday before the wedding Lady Bessborough took Caroline to Roehampton to see William. The bride acted depressed, and her mother reproached her. It would hurt William's feelings if she seemed reluctant. Lady Caroline pulled herself together for a little speech, as much for her mother's benefit as for his: "My dear William, judge what my love must be, when I can leave such a mother as this for you. Girls who are not happy at home may marry without regret, but it required very strong affection indeed to overpower mine."[7]

On 2 June, a concert and party honoring Caroline took place at Devonshire House. The presents included a burnt-topaz cross from Harryo, and from Hartington some "very pretty bracelets." Bess gave her a pearl cross, and from Lord Melbourne she received a set of amethysts. Cousin G, now Lady Morpeth (who was nine months pregnant) gave her an aquamarine clasp and some wrought gold amulets with cameos. Her grandmother offered her a magnificent cross encrusted with amethysts that would "suit the Melbourne set," according to the Duchess of Devonshire.[8] William sought to cement his relationship with Lady Spencer by giving her a portrait of Lady Caroline. Lady Spencer was so touched that she proclaimed the portrait would be returned to the gallant husband upon her death.[9] Lady Melbourne presented Caroline with a diamond tiara in a flower design set "en tremblant," so that when she moved the stones shifted and shimmered.[10] It was a grand gesture from possibly the most astute

English woman of the age, who hoped William was about to make a magnificent match.

The Reverend James Preedy from Hatfield, renowned for his befuddlement, married William and Caroline on 3 June 1805 in the Bessborough residence at 2 Cavendish Square. The wedding gown, with its fine lace sleeves and lace high up around her neck, gave Caroline an "Eastern" appearance to the eye of her Aunt Georgiana. She wore one strand of pearls, and under her veil the aquamarine clasp that Little G had given the day before, while she held another similar clasp in her hand. Looking "light and beautiful," Caroline walked steadily to join William. When the vows were exchanged, she spoke without hesitation.

Afterward, however, Caroline began to weep. A large and noisy crowd had gathered, and William, calmly picking up the slight figure in his arms, carried her through it to the waiting carriage. Everyone was relieved as they left for Brocket Hall, especially Harriet, who confessed, "the agitation has been too much for me." Georgiana sat up with her sister until midnight speculating on what might be transpiring in the nuptial bedroom.[11] Harriet finally fell asleep, and Georgiana departed, but the party went on. And on. The tabors and the fiddles were reportedly still striking up and the servants still drinking their mistress's health more than a week later.[12]

To assuage Caroline's feelings of exile from the female realm, William wrote a letter of reassurance to Lady Spencer saying that he would bring his wife to visit "the moment Caroline says she wishes it, and to stay there as long as you will allow us, and this not only now, when I may be supposed to act so for the sake of appearance, but at any time and at all times in the future."[13] William acted in his own self-interest, but also with sensitivity for the feelings of the woman he loved. This augured well, and helps explain the hopes of the women who cared for Caroline that, in the end, he would know how to make her happy.

The couple honeymooned at Brocket, where they had not much chance to establish a rhythm in their own relations. In fact, they were almost constantly under scrutiny, like a patient with a rare disease. Lady Bessborough wrote sentimentally to Caroline that only someone with William's kindness could have stolen her lone female child, "but as I told you so gravely the other day, he really appears to me like my *natural son*." This comment seems rather daring, given the fact that William was in fact a "natural" (that is, illegitimate) child, that he had been one of Harriet's admirers, and that Harriet had but recently given birth to another "natural" child of her own by Granville.[14]

Despite maternal encouragement, Caroline was unwell after her marriage. Harriet made a visit four days after the wedding trying to calm her daughter's nervous indisposition and soothe the discomfort and shock of losing her virginity. Lady Bessborough wrote to Granville: "I do think it very hard that men should always have beau jeu on all occasions, and that all the pain, Moral et Physique, should be reserv'd for us."[15] After Harriet left, Lady Spencer and her sons (Caroline's uncles) arrived. When Caroline came downstairs she began flinging herself into one chair after another. Lady Spencer chided her and bundled her into their new Cabriolet for a drive around the park.[16] By 19 June, Lady Bessborough thought her daughter looked better, "but so unlike a *wife*"—more like a "School Girl" than a married woman. Bess's son Augustus could not even imagine this "Ariel, the little Fairy Queen" in her new role.[17]

Hartington had not entirely forgiven Caroline for jilting him, so she wrote him a poem three weeks after her marriage casting herself in her favorite role as the Fairy Queen Titania, and him as Oberon.

> The wand was broke her elves dismiss'd
> The Deamons yell'd—the serpants hist
> The skies were black the thunder round
> When sad Titania left her lord
> And thus in plaints both loud & long
> To stones address'd her mournful song.

Bidding her Oberon goodbye, this queen admits she has traded a fairy kingdom for the love of an all-too-mortal being, "a man whose very gentlest breath / Might blow a thousand elves to death." Titania enumerates the things she has left behind—jokes and games and childhood delights, gone now that she is "another's wife."

> Thus spoke Titania then she sigh'd
> Doomed to become a Mortals bride
> What since befel her no one knows
> but certain 'tis overwhelm'd with woes
> she deeply mourns her broken vows.[18]

The poem is accompanied by a sketch of the fairy queen flying amid spirits fleeing from a planetary globe—a world no longer hers.

Caroline's new world posed the first true intellectual challenge of her life. Not two days had passed after the wedding when she wrote to her mother asking her to send a book on education and Charles Rollins's twenty-four volume *Histoire*

Ancienne. Lady Bessborough teased her gently that her happiness no doubt depended upon "that dear, beautiful, light amusing book." "Could you not contrive," she inquired, "a little rolling booke case you might draw after you, containing these precious volumes?"[19] Conscious of her scattered and inferior learning, Caroline now conceived a passion to become properly educated and an equal partner to William. Into her scrapbook she pasted a printed copy of William's "Essay on the Progressive Improvement of Mankind," for which he had won the declamation prize at Trinity, Cambridge.[20]

When the newlyweds were fixed in Melbourne House's first floor apartments, Harryo commented that Caroline looked "amazingly improved" by her marriage and "as gentle and *posée* as if she had been a matron in the country for 20 years instead of days."[21] Caroline was playing nurse to William, who had a bad cold. She could rise to an occasion and loved role-playing, of course. The role of wife proved complicated, however.

She wrote to Lady Morpeth, now a mother: "You told me the happiest time in your life was three weeks after being married. I am not quite arrived at that period but am much contented with my present state and yet I cannot say I have never felt happier." Perhaps to negate any imputation of dissatisfaction, she added that she had married "not a Man but an Angel" who was beautiful, clever, sensible, and "kinder more gentle more soothing more indulgent talks nonsense better and coaxes me more than a woman could and with all that he is in short perfection."[22]

Caroline and William had a separate entrance to the house in Whitehall, but separation of their affairs from the Melbournes was impossible. Under the marriage settlement, William and Caroline together had been allowed £2,200. While this would have been a fortune in the eyes of most young couples, it allowed little independence to those in William's and Caroline's class, and their habits and expectations led them into the usual problems. They were constantly in arrears to tradesmen. Lady Caroline kept several pages, and she clothed them in an extravagant livery of her own design. Mr. Baker, her tailor, received very specific directions with accompanying drawings for red waistcoats and breeches to accompany a brown Hussar jacket trimmed in red with six rows of round silver buttons, also with cuffs and collars.[23] Henry Dunckley's early biography of William reports that on at least one occasion he was served a writ for debt by his own tailor, Francis Place, the future Radical politician.[24]

In addition to the indignities of summer colds and short funds, the young couple also felt overshadowed by the impending marriage of Emily Lamb to Lord Cowper, which was set for 20 July. Emily was ecstatic at her prospective union to this powerful and wealthy man considerably her senior. "I am happier than any person ever was before," she wrote to her mother, signing her name and drawing a circle around it, signifying a "Mystical ring" of "unaccountable power."[25] Emily disliked Caroline and would prove a formidable foe.

Conspicuous by his absence at Caroline's wedding, Sheridan nonetheless continued to haunt Lady Bessborough. At a ball at Devonshire House in late June 1805, Sheridan followed her around "like a Shadow" and tried to sit by her at supper, "always pretending to cry."[26] In July, with Lady Caroline still feeling unwell more than a month after the wedding, Lady Bessborough attended another party at which Sheridan made himself a nuisance by taking a seat opposite her and staring at her with alternating looks of supplication and ferocity so that no one could miss his behavior. Excusing him by saying he was drunk, Harriet tried to make her escape, but he seized her by the arm and begged her to shake hands with him. When she extricated herself from his grasp, he followed her, reproaching her in loud tones for her "cruelty." Escaping into the company of the older women at the party, Harriet was appalled to find Sheridan undissuaded from making a further spectacle of himself, which he did by apologizing profusely for "all the offences he had ever committed . . . either on this night or in former times" and protesting his undying love, respect, and adoration.[27]

Lady Bessborough did not mention Sheridan's actions to Caroline, who had enough problems at Melbourne House. The potential sources of friction there were many, including the Lambs' informal and irreverent habits. Lady Caroline drew sketches that showed William and George Lamb in the "family attitude," sprawled on a couch, one leg draped up on the back or leg of the furniture, reading. They were a close-knit group of practical jokers—hardheaded and unsentimental. The Lamb children tended to be cast in the mold of their mother.

Lady Caroline fictionalized Melbourne House in *Glenarvon,* calling it "Monteith" and describing herself (in the role of Lady Calantha), as an alien being: "What talents she had were of a sort they could not appreciate; and all the defects were those they most despised. The refinement, the romance, the sentiment she had imbibed, appeared in their eyes assumed and unnatural; her strict opinions, perfectly ridiculous; her enthusiasm, absolute insanity; and the violence of her temper, if contradicted or opposed, the pettishness of a spoiled and wayward child."[28] The Lambs viewed Caroline as William's hobby, and they laughed when William treated her desire for book learning seriously.

A rich intellectual cuisine, combined with daily object lessons in the cynicism and hypocrisy of Whig society, shook Lady Caroline's rather naïve view of the world. This she also transcribed in *Glenarvon:* "Calantha's principles had received a shock, the force and effect of which was greatly augmented by a year of vanity and folly."[29] Caroline would later reproach William for calling her "prudish" and "straight-laced," as well as for talking of his previous love-affairs, perhaps in the mistaken notion that such descriptions would arouse her sexual appetite. He even confessed to her that he had been in love with her cousin G before she married Lord Morpeth. She said William "amused himself with instructing me in things I need never have heard or known."[30]

In his biography of Caroline, David Cecil expresses disbelief at Caroline's apparent ignorance of the facts of life when she married, pointing out that she spent nineteen years in households where affairs and illegitimate children were the rule and where couples paired off at parties and searched for vacant bedchambers.[31] But Lady Caroline's relative innocence at the time of her marriage is corroborated by others, especially by her mother and her husband. If it seems incredible that someone brought up in the Devonshire House circle should have been prudish, we should remember that her cousins G and Harryo seem also to have been raised in similar ignorance. Six years Caroline's senior and not himself highly experienced, William posed as cynical and world-weary. Hypersensitive over his father's rejection, he took a paternalistic attitude toward his wife's naïveté and simply laughed at her pretensions as a *femme fatale.*

Whatever the frictions, William and Caroline knew their duty. She soon became pregnant, and this happy event caused excitement and confusion in her. She wrote to cousin G to ask what symptoms she should expect, and whether during this period "it is bad for you to *sleep* with your husband in the most significant sense of the word."[32] William was very happy, and for a time all was smooth. Lady Elizabeth Foster reported that Caroline looked back to normal in September: "She is the same wild, delicate, odd delightful person, unlike everything."[33] By October, Harryo thought Caroline looked pretty but "pale and ill" and "pale and thin." Caroline's pregnancy gave her a terror of miscarriage, and she drifted about Melbourne House as if afraid she might be about to step on broken glass.[34]

Perhaps Lady Morpeth had indeed advised sexual abstinence, or perhaps there were other causes for annoyance, but William sometimes seemed cool and distant to everyone, and the young couple quarreled over trifles—for example, whether Caroline's maid Betsey should travel in an open or shut carriage. This particular argument resulted in William's abruptly going out "on business" and sending word he would not be home till late. Caroline retaliated by calling a carriage for Devonshire House and dining with Harryo and her Aunt Georgiana. Impulsively, she then sent her wedding ring home and attended a play with her cousin, wearing gaudy jewelry and heavily rouging her cheeks. Unable to contain what was already obvious, she confessed to Harryo that she was having a tiff with William, swearing her to secrecy. Harryo promptly broke her promise by writing to her sister G. It appears the quarrel was made up shortly thereafter. Not much later, Lady Bessborough found the couple sitting in one chair together, reading a book.[35]

In late October news of the victory at Trafalgar on the twenty-first and the death of Admiral Horatio Nelson arrived in London. It stunned the city, and Devonshire House was no exception. A long shadow of mourning for the fallen hero would stretch across the approaching Christmas and New Year's celebrations in England. It would be weeks until the battered ship "Victory" would sail into London bearing Nelson's body to lie in state in the Painted Hall at Greenwich. Caroline's brother Frederick rode as part of the mounted guard in the funeral procession. Frederick was a handsome and easygoing young man now, but also the only one of the Ponsonby children to have inherited the gambling addiction that had blighted the lives of his mother and aunt.

Caroline and William flirted incessantly, and Lady Bessborough thought it was "delightful to see two creatures so happy."[36] Yet William could not fathom Caroline's "irrational" belief in Christianity. He had been raised with only such religious training as was necessary to the social and political schemes of his mother and sister, who attended Sunday services but held no real religious convictions. Despite his lack of any creed, however, he took an avid interest in theological questions, enjoyed the company of educated religious men, and despised church officials who appeared to be "theological simpletons."[37] He viewed the Church of England as an important institution regulating the religious instinct, even while its doctrines were laughable. At the same time, he had a lifelong fear of excessive religious fervor because it led to intolerance and persecution. This was an idea he articulated frequently, and which he later attempted to inculcate in young Queen Victoria when he became her first Prime Minister. The church must know its place, William believed. After sitting through a long evangelical sermon, William Lamb commented dryly: "Things have come to a pretty pass when religion is allowed to invade the sphere of private life." He is also reputed to have said that he could not be considered a pillar of the church, but rather a "buttress," for he "supported it from the outside."[38]

The Lambs' pragmatic atheism and thorough materialism posed a riddle for Lady Caroline, whose faith had been planted by her pious grandmother and inconsistently watered by her mother. William's attempts to disprove the existence of God and disabuse her of her "superstitions" caused quarrels in which crockery flew. William was adamant that he would make his fairy-wife into a worldly woman. The battle would never be won, though Caroline would later go through a period of manic dissipation resulting partly from William's strong attacks on her belief system. It was upon this subject that she probably meditated in an ambitious poem written in her commonplace book and illustrated by water colors with captions in French. The verse is reminiscent of Blake's *Songs of Innocence and Experience:*

> Winged with Hope & hushed with Joy,
> See yon wanton blue-eyed boy
> Arch his smile, & keen his dart
> Aim at Laura's youthful heart!
> How could he his wiles disguise
> How deceive such watchful eyes?
> How so pure a breast inspire,
> Set so young a Mind on fire?

The poem continues in this vein, recounting the bewilderment of the heroine, who can scarcely defend her heart against this assault from a "friend." Thus trapped, the heroine confronts her own alienation in the form of her lover:

> Now I know thee tyrant boy
> Who can worlds of bliss destroy
> Yet oh speak tho' all in vain
> Speak and bless me once again
> Better twice a dupe to prove
> Than view the alter'd looks of love.[39]

William was that wanton boy whose protestations of holding only her best interests at heart served as an excuse for cultivating her cynicism. "Oh those Lambs how they do enlighten one's mind," she later wrote sarcastically to cousin G. They are "the best of masters," she said. "They can teach everything but not to love them."[40]

William's blasphemous views were also reflected in the family predilection for cursing. He had formed the habit of liberally seasoning his comments with Anglo-Saxonisms and sacrilegious exclamations. Lady Caroline wrote a poem of admonition:

> Yes, I adore thee, William Lamb,
> But I hate to hear thee say God d——:

Frenchmen, say English cry d——d——
But why swear'st thou?—thou art a *Lamb!*[41]

Dinner-table interactions at Melbourne House and Brocket Hall were conducted in a rowdy argot, basically a conversational free-for-all with a generous garnish of expletives. The sass, effrontery, and low tone of this Whig household are embodied in George Lamb's musical play, *Whistle For It,* which was produced at this time at the Priory, Stanmore, the residence of Lord and Lady Abercorn. In this home-made production William was cast as the Captain of the Banditti, and Caroline watched jealously, causing her husband to steal looks at the audience and underplay his part because he feared Caroline's reaction "if an expression or look of well acted tenderness" toward his female counterpart were to escape him.[42] The play then went for a disastrous opening (with a professional cast, of course) at Covent Garden Theatre in London. George Lamb was proud, despite the bad reviews, though his family's warm congratulations could not remove the sting of Byron's comments upon his failure in *English Bards and Scotch Reviewers.*[43]

Caroline's moral intensity was a mystery to her in-laws. William had married a mere child. Everyone wondered how this waif-like creature would produce any offspring, let alone the large brood required in a world of smallpox, tuberculosis, cholera, and the attrition of any number of fearsome childhood diseases? Caroline's brother Lord Duncannon (John William Ponsonby) had married Lady Maria Fane in November, and Maria Duncannon was herself pregnant. As her own belly swelled, she predicted Caroline's child would be a fairy with wings, one that no one could catch. It was a prophetic remark.[44]

After Christmas 1805, Sheridan's first play, *The Rivals,* was revived on its thirtieth anniversary, and Caroline attended. With its famous characters, like Mrs. Malaprop and Lydia Languish, *The Rivals* is a satire of the world of the Lambs, Ponsonbys, and Cavendishes, with all its love affairs and jealousies, mistaken identities and private codes—masquerading in the play as garbled communication. Above all, *The Rivals* satirizes that world's conventions of courting. Lydia's idealistic longing for a flamboyant elopement has to be overcome before she will accept her lover's hand in conventional marriage. The drama held up well, it seemed to Caroline.

At its six-month mark, her own marriage was unsteady. Harryo reported contradictorily that Caroline "was very amiable but looked extremely ill. She worries herself to death about a pain in her chest." William acted both "grave and disagreeable."[45] Caroline continued jealously aware of William's every movement, while he sustained a constant, no doubt exhausting, attentiveness to her. Together they read Hume, Shakespeare, and "Newton on the Prophecies with the Bible."[46] Despite this constant companionship, Caroline continued to be and look ill. She wrote to her grandmother that her milk had begun to flow, but that "the child has not moved yet."[47] Worry wore her down, and she suffered an attack of influenza in January of 1806. Again, Harryo wrote evocatively: "[T]hey seem the happiest of human beings. She looks very ill."[48]

Partly to escape the claustrophobia, William now succumbed to the pressure and stood as the Whig candidate for a vacant seat at Leominster in early 1806. On 23 January, Pitt the Younger had died, and this caused a surprisingly strong emotional outpouring from the Whigs, though they had fought him for so long. The passing of this statesman created unease, as many British politicians read the news from Austerlitz, where Napoleon had defeated the Austrians and the Russians. Fox formed a new administration and made Sheridan treasurer to the Navy, putting Charles Grey (now Lord Howick) in the Admiralty and appointing Caroline's Uncle George (Earl Spencer) to the Home Office. All this made the political landscape more friendly to William's cause, and he threw himself into election canvassing.

At the climax of the campaign, on 31 January, Caroline went into labor prematurely. The child clung to life and a messenger sped off to summon William. Though he traveled all night, William arrived too late. Their baby was buried at Hatfield. William won the seat at Leominster, but this was little consolation for the "cruel disappointment" that left Caroline broken in health and spirit, William silent and brooding.

Sadly, other grief was looming. In February, the Duchess of Devonshire began to have severe headaches. The previous September, when she had passed "a gall stone of amazing size," she had felt her health going.[49] Now, pain she recognized from previous attacks also returned. In early March, sensing that she would not survive another bout of illness, she began to write letters to her children and friends, including one to her mother that ended pathetically with a request for £100 to help her pay off some small debts. She showed signs of jaundice, which her doctor Sir Walter Farquhar mistook for a positive indication that the illness would pass. She was dying of an abscess of the liver, though no one recognized it.[50] She managed to endure a visit to court, then caught cold. It worsened, despite optimistic predictions, and the spasms she had experienced before returned.

Though she had confessed her debts only a year previously, Georgiana had actually begun to borrow again, and this unrelenting anxiety, continued for thirty years, had exacerbated her many physical ailments, destroying her will to live. Believing her Aunt Georgiana's end had come, Caroline wrote:

Gentle sleep, thy blessings shed—
Soothe her weary soul to rest;
Angels, guard her suffering head,
Calm the troubles at her breast

'Tis for others' woes she weeps,
By their sorrows quite opprest;
Angels, guard her while she sleeps.
She who blesses, should be blest.[51]

Whether Georgiana was grieving for *others*' woes is debatable. She was the proverbial survivor, and up to the last moment her numerous doctors, including Farquhar and Matthew Baillie (brother of Scottish playwright Joanna Baillie), expected a reprieve. Her head was shaved and a blister was applied to her scalp. She was almost completely blind, now, and spoke only in whispers.[52] Harriet sat by her bedside and listened to her sister's "inarticulate sounds which it was impossible to understand."[53] Georgiana now suffered hallucinations and went into an eight-hour attack of convulsions. Nonetheless, it seemed unimaginable that she would die. She staved off the end until 3:30 A.M. on 30 March. Harriet was almost destroyed by attending her sister through her final illness: "Anything so horrible, so killing, as her three days' agony no human being ever witness'd."[54]

The Duchess of Devonshire lay in state until Easter Sunday 1806. An unusual chill had descended upon the countryside, and snow fell. Similarly, cold winds were blowing in Caroline's heart for Lady Elizabeth Foster. She had often discussed how to resolve the "Bess Problem" with Hart and Harryo. Now, if ever, was the time to act. On 4 April, the night before the hearse arrived to take Georgiana's remains to Chatsworth (the Devonshire estate in Derbyshire), Little G and Harryo confronted Bess and told her that it was time for her to leave. That evening, Hartington tapped on her door and made it a unanimous verdict.[55]

Lady Elizabeth's resolve never wavered, however, because Georgiana had left her with absolute control over her papers. Bess had authority to do anything she wished with thousands of letters and other documents.[56] Canis refused to act. It was a stalemate. Temporarily, Bess went with Harriet to Roehampton.

Caroline continued unwell through the summer, and her maladies must have made her husband an infrequent visitor to her bed. She consulted doctors who prescribed various remedies, including a "laudanum plaister" worn on her back and a regular dose of laudanum mixed with egg whites. She was given other advice to imbibe "tonic medicines" and to bathe in the sea.[57] It would not do for her to become pregnant before she was physically stronger. Lady Melbourne found it all mystifying. She had given birth eight times and lost three children. She did not understand Caroline's frailty.

Ill or well, Caroline had no particular role to play in the Melbourne household, which was entirely controlled by her mother-in-law, right down to Brocket's orchards and gardens, which turned a profit under her able management. Lady Melbourne had an uncanny ability to succeed where others failed. When he was in the last period of his unhappy life, her nephew M. G. ("Monk") Lewis wrote to her in frustration, misery, and astonishment: "You go up, up, up, and I go down, down, down."[58] Caroline and William still owed their financial security to Lady Melbourne's diplomacy with Lord Melbourne. In contrast, Emily Lamb stood within her mother's ring of power as the wife of Lord Cowper. She was having the Cowpers' country home, Panshanger, torn down and rebuilt magnificently.

Perhaps because she was not only not needed but not wanted, Caroline went for an extended stay with her mother to Littlehampton in Sussex. In her sketchbook she drew *putti* like little devils wielding blades. One picture shows a serpent-like creature pinning a human figure to a rock. It is accompanied by the following verse:

Sorrow lost—reproaches vain
Love will never come again
Soon despair with ruthless dart
Took possession of her heart
Bursting grief her bosom fired—
And love, & hope, with life expired.[59]

These figures represent the demise of marital bliss. William was still loving, but also still reserved. Caroline's desire to be petted and coddled went unfulfilled, and despite her sexual initiation, she remained immature. Unable to find the right method with Caroline, and feeling directionless, William tended to brood in his study.

These problems were exacerbated by the fact that William's attitude toward his marriage was one of great seriousness. As a young man he had adopted the glib and sardonic attitude of his contemporaries when discussing matrimony. However, it is clear that he believed that once a match had been made only disaster warranted its dissolution. Despite any miscalculations he made about the effect of his worldly wise manner on his impressionable spouse, he loved her and was in it for the long haul. Whatever his shortcomings, he seems to have remained faithful to Caroline until the very last period of her life. "By Whig standards," as William's biographer Leslie Mitchell admits in some puzzlement, "he showed an almost unbelievable chastity." The view that William fell carelessly into his marriage cannot be supported.[60] The reason that William Lamb's behavior seems incomprehensible to many biographers is that they fail to take his relations with Caroline seriously as the partnership it truly was.

Caroline now had an experienced position from which to observe how other couples wooed and wed. Caroline St. Jules and George Lamb were obviously beginning a courtship. As it developed, she "could not help remarking," she wrote to her mother, "the difference between a husband and lover!" She also observed, however, that the transformation was not an inevitable one, for she observed other married couples who seemed still very much in love: "How comes this wonderful phenomenon? Why—when the honeymoon is over, does [the husband] still remain a lover?" she asked.[61] No answer came.

That summer of 1806, Corisande de Grammont married Lord Ossulston. This was an excellent match that pleased the various members of the Devonshire-Bessborough circle. Lady Elizabeth, however, was now a source of unhappiness in that same circle. She kept up her pressure on the Duke of Devonshire to marry her. He, as usual, seemed disinclined to do anything one way or the other. His health was bad, and his temper short. Why couldn't things simply limp along as they were? This domestic drama was suddenly overshadowed by the news that Charles Fox was dying, a tremendous blow to William. The Duke of Devonshire had kindly allowed Fox to stay at Chiswick House in London. A moderate in politics, Fox had been immoderate with food and liquor for years. He passed away there on 13 September, and William Lamb grieved profoundly at the loss of this scion of liberalism and humanism. William had been a Foxite since Cambridge, and he wrote an adulatory epitaph intended for the memorial sculpture of Fox erected at Wimbledon Parish Church:

> This was the man whose ever deathless name
> Recalls his generous life's illustrious scenes;
> To bless his fellow-creatures was his aim—
> And universal liberty his means![62]

William had lost a family friend and a personal protector—almost the father he had never had. Now that Fox was gone, the leadership went to Lord Howick, with whom William was on polite but not warm terms. William occupied himself with parliamentary business as member for Leominster, a market town on the Welsh border.

Caroline at last began to feel better, and this meant the sun seemed to shine once more for William. William's attention to his political future may have calmed both of them. Her grandmother observed that she and William were "on the best terms possible & very happy in each other."[63] Lady Caroline decided to pay a tribute to William and show off her artistic abilities by copying a portrait of him that had been done by Maria Cosway and hung in Melbourne House. The picture—reportedly William's favorite—was being constantly taken down and then put up to "an amazing height" at the end of each session, because of Caroline's anxiety that it should not be damaged. Of course, in the process of remounting it, the ladder itself was thrust through the painting, making "the Devil of a hole," in Lord Melbourne's words. Caroline could do nothing right. Lord Melbourne grumbled that it seemed she had damaged the painting on purpose. Acutely embarrassed, she sought escape from the Melbournes' noisy dinner table by retiring to her rooms.[64] She also spent time at the residence of Lord and Lady Holland, where a coterie of liberal-minded intellectuals gathered. It concerned her grandmother that Caroline kept company with the divorced (and remarried) woman with politics as permissive as her morals. Holland House was not "a good place for her to frequent if it could be avoided."[65] Caroline also vented her overabundant energies and took out her frustrations by riding, fox-hunting, and shooting.

Her cousin Harryo's latent sympathetic feelings were aroused by the story of the fiasco with the painting: "This was very unlucky," she said, acknowledging that Caroline was out of favor with the Melbournes. Harryo wanted to please Lady Caroline by currying favor with her sister-in-law Emily (Lady Cowper), but hesitated, rightly suspecting that she could not trust Emily.[66] Caroline now had only a handful of strong supporters, besides her grandmother: William, her cousin Hart, and her own mother.

Lady Bessborough was preoccupied, however, with the problem of Bess. Harryo was outraged because the Duke had encouraged Bess to take on the duties of hostess for the Devonshires, whereas this was Harryo's right as eldest daughter. Caroline agreed. At a dinner party on 18 November Caroline read out loud to the Devonshire-Bessborough clan a letter of Madame Maintenon excusing her sly conduct in making herself a confidante of Louis XIV. The parallel to Bess was obvious: "I fancied Lady E was embarrassed," wrote Harryo the next day.[67] Not embarrassed enough to leave, however.

Now, to her joy, Caroline found herself pregnant again. Her grandmother recommended a new physician, a Dr. Penrose, and under his care Caroline struggled through morning sickness, headaches, and dizziness. Once again she suffered from some sort of nervous prostration vaguely reminiscent of her obsessive behavior as a child in Italy. Her grandmother wrote to Harriet on 23 December 1806: "I do not like Caroline's still having these nervous attacks & I dread their becoming habitual. I think the physicians (not you) should tell her that much might be done by her trying to resist them . . . but I do not know whether it will have any effect in fainting and giddiness."[68]

William fought any anxiety about Caroline's pregnancy by busying himself with politics. In November, he canvassed rather ineffectively for Sheridan and for Caroline's brother Frederick Ponsonby. The former won and the latter lost election. In December, Lord Howick kindly asked William to move the address at the opening session of Parliament, a task generally reserved for younger members who were potentially ready to assume some office in the administration. William had attended the sessions in the House of Commons religiously, and he had been on the verge of speaking impromptu a number of times, but found himself tongue-tied, nervous, and "too vain to expose myself to the disgrace of speaking in a hesitating manner."[69] He knew his limits all too well. Now, he would have the chance to prove his leadership potential with a prepared speech.

The opening of Parliament would be a subdued event, since war continued in Silesia and Breslau, and the incapacitated George III would not preside from his throne—nor would his retinue of secretaries, ladies-in-waiting, ushers, and yeomen of the guard be present. Nonetheless, William wrote and revised his speech, rehearsing it with Caroline as if he were about to play Captain of the Banditti. Caroline knew his vulnerability and admitted that she felt "frightened to death" on his behalf.[70] She wanted to attend—but women were prohibited from entering the Chamber.

William's maiden speech on 19 December was preceded by the King's message, read by the Speaker, which asserted that the country was in danger, still at war, and must punish the French navy, which threatened its lifeblood: overseas trade. William then spoke of the need for a strong Army, cautioned against the duplicities of the French, and applauded British society's care and concern for all, including "the meanest and most illiterate of people." There was warm applause for these platitudes. Sheridan congratulated him.[71]

At the conclusion, a slight figure in men's clothing slipped from the gallery and pelted back across Westminster Bridge to Whitehall. Caroline had pretended to go Holland House but instead had changed into breeches, shirt, and coat supplied by her little brother Willy. She had entered the Houses of Parliament in company of a family friend, Mr. Ross. Delighted and agitated by her own daring,

Caroline passed through the private entrance to Melbourne House, changed out of her disguise, and reappeared in time to welcome William. She hadn't fooled Lady Melbourne, however, who expressed her displeasure but agreed that she would say nothing if William was not angry.[72]

When William returned with a throng of well-wishers he could hardly have been angry with anyone. It was not long, however, before he realized that he had achieved a very modest victory. He had escaped without embarrassment, but he had not impressed those with power to choose future cabinet officers. Sheridan's congratulations were superficial. William was far from making his mark. As it turned out, he was never able to do more than offer prepared speeches, and when surprised in debates, would lose his train of thought and flounder ridiculously. Over the twenty-two years between 1806 and 1828, William spoke in Parliament only 79 times, often so briefly that the speech was less than a paragraph. Whole years would elapse in which William failed to speak at all.[73]

Still, on this day in Caroline's eyes he was a hero.

Parenthood

1807–1808

C aroline's first trimester difficulties continued. She had fainting spells, and on 22 January 1807 Harryo reported that she was "very weak and full of pains and fatigue."[1] As always, she maintained regular communication with her mother, who was feeling in poor spirits herself over relations with her brother George (2nd Earl Spencer), with whom she continued on uneasy terms due to the family politicking of his wife Lavinia. The friction this woman caused Harriet never abated, despite many efforts to appease her. Almost ten years earlier, she had noticed Lavinia's habit of becoming warm and friendly just in time for visits from Lady Spencer.[2] Little had changed. "I admire her cleverness," she eventually concluded in a letter to Granville. "[A]t times when I have seen her ill or unhappy I have felt as if I lov'd her; but there is something in her Character and manners wholly repugnant to me."[3]

Feeling "very low" about the undesirable distance separating her from her brother, Lady Bessborough went to check on Lady Caroline in her apartments at Melbourne House, and on alighting from her carriage discovered she was being followed by "a ruffian-like looking man" who pursued her into the dark entryway and up the stairs into the house. At first frightened, she was put out to discover it was Sheridan, whom she did her best to ignore, but who spent the whole evening causing Harriet to laugh in spite of herself with his witty remarks, "tho'

I persever'd in my determination of not speaking to him. I do not like his having got the entrée [at Melbourne House], and think him, even old as he is, a dangerous acquaintance for Caroline."[4]

Sheridan was still haunting Lady Bessborough, and plainly she perceived him as a threat to her daughter. He had already visited Caroline in January, when she described him as "very pleasant," with no "mysterious intents."[5] After chasing Harriet into Melbourne House, he returned at least once to visit Caroline without incident, but there remained something menacing in his omnipresence.

William's education of Lady Caroline continued, but the pupil grew restive at her teacher's unrelenting assault upon her religious beliefs. She purchased and had bound a gilt Bible inscribed, "[t]o the Hon. William Lamb. Given to him on his birthday by Caroline Lamb who begs him to value it for *her* sake. March 16, 1807."[6]

There were four women expecting babies in the summer of 1807: Emily Cowper, Caroline Lamb, Maria Duncannon, and Corisande Ossulston. Harryo, who constantly fought her weight, was bored and annoyed by the comparisons being made between the ripening mothers. It was as if "there was a second apple promised to the biggest and I am quite worn out by all the discussions and comparisons on the subject," she wrote in July.[7] Caroline stayed at Brocket, which she never tired of describing as the most beautiful place on earth. The first to give birth was Lady Ossulston. Maria Duncannon's baby arrived next, and it alarmed everyone by appearing listless and weak. As she prepared to "begin my agonies," Caroline found it heartbreaking to see a newborn unable to eat, and so weak "it could not hold up its head or open its eyes."[8]

As Caroline's time approached, Sheridan reappeared. It was one of the hottest summers in memory, and on 1 August he forced his way into Lady Bessborough's sweltering box at the opera and smirked while she tried to ignore him.[9] Two and a half weeks later, Lord Howick (the former Charles Grey) sought out Lady Bessborough to talk about his affair with Sheridan's wife, Hecca. Lady Bessborough reproached him bitterly for his abominable conduct, which was an affront to the memory of Georgiana, who had borne him two children. Perhaps because they both mourned Georgiana, Harriet's reproaches stung Howick to tears, and eventually he became violent: "[H]e beat his head, call'd himself by a thousand harsh names, cried, and threw himself at my feet . . . clasp'd both my hands in his, press'd them to his forehead as he knelt before me quite sobbing aloud, and then at once when I least dreamt of it clasp'd me in his Arms."[10] It was overdone, and Lady Bessborough confessed that this scene with Howick made her "ashamed of it for him, and for myself." She really could not account for his behavior: "was it resentment at my just indignation for his conduct to [Hecca]?" It was a peculiar event, but not as strange as what followed.

On 27 August 1807, Caroline began her labor. Lady Bessborough came to her at Melbourne House, where she received a note from Hecca Sheridan begging her to come. Harriet put off this visit until midnight. Since Caroline had still not gone into the last stages of labor, she left for what she believed would be a short while. She had arrived at the Sheridans' apartment and been in conversation with Hecca a few minutes when Sheridan burst drunkenly into the room. A bizarre interchange ensued in which he apologized, asking for mercy and compassion, admitting he was a "wretch," and told Harriet she was the woman he was most in love with, whereupon Hecca indignantly cried, "Why, you always tell me *I* am the only woman you ever were in love with." Sheridan then replied, "So you are, to be sure, my Dear Hecca," upon which she shouted, "Except *her?*" pointing at Harriet. This went on for almost three hours, according to Lady Bessborough. During the altercation, Sheridan grabbed her violently by the arm, accusing her of setting Hecca against him. Finally, the two women, with the help of the maid, succeeded in locking Sheridan in, and Harriet made her escape into the early morning streets to rush back to her daughter.[11]

Caroline's labor ended that morning, 28 August, with the birth of "a very fine boy," delivered by Dr. Penrose. The child was named George Augustus Frederick after the Prince of Wales, with the dowager Lady Spencer's blessing. William wrote to their friend Lady Holland (who was herself seven months pregnant) the next day that the child was "very large," especially "for so small a woman, which quality of the child made the labour very hard and painful, tho' it was very short lasting."[12] Lady Caroline insisted on nursing Augustus, against the wishes of her mother-in-law. At the end of September Caroline brought Augustus to Manresa House in Roehampton, accompanied by William, to visit her mother and father.[13] She had recovered well and seemed ecstatically happy with her infant boy. The Prince of Wales was to be the child's godfather.

The christening took place at Melbourne House in October. Sheridan tried to get an invitation from Harriet, who referred him to Lady Melbourne. He then approached Caroline, who gave him the same response. Finally, he asked Lady Melbourne, who told him flatly "no," and gave the excuse that if she began to let strangers attend, the place would be overrun. Harriet, Caroline, and Lady Melbourne held firm. But the ingenious Sheridan was not to be denied. Melbourne House had been illuminated inside and out, and the flow of guests had been constant. When the doors were thrown open to admit the Prince of Wales, in walked Sheridan. He had gotten the Prince to designate him as his attendant for the day.[14]

After the christening, conducted as had been their marriage ceremony by genial bumbling Reverend Preedy, a huge meal was served. The Prince, who had arrived at 5:00 P.M., obviously wanted to stay, along with his "attendant." Time, as Harriet wrote, "hung Heavy." Someone suggested writing short verse impromptu to which one's "opposite Neighbour" would write an impromptu reply. Sheridan managed to gain the seat immediately opposite Caroline, and he handed her these lines, which she read aloud:

> Grant Heav'n, sweet Babe, thou mayst inherit
> What Nature only can impart—
> Thy Father's manly sense and spirit,
> Thy Mother's grace and gentle Heart;
> And when to Manhood's hopes and duties grown,
> Be thou a prop to thy great Sponsor's throne.

This verse was certainly well-received, since it paid tribute to Augustus's "sponsor," the Prince. Yet it had an extraordinary effect on Caroline, usually at no loss when composing impromptu verse. Claiming to feel unwell, but also, as her mother wrote to Granville, looking frightened, she got up and abruptly left the room.

After her daughter's exit, Harriet wrote a response and passed it to Sheridan to read:

> May he who wrote ye verse impart
> To thee sweet Baby whom he blesses
> As shrewd a head, a better heart,
> And talents he alone possesses.

When Sheridan read the response aloud, he stammered at the third and fourth lines, according to Harriet, and then he substituted these lines for hers: "A wiser head, as pure a heart, / And greater wealth than he possesses."[15] Undoubtedly these lines were meant to reprove Sheridan for driving Caroline away. They scold him for having marred his intelligence and talent with emotional weakness.

What was in Sheridan's poem that could have offended Caroline? Was it his manner? Had some double-entendre been perpetrated, one that only Caroline and her mother would understand? Sheridan's behavior stemmed partly from his alcoholism. He behaved erratically even on the floor of the House of Commons during this period. But Caroline's behavior suggests that there was more to it.

His attentions were never directed to any of Harriet's other three children, only to Caroline. It was an idée fixe that originated in some rational conclusion of years before, and not merely from his sexual obsession with Harriet and her daughter. One proof of this is that he turned up unexpectedly at Brocket Hall a month after the christening.

Lord and Lady Bessborough had arrived at Brocket to spend a quiet visit with Caroline, the new baby, and William. Sheridan had arrived after them. When Sheridan showed up in a barouche, they were flabbergasted. Harriet gave him the silent treatment, but as usual the man was immune to embarrassment. He followed her pathetically around the house, spewing forth "Epigram upon Epigram, and joke upon joke" in a vain attempt to get her to shake hands with him—he was still seeking forgiveness, apparently, for the cruel and obscene letters he had written two years earlier. Harriet's husband was present, but whenever his attention was directed elsewhere, Sheridan implored Harriet "to forgive and shake hands." Despite her protestations, he stayed through the next day.

As he was about to get into his carriage to depart, Sheridan feigned a cough and mumbled that "he had never met with so good a bed." Everyone was silent, according to Harriet, though one may imagine an eyebrow or two being raised. Sheridan reiterated that he "lik'd being at Brocket of all things." The assembled company remained quiet. Finally, he asked directly to be allowed to stay—"They could not refuse: he stayed."[16] He had been entertaining to everyone but Harriet the night before, and now he outdid himself, both in wit and "in following [Harriet] in and out of the room, up and down stairs, and even into the Nursery," where she kept watch over her grandchild, waiting for the return of Caroline and the nurse. In an attempt to stanch the flow of his monologue, in which her "beautiful eyes" kept recurring, she held up the child and asked him "if his Grandchildren were as pretty as mine."

An instant transformation took place. Sheridan turned red and spluttered a vow of vengeance. Muttering curses, he left and did not see her again until his carriage arrived. The Bessboroughs were also departing, and Sheridan waited to hand Lady Bessborough up—a gesture she claims she could not easily or gracefully refuse, for fear of embarrassing her family. Sheridan viciously gripped her hand so powerfully that she almost screamed. She was left with bruises, swelling, and a badly cut ring finger.

It is difficult to take Harriet at her word. Sheridan had grown used to protestations that changed suddenly to embraces and disgust that became delighted laughter. Her letter to Granville admits that being pursued so recklessly at her age gratified her: "Imagine a grandmother being injured because of her beautiful eyes!" she wrote in French. "One may boast a little when that happens to one."[17] She even transcribed one of Sheridan's epigrams for Granville.

But why, when Harriet asked whether Sheridan had grandchildren so attractive as Augustus, did he grow furious and speak of "vengeance"? Sheridan's biographer Fintan O'Toole guesses that this was a reference to Sheridan's son Tom's "sexual embarrassments."[18] Tom had recently been involved in a highly publicized and scandalous case of "Criminal Conversation" which had embarrassed his father both personally and financially. Tom had been bailed out of his unhappy situation by loans his father couldn't repay, and he stood to lose his seat in the House of Commons. Tom, however, did have a legitimate male child, Brinsley (christened in 1806), and a daughter, Helen Selina, who had been born that year (1807). The reference to "grandchildren" could have been intended, O'Toole says, as a barb to torment Sheridan about his son's predicament. But Lady Bessborough concluded her account to Granville by saying, "I hope the revenge will end here; it is quite sufficient." What, indeed, was being revenged? If Sheridan believed himself to be Augustus's grandfather, the scenes at the christening and Brocket Hall make a bit more sense. Harriet's question was, then, retaliatory, and Sheridan's response in proportion to the offense taken.

In the late 1930s, biographer Kenelm Foss argued against the theory that Sheridan was Caroline's father. He pointed out that Lady Bessborough had many lovers, and that the parentages of many other high-born personages, including William and George Lamb, for example, were commonly spoken of and "transmitted to posterity."[19] These are convincing points. They leave us with little explanation for Sheridan's behavior, however, other than sheer perversity and the madness of alcoholism, drug addiction, or manic depression. If Sheridan was Caroline's father, Harriet might have wished to conceal that fact because he was not a Duke, Prince, or Earl, though he could claim to descend from a former King's mistress. Sheridan's reputation, jealousy and violence might have made Lady Bessborough reluctant to allow knowledge of Caroline's true parentage to become known even to Sheridan himself. We don't know. His actions stemmed from some obsession that went with him (and her) to the grave.

The memory of the christening faded, and Caroline was entirely taken with her infant son, much to the amusement of the Lambs. George Lamb maliciously reported that she rode out on the high road on a horse or ass led by one of her troop of pages in full uniform, with the baby on her lap and her maid and nurses following on foot—as if she were the queen with a royal retinue—and then was mystified when she stopped to pay the toll and the Turnpike men laughed at her.[20] She was writing poetry again, and sent her mother some verses. She had some chest pain, but she did not worry because it seemed to come from "carrying the dear heavy boy."[21]

Augustus grew rotund, healthy, and attractive. Harryo wrote on 12 November 1807: "[Caroline's] baby is really beautiful, from a degree of strength, animation and vivacity that you do not often see in a child of a year old." Yet Harryo describes Caroline as having "grown very thin" and looking "heated, though in very good health," though not so good health as she displayed while pregnant: "[C]ertainly there never was anybody whom being with child became so much, as when I left Town I thought her excessively pretty and yesterday almost as much the contrary."[22]

Harryo's disparate descriptions of Caroline raise an issue to which we shall return in discussing her relationship with Byron. Lady Caroline gave contradictory impressions. This was partly because of her mood swings, but it was also partly because she became a person about whom stories were told, embellished, and retold. Such stories often followed the inclinations and agenda of the teller, as Harryo herself candidly acknowledged in a letter to her sister G (Lady Morpeth):

> One hears such wonders of her both ways and every way when one is away from her, that I always feel an involuntary surprise to find her, as I did, at Hadley, like another, to quote Lord B[essborough], and when she is quiet, gentle and reasonable I am glad to see her and to believe that much of what we heard must have been exaggerated. I do not mean to say that there is not too much reason to wonder at her oddity, and blame her conduct at times. Lady Elizabeth [i.e., Bess Foster] (who in general takes her part in any attacks upon her) says she stood in a corner one day flinging cups and saucers at William's head (a pretty pastime for him, poor man), but she says they all worked one another up and all had a share in the blame they so plentifully heaped upon her head.[23]

Bess thus indirectly corroborates Caroline's later claim that William's "violence was as bad as my own."[24]

William's violence was also more ritualized, however. From correspondence subsequent to Caroline's death, we know that William found whipping highly arousing. After Caroline died, William urged his lover Lady Brandon to flog her children and even her maid, imagining how much he himself would enjoy wielding the rod "upon that large and extensive field of *derrière*, which is so well calculated to receive it." William was obsessed with anecdotes and disquisitions on the theme of flogging, and with pictures of women beating nude children. In a sequence of forty letters sent between William and Lady Brandon around 1830, all but four allude to flagellation, and in several William promises to practice it upon his correspondent.[25] Later in their marriage, William and Caroline served as guardians for a girl (Susan Churchill, about whom more presently), and he whipped her: "I remember as though it was yesterday," Susan told him when she was grown, "the *execution,* then being thrown in a corner of a large couch there was at Brockett—you used then to leave the room and I remember your coming back one day and saying 'Well cocky does it smart still?' at which of course I could not help laughing instead of crying."[26] Caroline Norton (William's paramour after Lady Brandon) wrote to him that she had almost bought him an inlaid box because it depicted "your favourite subject of a woman whipping a child."[27]

William would certainly take the rod to Augustus. He may also have tried to discipline his childlike wife along the paternalistic lines that gave him so much pleasure. But as the stories have come down Caroline is the one flinging crockery, and William the long-suffering husband. Already, one can see that the repetition of such stories became part of a pattern of vilification intended to drive a wedge between Lady Caroline and her husband, and eventually undermine her sanity. As Harryo said later in the same letter to her sister quoted above, the Melbournes had already conceived "much spite . . . against her." It was William's sister Emily Cowper who had expressed the family verdict, cruelly sneering at the defenseless Augustus. As Harryo reported:

> George [Lamb] said last night that [Caroline's] child was the most frightful creature he had ever beheld. I said really angrily (for if you could see it you would really think it impossible anybody could say so but from ill-nature or jealousy), that it was quite ridiculous to pretend it. He coloured, muttered and seemed anxious Lord Melbourne and Lady E[mily Cowper] should not hear us, but she did and told me afterwards that Lady Cowper had persuaded him to think so, for that when the boy was first born they were all in admiration of it till she began sneering about it.[28]

In addition to this meanness on the part of William's sister Emily, Harryo reports that one day in November Corisande Ossulston began abusing Caroline to Lady Melbourne. In one of those predictable turnabouts, however, Lady Melbourne became angry. "Though the first person to [attack Caroline] herself," said Harryo, Lady Melbourne "is the last to hear it from anybody else." Harryo kicked "Corise" under the table and cut short an unpleasant encounter.[29]

Obviously, Caroline-bashing was a popular pastime for the Melbournes and their circle. Harryo also indulged in it, even if she sometimes yielded to sympathetic feelings toward her cousin, as she did on 21 November 1807, for example, when Harryo described Caroline as looking "uncommonly well." Within this women's world there were many opportunities for hurt feelings. The rivalry between the three babies of Corisande Ossulston, Maria Duncannon, and Lady Caroline continued. And at first, Harryo voted Augustus the "finest" in the contest.[30]

In the fall of 1807, Caroline continued to correspond almost daily with her mother, who sought solace in food from her money anxieties and low spirits after the death of her sister. She was gaining weight rapidly.[31] Cheered by Caroline's euphoria in her role of mother, she grew gloomy when in November and December news came of the October declaration of war from Russia. Its probable impact on the nation, her two sons, and Granville scared her. Harriet's long-absent lover started home and finally reached England in January 1808. Over the next three months, he saw Harriet often. One proof of this is that she wrote him few letters.[32] He must have found her altered in many ways—heavier, older, less attractive. She had lost none of her vanity, but she had no doubt recognized that Granville must soon marry. He had considered a match with the Russian Princess Galitzin, whom Harriet called the "Little Barbarian," but nothing had come of it.[33]

Lady Bessborough chaperoned her niece Harryo while the "Bess Problem" remained unresolved and noted that Harryo obviously thought Granville handsome and brilliant. But Harryo considered Granville her aunt's property and resisted any attempt to bring her together with him. Patiently, and with understandable misgivings, Lady Bessborough set to work bringing about this match.

In the meantime William and Caroline seemed happy parents. William grew fond of Augustus, though Caroline admitted he was "less so than I am in outward demonstrations."[34] She went to visit her grandmother in April 1808, and William dined with them on the nineteenth. He then walked home through a late but heavy snow all the way to Brocket Hall, rather than ride back with his sister Emily in her carriage. Caroline stayed on with her grandmother, reading romantic history books like William Robertson's *History of Scotland* (1759) and Madame de Genlis's *Le Siege de la Rochelle* (1808), which described how Richelieu's forces had taken the French port in 1628 after a fourteen-month siege. William praised Caroline's youngest brother Willy, and this naturally pleased her, for she had loved him from the start and still thought him "so agreeable, & his figure . . . quite beautiful." And yet she dreaded her own son's future. Her grandmother wrote on 26 April: "Caroline writes that she does nothing but nurse [Augustus]. I fear by that & by the tone of her letter that she does not feel quite easy about him."[35]

The first definite sign that Augustus was not normal appeared only weeks later. He was nine months old and teething. He suddenly went into a convulsion and lost consciousness.[36] Doctors assured Lady Caroline that the convulsions were not unusual. They occurred more frequently in boys than girls, and would probably cure themselves as the child grew older. Teething was given as the cause, although his diet was also checked carefully and momentary consideration given to the possibility of a disease of the brain. Augustus might continue to suffer from giddy fits or epilepsy—after all, Lady Caroline herself had fainted several times during her pregnancy, and the medical men thought this a probable origin of the child's affliction. Augustus's face became vapid, and now Harryo admitted that he looked a little peculiar after all, certainly not as "pretty" as Corisande's child. Perhaps George Lamb and Emily had some justification for their cruel remarks on their nephew's appearance.[37]

As summer waned and Augustus's first birthday came on the horizon, Lady Caroline found herself pregnant again, much to William's pleasure. The child's convulsions had not recurred, and Caroline wrote to her mother, who was in Ireland visiting the Bessborough estates, that "Augustus continues well & I grow very rondelette."[38] Caroline, her mother, and grandmother exchanged a number of letters that autumn about the British victory at Vimeiro on 21 August 1808. Having defeated the French and Russian forces in Portugal, the British signed an armistice, called the Convention of Cintra, that was so generous to the defeated armies that it provoked outrage in Britain, with calls for investigations of the principals and appropriate punishments. "Britannia sickens, Cintra! At thy name," Byron wrote of this event, "and folks in office at the mention fret."[39]

By November, Harriet was back from Ireland and visiting Caroline, who was already preparing for her lying-in at Brocket, which would not be until early March. There was a heavy snowfall that winter, and the dowager Lady Spencer went out to visit the poor and needy in St. Albans wearing snowshoes "like a Lapland witch."[40] On 29 January 1809, Caroline went into early labor and delivered a premature little girl. The child died in Harriet's lap the following morning and was buried at St. Ethelreda's Church in Hatfield along with the child Caroline had lost in 1806. In their grief, William and Caroline were both attended by Sir Walter Farquhar.[41]

On 8 February 1809 Harryo reported that Caroline was ill from her miscarriage, but improving.[42] Caroline seemed to recover from this tragedy more readily, perhaps because she still had Augustus, about whom she had written in her commonplace book:

His little eyes like William's shine

How great is then my joy,

For while I call this darling mine,

I see 'tis William's boy.[43]

But William's boy lagged behind the others. He could neither walk nor talk. Worse, his convulsions returned with frighteningly regularity, accompanied by screaming fits.

While Caroline fretted over Augustus, William became more absorbed in his political career. Husband and wife were changing. For Caroline, the changes proved wrenching. The death of her child preyed upon her emotions, and she could not, like William, easily escape the household. Her in-laws were omnipresent; they called her "the little Beast" in private.

In April, just as she recovered physically, she suffered "a sad trying operation on her mouth," according to Harriet. One of her front teeth had decayed so much that she had to have "half of it pik'd away which was very painful." Harriet's description reminds us that Lady Caroline had inner strength: "[S]he bore both the pain & the alteration with that wonderful fortitude which she has always commanded."[44] No doubt Harriet wished she had the financial resources to make Caroline independent of the mocking, acerbic Lambs. Saddened by her Uncle Charles Spencer's death, Harriet was further disappointed to find that he had left little provision in his will for Caroline and William. But then, everyone assumed that William's father would not live long, and that they would soon be wealthy.[45]

In William's absence, Caroline turned to Hartington for emotional support. In late April 1809 she wrote him a typical letter, full of news about the opera and theater, saying she had been "much disappointed" not to see him at Mrs. Montague's ball and that she longed to see him "more than I can say, God bless you." She impulsively announced her intention of taking lodgings on that side of town for future socializing.[46] But the madcap tone of such letters is belied by the anxieties of parenthood. When at last Augustus took "a few steps very tottering— but still without support," reports of a fever spreading over Hertfordshire caused her to abandon her beloved Brocket and take her son to the city. How could she have borne to lose Augustus, even with all his problems?[47]

Indiscretions

1809–1811

I hate to go slow do not you—it is the only thing I much care
about—I run—gallop—or drive as for a wager.

—Lady Caroline Lamb[1]

1809 was a year of marriages.

Caroline St. Jules married George Lamb on 17 May 1809 in the great salon
at Devonshire House. To distinguish the two Carolines, family members now
referred to Lady Caroline as "Caro William," and to the new bride as "Caro
George." Unbelievably, the newlyweds resided initially in Melbourne House, so
that the two Caros had to "live cordially together without the little jealousies which
in their situations are so much to be dreaded," as Lady Spencer put it. She
concluded sagely: "[M]uch will depend upon their not having tittle-tattle gossiping
servants," an amusing statement coming from one who had employed a governess
as a spy.[2]

Recovered from her miscarriage, "Caro William" felt mounting frustration
with her husband's taciturnity, and they quarreled. It is sometimes asserted that
on such occasions she called him "Black William" as a token of her anger, but the
epithet was actually a fond one, based on William's swarthy appearance. She
sometimes called him her "abler Assistant my Black William" when she wrote to

Hart.[3] No doubt she hurled other insults at him along with the crockery during arguments that sometimes required that half the dish pantry be restocked. On 27 May 1809 she wrote in a conciliatory tone to "Black William" from Panshanger (Lord and Lady Cowper's country residence not far from Brocket Hall), where she and the newlyweds were visiting and awaiting William's arrival. It was a newsy, chattering letter with an undercurrent of jealousy. Seeing Caroline St. Jules married had reminded her how much she loved William: "I only want my Angel boy & Man to be perfectly happy," she wrote coquettishly, and then chattered on about the Lady Mary Wortley Montagu's newly published letters: "[Y]ou cannot think how clever they are—unlike the stile of a girl of fourteen but really as so many married women are so like children in body & mind it is well now & then the reverse should take place—*Tunc*. I have just been stung." Caroline then inserted Greek phrases which translate as "the writer has had a lapse," and "the little beast makes both honey and grievous wounds." Keenly aware she might suffer by comparison with his new sister-in-law, she promised, "I will study to be as pleasant a friend to you as Caroline George is to her husband." She continued,

> we seemed all of us acting a play last night—in a new House—old people & all met together from odd quarters—I think lately my dearest William we have been very troublesome to each other which I take by wholesale to my own account & mean to correct leaving you in retail with a few little sins which I know you will correct also . . . condemn me not to silence, assist my imperfect memory & occasionally call me friend-girl Darling (though Mrs. Clark [?] shares that appellation) & all such pretty names as shew great love. I will on the other hand be silent of a morning—entertaining after dinner—docile—fearless as a heroine in the last vol. of her troubles strong as a mountain Tiger & active as those young savages Basil's boys to whom by the by you will give one shilling apiece—you should say to me *raisonnéz mieux et repliquéz moins* [Reason better and reply less].
>
> —[your] own Queen—Car Lamb[4]

The "sting" of love came into the text via the Greek that William had taught Caroline, as she struggled to make herself his equal in learning. In July she wrote to ask her mother to write down "the principal dates & events, wars, risings, &c. from Romulus till the time of Constantine the Great" so that she could better follow the history book William was reading aloud to her.[5] She had come a long way from the simplicity that characterized her letters and conversation before she was married. She had also become pretentious. Caroline's jealousy produced that letter, and it also produced a poem on her doppelgänger: "There is Caroline Jules / With her laces & thules, / is good yet makes men sigh / While her sister runs wildish, / And seems rather childish, / but oh she's a roving eye."[6]

There was yet another reason for Lady Caroline to feel jealous of her new sister-in-law. In addition to some lavish presents of jewelry, Caro George had received £30,000 as a dowry from the 5th Duke of Devonshire, the identical amount that had been given to his eldest daughter, Georgiana, when she had married Lord Morpeth. The news got around, and it made Caroline's grandmother uncomfortable, for though she felt that Caro George should be treated well, Caroline and William had no comparable assets.[7] Lady Spencer would have been more disquieted had she known that the Duke had also arranged for the newlyweds to receive an additional £500 a year.[8]

After the Duke's lavishness to Bess's daughter, his marriage to Bess became inevitable. She had maneuvered brilliantly, and Lady Bessborough acknowledged to Granville that "she has more *calcul* and more power of concentrating her wishes and intentions than I ever before believ'd."[9] On 5 September Harriet wrote to Willy, "I fear the scene I have so much dreaded is likely to take place, if it has not already done so."[10] The union was a foregone conclusion, but Lady Caroline opposed it strenuously. Harryo described her as being "like a Volcano on the subject."[11] Harryo kept Selina Trimmer with her as much as possible to avoid having to appear in public with the "usurper," but that, she said, did "not in the least prevent [Bess] persecuting me from morning till night to go out with her to the park, play, etc."[12] Hart was caught in the middle. Lady Caroline demanded that he "censure that old witches conduct" and said that it disgusted her to hear Bess referred to as the Duchess. She said Bess had manipulated him: "Oh she is a deep one! She has flummeried up a certain young Marquis from his cradle."[13] Though Caroline called him the "Hypocritical Hart," he responded unflappably to the "dearest of wild young women" that he had no use at all for Bess, "that crocodile."[14]

None of this fulminating had any effect. Canis succumbed on 19 October 1809 in a private ceremony arranged to take place when the blundering Reverend Preedy came, as he thought, on an innocent visit to Chiswick. Believing that the marriage had already taken place, he was easily tricked into performing it himself as if for family "show."[15] As a peace offering to the Lady Spencer, Bess promised that she would not use the title of "Fifth Duchess," but no one expected the promise to be fulfilled. The new Duchess of Devonshire copied into her journal a line from an Italian poem she had memorized years before: "*E al fine il nome ancor*'" [and at last the name also].[16]

Lady Caroline's intense hatred of Bess seems out of proportion to the situation—unless one remembers that Bess's illegitimate child had become her sister-in-law. Moreover, she was at severe odds with her in-laws, for the Lambs openly attributed Augustus's seizures and retardation to lax parental discipline. It was a point of view unfortunately shared by her own grandmother, whose physician would tell her that Augustus's screams were "nothing but temper, & must be corrected."[17] For better and for worse, Caroline ignored their advice. She had no intention of letting Augustus be carried off by a disciplinary "nurse," at whose actions she could guess from experience. Nonetheless, she sought distraction from her maternal duties.

Caroline spent the greater part of August at Cowes, partying and playing cards. She wrote her mother that she had been to "a very odd dinner at Mrs. Day's" where the food and entertainment were so lavish that she "could not help regretting the expence those poor people put themselves to."[18] After dinner, she found little pleasure at the card table, for the players quarreled over how she should execute her hand:

> Words grew high & I grew frightened, when they all turned to me & asked me if I ever had play'd at Loo before. "Yes," I replied, "at the Princesses last night"— "And what sort of Loo was that?" they said eagerly, "what sort of Loo was that?" "A very different one," I answered, and they all eagerly asked in what respect. "A much quieter one," I said, & it allay'd the rage for the moment and made them all laugh, but after a time it broke out again worse than ever.[19]

Though glad to leave this raucous party, she nonetheless continued to attend such affairs as an escape from Melbourne House.

Now Caroline felt the first erosion of her character. She wrote to an unnamed correspondent in typical stream-of-consciousness style: "What is the meaning of right & wrong—all is but appearance—who that looks innocent can be thought guilty—what is guilt—there is no such thing as conscience—people may go into the World and what is the use of thinking if I cannot sleep in my Bed why then should I try to lie down there are balls & Assemblies & operas & plays—& who dances more gaily than I can—who shall dare say I am not good or happy."[20] She delighted in outrageous behavior. She described to Lady Holland one masked ball for which she

> put on boys shoe buckles a red Emery wig a boarding school frock so that I looked like a boy dressed up for a girl & in that character told everyone that I personated

Lady Caroline Lamb had died my hair red &—I jumped like a Harlequin laughed heartily & had no mercy on any one—likewise heard pretty home truths saw who were my friends & shrugged my shoulders at those whose malice more abundant than their wit treated me Cavalierly—having tired myself with these juvenile freaks I slipped behind a curtain & pulling a gown & cassock hid for that purpose over my frock returned in the character of Sidney Smith & as well as I could personated a Scotch Reviewer a Yorkshire Clergyman—a London wit.[21]

This was the London that seduced Caroline. The balls and assemblies were principally venues for feminine display—occasions of the marriage market, certainly, but now also a region of feminine privilege. Costumed masquerades allowed women to interact freely with members of either sex, and attempts to establish their identities were proscribed. As the famous courtesan Harriette Wilson put it: "I love a masquerade; because a female can never enjoy the same liberty anywhere else."[22] While provincial events were more egalitarian, the London assemblies were dominated by the affluent members of the *ton*.

The rich were far too rich, and Caroline moved among the wealthiest in their surroundings of stunning profligacy. Ladies—though not she—might spend thousands of pounds on their wardrobes, with handkerchiefs costing fifty guineas a dozen. The English were principal consumers of turbot, plover's eggs, truffles, champagne, curry, ham, caviar, and delicacies like reindeer tongue from Lapland. Byron described the dinner tables of the wealthy:

Fowls à la Condé, slices eke of salmon,
With sauces Genevoises, and haunch of venison;
Wines too which might again have slain young Ammon—
A man like whom I hope we shan't see many soon;
They also set a glazed Westphalian ham on,
Whereon Apicius would bestow his benison;
And then there was Champagne with foaming whirls,
As white as Cleopatra's melted pearls.

The main courses, a "tumult of fish, flesh, and fowl," including, "young Partridge' fillets, deck'd with truffles" gives way to "fruits, and ice."[23]

It was the era of the dandy, personified by Beau Brummel, whom Byron mockingly dubbed more important than Napoleon, and whose imitators gathered in the bow window of White's and drank and ate at clubs like Brooks's, or, if they sought female companionship of their own station, Almack's—the only club in

London to which women were admitted, and in which they had the final say. More than one gentleman was unpleasantly surprised to find himself blackballed for Almack's membership by the weaker sex.

In the evenings, carriages rolled into the West End with lamps glowing, and liveried footmen knocked at the doors of the clubs and great houses, which were lit up with chandeliers and sconces. When a masked ball or assembly was hosted by one of the upper crust, it wasn't unusual for several hundred splendidly coifed, gowned, and bejeweled guests to attend, as private orchestras played quadrilles and servants replenished the supper tables. Famous talkers like Samuel Rogers, Sydney Smith, and Henry Luttrell prepared *bon mots* for such parties. On Sundays, Lady Caroline liked to join one of the parades of horseback riders that passed through Kensington Gardens or down Rotten Row. And when these amusements palled, there was always a play or light opera to attend, in boxes held open for the pleasure of the duennas of the *bon ton* and their husbands, whose marriages were almost without exception rife with license and prevarication.[24] "What a world it is dear sweet boy," she wrote to Hart, "what a flimsey patched work face it has, all profession, little affection, no truth."[25]

Yet Caroline fell for it: "I know well the force of thick gold chains crosses & emerald Clasps," she subsequently admitted to Lady Holland, "—how then can any heart be callous to diamond necklaces earrings live Horses & Chandeliers?"[26] She was pressing the limits of pardonable behavior, yet she denied it. In letters to her uncle she attempted to defend herself against crimes she seemed scarcely to understand herself:

> Your letter my Dearest Uncle has more than made up to me for the St. Joseph or 50 such Balls, & had you seen me receive it you would believe that if ever I should be going to doing any thing foolish & unreasonable the remembrance of that kind letter written in your own dear hand shall prevent my doing it. I say any thing *foolish,* for I trust better motives will prevent my doing any thing wrong & so as I know you hate professions I shall only say this & conclude my letter—just however telling you that William had most excellent sport killed 13 Brace himself the first day & 10 the 2d.[27]

Caroline's attempt to distract her Uncle from her initial awkward confession of bad behavior continued with a litany of William's hunting accomplishments and the robust health of poor Augustus.

In a subsequent letter to her uncle she preens herself on having resisted the temptation to go dining and dancing on board the yacht of Dr. and Mrs. Howley:

"I made 3 attempts to say no decidedly but always came out with an but if my Uncle had not said I had better not go to sea and if Mr Lamb was here & if . . . till at last I shut my eyes opened my mouth and said no at once which perhaps you will think I might as well have done at first, but I really think if you had been here & heard of Doctor Howley and Miss Bells even you would have permitted me to have gone." With this dubious attempt at reassurance in a shambles, Caroline concludes by saying that her act of self-denial ought to "balance any of the numberless little occurrences you may have heard of in my conduct which have at times given you displeasure."[28] There was plenty to be displeased about. Whole weeks went by during which she returned home after 6:00 or even 8:00 A.M., and she was "thickly pursued with cards notes, walzing matches dinners & blue stocking meetings."[29]

Caroline had now adopted the world-weary nonchalance of her class, and she pretended to view marriage with the jaded eye of four years in wedlock. Once she had trembled in her husband's embrace. Now she was flirting with the rest. She herself bore the responsibility for her loss of integrity, but it is only fair to note that she typifies a period of public piety and private debauchery. Lady Caroline's passage through this moral thicket, and the radicalization she experienced as a consequence, paved the way for her liaison with Byron, who would so brilliantly capture the political and moral bankruptcy of the times in the sullen ennui of *Childe Harold's Pilgrimage*. The Tories, who maintained a constant paranoia about French invasion, had held the reins of government almost constantly since 1783. The House of Commons was practically bought and sold by landed gentry in the boroughs, despite an attempt at reform in 1793 by the liberal faction of the Whigs, "The Friends of the People." The political climate under the Tory regime had been one of anxious repression of reform, out of fear that, with the slightest flinch, England might self-destruct, like France. A man could be hanged for petty theft. The brutal repression of the poor was complemented by the license of the rich, in whose households cards, drink, dice, and adultery were the entertainments.

Lady Caroline was a passionate participant in political discussions, bringing the perspective of the Whig party's liberal wing. She corresponded with activists like the Reverend Sydney Smith, co-founder with Lord Jeffrey of the *Edinburgh Review*. Smith had embraced the fight for Catholic emancipation and opposed the Game Laws, involuntary transportation, and slavery. Renowned for his sharp wit as well as his personal warmth, Smith agreed with William Lamb, and therefore also with Caroline, who had inherited her mother's keen interest in the Whig agenda. He had written to Lady Caroline in June to send his regrets for not visiting.[30]

As is so often the case with fearful governments, war abroad proved indispensable to stability at home. The Bessborough circle were typical of families whose young men fought battles on the Continent. Frederick Ponsonby was wounded at the battle of Talavera in Spain in late July. Lists of those killed or wounded in action were posted in the towns from which their regiments had been drawn. Caroline saw a man collapse when he found his nephew's name among those killed.[31] She read Sir John Moore's *Narrative of the Campaign of the British Army in Spain* (1809) in September, scarcely a month after the Battle of Talavera, and she was "very much struck if the account is true with the bad management there seems to have been at first setting out." She was also impressed that everyone had been duped into supporting the Spaniards by "a pack of stories which seem to have been perfectly groundless." Jingoism appeared even in church. She heard a "Methodistical" preacher "who so entirely lost himself at the conclusion in the military simily he had adopted that he addrest 3 old women in a voice of thunder which stirred them up amazingly calling to them to fight & strive & obtain the Kingdom of heaven by blood & loudly addressing them by the appellation of ye Veteran Christian Warriors—"[32] Her brother Frederick made Caroline believe that British soldiers had been sacrificed for an unworthy ally who showed "Cowardice & inhumanity."[33]

Heightened political awareness made Caroline's behavior more extravagant. In September, Harryo saw her at Cowes, where she appeared

> much more extraordinary and entertaining than ever, leading the sort of life people do in a Harlequin farce, perpetual shifting scene, dress and company, lodging at an apothecary's, dining at the Duke of Gloucester's, *enfant de famille* at Mrs. Knox's, an Irish lady who gives assemblies in London, one minute on a Pillion, the next in a boat, but the wand to effect these changes always in Columbine's hand—Lady Spencer [Lavinia, the wife of George John] exclaiming— "William Lamb is an angel, nothing like the school of adversity!"[34]

William maintained silence because he had learned that escalation of the stakes did not work with Caroline. At the same time, silence tended to stimulate her to greater outrages. To this quandary he had no solution.

Things went uneasily along. Lady Caroline wrote to Hart reproaching him as a bad correspondent: "I have read Rights of Woman, am become a convert, think dissipation great folly, & shall remain the whole year discreetly & quietly in the country." She continued to flirt with him, saying he should give Caro George "3 kisses for me, & mind I never will give you another while you live—

you are a bad good for nothing boy."[35] Caroline had read not only *Vindication of the Rights of Women* (1792), but also *Thoughts on the Education of Daughters* (1787), both by Mary Wollstonecraft. She found much to criticize in her female friends, who, in "contrast to myself & other more liberal minded women who like Mary Wollstonecraft stand up for the rights of the Sex & wear our shackles with dignity." She chafed at the vision of "these Lords of Creation who pretend in England to trample us under foot," men who were really "just as much our slaves & just as little can do without us as any others with less big pretentions— only like other noble animals we let them bridle & Curb us for want of knowing our strength."[36]

Reading nourished Lady Caroline's emergent feminism, and she even picked up a book on metaphysics by Dergal Stuart, though it didn't take: "Since I looked into his first Works I have never felt sure of any thing it is therefore my belief if I read his second I shall go quite Mad."[37] She became more strident, demanding that Hart answer her letters immediately: "write write write write write write write write—I will add nothing but write till I have an answer."[38] Around this time she attended a party given by Lady Cork in honor of Prince Blücher (1742-1819), the Prussian Field Marshal who was to play a decisive role at Waterloo. Blücher had apparently forgotten the engagement, however, and everyone grew weary of anticipating his arrival. Lady Caroline had acted a charade, then disappeared. A violent knocking at the door suddenly stirred hope that the guest of honor had arrived. A servant announced General Blücher and there was a chorus of "hurrahs." Lady Caroline strutted in wearing a cocked hat and great coat she had found somewhere in the house. She capped this performance by tricking a late arrival to the party, Lord Hardwicke, into giving her the money to pay the servants for their "pretty hurrah."[39]

Lady Caroline had survived two relatives' marriages, but now another loomed. Harryo was in an untenable situation, living with her hated stepmother. The stage was set for Granville to propose. "For this I am not prepared & cannot reconcile myself," Lady Caroline wrote to her mother in October, "but somehow or other one gets used to everything."[40] Granville and Harryo were married on Christmas Eve 1809 in a private ceremony to which Caroline was not invited. The Duke gave Harryo a relatively modest £10,000 settlement, only a third of the jointure he had made over to Caroline St. Jules earlier that year. Caroline protested at "being excluded from my own Cousin's wedding" and demanded "a favour & Cake" of Hart, who had attended.[41] To her Uncle George John, the Earl Spencer, she wrote tellingly, "of course you have heard of Harriets marriage and I hope you approve of it, she has liked Ld G a great while and I am all for Marriages with love and affection though Mrs Malaprop in the Rivals says it is safer to begin with a little Aversion."[42] The aversion here was all Caroline's.

She had time to brood over her cousin's marriage, for she was nursing two-year-old Augustus through the croup. She wrote a poem to Hartington during one of these vigils:

> I'm writing to you lovely Spark,
> With Nurse and Sally in the dark.
> so that I neither care nor ken
> which way I turn my crazy pen.
> But when some light assists my hand,
> Ile draw the picture you command,
> paint Flora in a flowing robe
> with either breast just like a globe.
> her skin like snow on frozen river,
> her hair the colour of your liver.
> her wide jaw bone and figure tall!
> leave it to me, I'll paint it all . . .[43]

Caroline had attended the Opera the previous April, where she saw the character of Flora portrayed by the actor Des Hayes, who impersonated the goddess and then exchanged roles with a gargantuan actress: "[T]he fattest biggest animal ever yet noticed by naturalists," thinly disguised in a gauze costume. "This animal," she wrote to her cousin Hart, "for Woman I cannot call her, hop'd & danced & showed her leg."[44] In Caroline's transmogrification of the goddess from ideal creature to appalling animal she offers the conventionally perfect surfaces of Flora's globe-like breasts and snow-white skin, then gets visceral with the liver-colored hair.

To titillate and startle became her goal at parties, like the large one thrown at Roehampton in July 1810 for the Prince of Wales and his retinue, who ate and drank prodigiously as usual until after 2:00 A.M.[45] After such occasions she often went madcap, especially with Hart, who had sent her an antidote for a hangover:

> My most sanative Elixir of Julep—my most precious Cordial Confection—my most dilutable Sal Polychrist & mash mallows paste. Truly comfortable spirit of Hartshorn Tincture of Rhubarb & Purgative Senna Tea—it is impossible, my most exquisite medicine chest, to describe the delightful effect the potion you sent me this morning had upon me. Prescribe such powders to all [those] who die for love

of your Lordships tricoloured eyes, & remember Cousin of my heart & heart of my cousins that your all faithful gallipot was only awaiting for a line to dose you with letters every day. Grandmother very well; went there to sleep on Tuesday & Wednesday, monstrous pretty party & supper gave on Sunday as a farewell, & now mean to adjure the delights of the flesh & all the pomps and vanities of this wicked world.[46]

At the conclusion of this letter she calls Hart "my Dearest Tartar Emetic." These effusions evince a bubbling linguistic creativity. When that mood came, she curved her words down at the edges of the paper to get them to fit, so that the page looks like strands of curly hair. Her poetic improvisations sometimes contained rebuses or sketches and were signed with real or invented names, like "Citizen Lamb," "Emily Cowper (oh how improbable)," "Sophia Heathcote," "Syrop of Elderob," "Molly Teacok," "William Rufus-Rex," and "Molly Bradby." In return, Hart sometimes signed himself as "Yr. affectionate treasurer" or more simply "Devilshire." Her frequent request to Hart was "send me more nonsense."[47]

Despite their wit, these letters reveal her emptiness. She confessed that she had "behaved a little wild—riding over the Downs and about the sands, with all the officers at my heels, in a way not very decent for one of my Cloth—I am like the song of Rosa in love with every body & am always abused for it." No doubt she exaggerated the picture of herself dallying with the regiment, but flirtation had become a more serious business for her, and it threatened sober consequences. She presented herself to Hart as one who had undoubtedly sinned (as who did not?), but in a superficial way: "I am pitted all over but it is but skin deep. Many a fair outside covers a blacker heart. . . . When we meet in a better & happier World we will be unco virtuous."[48] Anxiety stirs behind this façade. Her marriage vows were in danger.

Augustus's illnesses continued. Despite the doctors' reassurances that he would outgrow his problems, the child had seizures during which he foamed at the mouth and bit his own tongue before lapsing into unconsciousness. Since these attacks were often preceded by earsplitting screams and followed by vomiting and incontinence, they naturally caused panic. Augustus might go days without a seizure. Then again, he might have three in a twelve-hour period. His size and strength were beginning to make him a formidable problem when the fit was upon him. Doctors still ascribed those fits to temper, saying bluntly that he was being spoiled. Again they recommended that Augustus be assigned to a strict nurse. Caroline refused. But as time wore on, the truth became inescapable: Sedation was the only available treatment. Still, life went on, superficially calm, and Caroline's grandmother insisted that "Nothing can be quieter or more amiable than Caroline & William are."[49]

Though William undoubtedly worried about Augustus, he had an escape. He gave prepared speeches at Westminster, and met with Whig strategists. When he was home, he discussed politics with his mother. Naturally, Lady Melbourne's political experience and acumen far exceeded Caroline's, but this did not make it easier for the wife to accept her husband's preference. One consequence of his choice was that Lady Caroline's acquaintance with Lady Holland, whom she continued to visit in her Elizabethan mansion west of central London, now blossomed into friendship. Elizabeth Holland had divorced her alcoholic first husband, Sir Godfrey Webster, had remarried respectably, and was the mother of nine children by her new spouse. As a divorced woman, Lady Holland could not be received at court, but she and her husband served as the nucleus of a large social and political circle of liberals. As Annabella Milbanke, the future Lady Byron, put it, if offered introduction to Lady Holland, the proper thing to do would be to decline, but "no one will regard me as corrupted by being *in the room* with her."[50] Caroline enjoyed the liberating conversations and polite manners at Holland House, so different from the crude yet inhibited atmosphere of Melbourne House. Lady Holland, though in poor health and overweight, radiated a commanding presence.

Caroline's grandmother correctly feared that the influence of the Hollands would prove dangerous, for it was here that Caroline met Lady Holland's eldest son by her previous marriage, Sir Godfrey Vassal Webster. Webster had entered the Army at nineteen and had fought in Spain, like Frederick Ponsonby. He was a war hero who had returned with the skull of a French soldier, which he had reputedly converted into a macabre-looking gold-encrusted drinking cup. He had a bad reputation. Even the Whips Club, with its lax rules and standards, would not accept him.[51] He was twenty and an object of clandestine interest by many young women. Caroline was twenty-four. The season would be packed, including preparations for the celebration of George III's seventy-second birthday. There would be various theater events, including an outdoor spectacle called "The Blood-Red Knight, or The Fatal Bridge," which involved the staging of battles between mounted attackers and foot soldiers defending a "castle."[52] Webster, an experienced soldier, probably found such entertainments laughable. But he apparently found Caroline the opposite.

He brought her gifts and escorted her in public. Perhaps she consciously hoped to make William jealous. If so, the strategy was not a good one, for she underestimated his forbearance. Could she have kept Sir Godfrey's attention for very long if their affair remained unconsummated? Perhaps, but it seems more probable that, as Caroline's previous biographer Margot Strickland has guessed, Sir Godfrey Vassal Webster introduced Caroline to a sexual pleasure she had not experienced in her marriage bed.[53]

Lady Bessborough, Lady Holland, and, most importantly, Lady Melbourne cared little for Caroline's chastity, but she had failed to keep her affair secret and must be punished. After observing Caroline and Webster at a party, Lady Melbourne wrote a scathing letter:

> I see you have no shame or compunction for yr past conduct every action every impulse of your mind is directed by Sir Godfrey Webster—I lament it, but as I can do no good I shall withdraw myself and suffer no more croaking upon your hurt— Yr behavior last night was so disgraceful in its appearances and so disgusting in its motives that it is quite impossible it should ever be effaced from my mind. When one braves the opinion of the World, sooner or later that will feel the consequences of it and although at first people may have excused your forming friendships with all those who are censured for their conduct, from yr youth and inexperience yet when they see you continue to single them out and to overlook all decencys imposed by Society—they will look upon you as belonging to the same class.[54]

Caroline had been seen with undesirables; she would find that Lady Melbourne's warning about flouting public opinion was not hollow.

From this point, Lady Melbourne viewed Caroline as a liability, and she supported a campaign to freeze out her daughter-in-law that would last longer than the Napoleonic wars. Lady Melbourne was particularly outraged that Caroline's affair had temporarily damaged William's line of communication with Webster's stepfather, Lord Holland, a major figure in the Whig power structure. Worse, Lady Caroline had not scrupled to keep company with people who were at all costs to be kept out of the fold—like Lady Wellesley. "You are the only woman," fulminated Lady Melbourne in the same letter, "who has any pretension to Character who ever courted Lady Wellesley's acquaintance." Lady Wellesley, of French extraction, was divorced and took lovers, and she must be "cut" by anyone of stature. Lady Melbourne condemned Caroline with prejudice, venting months of pent-up frustration, upbraiding her for compromising William's position, and promising an unremitting glaciality: "I will have no more conversation with you upon this hateful Subject—I repeat it let me alone, & do not drive me to explain the meaning of the cold civility that will henceforward pass between us."[55]

Lady Melbourne had previously explained the rules for extramarital affairs to the Duchess of Devonshire and her own daughter Emily. No doubt she had offered such advice to Caroline, only to find William's wife had no talent for observing the "decencies." For a while, Caroline refused to give up Sir Godfrey. Then, anonymous letters were sent to William divulging her infidelity.[56] The terror of her mother-in-law's estrangement sank in. Caroline panicked and retreated, admitting that she had been foolish to accept Sir Godfrey's gifts of jewelry and even a puppy: "I tore the bracelet off my arm & put it up with my chains in a Box by itself I have written to desire some one will fetch the dog."[57] She tried to clean up the mess as best she could. Unfortunately, she chose to confess: "[O]n my knees I have written to William to tell him not any falsehoods not as you say any stories to conceal my guilt but the whole disgraceful truth. I have told him I have deceived him I have trusted solely to his mercy & generosity." Caroline had once again violated the rules. William accepted the confession in embarrassed silence.

Unaware of her further offense, Caroline appealed to Lady Melbourne to help her patch things up. One can imagine how her overdramatization of the transgression of adultery must have struck the worldly Lady Melbourne:

> Dearest Lady Melbourne write & tell me you forgive me for I am indeed very miserable very repentant. . . . I am very superstitious and believe all those who are wicked are. this Morning the dog the beautiful little Peppeo playing & running about me snapped at the child but did not bite him—it was this occassiond my fear great God I thought if this dog should go mad & bite Williams child what would become of me I went into the garden & took a long walk the dog suddenly droppd before me in a fit foaming at the mouth—it turnd my heart sick I trembled all over I took it home & prayd that I might be forgiven then it was I tore my bracelet off & wrote to William I wish he could shew you my letter as you would see in it that I have told no stories used no deceits . . . Good God I tremble when I think of it I was indeed on the brink of perdition & about to encounter misery infamy & ruin with perfect levity.[58]

What was Lady Melbourne to do? Remonstrance seemed to drive her daughter-in-law into paroxysms of self-abnegation: "I must indeed have a heart of iron if it was not most deeply wounded and affected by your letter," Caroline wrote, promising she would avoid Sir Godfrey and stop any correspondence with him: "I will write no more—no indeed indeed I will not it shall end here."[59]

Yet, along with the hysteria and self-condemnation, Caroline made it clear that there was blame to share, blame that she put upon William, and that by implication must be laid also at Lady Melbourne's door:

those principles which I came to William with—that horror of vice of deceit of any thing that was the least improper that Religion which I believed in then without a doubt & with what William pleased to call superstitious enthusiasm—merited praise & ought to have been cherished—they were safeguards to a character like mine & nobody can tell the almost childlike innocence & innexperience I had preserved till then—all at once this was thrown off & William himself though still unconscious of what he has done William himself taught me to regard without horror all the forms & restraints I had laid so much stress on—with his excellent heart right head & impervious Mind he might & will go on with safety without them he is superior to those passions & vanities which mislead weaker characters & which however I may be ashamed to own it, are continually misleading me.[60]

Accurate as this might be, it sounded like finger-pointing. What else could she say at that juncture, except to add the assurance that her affair had ended, "not for a month not for a year but for ever."

Of course, it hadn't really. Caroline's and William's passion had cooled, and "contrary to the general opinion on this subject . . . lasted far longer on his side than on mine." Now, William's love was not enough. She confessed that "gratitude affection even love" remained, "but those feelings which carry with them such a charm and existed so many years unabated" were on the decline.[61] Perhaps this explains the fact that her affair with Webster, slated to end in April, still smoldered in June, when she begged permission from her mother-in-law to hold a final meeting with her lover:

> [I]f I may see him tomorrow & if you will not tell my mother the Dss [of Devonshire] or Fredric [Ponsonby] what passed tonight I will be as gentle as docile as a Lamb I will try & conquer feelings which are now too strong for my reason to command I will put my self in your & my Mothers hands & be guided by you—but if I am driven to dispair I will deceive you all. I speak not as a menace & I care not for what may be thought or said.[62]

Half-pleading, half-threatening, Lady Caroline did not fear Lady Melbourne as much as she might. She wanted to see Webster, and *she would,* regardless: "I have faults but I am not a brute & a beast without a heart," she told Lady Holland, "if the 8th of June would not do the 14th shall—& if I cut my hands off I will give up writing seeing thinking of any one may displease you."[63] Presumably this "last meeting" took place on one of the dates mentioned.

No wonder Lady Melbourne grew weary of her son's wife. She must have been quite relieved when Caroline left for Brighton with her mother and father in late summer. A heat wave made bathing pleasant. Caroline threw a benefit party at a local tavern to raise funds for the poor. "This place delights me," she said, and "I make acquaintance with every body—love & like every one without taste or discrimination." To Lady Holland she admitted the obvious—"I am easily flattered"— while to her mother-in-law she wrote a long letter in her "short style" with descriptions of whist games, dresses worn by various ladies to the theatre, and sundry details of her reconsecrated married life.[64] She tried to repair things with the Hollands and had some success. By the fall, the stinging embarrassment of this affair had begun to fade. Caroline was at Brocket Hall with William and Augustus, and she reported her husband "looking better than I ever remember seeing him, quite fat & blooming," though she herself had suffered from what she called "puffs on my brain," which were treated with "friction & spirituous applications."[65] Her cousin Harryo described this odd malady: "[T]he whole skin of her head is raised in lumps containing water. She says it has the appearance of a ploughed field, but that she believes it is only the exuberance of her fancy which has mounted there."[66] For many months, Caroline had been plowing through Samuel Richardson's *Clarissa,* and, bedridden, she now found time to finish that pathetic story. The experiences of the novel's doomed heroine were to be echoed later in her own *Glenarvon.*

In October 1810, Harryo gave birth to Granville's first legitimate child. And in November, William's sister had another son. "Lord Cowpers wife has brought forth a little healthy brat," Caroline remarked jealously to Hart.[67] She had Augustus, for whose improvement she prayed. Whenever she could paint a picture of normalcy, she did so. On a visit with her grandmother in St. Albans Parish, she laughingly wrote that Augustus "insisted on being carried up stairs from the Summer Parlour his head by Mr Bone his Feet by [the] Apothecary," to the amusement of everyone present. Her refrain was always the same: "Augustus improves every day."[68]

Not so for George III. Caroline wrote Hart: "Nothing could be sadder than the news about the King."[69] Indeed, after many relapses, the King had become a complete liability. On 31 December 1810, Parliament appointed the Prince of Wales Regent. Sheridan drafted a letter for the Prince's signature, disclosing the Regent's intention to make no change of ministers. The Whigs were learning that they could expect no shift toward a more liberal government now that Prinny was in power. On 5 February 1811 the Regency bill became law and the next day the Prince took his oaths before the Privy Council.

The war in Spain was going better, and Caroline's brother Frederick wrote home describing fierce fighting on the heights of Barrosa in which the French were defeated but the British were unable to follow up their advantage.[70] In the meantime, Caroline had continued her regimen of reading, including Byron's *Hours of Idleness* (1807) and *English Bards and Scotch Reviewers* (1809), already in its fourth edition. In the latter work, Byron declares himself "Unscared by all the din of MELBOURNE House, / By LAMBE'S resentment, or by HOLLAND'S spouse."[71] Perhaps Caroline enjoyed the puzzlement these references produced in the Lambs' dinner-table conversations. Byron could have known nothing of Lady Melbourne's political gatherings, except by hearsay.

Despite the truce with her mother-in-law, Caroline continued to invite trouble. She had fallen in love with a new dance called the waltz, banned in Switzerland and Swabia because of the unseemly closeness and dangerous invigoration it enforced on dancing partners. She danced with "Prinny" to such popular tunes as "Ach du lieber Augustine," and heaped scorn on the hypocrisy of those who feared to be seen waltzing: "I have always been of opinion & still am that those who like it like it because it is doubtful—those unco good young Women who shudder at the thought of vice like to venture to the edge of the precipice down which so many of their frail companions have been thrown."[72] Her grandmother was annoyed to hear that she had leapt over a couch during a party in early summer 1811, and she bemoaned Caroline's inability to grasp that she "lowers her character by such improprieties." Prophetically, Lady Spencer commented a few weeks later that Caroline was preparing a miserable future for herself "not from vice but vanity," presumably from riding out alone without her husband beyond St. James' Park.[73]

Indeed, Caroline was courting disaster. She had broken her promise not to communicate any further with Sir Godfrey Webster, with whom she was now in contact through his brother Henry. Lady Bessborough observed signs in her daughter's behavior that made her suspicious, and when she saw Caroline receiving one of Sir Godfrey's letters, she confronted her. After several attempts at prevarication, Caroline gave up and tearfully agreed to break off the affair *yet again*. She wrote a long letter of confession to Lady Holland which she unwisely combined with advice meant to bring mother and son closer together. After yet another last meeting with Sir Godfrey, Caroline wrote again to assert the uprightness of her future conduct, but without saying that she would give up *all* acquaintance with the younger man. She and Lady Holland held a brief interview during which Lady Holland said "cutting" and "heartrending" things to Caroline about the damage she risked doing to William and their marriage through her thoughtless and selfish behavior.[74] It had been less than a year since she had confessed to William.

Not surprisingly, Caroline's sixth wedding anniversary was unhappy. They attended a ball on 3 June 1811, but she paid William little attention. Finally, he left alone. Caroline stayed another three hours. When she returned home, she wrote again to Lady Holland expressing remorse for "the infatuation that seems [to] have overcome all my principles & right feelings but if a life of very constant attention & thorough amendment can make up for the past believe me it shall immediately take place my husband is angry with me I do not wonder."[75] Lady Holland apparently accepted Caroline's apologies, but not her excuses. She diplomatically but accurately told Caroline that she had acted like a spoiled child seeking attention. Caroline did not like this at all. "In our last reconciliation," she said, "you vexd me more than during our quarrel—you said hard things to me under the appearance of kindness." Caroline insisted that she hadn't behaved badly to gain attention, but because "I cannot help it . . . my passions have so long been used to master my Reason that although it exists it is not every body who knows it does—promises are but so many additions to sin I therefore make none but if you chuse to believe me you may."[76]

Unimpressed, Lady Holland said nothing more. However, when she threw a party at Holland House later that month, she made sure that Caroline knew she was not welcome. Infuriated, Caroline wrote a letter to Lady Holland which would be conveyed by Sir Godfrey himself—a sort of gauntlet. When she realized that her lover might balk at passing along her missive, she sat down and tore off another letter directly to Lady Holland. It is a typical example of her pique, boiling with self-righteousness and glib phrasing: "I shall never offer you any childish or public incivility—but neither by writing or by conversation or by any other means will I from this hour hold the smallest communication with you," she wrote. "I would as soon Waste my affections on a stone." Then she counterattacked, telling Lady Holland that she had neglected her son:

> I would have you learn that no human power shall ever dissolve the Friendship or allow the sentiments I feel for him some call your son but you do well to renounce a Mothers name—& to leave him to the false friends & bad Company your neglect of him has early brought him to—for were you to call him son & speak of him still as I have sometimes heard you it might be deemd no greater impertinence in me to remind you of the Duties of a Mother than in you to taunt me with those of a Wife—

Her rage was equaled by her powers of language and her consciousness that those around her—including Lady Holland—blew with the social currents:

as to the gnats & mites that dare to peck at me let them look to themselves—I will turn upon them before long with the vengeance which one baited & pursued at length is taught to feel & level them to the dust from which they sprung—what are these things that dare to speak of me—at best only my equals & by what I can find many of them inferior to me in the satiric powers they would stab me with—grant me but health & life & if I chuse it you shall see them flatter & follow me & lick the dust I tread on—Lady Holland if this is the case I shall be courted by you—that which is loved becomes lovely in your eyes—[77]

The thunderstorm passed, and when it did, Lady Caroline was horrified at her own imprudence. At 6:00 the next morning she wrote to apologize abjectly: "I shall on my death bed be miserable for the letter I wrote last night." Ever hopeful, she wondered whether she could "[g]allop over to see you at eleven tomorrow morning."[78]

Denied immediate absolution by Lady Holland, Caroline wrote at greater length from Brocket promising "upon my honour never willingly to enter your door when there is the least chance of my meeting with your son" and retracting all the charges she had made against her Lady Holland and her circle. More conciliatory letters followed expressing abhorrence for her behavior "these 2 years past."[79] Desperate to gain forgiveness, she also wrote a verse epistle to Lord Holland during William's convalescence after a bout of influenza:

> I am at home with William Lamb
> And he, I think, is rather better.
> He says he does not care a d—n
> Whether I prate or write a letter.
> So as you sent this morning early
> And as you know I love you dearly
> And as I am not prest for time
> I answer you in Doggrell rhime
>
> . . . . .
>
> By Heavns I'm sick of Dissipation
> And want some serious occupation.[80]

The comment on dissipation underscores her promise to mend her ways and spend her time conjugating Greek verbs (as she said) rather than dallying with Sir Godfrey. Under a renewed barrage of promises that Caroline would henceforward be a "Pattern Wife,"[81] Lady Holland gave up her animus; it was not in her nature to hold grudges, and Caroline was relentless in her pursuit of clemency.

Lady Caroline's determination to intensify her study of ancient Greek at this time may have been a conciliatory move toward her husband, who delighted in the role of tutor, but Greek also formed part of her new relationship with yet another questionable acquaintance, Jane Elizabeth Harley, Countess of Oxford, the daughter of a classics scholar who had translated Catullus. Like Lady Melbourne, Lady Oxford boasted a set of children whose fathers were an eclectic group of former lovers. The Oxfords also supported the estranged wife of the Prince Regent, Princess Caroline, who had aligned herself with the republicans.

The veteran Lady Oxford quickly divined that Caroline was inexperienced, and she decided it would be amusing to initiate the younger woman into "Greek" mysteries. Harryo recorded in her diary that Lady Oxford and Lady Caroline "have been engaged in a correspondence, the subject whether learning Greek purifies or inflames the passions." She concluded that "Caro seems to have more faith in theory than in practice."[82] True, Lady Oxford only argued purity in theory, but she nonetheless promoted scholarship to remedy Caroline's moods, and told her that "Greek would alone repress or depress the ardour & activity of [her] congenial soul." "Let us my sweet friend," she wrote, "improve the passing hour & turn our minds from the vulgar & trivial to the contemplation of true wisdom."[83]

With renewed desire to become educated, Caroline embarked on a course of study that inaugurated a lifelong passion. She copied out ancient Greek poetry and tried to write in Greek to Lady Oxford. William, reprising his tutorial role, approved of this new hobby and gave some assistance to her in translating a passage from Euripides's *Hippolitus*. The theme of the passage harmonizes all too well with the disillusion against which Lady Caroline now struggled:

> I am not a derider, my Father, of those with whom I live, but am always the same
> to my friends whether present or absent—
> Strophe 2
> My mind is no longer chaste and pure
> and hope dies within me—[84]

Presumably, the passage was the choice of Lady Oxford. Its emphasis on faithfulness to friends would become a grim echo later when Lady Oxford would betray her protégée.

William and Caroline had both changed since he had first tutored her in Greek and Latin, and it was no longer possible for him to keep her in awe of him, any more than it was possible for him to play cricket as he had done at Harrow. He tried it that summer and sprained his thigh in the attempt.[85]

At this time, after a long illness, Canis died on 29 July 1811, and Lady Bessborough went again to Chiswick, this time to comfort Bess. The visit proved painful, for the Duchess had unrealistic hopes for what Hart, as the 6th Duke, would do to accommodate her and her children. "Her expectations are much too high," wrote Lady Bessborough to Lord Granville. Nevertheless, Harriet tried to engage the young Duke's sympathies by pointing out how poorly Bess looked, to which Hart replied dryly, "I see she wears no rouge."[86] Caroline and Harryo commiserated with Hart about Lady Elizabeth's demands for money and property, for he had been uncharacteristically firm with Bess, turning her out of Chiswick and Devonshire House, only to suffer pangs of guilt. In November 1811 Lady Caroline wrote to him in sympathy: "I know why my Duke felt melancholy—he has the heart of an Angel & he knew he had been too hasty too suspicious. . . You felt that you had ferrited the maim'd fox out of its last hold—the safe corner to which it still clung from the dangers & taunts of a rigidly Just World."[87] The Duke replied that he had assuaged his own guilty feelings by begging Bess to accept liberal support for her "old age & crepitude," allowing him to feel that he had finally achieved an "amicable riddance" of the "fox."[88]

The debacle with Lady Holland having now subsided, Caroline basked (as she thought) in the sunshine of her mother-in-law's renewed acceptance: "Lady Melbourne like an Angel receives me as she did & *seems* at least to love me as she did." It was another beautiful fall at Brocket. "In my opinion," Caroline wrote to Lady Holland, "there is nothing perfect in nature but Hertfordshire." She had acquired a Blenheim spaniel—a rare privilege—and she offered to give it to Lady Holland to secure her improved status at Holland House.[89] The Blenheim spaniel, so called from Blenheim Palace in Oxfordshire, was bred there after the palace was built in 1704. The breed continues to this day.

Caroline now joined her mother at Brighton for a seaside holiday at the resort where the Prince Regent had become accustomed to take his leisure, and to visit the oriental pavilion he had built at nearby Brighthelmstone. Here she avoided dances and parties, returning to her love of horses and riding. It was probably here that she first made the acquaintance of Sidney Owenson—later, Lady Morgan. Lady Morgan was remarkable—barely over four feet tall, and with a curved spine that may have been the result of scoliosis. The two women planned to get together that fall, but when Lady Caroline summoned the coach she realized she had forgotten the address and had to write an embarrassed note of apology: "If it had not been near making me cry, what I am going to tell you might make you laugh," she wrote in a letter for which she still had no address. It was the start of an enduring friendship. Lady Caroline came to think of Lady Morgan as "my Earliest friend."[90] Lady Morgan in turn saw Caroline as "gifted with the rarest powers, at once an artist, a poetess, a writer of romance, a woman of society and the world," and "a woman of genius," though also of course prey to that "sublime discontent" and restlessness to which all genius is subject.[91]

Caroline's relatives judged her discontent to be less than sublime. Harryo wrote: "I wish the learned could explain the incongruity of [Caroline's] behaviour. They would be put to it indeed."[92] Caroline shared the bafflement others felt at her eccentricities. In one of her letters of self-justification to Lady Holland, she added an editorial footnote: "A monstrous silly Passage—the common cant of every Woman in similar circumstances!"[93] In surveying the cracked foundation of her own morality, she found she had a spark of writing talent. This knowledge was not so much repressed as rendered silent, however, by her instinctive awareness that it was not wanted and would be considered pretentious. However ludicrous her behavior, she had no desire to be laughed at.

Lady Caroline had been submissive to Lady Melbourne after her affair with Sir Godfrey, flattering her mother-in-law with thanks for her kindness and patience. But now she chafed again at the barriers that constrained her. She felt that "no time will ever bring me back the perfect innocence & enjoyment I once possessed nor shall I ever hear William's name or meet his eyes without feelings of bitter reproach."[94] This loss of innocence and this disillusionment helped prepare her for the most famous chapter of her life, her affair with Lord Byron.

Byron

1812

*Y*oung Lord Byron had returned in 1811 from an extended tour abroad. He celebrated his twenty-fourth birthday on 22 January 1812 and attended the sessions of the House of Lords at the end of the month, feeling this might be the moment to deliver his maiden speech. Two thousand troops had been sent in late December to repress the violence of the frame-breaking Luddites, who were protesting against the textile manufacturers' having replaced the narrow stocking-frames with wider ones that required fewer workers. Masked protesters had been destroying the new frames, and mobs advocating open insurrection were clashing with authorities. When a bill was introduced to stiffen the penalties against the protests of the "framebreakers," Byron resolved to make his opposition the subject of his first address, which he delivered on 27 February. He had taken an unpopular stand in favor of the workers, for even among Whigs the Frame Work Bill was thought a reasonable measure to prevent an uprising. At this time, Byron was also correcting the final proofs of *Childe Harold's Pilgrimage,* a poem based loosely on his travels. Suddenly nervous about the parliamentary leadership, he worried that *Childe Harold* contained an attack on Lord Elgin for taking marble statues from the Parthenon. His publisher, John Murray, commissioned the shrewd Samuel Rogers, poet and banker, to test out reactions to *Childe Harold*. Rogers, like Byron, was a contradictory mix: generous and witty, but also acerbic and fractious. He appeared so emaciated (so one story goes) that once when he was emerging from the Roman catacombs, a friend turned to him and shook hands, saying to his skeletal friend, "Good-bye, Rogers."[1]

As an intimate of the Holland House circle, Rogers loaned an advance copy of *Childe Harold* to Lady Caroline to get her reaction. Byron's previous work was already familiar to Caroline, and she had heard stories about him from her brother Willy and cousin the 6th Duke of Devonshire, both of whom had known the poet through connections at Harrow and Cambridge.[2]

As Caroline began to read the first canto of *Childe Harold's Pilgrimage,* she was immediately struck by the moving portrayal of loneliness in the crowd: "And none did love him: though to hall and bower / He gather'd revellers from far and near." She was also moved by Byron's attack on the "heartless parasites" of society, by the encomium to his mother (who had died the previous August), and especially by his declared intention to leave England's pretension and hypocrisy behind.[3] The first edition of the poem was also published with three of the so-called Thyrza poems appended. These verses are now widely acknowledged as expressions of Byron's grief for John Edleston, a young chorister with whom he had fallen in love at Cambridge. Disguising the homoerotic impulses behind the poems, Byron misled his readers into thinking he was pining for a female lover. Lady Falkland, who had met him earlier, fancied that she was Thyrza. She was by no means the only woman to do so.

Lady Caroline promptly asked Rogers for an introduction. He was at this time besieged by "the manoeuvres of certain noble ladies" who sent him invitations to dinner parties with the hint that he contrive to bring along his popular friend, and he demurred.[4] Years later, Lady Caroline said that Rogers resisted introducing her to Byron, warning her that the poet was unattractive—a nail biter with a club foot. Her reply was, "If he is as ugly as Aesop, I must see him."[5]

Childe Harold's Pilgrimage was officially published on 3 March. Taking the poem as a *cri de coeur,* Caroline wrote her first letter to Byron, dated 9 March:

> Childe Harold
>
> I have read your Book & cannot refrain from telling you that I think it & that all those whom I live with & whose opinions are far more worth having—think it beautiful. You deserve to be and you shall be happy. Do not throw away such Talents as you possess in gloom & regrets for the past & above all live here in your own Country which will be proud of you.

She told him not to try to find out who was writing to him ("it is one very little worth your notice"), though she wished more than anything in the world to meet him in person.[6] Fearing Byron might take her desire for anonymity seriously, Lady Caroline wrote again within forty-eight hours. Like many of his female correspondents, she honored him through imitation. Byron's *Childe Harold* begins,

> Oh, thou! in Hellas deem'd of heav'nly birth,
> Muse! form'd or fabled at the minstrel's will!
> Since sham'd full oft by later lyres on earth,
> Mine dares not call thee from thy sacred hill . . .[7]

Lady Caroline cast her response similarly in iambic pentameter:

> Oh that like thee Childe Harold I had power
> With Master hand to strike the thrilling Lyre
> To sing of Courts & Camps & Ladies Bower
> And chear the sameness of each passing hour
> With verse that breathes from heaven and *should* to heaven *aspire*
> Then all confiding in my powerful art
> With Friends attentions & expressions kind
> Ev'n I might Hope some solace to impart
> To soothe a Noble but a wounded heart
> And pay homage due to a superior mind . . .
> Strong love I feel for one I shall not name—
> What I should feel for thee could never be the same—
> But Admiration interest is free—
> And that Childe Harold may receive from me.[8]

She followed this "homage" and disavowal of illicit intentions by identifying herself as the author of the previous letter and asking Byron to leave a note for her under the alias "Mr. Sidney Allison" at T. J. Hookhams' Circulating Library on Bond Street. Book purveyors often provided customers with this service, which was a means of exchanging messages more efficiently and secretly than by post.

By now, Byron was deluged by letters from "star-gazers," as Thomas Moore dubbed them.[9] Byron wrote simply, "I awoke one morning and found myself famous."[10] While Lady Caroline's was among the first verse-epistles Byron received after the publication of *Childe Harold,* there were many others, including some that were immediately published, such as *Lines to Harold* (London, 1812), cast in sixteen Spenserian stanzas ("Cold is the breast, extinct the vital spark, / That kindles not to flame at Harold's muse.") But Caroline's poem impressed Byron enough that he showed it to his friend, Robert Dallas, telling him he thought the letter came from Mrs. Dallas. Robert apparently never got the joke. On finding out his correspondent was the eccentric and aristocratic Lady Caroline Lamb, Byron immediately broke his resolution not to answer such letters.[11]

Childe Harold opened the doors of Regency society to Byron. As Byron's friend, rival poet, and first biographer Thomas Moore remarks, "in place of the desert which London had been to him but a few weeks before, he now . . . saw the whole splendid interior of the High Life thrown open to receive him."[12] The poem was a subject of discussion in Melbourne House, when Lady Melbourne's niece, Annabella Milbanke visited on 15 March.[13] Not long after, Caroline found an opportunity to meet Byron at a ball at Lady Westmoreland's, but on seeing him attended by a number of women, she withdrew. She had seen his face, however, with its strong brow and nose, and its sensual mouth. Byron's pallor was exactly the fashion of the moment—fragile and spiritual, implying the ravages of fever. "How very pale you are," she later said, "a statue of white marble, so colourless, and the dark brow hair such a contrast. I never see you without wishing to cry. If any painter could paint me that face as it is, I would give anything I possess on earth—no one has yet given the countenance and complexion as it is."[14] Never mind that this pallid face might be the product of dieting and laxatives—"That beautiful pale face will be my fate," she claims she wrote in her diary. She also claimed to have written the phrase that would come to epitomize the Byronic character: "mad, bad, and dangerous to know."[15] The phrases may have been created later.

Byron was surprised to be told that Lady Caroline had left Lady Westmoreland's without being introduced. Subsequently at Holland House, he introduced himself and asked why she had avoided him, to which she made no direct reply. Intrigued, he asked for permission to call, and his request was granted. He wasted no time in visiting Melbourne House. Leslie Marchand, biographer and editor of Byron's letters, has said, Byron had a "psychological urge, built upon the whole background of his early life, to be accepted as a social equal in the aristocratic world."[16] Here was his opportunity. He arrived with Samuel Rogers just after Lady Caroline herself, who had been out riding. She was expecting Rogers, but when her page presented her with Byron's card, she was caught off guard: "I had just come in filthy and hot from riding when they told me that not only was faithful old Mr. Rogers in the drawing room, but he had brought with him another and a very different poet. Should I go up to my room and tidy myself before confronting him as I was? No my curiosity was too great and I rushed in to be introduced to this portent."[17] Soon thereafter, Byron was invited to attend a waltzing party thrown by Lady Caroline, set for 25 March 1812, a gathering of perhaps forty or fifty people who might dance from noon into the evening.[18]

Byron disliked the Waltz because of his club foot and skinny leg. He also thought the fad distracted public attention from himself. Nothing German appealed to him, in any case:

Seductive Waltz!—though on thy native shore
Even Werter's self proclaim'd thee half a w—re.[19]

Caroline acted thoughtlessly in inviting him to a dance, but he came, and here, as he watched with an aloof gaze, Byron first glimpsed his future bride, Annabella Milbanke. He left with an invitation to return the following evening with Thomas Moore, whom he wrote that day: "Know all men by these presents that you, Thomas Moore, stand indicted—no—invited, by special and particular solicita-tion, to Lady C L * *'s to-morrow even[ing], at half-past nine o'clock, where you will meet with a civil reception and decent entertainment."[20]

Catching a scent of the budding affair, Lady Bessborough tried to discourage Byron by telling him Caroline was not attracted. This quickened Byron's interest, as he later confessed to Lady Melbourne: "[H]er folly half did this, at ye. commencement she piqued that 'vanity' (which it would be the *vainest* thing on earth to deny) by telling me she was certain 'I was not beloved.'"[21] Perhaps because she had tried to throw him off the scent, Byron began to call Lady Bessborough "Lady Blarney." He determined to disprove her claim that Caroline was merely flirting with him, and to satisfy his curiosity about the Bessboroughs, Melbournes, and Devonshires.

Byron probably found Augustus's abnormality fascinating. The child had been placed under the care of Thomasina Webster, an unmarried woman of great kindness and real education. Caroline became more and more dependent on "Moome"—a Gaelic word for "foster mother"—relying on her to take dictation as well as care for Augustus.[22] Byron held the four-year-old on his lap on several visits to Melbourne House. He noted Caroline's interest in gardening and dogs, and when he returned he gave her a rose and some lines about his dog, Boatswain. He delivered the rose with the words, "Your Ladyship, I am told, likes all that is new and rare, for a moment."[23]

Whatever tortures followed, this relationship began as intellectual inter-course. Like William Lamb, Byron brought her books.[24] They talked about Hume's prose style and discussed romances and novels, like *Les liaisons dangereuses,* Walpole's *Castle of Otranto,* Beckford's *Vathek* and Jacques Cazotte's *Le diable amoreux.* On Good Friday, 27 March 1812, Caroline wrote to Byron on stationery decorated with seashells: "The Rose Lord Byron gave to Lady Caroline Lamb died in despight of every effort made to save it; probably from regret at its fallen fortunes. Hume, at least, who is no great believer in most things, says that many more die of broken hearts than is supposed."[25] She then sent Byron the flower she wished most to resemble—a sunflower, because it had a "noble and aspiring mind," and it followed with its gaze "the bright star to whom it pays constant homage." She begged him to avoid "any more Taunts and cuts about 'Love of what is New,'" and she concluded by praising the lines to his dog Boatswain, while complaining of the lines in *Childe Harold* that she couldn't approve:

> Perchance my dog will whine in vain
> Till fed by stranger hands;
> But long e'er I come back again
> He'd tear me where he stands.[26]

These lines from the first canto of *Childe Harold* had been plucked from a song that Byron inserted between stanzas 13 and 14 of the poem, in which Harold comforts his companion: "Come hither, hither, my little page! / Why dost thou weep and wail?" Such imagery and allusions illuminate the way that Byron and Caroline were drawn to each other. She loved cross-dressing, and sensed in the lines of the song the homoerotic attraction of Byron to young boys. Intuitively, Lady Caroline enhanced her own boyishness and began a set of illustrations, or "vignettes" for *Childe Harold's Pilgrimage* populated with her trademark *putti.* At least two of these drawings still exist. (See illustrations.)

After a short period of platonic devotion, they succumbed: "[N]ever while life beats in this heart," she told him, "shall I forget you or that moment when first you said you lov'd me—when my heart did not meet yours but flew before it—& both intended to remain innocent of greater wrong."[27] Byron's friend and first literary agent, Robert Dallas, described him as "so enraptured, so intoxicated, that his time and thoughts were almost entirely devoted to reading her letters and answering them." One morning in April, Dallas entered Byron's rooms at 8 St. James's Street and found the poet so absorbed in writing a letter to Caroline that he appeared not to notice when his friend spoke to him and sat down across the table for a while reading the newspaper. Byron had "a peculiar smile on his lips; his eyes beamed the pleasure he felt from what was passing from his imagination to the page." Dallas thought his friend so completely in love that he had practically entered another world.[28] The lovers wrote daily to each other, often multiple times. Sadly, little has survived out of a correspondence of more than three hundred letters.[29]

Caroline had captivated Byron. He had not yet perceived the failing in her that infuriated Lady Melbourne. Without concealment a romantic affair becomes impossible, and Byron probably counted on Caroline to know where the line must finally be drawn. He was fatally wrong. But this problem was yet a sprouting seed, and at first, all remained "piquant." Byron forbade waltzing, and Caroline acquiesced. Dancing classes stopped at Melbourne House. She sent him a lock of her hair, cut when she was fourteen. She arranged to meet him at the soirées of hostesses like the literary liberal Lydia White.[30] Rogers recounted his astonishment at Caroline's boldness: "She absolutely besieged him." One night, he recalled, "after a great party at Devonshire House, to which Lady Caroline had not been invited, I saw her,—yes, saw her,—talking to Byron, with half of her body thrust into the carriage which he had just entered."[31]

Everyone saw Caroline's posture: "Lord Byron is still upon a pedestal," wrote Harryo, "and Caroline William doing hommage."[32] It all disgusted twenty-year-old Annabella Milbanke, who deplored Caroline's erotomania, or "Byromania," as she called it:

> See Caro, smiling, sighing o'er his face
> In hopes to imitate each strange grimace
> And mar the silliness which looks so fair
> By bringing signs of wilder Passion there.[33]

This penetrating poem distills the elements of Caroline's disaster: In hopes of stimulating his love, she became an "ape." Annabella pitied Caroline as a woman infected by the "venom'd sting" of Byron's prurience who now infected others: "I really thought that Lady Caroline had bit half the company, and communicated the *Nonsense-mania.*" Thinking herself vaccinated, Annabella dwelt condescendingly on Lady Caroline's feckless, fevered worship: "Lady C has of course seized on him, notwithstanding the reluctance he manifests to be shackled by her." Yet, like Caroline, Annabella held back from a first meeting with Byron, believing that if she made no "offering at the shrine of Childe Harold" she would be protected from his spells.[34] Harryo also claimed to "feel no wish for any further intimacy. His Countenance is fine, when it is in repose, but the moment it is in play suspicious malignant & consequently repulsive."[35] The revulsion rings hollow.

Caroline used the trick of dressing in breeches to visit Byron *incognita* at his apartments in St. James's Street, and even Lady Melbourne was at first fooled into thinking she had hired a female page: "If so, do not hope to make me laugh. You always think you can make people laugh at your follies, but these are crimes."[36] Undeterred, Caroline duped Byron's page, Fletcher, into collaborating:

> FLETCHER—Will you come and see me here some evening at 9, and no one will know of it. You may say you bring a letter and wait the answer. I will send for you in. But I will let you know first, for I wish to speak with you. I also want you to take the little foreign page I shall send in to see Lord Byron. Do not tell him before-hand, but, when he comes with flowers, shew him in. I shall not come myself, unless just before he goes away; so do not think it is me. Besides, you will see this is quite a child . . .[37]

Robert Dallas also witnessed Lady Caroline's page-boy act:

> He was a fair-faced delicate boy of thirteen or fourteen years old, whom one might have taken for the lady herself. He was dressed in scarlet hussar jacket and pantaloons. . . . He had light hair curling about his face, and held a feathered fancy hat in his hand, which completed the scenic appearance of this urchin Pandarus. I could not but suspect at the time that it was a disguise; if so [Byron] never disclosed it to me.[38]

Dallas ended on an uncharacteristically dry note that he could not "precisely recollect the mode of [the page's] exit." Byron enjoyed these antics. While living temporarily with a young woman in London, he had taken her out with him in male clothing.[39] Now his lover voluntarily showed up in disguise. When she did so unannounced, however, Byron became irritated.

Indeed, the lovers often lost their tempers. Samuel Rogers found himself caught in the middle: "They frequently had quarrels; and more than once, on coming home, I found Lady C walking in the garden, and waiting for me, to beg that I would reconcile them."[40] Undoubtedly these reconciliations were sweetened by the *bon mots* on which they thrived, the witticisms that masked anxiety about the consequences of their behavior. Byron later told John Cam Hobhouse that at dinner one day Lady Caroline turned to her brother-in-law, George Lamb, and asked him whether he knew what the seventh commandment was. Into the pause she inserted the concise answer: "Thou shalt not bother," a phrase that distilled the Lamb credo.[41] It was a time of such glib phrases, and few talkers were so fluent as Byron and Caroline. Most had to prepare well in advance, as Byron later noted: "What unexpected woes / Await those who have studied their *bon mots!*" he wrote, noting that those who cribbed their witticisms ahead of time then had to "allure the conversation / By many windings to their clever clinch."[42]

Caroline provided Byron the right intellectual and emotional partnership at this moment. Just slightly more than two years older, she was no sycophant. She could play Byron to a draw at the mental and verbal games he devised, and their affair soon reached high temperature. Byron told her in April 1812:

> Every word you utter, every line you write proves you to be either *sincere* or a *fool,* now as I know you are not the one I must believe you the other. I never knew a woman with greater or more pleasing talents, *general* as in a woman they should be, something of everything & too much of nothing, but these are unfortunately coupled with a total want of common conduct.—For instance the *note* to your *page,* do you suppose I delivered it? or did you mean that I should? I did not of course.—Then your heart—my poor Caro, what a little volcano! that pours *lava* through your veins, & yet I cannot wish it a bit colder, to make a *marble slab* of, as you sometimes see (to understand my foolish metaphor) brought in vases tables &c. from Vesuvius when hardened after an eruption.—I have always thought you the cleverest most agreeable, absurd, amiable, perplexing, dangerous fascinating little being that lives now or ought to have lived 2000 years ago.——I wont talk to you of beauty, I am no judge, but our *beauties* cease to be so when near you, and therefore you have either some or something better. . . . All that you so often *say,* I *feel,* can more be said or felt?[43]

What woman could resist the imputation of a quality *better than beauty* to herself, or the delightful perplexity of her lover trying to solve the riddle of "me"? Perhaps Byron's affair with Caroline was a case of contagious narcissism, but it developed at an intellectual and emotional level that still astonishes.

He thought constantly of her, attending the sessions of the House of Lords only twice in March and thrice in April. On 21 April he spoke for the second time, giving an uproariously funny speech supporting the rights of Roman Catholics to be spared ill treatment under the law.[44] Though Byron had sexual relations with other women during this time, his attachment to Caroline was intense during the period of April to June, when the lovers were thickest. He became jealous of robust and manly William, with whom he contrasted himself, casting himself as the Devil and William as a Saint. He emphasized to Caroline that, unlike William, he was cursed in his family background and upbringing. Byron recounted his doomed love for his distant cousin, Mary Chaworth, and how she had said, in his hearing, "Do you think I could care anything for that lame boy?"[45] This stirred Caroline's sympathies, and yet she would not disparage William.

Byron castigated her for coldness, and this rankled even after the affair had ended. She wrote him two years later to reproach him: "But was I cold when first you made me yours? When first you told me in the carriage to kiss your mouth and I durst not—and after thinking it such a crime it was more than I could prevent from that moment—you drew me to you like a magnet and I could not indeed I could not have kept away—was I cold then—were you so?"[46] Byron had sought to destroy the inhibitions of his lover. He succeeded too well. Painfully, Caroline acknowledged that on at least one occasion her sexual desire was too strong for her partner's taste: "I saw you lift the vail up twice—it was a strange adventure— but you were not kind that night as formerly—you thought of others *even while with me*—of that I am sure—& the remembrance of that night and your accusation of wildness are disagreeable to me."[47]

Aware of her competition, Caroline persuaded Byron to go through a mock wedding ceremony. They exchanged several rings, including "a *wedding* one" that Byron insisted "she *bestowed* upon *herself* & insisted on my placing it on her finger."[48] The only poem surviving from the many that Byron wrote his lover while they were infatuated attests to the importance of these tokens of their relationship. On the manuscript copy of the following poem is Caroline's note: "These are the first lines Ld Byron wrote to me—I had made him a present of a gold neck chain and these lines were written at the moment."

> Yet fain would I resist the spell
> That would my captive heart retain,
> For tell me dearest, is this well?
> Ah Caro! do I need the chain?
> Nor dare I struggle to be free,
> Since gifts returned but pain the giver,
> And the soft band put on by thee,
> The slightest chain, will last forever![49]

Byron's resistance to the sentimental sacraments of adulterous lovers seems to have been weak, whatever he said later. The ring ritual temporarily assuaged Caroline's guilt over her erotic obsession with Byron.

Though she despised Lady Caroline's fixation, Annabella Milbanke could not resist the opportunity to give Byron some of her poems. Caroline reluctantly passed them to him, along with the gossip that Annabella was going to marry George Eden, who had attended waltz parties at Melbourne House. Byron read the poems and wrote a note praising Annabella's work. Byron knew that Annabella Milbanke had been a supporter of the cobbler-poet Joseph Blacket, who had died in 1810, and he compared her poetry favorably to Blacket's. He ended by trying to strike a note sensitive to Caroline's jealousy: "You will say as much of this to Miss M. as you think proper.—I say all this very sincerely, I have no desire to be better acquainted with Miss Milbank, she is too good for a fallen spirit to know or wish to know."[50] It is hard to believe Caroline felt comforted, for Byron easily made inroads into hearts like Annabella's.

After Miss Milbanke came the very next morning to hear Byron's opinion of her poetry, she wrote in her diary, "Went in morning to Lady Caroline Lamb, and undeceived her by a painful acknowledgement." Annabella had been forced to admit that she was not engaged to George Eden and had no intention of marrying him.[51] Still jealous, Caroline composed some verse of her own, addressed to Annabella, but for Byron's eyes—intended to block any inroads *she* might have made into *his* affections:

> Cousin of mine thy verses stray & Quaint
> Shall soon unrivald all his favour share
> For love requires but little art to paint
> Such one as thee in colours bright & fair
>
> Thou hast the charms of innocence & youth
> Thy thoughts & passions under firm controul
> Thy lips untainted pure as spotless truth
> & faith & Principles to guard thy soul.

Caroline goes on to express the hope that Annabella would never know "storms and passions" and "moments of rapturous bliss or frantic woe," but instead become a "fond Mother & a faithful Wife." She finished this letter in direct address to Byron:

> [G]ive me credit for writing off such an address my Horse waiting my Gdmother calling my boy crying my husband swearing my Maids scolding—though metre sense music poetry are rather withheld but it is not to all that these are granted & from an Infant I wrote Rhimes as you see—much as shoe blacks & bell men & love sick Maidens when abandoned oftentimes break out in—take Annabella's

far worthier productions be not over in love with her this one Evening and afterwards you must do as you will—I send your ring would it were more to my liking but before long I will have one quite so—

Distrust consumed her as she sought to keep Byron's attention, hoping that her slight figure, matron's status, and fallen character could be somehow turned to her advantage in her battle against the apple-cheeked, petite, and "perfect" Annabella. She ended her letter with a brisk assertion of her rights as his lover, and a reminder of her willingness and ability to sacrifice: "I am ill this Morning—but I shall come living or dead to the Play—& take you up in my way—write to me—"[52]

While she worked at keeping Byron's attention, Caroline also sought to forestall Annabella's inclination toward the poet, now that she knew Annabella was not engaged. Caroline wrote to her on 22 May a long letter which Annabella succinctly deemed "very remarkable." She urged Annabella to "shun friendships with those whose practice ill accords with your Principles," for "Christian Charity" itself might make her tolerant of evil in "those we love." In what seems a transparent allusion to Byron, she warned Annabella against "befriending & protecting those falling Angels—who are ever too happy to twine themselves round the young Saplings they can reach—but if they are falling you cannot save them—depend on that."

As the fallen woman, Caroline sought to advise the inexperienced Annabella about the pitfalls of London,

> for every thing that enters into this fair City is tainted more or less—your danger will not arise from Balls—roués Coxcombs & Gossips—but beware of what may come across you in the shapes of Genius' superior abilities—Heroic sentiments, affected innocence—look to the conduct & do not attend to their prating—avoid Friendships with Women—you are a little inclined to be taken by a certain Frankness of manner—never let them make you their confidantes & when you hear them killing character answer them coldly—there is no wit in this species of conversation & a word a look a very trifling addition may make a world of difference—& blast a name for ever—and as I am giving you a sermon—like an Apprentice when about to be hang'd—never give in to speaking what is false that good may come of it.[53]

This letter typifies Caroline, whose motives were often transparent to everyone but herself, yet who somehow seems to lose her way as she goes on, so that she ends in sincerely feeling the emotions she first brings forth to forestall others' criticisms. Along the way, she even confessed to Annabella that her own poetry was inferior:

> [M]y beautiful Rhapsodies like every thing else I do—burst forth on every event to perish with it—witness all the Elegies I have written since five years old for every dog cat monkey & squirrel that left this goodly world & where is the young Lady who has not addrest Cynthia bright Goddess—Hygea—innocent Doves—Lambs playing on the Green—the return of Spring—the Fall of the Leaf—a cow ruminating after its dinner & all the other Images that awaken sympathetic emotions in the youthful heart.

Despite all this advice and confession, Caroline's jealousy comes through. It is the jealousy of a rival lover *and* writer aware of the triteness of her own literary productions.

Even Caroline's covetousness became confused, however, for it had been aroused also by a developing intimacy between Lady Melbourne and Byron. Caroline tried vainly to encourage Byron's appreciation of her mother, Lady Bessborough, through invidious comparison with "The Thorn": "If I feel jealous of [Lady Melbourne] I will remember her age and respect her. . . . She has every fine quality and much good, but if *I* have too much of it, I think she is too wholly without sentiment and romance. She also wants that softness which my mother and yourself have." Even at age sixty-two, however, Caroline's mother-in-law was a dangerous rival for Byron's affections. Lady Caroline was careful to promise, tongue-in-cheek, "I love Lady M. and I think she has the law on her side, and therefore I will be very submissive and kind—for your sake also, for she is only too dear to you."[54] Lord Byron felt a real attraction to Lady Melbourne, however. She became his mentor, and he was her last conquest, though proof of physical intimacy was undoubtedly destroyed by her children.

Lady Melbourne feared that Byron's affair with Caroline would ruin them both. Byron himself seems to have suggested an elopement to Lady Caroline in May 1812. Others anticipated it. The Duchess of Devonshire, Lady Elizabeth, wrote on 10 May to her son Augustus that Byron's impending departure for Greece might relieve some husbands' minds, but that she would "not be surprised if Caro William were to go with him, she is so wild and imprudent."[55] Discussion in the Bessborough and Melbourne households of Caroline centered on the obvious: How to get her out of town.

Caroline left for Brocket Hall on 18 May 1812. Byron had stayed up all night to observe the public hanging of John Bellingham for the murder of Prime Minister

Spencer Perceval in the House of Commons, committed one week earlier. Apparently, the assassin had mistaken Perceval for Granville Leveson-Gower—a bizarre twist.[56] Justice was swift, and Bellingham would swing for his offense early in the morning. Byron and two acquaintances had rented a room with a good view of the scaffold at Newgate Prison, where groups of up to eight convicted felons were often hanged while street-vendors and shopkeepers hawked their produce and bread. They arrived well before dawn to be sure not to miss the show, and during a delay in gaining entry to the house, Byron noticed a destitute woman lying in a doorway. In a typical gesture of compassion, he offered her a few shillings. She, however, struck the coins from his hand and, "starting up with a yell of laughter, began to mimic the lameness of his gait."[57] It was an ominous beginning to a day that would sear Byron's memory. He was repulsed by the hanging, then spent several hours with his exhausting lover. "I saw Bellingham launched into eternity and at three the same day I saw [Lady Caroline Lamb] launched into the country," Byron quipped in a note to Thomas Moore.[58] But the flippant tone belied strong feelings of revulsion at the execution and a sense of doom overshadowing his affair.

Lady Caroline opposed capital punishment, and she told Byron she was disgusted that he wished to be an observer at that loathsome ritual. Perhaps the image of the madwoman in the doorway lingered as Byron contemplated his lover's departure, for their conversation had been serious and painful. Caroline later told Lady Melbourne that they had talked "many hours." "3 things I swore," she went on, "never to let our attachment end in wrong—never to go away with him never even to say I preferred him to William."[59] The death of Perceval and the execution of Bellingham had made an indelible impression upon her: "I remember you at the time when Perc[e]val was shot & how much you felt it—your coming here—your seeing William affected—your being deeply so yourself."[60] Under the influence of Perceval's sudden demise, the hanging, and the woman who had mocked his charity, Byron may have confessed to crimes for which he might be hanged, leaving the specifics vague. Whatever he said, Lady Caroline was appalled, yet gratified that he would divulge to her his darkest secrets.

Byron was a master of such narrative shocks and recoils. The very day after Caroline's departure for Brocket, he wrote her to say, "[t]his dream this delirium of two months must pass away." They should, he continued, take the opportunity presented by her absence to reflect and allow rationality to take hold: "We have both had 1000 previous fancies of the same kind, & shall get the better of this." He promised he would also leave town to "cease to make fools talk, friends grieve, and the wise pity."[61] He took his time, however, attending several parties before leaving for Newstead two weeks later. Caroline, who had not had a thousand other infatuations, was unprepared to let go.

While at Brocket, she paid several visits to her grandmother, with whom she dined on 4 June, the day after her seventh wedding anniversary, which she seems to have celebrated without her husband.[62] She wrote letters to Newstead, begging Byron to return.[63] The increasing oscillation of his feelings made their reunions more poignant. Thomas Medwin reports that Byron mentioned "several quarrels" as the end approached: "One was made up in a very odd way, and without any verbal explanation. She will remember it."[64] Byron's meaning is unclear. Some have guessed that he refers to anal intercourse. Perhaps Lady Caroline understood—and even accepted, difficult as that was—the "predispositions," as critic Bernard Grebanier calls them, "fixed by his experiences at school and in the East."[65] Whether that meant she would accept such advances is, however, an entirely different matter. But Byron's phrase (again, if correctly reported by Medwin) probably refers to some taboo.

The quarrels continued. Some time during this period, Caroline wrote Byron one of many conciliatory notes:

> My dearest Byron
>
> There is no cause for alarm—but I have had a wretched night and am still painfully irritable. I am therefore going out and to occupy myself in the air. I am exceedingly grieved I gave you so much uneasiness. I will endeavour by all possible means to avoid a return of any thing so painful between us—In justice to myself however I may say that I should not feel this irritation if it were not for my present circumstances. These seem both cause & effect.[66]

Her domestic conditions had darkened. Yet William's attitude toward his wife's infidelity was basically what it had been during the Godfrey Vassal Webster affair. He grew silent and withdrawn, and this gave Caroline the impression that he condoned her behavior. William did not believe Byron would prove to be more than a temporary sensation, once the poet left London and Caroline went to Ireland, as planned. However, even Caroline's mother began to think that, "*neither* wish nor intend going, but both delight in the fear & interest they create."[67] Both lovers craved attention above all.

William's circumstances grew complicated because of political setbacks his party suffered during the year and a half since the inception of the Regency. In March 1812, Canning had been staggered by the Prince's embrace of the Tories. William had turned down a Tory cabinet post out of loyalty to the Whig party with which he now found himself in disagreement. He and Caroline were in debt, and William saw no way to afford the expense of an election set to take place in July. With gloomy satisfaction, he informed his mother he would not stand for a seat. She promised to get the money from his father, but William refused.[68] He thus found himself in limbo. He had married Caroline because she had awakened his protective as well as passionate feelings. Now, he seemed unequipped to confront his wife or the man who was having her publicly. As one of William's biographers, Philip Ziegler, has put it, "a thin streak of indifference ran pallid through [his] life."[69] Painfully aware of his own shortcomings, William spent time in the library, attempted to comfort Caroline, whom he pitied, but said nothing on the subject that was rendering her guilt-ridden to the point of collapse. Into the vacuum left by the husband's seeming indifference flowed again the power of Byron, who was now on one of his periodic crash diets.[70]

The family returned from Brocket. Lady Caroline's emotional instability increased. Harriet begged Byron's close friend, Hobhouse, to prevent an elopement, and he called on her in mid-July. When Caroline found them together, she outraged Hobhouse by pointing out that they looked "guilty," like conspirators.[71] Lady Caroline kept in touch with her grandmother, who gave her advice in a "serious letter." On 24 July she and William dined with Lady Spencer and managed to convey the impression that there was not a cloud in their sky.[72] The weather would change abruptly.

On 29 July, Hobhouse and Byron were just leaving for Harrow when a diminutive person wearing a greatcoat arrived amid a small crowd on St. James's Street, jerked to a halt on seeing Hobhouse, then fled past him up the garret stairs. Hobhouse descended, entered a shop on the first floor belonging to a Mr. Dollman, ordered a hat to kill time, then returned to Byron's apartments. He found Byron waiting for Lady Caroline, who was in the bedroom "pulling off her disguise—under which she had a page's dress." They persuaded her to don some clothing loaned by one of the women servants of the house, whereupon Lady Caroline insisted, "[w]e must go off together, there is no alternative."[73] She had persuaded William that she was on her way to Roehampton while he himself headed to St. Albans.[74] The stage had been set for an elopement.

Hobhouse remonstrated, and Lady Caroline threatened, "There will be blood spilt." Getting no clear assent from her lover, Caroline cried, "It shall be mine, then" and, snatching at a court sword lying on the sofa, struggled briefly with both men. Regaining some composure, she requested a private meeting with Byron in his friend's apartments, but Hobhouse refused. Finally, she went to Hobhouse's and changed back into her own clothing while Hobhouse and Byron paid a visit to a coffeehouse.[75] Byron went home, and, in a typical act of ambivalence, immediately sent a note to Caroline at Hobhouse's saying he wished to see her before she left London.[76] She extracted a promise from the exasperated Hobhouse not to prevent this meeting.

Having dodged an elopement once, why would he wish to see Caroline alone? Perhaps for another poignant reunion? His behavior seems paradoxical. On the 29th, the same day , he had written to Miss Mercer Elphinstone, an heiress, that he might be able to visit her at Tunbridge Wells.[77] His escape routes from London were many—and yet he stayed, much to the frustration of Lady Bessborough and Lady Melbourne—whom Caroline had dubbed the "Queen Mothers."[78] They pressed him to leave town, and he agreed, yet made no arrangements to do so.[79] Harriet thus began preparations for a trip to the family seat in Ireland. She let her guard down and told Lady Spencer that she feared for Caroline's marriage. Then she regretted her candor and wrote that it looked like everything would be well after all.[80]

But all would not be well. Lady Caroline had fallen for a man whose ambivalence left her no escape. And, like other women before and since, she had confused loving a writer with being a writer herself.

Ireland

1812, continued

𝓘 t was common for lovers to exchange locks of hair. It was less common to give what Lady Caroline now sent Byron. It was a clipping of her pubic hair with a note:

> "Caroline   Byron— August 9th, 1812
> next to Thyrza Dearest
> & most faithful—God bless you
> own love—ricordati di Biondetta
> From your wild Antelope[1]

This note alludes to the character of "Biondetta" in Jacques Cazotte's *Le diable amoureux* (1772),[2] in which a young man of twenty five (Byron was twenty four when he met Caroline) is seduced by an "enamored spirit" who appears to him in the guise of "Biondetta," a fair-haired woman dressed as a page carrying a platter of fruit and accompanied by a spaniel. The reader needs to know that the devil first appears to Marlowe's Faust in the form of a spaniel, and Goethe, playing on this same theme, changed the animal to a large poodle in his masterwork, *Faust, Part One*. This background explains the meaning of the allegorical portrait of Lady Caroline begun by Thomas Phillips sometime in 1812 (now at Chatsworth). The painting depicts Lady Caroline in livery holding a platter of grapes and being gazed upon by a spaniel.

In the letter which accompanied the pubic hair, Lady Caroline asked for a gift in return: "I asked you not to send blood but yet do—because if it means love I like to have it—I cut the hair too close & bled much more than you need—do not you the same o pray put not scizzors points near where quei capelli grow—sooner take it from the arm or wrist—pray be careful." This carnal exchange would not be completed. But though he gave Lady Caroline no clipping of hair, he did give her a gold locket inscribed with his family motto, "Crede Byron" (have faith in Byron). Thus, Caroline did not realize he was pulling away. Instead, she fantasized about living with Byron at Newstead: "Newstead—that is a pity—why not have kept it & taken Biondetta there & have livd & died happy."[3]

Annoyed as he was, Byron still feared Caroline's influence, because she had such power that "he could only do what she pleased." He admitted to Hobhouse he had never been so in love, despite the fact that she "teazed him to death and made him wretched—that a few weeks absence would cure him—but that if she got on him again she would force him to go away with her, & that he should blow his brains out a week after." Lady Bessborough reported all this directly to Caroline herself in hopes of convincing her to give up on the idea of an elopement.[4] On 12 August Harriet went to Melbourne House to beg Caroline to leave immediately. Lord Melbourne entered the room and grumbled about Caroline's bad humor. Caroline spat back in anger, and Lady Bessborough left to fetch Lady Melbourne from the lower apartment. While they were gone, Lord Melbourne lost his temper completely. When Caroline threatened to go to Lord Byron, he said "Then go, and be damned!" adding that he doubted Byron would have her.[5] Caroline turned and ran into the street.

When mother and mother-in-law returned, they found Lord Melbourne on the stairs yelling "Stop her!" to the porter. The servants canvassed the area; Harriet took her carriage and drove up and down Whitehall—all to no avail. Lady Bessborough and Lady Melbourne went immediately to Byron, who expressed bewilderment. "Oh G.," Harriet wrote to Granville in desperation, "Caroline is gone. It is too horrible. She is not with Lord Byron, but where she is God knows."[6] As soon as the "Queen mothers" had gone, Byron sent a note after Lady Melbourne saying he was "extremely uneasy" and wondering what part he must play in "this unfortunate drama." Byron stood ready, if necessary, to elope: "I must not shrink from anything." Byron had thought "everything was well & quiet," and now could do nothing but wait "in the most painful suspense" to hear Lady Caroline's—and his own—fate decided.[7] Lady Bessborough returned to Cavendish Square about nine that evening, exhausted, to have dinner with Hart.

After running out of Melbourne House, Caroline had fled across St. James's Park and up Pall Mall to St. James's Street, where she ducked into an apothecary's shop and persuaded the chemist to take a small ring in exchange for the hire of a hackney coach. She told the coachman to stop at a pawnbroker's and moneylender's in Kensington. Here she pawned an opal ring for £20 and purchased a ticket for a stage coach that would take her to Portsmouth for embarkation on "the first Vessel that sail'd from there, where-ever it might happen to be bound for." But where would she conceal herself until the coach departed? It was then that she thought of Dr. Thomas, a surgeon she had met once or twice before, and whose address she now recalled. She scribbled hasty notes of farewell to her mother and Byron, and tipped the coachman to deliver them to the Bessboroughs' residence in Cavendish Square, keeping her location secret. As she alighted in front of Dr. Thomas's home, she gave the coachman one additional note, to be delivered to Lord Byron's footman, Fletcher, telling him that a letter awaited him at Cavendish Square.

Dr. Thomas, if he remembered Caroline at all, must have been very surprised by the appearance of a disheveled and pale young woman at his door as he was sitting down to his evening meal. She was evidently in great distress, but refused all offers of help. She could not return home. She needed only to be concealed for a short while, until the stage left in the morning. Would he be so kind as to grant her this one request?

Meanwhile, the coachman stopped first at Byron's residence in St. James's Street. Once he recognized the handwriting of the note, Byron immediately pursued and caught up with the man, demanding to know the whereabouts of the author. Threats, and the proffer of a cash reward, convinced the coachman to break his oath. After scribbling a note of his own to be delivered by the coachman to Cavendish Square with the packet of letters, Byron went immediately to Dr. Thomas's, where he pounded on the door. Primed by Lady Caroline's stories of being pursued by malevolent enemies, the doctor at first refused Byron entry, but he forced his way in and stunned the room by declaring himself to be the lady's brother. Before anyone could react, Lady Caroline picked up her cue, crossed to Byron, and was gone. The "wild Antelope" had been run to ground.

Caroline was still defiant, however. When they arrived in Cavendish Square, Lady Bessborough was at the point of collapse, and Byron did all the talking. "I am mortified to say," wrote Harriet to Granville, "it was more by his persuasions than mine, and almost reproaches at her bearing to see me suffer so much, that she was induc'd to return with me to White Hall."[8] Harriet mustered her remaining strength and went in first to plead the rather thin case for commutation of Lady Caroline's sentence. William immediately promised he could and would forgive her, and the Melbournes ratified this decision with a sullen silence—the best that could be expected under the circumstances. Caroline made her entrance back through the portal she had exited scarcely twelve hours before. It was ignominious. It was painful. And it was not over yet.

Later that night, Lady Bessborough began spitting blood. This lasted until morning, when a physician succeeded in stopping the flow by administering a medicine Lady Bessborough described eloquently as "some very nasty thing." Ill as she was, her only thought was to depart with Caroline for Ireland as soon as possible. Unfortunately, Byron had been too much affected by the drama of the moment, and he now exacerbated the problem of Caroline's resistance to departure by writing a letter:

> My dearest Caroline—If tears, which you saw & know I am not apt to shed, if the agitation in which I parted from you, agitation which you must have perceived through the *whole* of this most nervous *nervous* affair, did not commence till the moment of leaving you approached, if all that I have said & done, & am still but too ready to say & do have not sufficiently proved what my real feelings are & must be ever towards you, my love, I have no other proof to offer; God knows I wish you happy, & when I quit you, or rather when you from a sense of duty to your husband & mother quit me, you shall acknowledge the truth of what I again promise & vow, that no other in word or deed shall ever hold the place in my affection which is & shall be most sacred to you, till I am nothing I never knew till *that moment,* the *madness* of—my dearest & most beloved friend—I cannot express myself—this is no time for words—. . . .[9]

But indeed this was a time for as many words and as few actions as possible. Byron was counting on Caroline to be drawn inexorably back into the fold by the queen mothers. Thus, he felt he could affirm his deepest love, signing himself "ever & even more than ever yr. most attached Byron." And in a postscript he even reaffirmed his willingness to "give up all here & beyond the grave for you," and declared, "I was and am *yours,* freely & most entirely, to obey, to honour, love—& fly with you when, where, & how you, yourself *might & may* determine."[10] These protestations may have been meant as a consolation to Caroline as she reconciled herself to her husband and child. Instead, by dangling a possible escape with him, Byron increased her resolve to stay in London.

Caroline sent her mother a note telling her she believed she was "breeding" and had persuaded William that they would be risking a miscarriage by traveling. This was a plausible strategy, because the Lamb succession was far from secure, despite Lady Melbourne's large brood. Augustus was retarded. George Lamb's marriage to Caroline St. Jules had apparently gone unconsummated, and Frederick was yet unmarried. Caroline remained alert to any sign of desertion by Lord Byron. If he left town, so would she, with or without him.[11] Was she pregnant? No, she had probably lied, though it's possible Caroline herself might have been deceived. Enervated from her blood-spitting, Harriet mobilized her considerable body, dressed, and called the carriage to take her once again to Melbourne House.

En route, she was discovered by the footman to have lost consciousness. She had suffered an apparent stroke and had to be carried—no easy task—back into her home on Cavendish Square. Indignation spread among the servants. Mrs. J. H. Petersen, Lady Bessborough's maid, had served Harriet for almost thirty years, and she was so enraged that she wrote a letter of reproach to Caroline: "Cruel and unnatural as you have behaved, you surely do not wish to be the Death of your Mother." She went on to say that Lord Bessborough had refused to summon Caroline for fear it would actually worsen his wife's condition: "You have for many months taken every means in your power to make your mother miserable and you have perfectly succeeded but do not quite kill her—you will one day or other fatally *feel* the wickedness of your present conduct. O Lady Caroline, pray to God for strength of mind and resolution to behave as you ought for this is dreadful."[12] It was déjà vu: a return to the Italian sojourn of her childhood, when Caroline's misbehavior had worsened Harriet's choking fits, and the tutors had scolded and isolated her. She went to nurse her mother, and, after a few days, Harriet had made enough progress to be taken to Manresa House in Roehampton for further recuperation. She had in the meantime received the good news that her son Frederick had survived the Battle of Salamanca, distinguishing himself in Wellington's great victory.[13] Her primary goal remained to take Caroline to Ireland.

Caroline begged her father's forgiveness, taking responsibility for having caused her mother's illness through "foolish and wrong conduct," but attempting once again to forestall her banishment to Ireland, this time because Lady Bessborough was too ill to travel. She asked her father for a ten-day reprieve, promising she would do nothing improper: "[L]ock me up if you chuse during that time, but do not refuse this to your own child, your only daughter, who with all her faults loves you dearly." She appealed also to her mother: "I do promise upon my honour and soul, that at all events, whether you grant [the delay] or not, I will not see Lord Byron. . . . Trust in me at least at this moment; all deceptions are over now."[14]

Of course Caroline was lying. She wanted to see Byron again, although she was leaving herself vulnerable to a dismal incarceration if William retaliated, for his support alone stood between her and an ignominious separation. This made her understandably nervous when she attended a party to which Byron had been invited: "You have been very generous and kind *if* you have not betray'd me, and I do *not think you have*," she wrote Byron the next day:

> My remaining in Town and seeing you thus is sacrificing the last chance I have left. I expose myself to every eye, to every unkind observation. You think me weak, and selfish; you think I do not struggle to withstand my own feelings, but indeed it is exacting more than human nature can bear, and when I came out last night, which was of itself an effort, and when I heard your name announced, the moment after I saw nothing more, but seemed in a dream.[15]

She confessed that she had just sent him one of those compulsive, maddening notes that later convinced Byron she was merely acting: "I sent a groom to Holmes twice yesterday morning, to prevent his going to you, or giving you a letter full of flippant jokes, written in one moment of gaiety, which is quite gone since. I am so afraid he has been to you; if so I entreat you to forgive it."[16]

To amuse him, she sent caricatures she had drawn of Madame de Staël. She also wrote in an elaborately offhanded tone asking him to give her advance warning if he decided to marry: "I shall not suffer, if she you chuse be worth you, but she will never love you as I did." Then she tried to entice him into meeting her as if by accident at church:

> I am going to the Chapple Royal at St. James. Do you ever go there? It begins at 1/2 past 5, and lasts til six; it is the most beautiful singing I ever heard; the choristers sing "By the Waters of Babylon."
>
> The Peers sit below; the Women quite apart. But for the evening service very few go; I wonder that more do not,—it is really most beautiful, for those who like that style of music. If you never heard it, go there some day, but not when it is so cold as this.[17]

In the aftermath of Caroline's hysterical flight from home, Byron had shown restraint and common sense, shouldering his "just share of the consequences" of their affair, begging Lady Melbourne to "comfort & be kind" to Caroline, and admitting that in such affairs, "the *man* is—& must be most to blame.[18] Some of this may have been posturing for the sake of his relationship with Lady Melbourne. Nonetheless, it appears he kept the secret of Caroline's many attempts to see him.

Caroline finally gave up resisting the journey for which her mother had been begging. She purchased a blank book and ruled pencil lines on several pages, dated it 1812, and began thus:

This comes from one that suffers—when you open this Book—you will be as far from me in distance as you are now in heart—yet I believe Time which softens all resentment—will make you forget many of my faults & you will perhaps remember then—that I was affectionate & true to you—that however separated I have been yours & though Men can forget Women do not—neither do they ever resent & what you bound to you once will be still yours while it exists however you may think to cut the chains no one knew how to unloose—I hope you will forget all that was wrong in my attachment . . . you will never see me again."[19]

This mood, of course, could not last. She began to write something else, then razored out two pages. She then started a short story titled "Biondetta"; the pathetic tale of a "small spaniel *Bitch* whom Lord Byron took a fancy for."[20] The canine Biondetta's fierce possessiveness leads Byron to give it back to its owner. Soon, "a new favourite filled its place." When Byron sees Biondetta, chained and furiously barking at its rivals, he is sickened and angered, spurns the dog, and it dies. Its body is returned to him with its master's collar still around its neck. The story concludes with a quotation from William Cowper's works: "attachment never to be wean'd or chang'd."

Dissatisfied with this ending, Lady Caroline rewrote it. She abandoned the lines she had laid out with pencil and scribbled hastily. The spaniel needed more nobility of character, so she put down that it "was of the Blenheim Breed in a right line," and she increased the pathos by saying that Lord Byron refused to see it even after it died.[21] Caroline then started a story about a woman named Hanah whose lover has abandoned her. This story, too, must have led into unpleasant territory. Two more pages were razored out.

And then, almost reconciled to leaving, having indulged in morbid fantasies of contrition, she delivers the shock that Byron had seen her once more:

Only one word. You have raised me from despair to the joy we look for in Heaven. Your seeing me has undone me forever—you are the same, you love me still. I am sure of it—your eyes, your looks, your manners, words say so. Oh God, can you give me up if I am so dear? Take me with you—take me, my master, my friend. Who will fight for you, serve you in sickness and health, live but for your wishes and die when that can please you—who so faithfully as the one you have made yours bound to your heart of hearts? Yet when you read this you will be gone. You will think of me, perhaps, as one who gave you suffering—trouble. Byron, my days are passed in remembering what I once was to you. I wish you had never known me or that you had killed me before you went. God bless and preserve my friend and master. Your Caro.[22]

When she finally departed with her family for Ireland in September, Caroline had enshrined herself as Byron's most devoted lover and secretly believed he would wait for her somewhere in Europe, where he had told her he was bound. She did not believe her banishment would bring an end to the affair, and because she did not expect to be gone very long, she left Augustus behind in the care of "Moome."

After a quick but rough passage, the Bessboroughs, William, and Caroline reached Bessborough House in County Kilkenny. They arrived no later than the first week of September 1812 at the estate which had been conferred by Cromwell upon Sir John Ponsonby.[23] The house's crowning glory was a large hall adorned by four massive Ionic columns of Kilkenny marble, each an intact stone mass ten-and-a-half feet tall.[24] Lord and Lady Bessborough stayed there while Caroline and William moved into Belline House, half a mile from the main domicile.

Since the landlords had visited the estate only twice in recent memory, a great deal of posturing, drinking, and dancing now took place, spiced by animosity between two local groups, the Carrickers and the denizens of Piltown Village, who drank and ate together, then showed sudden interest in fisticuffs. Harriet was well enough to stand and make a speech, hoping to disperse the crowd that had gathered for a toast of whisky punch. She explained on behalf of the Bessboroughs that she "felt equally grateful to both Carrickers and Piltowners, and that [she] begg'd it of them, as a proof of (what they call) their Loyalty, to go home quietly without any disturbance or jealousies." She and Caroline then danced and sang with the revelers, who went home without major incident—no "broken heads" at least—"but it gave me a little notion," concluded Harriet, "how hard they are to manage."[25] Her patrician attitude typified the Irish landlords, who seldom considered that the suffering of the Irish peasantry filled their purses in England. Bessborough House would be burned to the ground in the Irish civil war of the 1920s.

Byron had gone to Cheltenham at the end of August to join several friends at the fashionable resort. "By the waters of Cheltenham," wrote Byron to Lord Holland, "I sat down & *drank*."[26] The ostensible buyer of Newstead Abbey, Thomas Claughton, was weaseling out of the contract, and Byron exchanged concerned notes with his lawyer, John Hanson. He wrote from Cheltenham to Lady Melbourne on 10 September that he presumed she was relieved that Caroline was "safely deposited in Ireland & that the sea rolls between you and *one* of your torments; the other you see is still at your elbow."[27]

The field being clear, Lady Melbourne had room to operate, and Byron hoped she would help him to a marriage that would protect his public character, allow him to escape Caroline and solve his financial problems. He appealed to her to help him bow gracefully out of any further relationship with Lady Caroline, telling her that he was simply tired of affairs. They were too exhausting: "It is true from early habit one must make love mechanically as one swims, I was once very fond of both, but now as I never swim unless I tumble into the water, I don't make love till almost obliged." But then he deferred to his sophisticated correspondent, "I will say no more on this topic, as I am not sure of my ground, and you can easily outwit me as you always hitherto have done."[28] Cleverly, Byron drew closer to the experienced woman who, though heavier and in her early sixties, still had a pleasing face and a charming demeanor to go with her razor-sharp mind. Byron was right to tread carefully. "Will you honor me with a line?" he concluded. He took care not to reveal that Caroline still meant something to him.

The young 6th Duke of Devonshire came to Ireland to take official possession of the long-vacant Devonshire estate at Lismore, and Caroline joined her family in visiting him. As they approached Lismore Castle, her imagination was fired by Gothic images of ghosts and knights in armor. She expected, she said, to "wind thro' extensive tho' deserted Parks up to the Portcullis on the out side, and wander about vast ruin'd apartments full of tatter'd furniture and gloom within." The reality was quite otherwise, for despite Hart's ambitious work on the castle's bridge and gardens, the grounds were small and the interior itself furnished "in the newest Inn fashion."[29] Caroline teased her cousin about this and the dampness of the air, and one evening suddenly opened a door and intoned in a loud voice, "Pray walk in, Sir; I have no doubt you are the rightful possessor, and my Cousin only an interloper usurping your usual habitation." When the practically deaf Hart had this message relayed to him, he turned in astonishment to watch with the others for this visitor's arrival. The pause was unbearably long. And then a frog hopped in, followed by Caroline holding candles as though she were a servant lighting her master's way.[30]

These zany moods alternated with depressions that renewed Harriet's fears that her daughter had been permanently unhinged by her disastrous affair. She still feared an elopement, knowing that Caroline had never given up hope. To her mind, Caroline was simply throwing away her own happiness.[31] Harriet wrote to Lady Melbourne, begging her to maintain her "hold" over Byron. We know this because Lady Melbourne in turn passed the letter to Byron himself.[32] Thus the mother-in-law became a spy for the lover.

Byron was delighted. "Pray don't [lose your hold on me]," he gloatingly echoed Lady Bessborough's request. He mocked Harriet and said that he was writing "the greatest absurdities" to Lady Caroline in Ireland to keep her in a good humor and yet forestall her return. He now rewrote his summer fling for the benefit of Lady Melbourne, claiming coyly "I do not believe in the existence of what is called Love."[33] And yet Byron still had not the courage to "snap the knot." He had not told Lady Caroline in so many words that their affair was over. He wanted Lady Melbourne to do the job for him.

He claimed to write to Caroline only twice or thrice in September—while she wrote almost daily.[34] The earliest of her letters contained hints that he should follow her to Ireland, a course he admitted that he actually entertained, for he still felt honor-bound to marry her, though in the same breath he sounded out Lady Melbourne on the question of Annabella Milbanke's inheritance. Byron told Lady Melbourne he would follow *her* (not Caroline) to Ireland if she went, and warned that "C is suspicious about our counter plots." This conspiratorial tone is sustained to the end of this chilling letter: "I am obliged to be as treacherous as Talleyrand, but remember *that treachery is truth* to you; I write [to Caroline] as rarely as I can, but when I do, I must lie like George Rose, your name I never mention when I can help it; & all my amatory tropes & figures are exhausted—I have a glimmering of hope, I *had* lost it, it is renewed—all depends on it, her worst enemy could not wish her such a fate as *now* to be thrown back upon me."[35] And yet, Byron dreaded seeing Caroline. This is a point to which he came directly in a letter posted in late September to Lady Melbourne: "It is not *I* who am to be feared now, but *her* with her *Pique*. . . . I do not at all know how to deal with her, because she is unlike everyone else." His anxiety to move ahead with any possible betrothal was also a strategy to ward off Caroline, though he obviously played up this angle to manipulate Lady Melbourne: "I would marry before they return, this would settle it at once. . . . I admired your niece [Annabella Milbanke], but she is engaged to Eden."[36] Only now would Byron discover that the engagement Caroline had told him about had never actually taken place. Until late in September, he continued ready to marry Caroline herself, if the fates decreed, and "to devote my life to the vain attempt of reconciling her to herself, wretched as it would render me."[37] It was a recipe for madness—as if either of them needed one. When Lady Melbourne advised Byron to try to get Caroline "into a quiet state" by agreeing to see her on the sly when she returned from Ireland, he responded sharply, "*Manage* her"!—it is impossible—& as to friendship—no—it must be broken off at once, & all I have left is to take some step which will make her hate me effectually, for she must be in extremes."[38]

Byron seemed to have fallen into a complete tangle of Lambs, Milbankes, Cavendishes, and Ponsonbys, for he was now hoping to disengage from one and engage himself to another of this "reigning race": "I am perfectly convinced that if I fell in love with a woman of Thibet she would turn out to be an *émigré cousin* of some of you."[39] All this was flattery. He misled Lady Melbourne into thinking that his acquaintance with Caroline actually began with the complimentary remarks he had rendered on Annabella's poetry, hoping to convince Lady Melbourne that he could love Annabella "if she would let me."[40] And soon he was more blunt: "I see nothing but a marriage & a *speedy one* can save me," he wrote to his benefactress on 28 September. "If your Niece is attainable I should prefer her—if not—the very first woman who does not look as if she would spit in my face."[41]

Lady Melbourne forwarded to Byron all the letters she got from Caroline. "You see how I go on trusting you, & putting myself entirely in yr power," she wrote.[42] Suspecting collusion, Lady Caroline copied out some passages from Byron's letters to send to Lady Melbourne, putting him in the uncomfortable position of justifying his posture of saddened lover. Ingeniously, he claimed he was trying to spare the feelings of Lady Bessborough, who would be hurt if he dropped her daughter too abruptly: "[S]he will *hate* me if *I* don't break my heart."[43]

Included in Byron's letter to Lady Melbourne was the penultimate stanza of a poem to Caroline that he had written that September. The peculiar thing about this poem is that it seems to have been written to counteract Byron's weakening determination to stay away from Caroline upon her return. Lady Melbourne apparently found enough cause for concern on this point that she sought reassurance from Byron, who copied the poem out in Lady Jersey's commonplace book at Middleton in the presence of Lady Melbourne herself. "To Lady Caroline" begins:

Go—triumph securely—the treacherous vow
Thou has broken *I* keep but too faithfully now,
But never again shall thou be to my heart
What thou wert—what I fear for a moment thou *art*.

Posing as the reproachful but still-constant lover, Byron has it both ways: Caroline was and (he "fears") still is beloved. He is the brave victim of overpowering emotion who is "[a]shamed of my weakness however beguiled," and who swears to "bear like a Man what I feel like a Child." The poem goes on to accuse the absent loved one of being "in pride of new conquest." Then came the stanza Byron had sent in his letter to Lady Melbourne:

> For the first step of Error none e'er could recall,
> And the woman once fallen forever must fall;
> Pursue to the last the career she begun,
> And be *false* unto *many* as *faithless* to *one.*

The final stanza of "To Caroline" reads:

> And they who have loved thee will leave thee to mourne,
> And they who have hated will laugh thee to scorn,
> And he who adores thee yet weeps to foretell
> The pangs that will punish thy falsehood too well.[44]

Caroline, in trying to make him jealous, handed Byron the stereotype of the fickle lover.

In October, Lady Caroline wrote a poem after she had given alms to an old beggar man near the Bessborough estate. These lines are dated 7 October 1812, and they show the first signs of the process by which she would turn her pain into literature:

> Poor Wretch thou hast nothing to hope for in life
> But the mercy of hearts long success has made hard.
> No parent hast thou, no fond children, no wife,
> Thine age from distress and misfortune to guard.[45]

By October Lady Caroline had been outgunned and outflanked. Lady Melbourne had won, and Byron now had "access to the lower regions of Melbourne House," as he put it, with ample opportunity to marvel at his mentor's skills: "I never saw such traits of discernment, observation of character, knowledge of your *own sex.* & *sly concealment* of your *knowledge* of the *foibles* of *ours.*"[46] At some point that autumn they exchanged rings: "I hope you will not reject the only thing I ever dared to present to you," he wrote later, "nor violate ye. conditions on which I accepted your own."[47] Byron may have been Lady Melbourne's last great conquest.[48]

She certainly acted as his spy with alacrity: "You may depend upon my giving you the earliest intelligence in my power of [the Bessboroughs'] return," Lady Melbourne wrote, taking pleasure in their presenting a united front. "I shall give no answer [to Caroline] till I hear from you or see you." And she excused him, as he had hoped, from responsibility for Caroline's distress, by saying Caroline could not "be looked upon as the Victim of a designing Man," since her previous indiscreet behavior "exculpates you entirely." Caroline was "no Novice" and need have no tears shed for her pain.[49]

In a tone of plain objective inquiry, Lady Caroline wrote Byron demanding that he tell her whether he could really live without her, despite everything he had said. He began writing a response, then threw it in the fire. He justified his silence in the face of her direct question by saying his answer "would only lead to endless recapitulation, recrimination, *bother*ation (take a Kilkenny phrase) accusation, & all other -ations but *sal*vation."[50] He may have been right that he could never finally hope to escape through direct response, but he found himself in a "diabolical dilemma," for he could suffer himself to appear neither jealous nor indifferent.[51] When Lady Melbourne urged him to write coldly, he balked, saying

> *what* you wished me to write would be a little too indifferent; and *that* now would be an insult, & I am much more unwilling to hurt her feelings now than ever, (not from the mere apprehension of a disclosure in her wrath) but I have always felt that one who has given up much, has a claim upon *me* (at least—whatever she deserve from others) for every respect that she may not feel her own degradation, & this is the reason that I have not written at all lately, lest some expression might be misconstrued by her.[52]

This is very different from the tone of bravado in his letters claiming no concern for Caroline's fate.

In the face of inscrutable silence, Caroline wrote less often, but when she did she tried to make Byron jealous by implying that she and William were reconciling and boasting she could cause anyone to fall in love with her, if she wished. Byron scoffed at this, saying that it wasn't so much making a man love you, but rather keeping him in love that counted. "*You* perhaps *can* show me such a woman," wrote Byron to Lady Melbourne. He also wrote to Lady Bessborough to make it plain that he hoped the family would not be returning soon. He wanted time to arrange a possible engagement with Annabella Milbanke. "Does Annabella *waltz?*" he asked in a letter of 28 September, "—it is an odd question—but a very essential point with me."[53]

Harriet's attention was not all on her daughter during this time, for the family were thrown into an election by the dissolution of Parliament on 29 September. Hart sponsored William Ponsonby (now age 25) for a seat at Youghal, and the family campaigned hard for Frederick Ponsonby, who was still fighting in the war in Spain but whose seat as the member for Waterford could still be preserved. Frederick had been wounded during a skirmish near Villemar at about the same time that news that the Russians were torching Moscow reached them in late October 1812. Lady Bessborough felt sorry for William Lamb, who was going to be left out. She wrote to Granville that it was a shame that "a man of such firm and conscientious rectitude of character, and of so good an understanding" should be lost to public life, though she admitted he was not "reckon'd a first-rate Speaker." And yet, when an election dinner was got up under a tent put over a gothic ruin, William did speak well. It was too bad that he was so dependent upon his father.[54]

William wrote to his mother in agony over his inability to take advantage of the political situation: "It is actually cutting my throat—It is depriving me of the great object of my life at the moment that I was near to its attainment and what is more, at a period when I cannot well turn myself to any other course or pursuit—But I have no money." He admitted to his mother that he had thought about approaching his father for assistance, but felt he could not, even though he faced "public ruin."[55] Harriet's good wishes were no doubt appreciated, but her energies were consumed with political maneuvering on behalf of her own sons.

It so happened that at this time Lord Clare, Byron's very good friend from Harrow, was in Ireland. Clare was one of Byron's great passions. "I never hear the word '*Clare*' without a beating of the heart," he would write in his journal in 1821.[56] But the friends were temporarily at odds, and Lady Caroline seized upon this opportunity of "intermeddling," as Byron told Lady Melbourne.[57] The attempt failed, nor did she make any impact through hints that she was much pursued. Byron ascribed it all to "ridiculous egotism," though it was obviously emotional flailing of the type that worked on William. Byron wrote to Lady Melbourne in a pique: "Can't she take example from me, do I embarrass myself about A[nna-bella]?—or the fifty B, C, D, E, F, G, H's &c. &c. that have preceded her in cruelty or kindness (the *latter* always the greatest plague)." "I am not her lover," he said, "& would rather not be her friend, though I never can nor will be her enemy."[58]

No fine footwork could obscure Byron's bad position, however. He contemplated leaving the country when Caroline returned. At the end of October he began an extended visit with Lady Oxford. In his letter to Lady Melbourne, he now openly played the victim: "I think *my loss* is the *most considerable*," though he was apparently ignoring her good advice to "flirt as much as you please, but do not get into a serious Scrape before you are safe from the *present* one."[59] He told Lady Melbourne coolly, "I mean (*entre nous* my dear Machiavel) to play off Ly. O against her."[60]

Byron's choice was not a happy one for Caroline. Encouraged by Lady Oxford, Byron now completely disbelieved Caroline's protestations of depression. He quoted her own letters back to her when she wrote him claiming to be suicidal.[61] Caroline's upbeat letters may have been the product of the emotional jags that had produced "flippant" letters in the past, or they may have been designed to make him jealous—it is difficult to say. If they were calculated, they make even sadder reading. Lady Melbourne once received two letters on the same day from her, "one full of Spirits, gayete, Dinner Parties, &c. &c. ye other *false* written to deceive me, talking of her unhappiness & affecting to be perfectly quiet & resign'd."[62] Though Lady Melbourne interpreted this as manipulation, it would seem unlikely that Lady Caroline really hoped to dupe her mother-in-law with appeals of this kind, which apparently included entreaties to intercede on her behalf with Byron.

One surviving letter to Lady Melbourne, written on 20 October 1812, is scrawled and smeared as if she had wept over it:

> here we are where all are gay one hour & sick with fever the other—as to me I can neither be ill or well I neither sleep nor eat nor am able to do any thing I am more out of spirits than it is possible to say—you bid me write to my mother I can write to no human Being—I receive no letters I wish to receive none—do not fancy I ever can return or remain in England do not deceive yourself or talk harshly & unkindly to me my mind my nerves my whole constitution is so irritated that Wm says he does not know what to do with me—& Jane the same—ask him if I am selfish or stubborn as you always say these are savage words & go to my very soul—I cannot forget their harsh sound—from you from him they come & dread driving me to utter dispair . . .

This letter is written in a scrawl that splashes ink across three pages and then shrinks smaller and smaller as it approaches the dam of the page's end:

do not write or speak to Lord Byron do not I implore you—I shall know if you do
& I do entreat you not but do not *you* also write harshly to one who is near mad
& soon very soon will be gone Wm promises me I shall see him once more it is
only once I wish only for one moment—had not my Brother prevented me before
I came all had been well—do not name me to Lord Byron for God sake do not—
do not write so cruelly to me.[63]

No doubt Caroline's childish allusions to suicide hardened Lady Melbourne
against the neediness that was in itself unappealing to her.

Adopting Lady Oxford's impatience with Caroline's puerile and histrionic
behavior, Byron also took a hardened attitude. He was amused when Lady Oxford
disclosed that Caroline had appealed to her to obtain Byron's forgiveness.[64] He
was less amused when Lady Melbourne expressed concern that Caroline's return
might bring a relapse of Byron's infatuation: "You never were more *groundlessly*
alarmed, for . . . I have gone through the experiment before, more than once, &
I never was separated three months without a perfect *cure,* even though ye.
acquaintance was renewed." He was feeling "sick & annoyed" and frankly
angered by the endless stream of letters from Ireland.[65]

Byron was doubtless smarting also from the rebuff of his marriage proposal
by Annabella Milbanke, whose belief that Lady Caroline still held Byron's heart
may have played a large role in her rejection. Annabella disliked everything about
Caroline, including her speech: "Lady Caroline baa-a-a-a's till she makes me
sick."[66] Annabella's was a sharp mind, and once she had fixed upon a subject for
analysis, she was thorough. Thus, she now took the time to compose a five
hundred word essay analyzing the defects of Lady Caroline's character. In this
essay, she charges that Caroline's imagination is in a "perpetual fever," and that
she is the epitome of self-indulgence, a "spoiled child" who had "almost forfeited
the *power* of self-command," and whose "coquetry is thoughtless & improvident
to excess." Contradictorily, however, Caroline also appears to her as a clever
manipulator who "*manages* every feeling as she sees it rise to the mind of those
whom she would persuade." She possesses a "peculiar grace in telling her story,
which engages our interest and tempts the judgement to take her part." This
master manipulator is, however, clumsy, and "tries to disarm the condemnation
of her friends by unreserved confession of her errors, and the generosity of the
hearer may at first be duped by that proceeding; but its frequent repetition
destroys all esteem for the *emotion.*" Though Annabella's criticisms were partly
motivated by her own attraction to Byron, she nonetheless put down a devastating
portrait of Caroline as a woman who knows "the misery to which she is devoting

her future years by her present disregard of Duty. Yet from want of resolution to reform, she still acts as if 'She thought it folly to be wise too soon'!"[67] Caroline did indeed attempt to preempt the retorts of her critics. Her attempts were also generally transparent. She seems to have confused an upswing in her mood with egotism, and this led her to ritualized (and therefore ineffective) apologies to her family and friends. It is a familiar pattern to those who have studied manic-depressive case histories. Virginia Woolf's response to questions about the strangeness of her own behavior sound like Caroline: "I owned to great egoism & absorption & vanity & all my vices."[68]

It is telling that Annabella's comments on the character of Lady Caroline have a companion essay, a shorter one on the character of the other Caroline, Mrs. George Lamb, who possesses a "strong feeling for the amiability of Truth," and who is "invariably good-tempered" and moderate in her passions and friendships. Without that "romantic force of feeling which suggests extraordinary acts of disinterestedness," Caro George would seem to lack the very qualities which made Annabella care for Caro William—but through a sort of evasion of her own insights, Annabella came to prefer this well-regulated and conscientious companion to the passionate Lady Caroline.[69] Her essays testify to the invidious comparisons made by virtually every acquaintance of the two Caros.

After the rejection of his proposal, Byron finally wrote with a direct answer to Caroline's question. His purpose was to hurt and offend, and he probably worked on the letter over a period of days, with the help of Lady Oxford, upon whose friendship Caroline had so naïvely counted.

> Lady Caroline—our affections are not in our own power—mine are engaged. I love another—were I inclined to reproach you I might for 20 thousand things, but I will not. They really are not the cause of my present conduct—my opinion of you is entirely alter'd, & if I had wanted anything to confirm me, your Levities your caprices & the mean subterfuges you have lately made use of while madly gay—of writing to me as if otherwise, would entirely have open'd my eyes. I am no longer yr. lover—I shall but never be less than your friend—it would be too dishonourable for me to name her to whom I am now entirely devoted & attached.[70]

Note that Byron makes a major point of the contrast between Lady Caroline's actual gaiety and purported melancholy. Accusing her of "unfeminine persecution," he admitted that he would still ever remember with gratitude the many instances I have received of the predilection you have shown in my favour. I shall ever continue your friend, if your ladyship will permit me so to style myself; and, as a first proof of my regard, I offer you this advice, correct your vanity, which is ridiculous; exert your absurd caprices upon others; and leave me in peace.[71]

Among many painful notes here, not the least is the echo of a phrase from one of Caroline's own letters to him, saying that she would seek to "correct my faults."

According to the account Caroline later gave Lady Morgan, Byron's letter arrived with a coronet on the seal under which she recognized the initials of Lady Oxford. "It was that cruel letter I have published in *Glenarvon*," Caroline wrote, "it destroyed me: I lost my brain. I was bled, leeched; kept for a week in the filthy Dolphin Inn, at Rock. On my return I was in great prostration of mind and spirit."[72] Byron probably never fully understood the power of the blow he had delivered. His letter is crucial to understanding Lady Caroline's deteriorating mental and emotional condition. It struck just before her actual departure for England at the beginning of November.[73]

Anyone would doubt Caroline's self-report of having "lost her brain," but it must be recorded that on 31 October her mother reported seeing Caroline in convulsions of agony, "rolling on the floor, throwing herself about and always with her eyes protruding out of her head." The paroxysms would abate, but then Caroline would become "wild with spirits dancing singing." When William declared his intention to cross in advance of the main party, Caroline told him that if he left without her he would never see her again.[74] Biographer Henry Blyth tells the story that Lady Caroline seized a straight razor and tried to cut herself with it but was prevented by her mother, who put her hand on the blade, so that Caroline would have had to slice open her mother's palm in order to hurt herself.[75]

On 3 November she to wrote Byron "an *Irish* epistle, foolish, headstrong," saying more than once that she intended to "revenge herself upon *herself.*"[76] Byron was unimpressed. Noting that Caroline had "hurt & disgusted me," he rejected her plea to see him: "I WILL NOT meet her," he told Lady Melbourne on 9 November. Caroline's "epistles shew that the *date* of my own letter had sufficiently expounded what was not stated."[77] By this he meant that the seal with Lady Oxford's initials had reached its mark.

Caroline reproached Lady Oxford pathetically, in a "long *German* [that is, longwinded] tirade," asking what Byron described as "unanswerable questions." Lady Melbourne continued to pass along intelligence that Caroline was only engaging in histrionic displays to gain attention. Comparing the two letters—one from Lady Melbourne, the other from Lady Caroline to Lady Oxford—Byron now pronounced Caroline "the most contradictory, absurd, selfish, & contemptibly wicked of human productions." He washed his hands of her, for "as she herself says she has resolved since she is 'not loved to be *detested.*'"[78] Byron was angry that Lady Caroline threatened to disrupt the screen of lies that allowed his continued presence under the same roof with Lord and Lady Oxford.

The Bessboroughs departed from Ireland by packet boat on 10 November. By the 12th, the Bessboroughs and Devonshires were together again, and Harryo was appalled at her cousin Caroline's mental and physical prostration:

> The Bessboroughs have been unpacked about a couple of hours. My aunt looks stout and well, but poor Caroline most terribly the contrary. She is worn to the bone, as pale as death and her eyes starting out of her head. She seems indeed in a sad way, alternately in tearing spirits and in tears. I hate her character, her feelings, and herself when I am away from her, but she interests me when I am with her, and to see her poor careworn face is dismal, in spite of reason and speculation upon her extraordinary conduct. She appears to me in a state very [little] short of insanity, and my aunt describe it as at times having been decidedly so. . . . Caro has been excessively entertaining at supper. Her spirits, whilst they last, seem as ungovernable as her grief. My aunt is very gay and amiable. Poor Lord Bessborough *me pe`se sur le coeur et l'esprit.* William Lamb laughs and eats like a trooper.[79]

This description reinforces the possibility that Lady Caroline was suffering cycles of manic-depression, though her symptoms might also have been due to emotional and physical stress compounded by drug use—laudanum and alcohol were already having their effect on her. One sign of the magnitude of her distress is that she apparently failed to keep a dinner date with her beloved grandmother.[80]

She was bedridden for some days after the family's return to England. Byron reported on 16 November that Caroline had written a "rational & calm though rather plaintive" letter to him, begging that he meet her just one more time.[81] Her divided mental state had begun to be mirrored by imaginative reveries—an escape into a fantasy-world in which she had already conceived herself the heroine of a story set in Ireland. Now, she found that writing Irish Gothic narratives became her "sole comfort."[82] As bad weather had made the roads temporarily impassable, Byron decided to stay put for a few days longer at Lady Oxford's. Caroline's condition improved, and she and William returned to Brocket

Hall where she took up a strenuous regimen of horseback riding. She would later tell the Italian novelist Ugo Foscolo that "there is nothing to compare with riding, dancing, or some other exercise," and that horseback riding "gave me new life."[83]

Byron, in contrast, had been putting on weight while he stayed with Lady Oxford at Eywood, Presteign, in Herefordshire, and gloating a bit in his messages to Hobhouse about his escape from Caroline. Hobhouse congratulated Byron "most sincerely on your release from one who was certainly not the Lamb of God which taketh away the sins of the world."[84] Feeling "much *fatter*" and unable to travel because of flooding in the vicinity of Eywood, Byron fretted, "If C makes her debut here we shall have a pretty scene!" Byron depended heavily on Lady Melbourne to avoid such a confrontation: "My hope now rests with you & your influence over her, which I know to be great over *all* who *know* you."[85] Byron wrote hopefully to Lady Melbourne on 18 November 1812 that a temporary lull in correspondence meant perhaps that "the task is over."[86] On the 26th he wrote her again, rather unconvincingly: "I do not mean to deny my attachment—it *was*—and is not." Besides, he continued, "I could love anything on earth that appeared to wish it."[87]

The silence was temporary, however. Caroline wanted an interview, which Byron declined. She demanded her letters back. He demanded his in return, then relented, saying he would return hers with no conditions, together with whatever gifts from her he still possessed. He had given most of them away to other women: "the trinkets are travelling . . . in all parts of England & Wales."[88] He suspected Caroline of planning to sell his letters to a magazine, and he took seriously her warnings that some of her male admirers (her "daring champions," he named them) intended to call him out.[89]

Byron returned to London briefly to discover that he still had not received a farthing on the contract for the sale of Newstead Abbey. He was in debt and distracted. By 14 December he had returned to the comforts of Eywood and Lady Oxford, where he received letters describing Caroline's gallop along the turnpike near Brocket in bad weather and worse roads. "You have told me how foreign women revenge; I will show you how an Englishwoman can," she told him. Gratified, in spite of his annoyance, by such theatrical posturing, Byron wrote to Lady Melbourne that he hoped "perhaps in the year 1820 your little Medea may relapse into a milder tone."[90]

In due course, Byron learned of her revenge. Shortly before Christmas, Caroline organized a bonfire ritual in the village of Welwyn, not far from Brocket. The villagers had participated before in Christmas celebrations organized by their eccentric hostess. Now, she arranged for the maidens to dance around a fire on which Byron burned in effigy. As they danced, they tossed onto the flames fakes of Byronic memorabilia, including his letters and gifts to her.[91] For the occasion, Lady Caroline composed a poem to be recited by one of her pages:

> Is this Guy Fawkes you burn in effigy?
> Why bring the traitor here? What is Guy Fawkes to me?
> . . . .
> Burn, fire, burn, while wondering boys exclaim,
> And gold and trinkets glitter in the flame.
> Ah, look not thus on me, so grave, so sad,
> Shake not your heads, nor say the lady's mad.
> Judge not of others, for there is but one
> To whom the heart and feelings can be known.
> Upon my youthful faults few censures cast,
> Look to my future and forgive the past.
> London, farewell; vain world, vain life, adieu!
> Take the last tears I e'er shall shed for you.
> Young tho' I seem, I leave the world for ever,
> Never to enter it again; no, never, never![92]

In honor of the occasion, her pages and footmen supposedly sported buttons on their livery with the motto "Ne Crede Biron."[93] The line, "Shake not your heads, nor say the lady's mad," cast her in the role of Ophelia.

The bonfire has been understandably ridiculed, but there is more than a hint of genuine emotional illness in it. In her current state, Lady Caroline seems to have been verging on a dangerous conflation of her identity with Byron's, just as the poet John Clare would adopt Byron's identity during a short-lived escape from custody in 1841. Caroline's suggestible imagination had also been exposed to a number of recent stories about bereaved and deserted women who fell into insanity.[94] In 1812 Monk Lewis had also published a small collection of verse including the poem "Crazy Jane," which had been popular as a street ballad for several years:

> Gladly that young heart received him
> Which never has loved but one!
> He seemed true, and I believed him;
> He was false, and I undone.
> Since that hour has reason never

Held her empire in my brain:

Henry fled: with him for ever

Fled the wits of Crazy Jane![95]

Byron's *Childe Harold* was an emotional trap. It painted a picture of a youth "sore sick at heart," and Caroline had responded by trying to comfort one who professed that "none did love him." But she soon discovered the truth that "maidens, like moths, are ever caught by glare," and that for Byron "[l]ove has no gift so grateful as his wings."[96]

The female figures of *Childe Harold* are reduced to the erotic fantasies of the speaker; they inspire him with their beauty, but never speak or intrude on the hero's self-dramatization. "To Inez," a poem within the poem of *Childe Harold,* describes how the speaker is "curst" with memory: "And all my solace is to know, / What e'er betides, I've known the worst." And then the speaker admonishes Inez:

What is the worst? Nay do not ask—

In pity from the search forebear:

Smile on—nor venture to unmask

Man's heart, and view the Hell that's there.[97]

The alluring women of exotic lands are lovely to Harold, so long as they keep smiling. They generally live in harems: "Here woman's voice is never heard: apart, / And scarce permitted, guarded, veil'd to move, / she yields to one her person and her heart, / Tam'd to her cage, nor feels a wish to rove."[98] Caroline now revolted against the poet who had inspired her passion, but whose women were given explicit directions for their behavior: "I love the fair face of the maid in her youth, / Her caresses shall lull me, her music shall sooth."[99] In escaping one trap, however, she tumbled into another. She became "Crazy Jane."

When Byron heard about the bonfire, he pronounced her a victim of "the foul fiend *Flibertigibbet,*" but he was flattered. He told his friends about it, and Hobhouse responded: "Your tale of the Brocket bonfire is almost incredible—well may you say with Horace, '*Me Phryne macerat*' adding at the same time '*nec uno contenta*'."[100] Hobhouse's Latin meant: "Not content with one man, Phryne [a whore or procuress] torments me."

Lady Melbourne felt uneasy as she tried to match Byron with Annabella Milbanke. Byron had put himself completely in her hands for this purpose: "You know I have obeyed you in everything, in my suit to ye. *Princess of Parallelograms*

[Annabella Milbanke], my breach with little *Mania* [Caroline], and my subsequent acknowledgement of the *sovereignty of Armida* [Lady Oxford]—you have been my director & are still for I do not know anything you could not make me do or undo."[101] Lady Melbourne had lined up her niece as best she could. Annabella had provided, upon request, a list of qualifications for a husband. Lady Melbourne ratified Annabella's preference not to marry "into a family where there was a strong tendency to insanity," but told Annabella frankly that she had set her sights too high: "[I]t is almost impossible while you remain on ye Stilts on which you are mounted, yt you should ever find a person worthy to be yr Husband." Annabella heeded her aunt, "you will perhaps take off my *stilts,* and allow that I am only *on tiptoe.*"[102] Caroline's antics threatened these negotiations. Two days before Christmas, Byron comforted himself by asking, "What can she do worse than she has done?"[103]

He got his answer within a fortnight.

Medea and Her Dragons

1813–1814

"If she will raise a storm, be it so, she will be the first to perish in it."

—Lord Byron[1]

$\mathcal{B}$ eginning with *Childe Harold,* Caroline had studied and imitated Byron's poetry, and she had since come to know also his handwriting and prose style. She put these to use in early January of 1813. Since November, she had been pressuring Byron to provide her a picture. Despite the fact that Byron had loaned her three portraits of himself, including one by Holmes, she preferred a small one George Sanders had done in 1812. She had asked Lord Clare to get Byron to give the Sanders portrait to *him,* and then pass it to her. Clare refused to cooperate. She tried approaching the artist himself for a copy, but Sanders said no.[2] At the time, Byron's publisher John Murray had the portrait in his offices because he wanted to use it as a frontispiece for a new edition of *Childe Harold,* but Byron had objected strenuously to having his face displayed on the opening page and insisted that "*all* the proofs be burnt, & the plate broken."[3] Byron had trusted him to keep the portrait safely until he called for it.[4]

Shortly after New Year's Day 1813—perhaps a fortnight after the bonfire—Caroline took a carriage to Murray's address at 50 Albemarle Street and told him she had been sent to fetch the portrait. She handed him a letter ostensibly from Byron to herself saying she could "take which Picture you think most like but do not forget to return it the soonest you can—for reasons I explained." The conclusion to the letter was—in Byron's characteristic fashion—scribbled over. The effect of the cross outs, together with denial of authorship of an anonymously published "satire" (probably "The Waltz") and a skillful rendition of Byron's scrawled signature convinced Murray.

Caroline made no secret of the theft. She had written to Byron in advance, and it appears that the forgery upset him much more than the prospective theft:

> Why she should herself say that she *forged my name* &c. to obtain it—I cannot tell—but by her letter of yesterday (which I shall keep for the present) she expressly avows this in her wild way and *Delphine* language—It is singular that she not only calumniates others but even *herself,* for no earthly purpose. . . . As Dogberry says 'this is flat Burglary'—will you recover my *effigy* if you can—it is very unfair after the restoration of her own—to be *ravished* this way.[5]

Lady Caroline had graduated from bonfires to burglary. It is understandable, therefore, that Byron would react badly when she entered his rooms a few weeks after the forgery and left a scribbled note in his copy of *Vathek*—"Remember me!"—echoing lines from *Hamlet*. He immediately scribbled out a reply express-ing anger and remorse. It was addressed "To Bd" ("To Biondetta"):

> "Remember thee," nay—doubt it not—
> Thy Husband too may "*think*" on thee!
> By neither canst thou be forgot,
> Thou false to him—thou fiend to me!

> "Remember thee"? Yes—yes—till Fate
> In Lethe quench the guilty dream.
> Yet then—e'en then—Remorse and *Hate*
> Shall vainly quaff the vanquished stream.[6]

As Byron scholar Andrew Stauffer has shown, this poem was revised before it got into the hands of Thomas Medwin, who published it after Lord Byron's death.[7] Byron never sent the original poem or any expression of frustration directly to Caroline, nor apparently did he share the incident with anyone else. He did not want to feed her lines of any sort.

Byron's sense of being "ravished" caricatures his real fear of women writers. The theft of the portrait stung, but the letter struck the mark, for Byron continued in a self-described "prodigious pucker."[8] He wrote to Lady Melbourne on 13 January in high dudgeon:

> I have seen the forged billet—the hand very like—now what is to prevent her from the same imitation for any less worthy purpose she may choose to adopt?—M[urray] does not know her name nor have I *yet* informed him of it—if known she will have the credit of being the authoress of all the letters *anonymous* & *synonimous*, written for the next ten years & the last five.——For aught I know she may have forged 50 such to *herself*—& I do not feel very much refreshed by the supposition.—I shall not write to *her* again—but I request once more as respectfully as I can that she will restore the picture—if not—as nothing but a scene will satisfy her—she shall have one performed which will be more edifying than entertaining.[9]

The forged letter was a clever performance in which Lady Caroline had emulated his orthography, punctuation, and blot-outs. She had even mastered the art of mimicking Byron's voice. On one occasion she entertained her friend Lady Hamilton & her sister: "I read to them in your voice," she told him, "& they nearly cried & kissed me till I was suffocated all for love of you."[10] Byron fulminated to John Cam Hobhouse: "Car L has been *forging letters* in my name & hath thereby pilfered the best picture of *me* the Newstead Miniature!!!—Murray was the imposed upon.—The Devil, & Medea, & her Dragons to boot, are possessed of that little maniac."[11] Byron's threats were empty. He caused no scene, and she held on to the picture.

Caroline's success at imitating Byron ("the hand very like") made her more confident. Upon first reading "The Waltz," she commented that the poem could not be Byron's because it was "too coarse."[12] When she discovered he *was* the author, she wrote a rejoinder which she copied into the sketch-book she had kept for years. Above the title she sketched two dancing cherubim. The concluding lines read:

> Man has so many true hearts grieved
> That woman thinks she does no wrong
> When she is false and he deceived.[13]

For his part, Byron simply wanted to escape all this waltzing about. On 22 January, his twenty-fifth birthday, he looked forward to a depressing prospect of "an endless correspondence" with Caroline. He decided to employ silence once again, hoping for remission from "Medea & her Dragons."[14]

In January 1813, Byron was introduced by Lady Holland to the Prince Regent's own nemesis, the Princess Caroline. Byron disliked the grossly fat Regent who lived in mind-boggling luxury at the expense of his subjects. Those who hated the Regent often supported his politically liberal and somewhat bohemian wife. The Princess of Wales was only too pleased to annoy her husband by supporting tradesmen and merchants, and they reciprocated. On 14 January, the Princess had written a letter complaining to her husband that additional restrictions had made it difficult for her to see her daughter, the Princess Charlotte, now age sixteen, whom the libertine Prince hypocritically sought to protect from her mother's bad influence. The letter was returned unopened, then published in the *Morning Chronicle* on 10 February. The Prince referred the matter to his Privy Council, which eventually decided not to intervene. A huge demonstration of support for the Princess took place, and Lady Caroline attended, riding her horse amid the crowd of well-wishers. Byron had corresponded with the Princess during this period, but he did not make his support public or even mention it to Lady Melbourne, who had literally gotten into bed with the Prince.

In late January Lady Spencer described her granddaughter as looking "sadly," but on 12 February "certainly better & happier."[15] The improvement in Lady Caroline's appearance was due to activities Lady Spencer would not have approved. On 6 February 1813, Byron was sitting in John Murray's office when "Miss W" (probably Thomasina Webster) entered and announced in a loud voice that Lady Caroline Lamb desired Mr. Murray to call upon her the next day. Byron held his tongue, for he had never confessed to Murray that the "pilferer" of the picture was Caroline, and Murray had other visitors. Lady Caroline had decided to "expose herself,"[16] in Byron's phrase, as not only the thief but a writer working on her first novel.

Chastised by Byron for letting Caroline have the portrait, Murray in turn tried to scare Caroline by telling her that she had committed a felony. She retorted, "So you give it as yr opinion that I might be convicted—for the Picture."[17] Murray's warning stimulated Caroline to begin a short novel with forgery as the fulcrum of its plot. It follows the career of George Morrison, a charming young man whose good looks and sweet voice allow him every latitude in his behavior. Morrison has the misfortune to meet with a gorgeous gypsy girl named Bessy Grey, a self-conscious manipulator:

1. Vignette of Childe Harold at sea, a scene from *Childe Harold's Pilgrimage*, by Lady Caroline Lamb (1812). By kind permission of Mr. Gerald Burdon.

2. Vignette of funeral scene from *Childe Harold's Pilgrimage,* by Lady Caroline Lamb (1812). By kind permission of Mr. Gerald Burdon.

3. Lady Caroline Lamb, dressed in page costume holding fruit tray and with spaniel, painted in 1813 by Thomas Phillips. Courtesy of The Devonshire Collection, Chatsworth. Reproduced by permission of the Chatsworth Settlement Trustees.

4. Brocket Hall. Contemporary photograph. By kind permission of Brocket Hall International. The house today is privately offered for corporate and private events.

5. Lord Byron in Albanian Dress, painted by Thomas Phillips. National Portrait Gallery, London.

6. William Spencer Cavendish, Marquis of Hartington, later 6th Duke of Devonshire, painted in 1811 (the year he inherited the Devonshire title) by Sir Thomas Lawrence. Courtesy of The Devonshire Collection, Chatsworth. Reproduced by permission of the Chatsworth Settlement Trustees.

7. Georgiana Poyntz, Countess Spencer, Lady Caroline Lamb's Grandmother, painted most probably in the period 1798-1810 by Henry Howard. Courtesy of The Devonshire Collection, Chatsworth. Reproduced by permission of the Chatsworth Settlement Trustees.

8. Isaac Nathan. Artist unknown. Portrait circa 1810-1820. Courtesy of Charles Venour Nathan.

9. William Lamb, by Sir Thomas Lawrence. 1805. National Portrait Gallery, London.

10. Lady Caroline Tired and Dispirited. From a painting by Eliza H. Trotter. Exhibited 1811. National Portrait Gallery, London.

To a lanky Cur I lov'd at that time —

12. Lady Caroline Lamb on horesback – E. Parocell (?) Private
Collection. Photograph: Photographic Survey, Courtauld
Institute of Art.

13. Lady Melbourne by John Hoppner. National Portrait Gallery, London.

14. Sketch by Lady Caroline showing winged cherub attacked by snakes and demons, with the caption "un soupçon cruel le dechire." By permission of Hertfordshire Archives and Local Studies.

un soupçon cruel le dechire

15. Lord Granville Leveson Gowe[r]
    after Sir Thomas Lawrence. By
    kind permission of the Courtau[ld]
    Institute of Art.

16. Sketch by Lady Caroline in he[r]
    Commonplace book at John M[ur]
    ray Archive showing her husba[nd]
    William, herself, and their son
    Augustus.

[H]er pride was such and her confidence in her charms so great, that she was not astonished at an honour paid her, and her morals early corrupted taught her to trust but little to the promises of Man; yet Bessy would love, if that word must apply to the fierce passion that mastered her bosom, when ever she beheld an object that excited such feelings in her, and when she did love jealousy and revenge and all the violent and unfeminine passions that can spring up in a perverted heart accompanied the feeling she thus cherished and indulged.

Morrison falls under Bessy's spell and agrees to steal for her, in order to gain her favors: "I am not a Maiden to be coy & think much of that which you desire[—] look at these eyes and lips is there any thing there that speaks a virgins fears— ere I had obtained my fourteenth year trust me I had lost the name. . . . I know mans nature well and would get from thee all I can, ere I make myself thy slave."[18] It isn't long before Bessy "sicken[s], & her shape betray[s] the cause." Morrison in turn sickens of the bargain he has made, and after becoming the prize at a gypsy "cat-fight," he alienates Bessy permanently. He tries to reform himself; there is, of course, another woman named Fanny Draper who urges him to return to God and the church, but Bessy intervenes: "I have turned King's Evidence," she declares, accusing him of burglary. He is convicted and sentenced to death, because his "guilt was of a nature that could not be pardoned: he had forged; all else had been perhaps overlooked but this was a crime the law could not overlook by reason of the facility for committing it."

Why should forgery be considered a capital offense? Is it that a person with such a facility *knows* better? Is it that the facility can never be eradicated? Is it, more simply, the idea that stealing another's identity is heinous? If Byron had read this little narrative, he would have mocked it, especially the ending: "The Babe that was born in guilt and shame was the cause of the death of its unnatural mother." Bessy awakens to the knell of her lover's execution. She has married an old man with plenty of money. But she dies giving birth. The story would have confirmed Byron's sinking feeling that Caroline's obsession was permanent.

Yet Byron could not keep silent, and he continued communications with Caroline, who wrote (he said) in a "melancholy and gentle*man*like" manner, certainly not "like a *gentle-woman*."[19] He wanted the Sanders picture back, yet was willing to forego it if Caroline would stay away. Avoiding her would be "no bad thing for the original whatever may become of the copy."[20] Eventually, he succumbed to pressure for a meeting, but stipulated it must be attended by a third party: Lady Oxford. The idea of taking his current lover to a meeting with Caroline astonished even the hard-boiled Lady Melbourne. She disliked the idea of exposing outsiders to Lamb dirty laundry, and she also felt that Lady Oxford endangered her position as Byron's principal confidante. She preferred to attend herself. Indeed, Lady Melbourne now sought every opportunity to see Byron in person, carefully informing him when her son and daughter-in-law were absent and asking him to come to her.[21] In turn, Lady Caroline treated her father- and mother-in-law with great circumspection. On 22 February 1813 she employed the ruse of having Augustus, who was only five, "write" to inform Lord Melbourne that she wished certain items to be sent to her.[22]

Negotiations for the meeting dragged on, probably fueled on Byron's side by continuing frustrations of his attempt to get the Sanders miniature returned, for which he was once again relying on Lady Melbourne's diplomatic skills.[23] Then, suddenly, Byron got the portrait back. In exchange, he agreed to allow a copy to be made. This promise was fulfilled, and Sanders himself was hired to copy his own miniature.[24] Byron also agreed to send Lady Caroline a lock of his hair. This treaty had been negotiated by Lady Melbourne, who reproached Byron on 25 March 1813 for balking at supplying such a "trifle": "[R]eally by yr reluctance to have yr Hair touched, or to part with any of it,—I am tempted to think there is some particular charm attached to it—& yt some of yr powers will be lessen'd, I will not say lost . . . something like Sampson."[25] Under this teasing, Byron acceded. But instead of his own hair he sent a lock of Lady Oxford's. He gloated that if she ever discovered the cheat, it would have an effect upon her comparable to a lock from Medusa's head.[26] Byron now believed he owed Caroline a comeuppance: "I have a long arrear of mischief to be even with that amiable daughter of L[ad]y. B[essborough]'s—& in the long run I shall pay it off—by instalments.—I consider this as payment for the first bonfire—a debt too heavy to discharge all at once."[27] Despite the fact that he had secured his picture, Byron felt angry: "There is but one way in which a man can write to ladies afflicted with these phantasies—& to her above all others—I must say *yes—yes—yes*—(like a crier in a country town) to keep her quiet."[28] No sooner had he regained the Sanders portrait than he gave it to Lady Oxford. Caroline would have to wait for her copy.

Lady Bessborough and Lady Melbourne now became convinced that if a meeting could persuade Caroline that Byron was now beyond reach, it was worth the trouble, and so Byron wrote to Lady Caroline on 29 April from his rooms in Bennet Street: "If you still persist in your intention of meeting me in opposition to the wishes of your own friends & of mine—it must even be so—I regret it &

acquiesce with reluctance . . . [I]t is in great measure owing to this persecution—to the accursed things you have said—to the extravagances you have committed—that I again adopt the resolution of quitting this country."[29] Byron noted that he intended to leave in June 1813, and that he'd like to get the meeting over with. He said he had "once wished for your own sake Ly. M[elbourne] to be present—but if you are to fulfil any of your threats in word or deed—we had better be alone."[30] He persuaded Lady Oxford to put her blessing on the interview. The meeting took place at 9:00 A.M. on 10 May.[31] He had not seen her for almost a year.

Informed that Caroline was ill, Byron believed it a ruse to gain sympathy, so he was shocked at her appearance. Always thin, she had become skeletal and subdued. Lady Melbourne—perhaps accompanied by Harriet—left them alone for a little while, hoping for a positive effect. But they were disappointed, for the meeting reignited Caroline's fanatical love, with disastrous results for her own health and that of her mother, who woke to recurrent nightmares of the lovers running away together.[32] Byron had once again failed to be firm. His natural sympathy had taken over, and he had told the pitiful woman that he still cared for her. Byron recognized his mistake and braced himself. "I think," he wrote on 25 May, "*terror* must be ye. order of ye. day." Caroline, who was "the oddest antithesis of *pipe*- and common-clay that ever was compounded since the first husband betook himself to stealing apples," might at any moment explode. She had reached a state of "*awful* calmness" Byron said.[33] To make matters worse, a newspaper printed a story that she had once been carried naked into the dining room at Melbourne House concealed under a huge silver platter. The false story fit too perfectly.

It wasn't the threat of such antics that made Byron fearful, however. It was Caroline's desire to publish something, starting with her quarto-sized vignettes of scenes from *Childe Harold*. She had reached an agreement with a printer named Prine who gave her £100 in advance for the work and had already begun the job. But Murray dissuaded her by agreeing in principle that she could make a specially printed one-of-a-kind edition of *Childe Harold* for Byron and include the pictures. She planned to make her own copy of Sanders' miniature of Byron as a frontispiece to go with her drawings. "[Y]ou do not guess how pretty they will be till you see them finished," she told Murray.[34] Caroline was also writing imitations of Byron's poetry that she intended to publish. She reworked one of his early short lyrics, "Maid of Athens." In that poem a departing lover swears his love "By that lip I long to taste, / By that zone-encircl'd waist, / By all the token-flowers that tell . . . ," etc. Caroline's retort substitutes "Belfont" for "Byron" and casts herself familiarly as "Biondetta":

By those eyes whose sweet expression
Many a deep design conceal
By those lips which preach discression
While they other trusts reveal—
By Biondetta's wrongs & woes
a ne crede—Belfont's Vows.[35]

Unaware of these developments, Byron was preoccupied with Lady Oxford, whom he planned to follow when she departed England with her husband. Caroline later said that Byron's affection was like "the wheels of a watch, the chain of [which] might be said to unwind from the absent in proportion as they twined themselves around the favourite of the moment, and being extreme in all things, he could not sufficiently devote himself to the one without taking from the other all that he had given."[36] His affections were not with her now, yet they might return.

Four days after Byron's final speech to the House of Lords, on 5 June 1813, *The Giaour* (pronounced "jower" and meaning "infidel") was published with a handsome dedication to Samuel Rogers. The theme of the poem was one Byron apparently assumed Caroline would recognize as deriving from his affair with her. Byron had predicted that she would understand it as part of his campaign to torment her, just as she tormented him: "If C gets hold of 'The Giaour' she will bring it in wilful murder against the author."[37] He thought that when she read that Hassan murders his wife, Leila, for her infidelity, Caroline would understand that Byron had imaginatively killed his ex-lover off. Instead, Caroline found the poem moving, especially the lines on the tomb: "Dark as to thee my deeds may seem: / My memory now is but the tomb / Of joys long dead . . ."[38] Lady Caroline strongly identified with Byron and felt that she still served as an inspiration for him when he wrote such lines as these:

I die—but first I have possess'd
And come what may, I *have been* bless'd.
Shall I the doom I sought upbraid?
No—reft of all, yet undismay'd
But for the thought of Leila slain,
Give me the pleasure with the pain,
So would I live and love again.
I grieve, but not, my holy guide!
For him who dies, but her who died. . .
She was a form of life and light,

That, seen, became a part of sight;

And rose, where e'er I turned mine eye,

The Morning—star of Memory![39]

Feeling that Byron's heroic monologue expressed her own unrepentance, she believed he was himself unrepentant. His image of the drowned Leila fit the Ophelia role in which she had cast herself. One of Caroline's letters to John Murray, undated, is signed, "[t]here's sweet Biron for you—Ophelia."[40]

Caroline now always wrote to Byron via John Murray, with whom she had formed a strong friendship. The likeable businessman was to be her confidante, bookseller, publisher, and friend until she died. She confided in him, and it appears he never betrayed that confidence—except, of course, that he ignored her incessant requests to burn her letters. Undoubtedly, Byron had counted on Murray's diplomatic skills: "[D]id not the Giaour tell me always to ask you,"[41] she said in one of her many letters to Murray, who somehow managed to find just the right note of response to Caroline's moods—supplying her with journals and books and patiently waiting for payment of her account. In return, Lady Caroline would be at times very generous toward him, inviting him and his family to visit Brocket, to shoot and fish and stay as her guests. At this time Thomas Phillips was completing his portrait of her in the role of a page carrying a tray of fruit. She half-thought she would give it to Murray, but instead offered him another picture to hang on his Chimney in 50 Albemarle Street: "[A] Lamb & a Page, can any thing be more appropriate to remind you of me?" She sent along the composition—almost certainly her own—and separately delivered a pair of candlesticks.[42]

On a late June evening not long before the Oxfords' scheduled departure, Byron attended a ball at Lady Jersey's, where he was startled to see Lady Caroline. He avoided her carefully, and believed that she had not seen him. But she had. When William Lamb found his wife crying, he was angry at Byron and wanted to know whether Byron had slighted her.[43] The absurdity of the situation was obvious to everyone except the husband and wife. In his bemused but annoyed comments, Byron noted that he was damned if he did and damned if he didn't talk to her. He wished that the "*correct & animated* Waltzer," his ex-lover, "would not call in the aid of so many compassionate Countesses." These women, he feared, in half-hating him and half-despising Lady Oxford, might "tear the last rag of my tattered reputation into shreds." And then, in one of those revealing twists, half-serious, he asked Lady Melbourne to elope with him and confound the world.[44]

Byron, who had talked of leaving the country with the Oxfords up until the last minute, decided to stay after all. Perhaps voluntarily, but more likely at his own request, Lady Oxford gave Byron back the Sanders portrait of him that had caused so much trouble. He now identified with Caroline's loneliness and jealousy when his lover departed for Sardinia in late June 1813. He asked Lady Melbourne not to mention Lady Oxford's name, since, "to tell you the truth—I feel more *Carolinish* about her than I expected."[45]

Byron's half-sister, Augusta Leigh, had come to London, and they began to spend time together. He continued to talk of going abroad, but instead attended parties like the waltzing party thrown by Lady Katherine Heathcote on 5 July 1813. It is hard to understand why Byron would have attended, given his feelings about dancing in general and waltzing in particular, but go he did, and so did Caroline, perhaps (as Lady Melbourne later guessed) because she knew Byron would be there and wanted "to pique [him] by her Waltzing."[46]

According to Caroline's own account, given years later to Thomas Medwin, Lady Heathcote asked her to begin the waltzing, so Caroline said to Byron, "I conclude I may waltz *now*," alluding to his earlier injunction against it. He replied sardonically that she was brilliant at partnering "every body in turn." Feeling faint, she sought refuge in a room where supper was being prepared. Entering the room with Lady Rancliffe—his neighbor in Nottinghamshire—Byron noticed that Caroline had picked up a knife and said, "Do, my dear, but if you mean to act a Roman's part, mind which way you strike with your knife—be it at your own heart, not mine—you have already struck there." Caroline then called out Byron's name, running away with the knife, which she claimed people tried to snatch from her. "I was terrified, my hand got cut, and the blood came over my gown."[47]

According to Byron's account, written the day after, Caroline had asked whether she should dance, and he replied that she *should,* for "it would be imputed to *me*—if she did not." As supper was about to be served, he and Lady Rancliffe had encountered Caroline, who "took hold of my hand as I passed & pressed it against some sharp instrument—& said—'I mean to use this'—I answered—'against me I presume'—and passed on."[48] Byron remained at the party until 5:00 A.M. and never knew a thing about it until he returned home and someone told him Caroline had tried to kill herself—though Lady Ossulston cut him around 4:00 A.M. with an angry look and what he described as "the usual feminine deduction that I '*must* have behaved very ill.'" Thomas Moore told Byron that the scene at Lady Heathcote's was "merely a safe exhibition of temper."[49] One pictures the women at this party hovering over the aggrieved Caroline and whipping up the drama. Byron would be given a piece of their minds. Lady Westmoreland scolded him, and he protested he remained "in stupid innocence and ignorance of my offence"—just as if he were a teenager who had accidentally insulted his friend's date.[50]

Lady Melbourne's version is different. She told Byron that Frederick Lamb had tried to subdue Caroline, and that Caroline had broken a glass, with which she scratched herself, then picked up a pair of scissors and attempted to wound herself—though not in a very determined manner.[51] Lady Melbourne made this tantrum seem both as hysterical and as calculated as possible. The story got into *The Satirist,* which published an account with a motto: "With horn-handled knife, / To kill a tender lamb as dead as mutton," and said that Lady Caroline had tried to hurt herself with a "dessert-knife" which she had "stuck in her wizzard." The article described how the "desperate Lady was carried out of the room, and the affair endeavoured to be hushed up."[52] The Duchess of Beaufort reported a rumor that Lady Caroline had "not only wounded herself in several places," but had gone into hysterics and been "carried out by several people actually in a straight waist coat."[53] Lady Melbourne's account underscored her assertion that Caroline was "a Barrel of Gunpowder."[54]

Lady Melbourne knew that Caroline suspected Byron's affections had been bestowed upon Lady Melbourne herself, for Byron said she was "eternally asking if I am not in *love* with you."[55] Caroline was made more miserable by the knowledge that she had once again put herself in the wrong with William, who she acknowledged had "ruined himself by excess of kindness for me." She appealed to John Murray to intercede on her behalf with the *Morning Herald:* "[W]hatever my faults or follies is it necessary I should bear real calumnies—and because part of a story is true am I to let my husband be dishonoured through my own imprudence?" She wrote wretchedly to Lady Holland, begging her not to "speak of this horrid scene any more than you can help," and melodramatically declaring herself "unfit" to appear in society again.[56] Disgusted, Lady Holland obeyed her correspondent's injunction not to reply, and when she passed through Welwyn that fall she avoided paying a visit to Brocket.

The fiasco at Lady Heathcote's reminded Byron why he wanted to depart England, and he pressed his half-sister Augusta to leave her husband and go with him. But Caroline approached Augusta and almost secured an invitation to go along! Hearing this news from Lady Melbourne, Byron responded with feigned indifference: "Ly. C[aroline] may do as she pleases—if Augusta likes to take her she may—but in that case she will travel by *herself.*"[57] The ill-conceived travel plans never matured.

That fall, Lady Caroline finally met Madame de Staël, whose son Albert had just been killed in a gambling duel in a town on the Baltic Sea. She visited the Bessboroughs at Roehampton in September 1813, but was apparently not then invited to Brocket Hall, for Lady Melbourne disliked her.[58] Nor did Lady Caroline herself get along perfectly with the prickly author, who was uninterested in the outdoor sports Caroline adored: "To air and water, not to mention soap, I think she has an antipathy," quipped Caroline to Murray.[59] When Madame de Staël bluntly asked Caroline about her affair with Byron, an argument started. For once Lady Caroline seemed to have met her match: "We came to an open rupture about Lord Byron, and yet I abused him respecting his conduct to me even as I felt, but I said he was, & ever would be most dear to me, and I do not see why strangers are to ask one these sort of questions."[60]

Despite this friction, Lady Caroline admired this independent woman who had received the respect of the literary world. "[T]o say that I have quarreled with her would be as ridiculous as if a butterfly were to abuse the sun—because it could not stand the lustre of its beam," Caroline acknowledged. When she was received in Madame de Staël's dressing room, she would find her in a loose cloth thrown over a gray silk pelisse, her gray and black hair covered with a bran conditioner and wearing a hat with a pen-box stuck in it. "I like her a great deal the better for receiving me so," Caroline confessed, "she is after all a very good hearted & good natured Woman."[61] De Staël's *De l'Allemagne* was being reprinted in honor of her visit to England—the 1810 edition had been expunged by Napoleonic censors. Murray asked Caroline, who was familiar with the work in the original French, to correct the proof sheets of the translation. She noted that two famous passages (one on enthusiasm), "so splendidly Eloquent in the original," were not well translated, and she proposed to Murray that William might help by translating them afresh. Murray could then insert them as if they were the corrections of Madame de Staël herself.[62] Murray agreed; William's talents were employed and Caroline pleased: "I delight in Staals booke, it seems to me a vast fund of erudition come together God knows why, but full of point, wit & ability."[63] Thus, Murray, Caroline, and William had already developed something of an affinity and a business relation. Caroline subsequently told Murray, "If you want any Greek translations or notes apply to Wm that is his favourite line of study. I think very few of the present day are equal to him as Grecians."[64]

Lady Caroline sought to cultivate further her business relationship with Murray, and on 7 October 1813 she wrote claiming, "this day my novel is going to the press," and offering to send him the manuscript of another "work," namely

"250 letters from a young Venetian nobleman—addrest to a very absurd English Lady." She described these as "no common love letters believe me . . . tell me will you accept the work will you read—mark & digest it?"[65] She was now seriously thinking of publishing not only a novel but all Byron's letters, just as he feared. Murray must have felt very uncomfortable at the prospect of his prize author being exposed in such a way. Perhaps she only threatened publication to see how her enemies within and outside the Lamb family would react. Murray must have been aware that such publication would constitute an act of war. He had also found Caroline's gift of the pictures of a Page and a Lamb, accompanied by candlesticks, somehow offensive—possibly because of her nocturnal cross-dressing exploits. Caroline responded that she was "sorry the candlesticks enrage you," but that he must admit that "the Page was *excusable*" and "a Lamb offering [is] even the custom among the Jews."[66]

Almost immediately, she had a change of heart about the letters, and wrote Murray to ask him to destroy any letters she had sent him in which she discussed or alluded to her "faulty conduct" with Byron: "I do assure you that in my heart I have and will return to my best and only friend," meaning her husband.[67] It was probably at about this time that she sent Byron a heart's ease flower and told him that she treasured all his gifts, including the rose: "the first Rose you brought me is still in my possession, you will find it in the Trunk with all yr other Gifts all that I could preserve."[68]

November was cold, and news of brutal fighting between the French, Austrians, and Prussians arrived in London. The Allies—Britain, Russia, Prussia, Sweden, and Spain—converged on Paris. Wellington's army, coming from the south, was encountering a poorly provisioned force of older men and young boys. A rumor that Byron had committed suicide was soon dispelled, and Byron now decided to seize the initiative and demand that Caroline return a miniature by James Holmes which she had kept for more than a year. Reluctantly, she sent it back. A surprised Byron wrote to Lady Melbourne to say, "C has at last done a very good natured thing," and promptly gave the picture to Lady Frances Webster.[69]

Portraits had a way of popping up in unusual contexts, however. Visitors to Phillips's studio in November were treated to an unusual display. Phillips's portrait of Lady Caroline in her page's outfit with the tray of fruit was hung beside his picture of Byron in robes that at least one visitor thought were intended to make him look like a friar. Phillips had carefully avoided any implication that he condoned the notorious love affair of his two famous sitters, even blocking Caroline's view as she sat: "What a prude I think Phillips," Lady Caroline remarked. "[H]e does all he can in civility do to stand before the picture which my eyes seek."[70] Now that the paintings were done, Phillips was so proud of his work that he set them up together. The result was that some viewers thought the portraits formed a single picture. "I was asked," Lady Caroline wrote Murray, "whether I was painted at Phillips as a Page Holding a plate of Fruit to Lord Byron as friar! Will you tell Phillips to put my picture out of sight—*really* he who professes to be so prudish might have obeyed my orders. . . . [E]very one going in sees us two together."[71] Her annoyance with Phillips made it almost possible for Lady Caroline to forget how badly she had behaved. "Life has glided by," Caroline told Lady Spencer. "I walk eat sleep & read a little—and think a little—Wm is most kind to me." She let down her guard a bit by admitting that "if you live out of Society the friends who sought you in it soon cease to remember you."[72]

Caroline now lobbied Murray to get the Sanders picture back and hold it long enough for her to have a copy made in secret, since Byron was resistant to fulfilling his part of the bargain. Reluctantly, he agreed, but having been burned once he refused to hand it over.[73] Instead, he insisted she must send a copyist to Murray's offices. "[H]ave you got the picture," Caroline wrote Murray at Christmastime, "when you have remember me—I will send one who will do it quickly and secretly."[74] She was in better spirits not only because she was about to get a good copy of the portrait she craved, but also because Madame de Staël had returned. This time there were no arguments over Byron, though Harriet admitted that she would have preferred to spend the holidays "here quiet with Caro & William."[75] The weather in January 1814 turned bad, and snow-choked roads prevented travel. An ice fair was held on the Thames with oxen roasted whole.[76] The Prince Regent planned to visit the Melbournes at Brocket, but then kept putting it off. Lady Caroline understood not wanting "to travel this Weather," though she told Murray she never shut the windows in cold weather: "Keep the feet warm, the head cool and the heart free, and you may defy the world, the flesh, and the devil—and Madame de Staal."[77] Finally, the Prince Regent arrived and settled in.

Caroline now resolved to emulate Madame de Staël's discipline in revising her novel. She stayed at Brocket with Augustus for a couple of days on her own while the others struggled through the snow to visit another household. When they returned, she seemed to talk more aggressively at the dinner table. Lady Melbourne complained to Byron in a letter of 16 January that Lady Caroline "is chearful enough to be very tiresome with her theory's and her discussions which she is eternally beginning & always turn upon some supposed ill usage, which Women receive from Men, evidently alluding to you."[78] Caroline asked Lady Holland to read the manuscript, then turned shy:

I looked at the novel as you were so good as to say you would read it—it consisted of nine vols—scribbled by various Pages—I waded through it with difficulty & found by erasing all that was bad & all that was dull—and all that was unnecessary that I just reduced it to 3 Pages—one of which was borrowed from an old Author the other was beautiful but too Poetical for the present taste & the 3d is still at your service & may serve equally for the beginning middle or conclusion of any work whatever whether tragic or comic is not this at least being candid.

Though not ready for a critique of *Glenarvon,* Caroline was not shy about telling Lady Holland, "I am now writing a Comedy & you are one of the Dramatis Personae."[79]

Murray had sent Caroline illustrations that were to be published with a new edition of *The Giaour.* "As long as I live," she told him, "& longer if memory lasts I shall remember with grateful thanks your kindness in trusting me with the drawings . . . how beautiful Leila & the dancing girl are—I am sorry to pack them up." For safekeeping, she returned the pictures to London with the Prinny.[80] Murray sent word in February 1814 that he had the Sanders portrait, but was terrified of letting anyone copy it. Caroline replied that he must nonetheless "permit a little Woman who perhaps will call to take a little miniature only see that it be *well* done & like . . . I am at this moment nearly as mad as Sharp—do not [make] me more so by refusing." She swore she would keep the secret: "I am most true & would not harm my friends for my life," and, she rationalized: "You know however harsh however false he is to me when I am away—he is only too indulgent & kind when I see him—& this is what all know—therefore do not you refuse what you know he would grant if I were to see him."[81] Murray earned Lady Caroline's gratitude by agreeing to permit the copying to proceed.[82]

In late January, Caroline took a bad spill on the ice. "I had liked to have broke my skull," she told Murray, but "Mr Lucas put some leeches & as you see what brains I had are yet my own."[83] In this letter she also told Murray (with sketches as well as words) how her drink-befuddled father-in-law had astounded her by inventing a snowplow drawn by four horses. The plow was capable of clearing a pathway for carriages through three-foot drifts. It required the weight of passengers, and six-year-old Augustus got so excited riding on it that "he stood up clapping his Hands & saying it was the most joyful moment of his existence." Augustus's high spirits often translated into danger for others, however. The next day he was brought to his mother because he had tripped up one of the servants. "How can you say so!" he protested, "I was trying all I could to trip him *down.*" It was an extraordinary winter, during which Lady Caroline had plenty of time to reflect on her many scrapes. "If we escape dying of a broken heart we may at all events finish with a broken head," she told Murray.[84] She was concerned to hear that her grandmother suffered from a cold that was as severe as it was persistent.

Lady Caroline loved Byron's *The Corsair,* which she preferred to *The Bride of Abydos.* "[T]his is in his very best style," she said with satisfaction, "quite as *Childe Harold* was," though she objected to a passage in the preface on Walter Scott that sounded like flattery.[85] She felt Murray should tell Byron to avoid pretentious phrases like, "[t]he soft triumvir" or "'*sol*' pauses on the hill." Byron should "speak English—it is a goodly language."[86] Thus, Lady Caroline demanded to be considered the teacher, not the pupil—mistress of poetry, not merely the poet's mistress, though now she felt she "*must* see him," signing herself "Gulnar," an allusion to Conrad, the Corsair's heroine, Gulnare.[87] No meeting was arranged, though Murray may have told Byron of Caroline's wish. In late March, the poet had moved into comfortable new lodgings on the ground floor of Albany House in Piccadilly, very near to his publisher's offices.

Driven half-mad with jealousy of Lady Melbourne, Caroline called on Byron at his new apartments: "I thought she was gaining your confidence and esteem as I was losing *both*. I acknowledge this & I was not wrong."[88] But Byron was not in, and Caroline instantly regretted going, then threw herself on his mercy in a letter: "I trust myself to your compassion. If you tell any-one that I attempted to see you I am lost—irretrievably lost. . . . Oh, Lord Byron, think how inexcusable it must appear to others when it does so to you and pray excuse what I have done."[89] This did not stop her from insulting him:

> Farewell, Mefistocles, Luke Makey, De la Touche, Richard the 3rd, Valmont, Machiavelli, Prevost, the wicked Duke of Orleans—for you are a little like them all. And Joseph Lancaster who is very ugly, and Kean in Othello also is ugly, both put me in mind of you. . . . I have a letter of yours written on this day two years ago [3 June 1812]—a most unkind one. Do not be angry—think of my situation, how extraordinary! my mother in law actually in the place I held—her ring instead of mine—her letters instead of mine—her heart—but do you believe either she or any other feel for you what I felt—ugly & thin & mad & despis'd as I am.[90]

Byron now described himself to a friend as being "haunted by a skeleton,"[91] for Caroline followed him, and undoubtedly saw him in public and even in private on a number of occasions. As she felt Lady Melbourne's power increase, she sent her mother-in-law the ring Byron had given her:

[H]ere is the ring Lady Melbourne—which was to have followd my fortunes through life & been buried with me when all this ends may it not give you the suffering it has caused me but do not ridicule this whim or refuse to wear it let me see when you come that it is on your hand it is the only thing he gave me I have ever worn lately—& I did swear so oh never never to take it off & he said in his letter that he had still his on—but ever after that I wrote my name Caroline Byron & he calld me his Wife & it was yet fresh from the stamp hardly polished that it might be quite new gold as he said—all his other rings are markd with his name but this has no mark.[92]

Whether she enclosed the ring remains unknown. If she did, it must have been returned, for it (or a facsimile) would turn up later.

Since Lady Melbourne held all the cards, Caroline enclosed a letter for Byron and asked her mother-in-law to deliver it: "As I will not disobey you and Lady Melbourne I give her this open—if when she has read it she sees no wrong in it I hope she will give it you—for I believe she is the only person alive who does not try to make mischief between us." If that made Lady Melbourne laugh, she was probably less amused by subsequent passages in the letter. "[W]hen they tell me you said such and such things of me I fire up & say ten thousand times worse of you and Lady Melbourne," Caroline wrote. She begged Byron not to believe stories he heard about her, but to "ask Lady Melbourne and see what she says," while simultaneously saying that Lady Melbourne accused her of "a romantic absurd wish to please you" by not waltzing. Caroline also quoted Lady Melbourne as saying that "love is all imagination and nothing else." She concluded by promising she would never write to any "Woman"—undoubtedly meaning his lover Lady Oxford.[93] Fury masquerades as humility in this enclosure, every line of which contains a double entendre. If Byron thought her unfeminine, she would counter him memorably: "[H]e has acted in all things as a Woman might—when anxious to pique and humiliate & irritate those over whom she has acquired influence & ascendancy."[94]

Spring 1814 saw the fateful events leading to the capitulation of Paris and the abdication of Napoleon to Elba. But for Caroline, these events were overshadowed by the death of her beloved grandmother on 18 March. Literally from birth Caroline had felt the protection of this controlling but loving woman. There is little record of the correspondence between Caroline and her mother and siblings at this time; the loss was too much. However, Lady Caroline did write to her uncle Earl Spencer to beg him to send her a few things: a red drawing book containing her sketch of Lady Spencer; the portrait William had given to her at Caroline's

wedding in 1805; a little Derbyshire china tea cup Caroline had used while at
Holywell; a prayer book; and a copy of the poems of bluestocking poet Elizabeth
Carter that had been a favorite of her grandmother's.[95] These sad mementoes
were complemented by a happier one in the form of the completed copy of the
Sanders portrait, which Miss Emma Kendrick finally delivered in April.[96] The
satisfaction, however, was bittersweet.

William's sister, Emily, and other members of the Melbourne family had
applied steady pressure on William to separate from his volatile wife, and they
now increased their lobbying. Caroline told Murray she had been portrayed as
"hateful even to her nearest friends."[97] Isolated, and without the comfort of her
grandmother's steadying presence, Lady Caroline felt panic at the prospect of
being parted from William. Now she regretted her aloofness to some of her own
family, including her uncle's wife Lavinia. She grew hypersensitive to signs that
she was being "cut," or frozen out. She wrote to her uncle when the cup and other
items were delivered to her as requested: "I thank you extremely & I assure you
it has been for these 10 months past & shall be my endeavour to regain the good
opinion of the Friends I have left—I never wish to allude even to what has passed."
And then, in a familiar turn, Caroline filled the next pages with hot frustration at
the frigid atmosphere of Melbourne House. The letter is blotted as if she had
actually wept over it as she wrote. The entire melodrama flashed once again
before her: "I said I would leave this House if those in it thought ill of me & did
not like me to stay—I once fled from it in a passion when as I thought unkindly
treated but never with any body or to any body as all those around me know—I
never did deceive a human Being all I did was as public as possible." Here, she
tried mightily to win over her uncle with candor: "[E]very one it is said who puts
themselves into the wrong always thinks they are wrong'd," she admitted, "& so
no wonder I think this my case—but it is this feeling which prevents my being
humble or penitent." She defended her actions and asked for reconciliation:

> I love you & my Aunt & my Cousins dearly—but I never come near any of you—
> not out of incivility but out of pride & resentment—no doubt it is a wrong feeling
> for me—& I have done very wrong things & ought to consider this, but I cannot,
> for if I were to have knocked a person down & the whole World accused me of
> having robbed & murdered I could not take the sentence deserved—nor stand the
> punishment quietly . . . I am lost—I feel it—but even that cannot make me
> humble—because I feel too much injured—to wish to conciliate any one—my
> family are desirous I should appear [in society]—people are pleased to show me
> much good nature, & I am not ungrateful, but I had rather my Aunt Spencer &

yourself sent for me than strangers. I wish before I return to the Country to see Georgiana & Lady Althorp—nothing however shall induce me to call upon them till my Aunt says so.[98]

After this unvarnished admission of her inability to submit to what she felt was unjust censure, Lady Caroline concluded her letter with an appeal to Lavinia to "see me as formerly" without any change in manner. Perhaps Lord Spencer was too familiar with Caroline's protestations to believe even so convincing a performance, or perhaps it was her claim (in the final paragraph) to possess "a heart that is at length grown wise"—but the letter did not elicit a response.

Lady Caroline was thus forced to write to her aunt. She employed the bluntest and most forceful language she could muster: "I defy you to hate me," she told Lavinia. "There is no stratagem no force I will not use if you banish me to see you again—in the mean time, if you are really inclined to mortify & cut me—you may." In her conclusion, she notes that Lavinia's sister was about to be married: "I wish her joy with all my heart but Ile be hang'd sooner than call on her or any one else in your House till I have seen yourself first & so theres the truth & if it looks unkind or rude I care not . . . you are safe now for I am too ill to move but when Ime well—unless you fire as they did at the mob—have at you—all short of it I defy— your most dutiful grateful affectionate & virtuously disposed niece, Caroline Lamb."[99] There is no indication that this appeal gained Lady Caroline readmission to her aunt and uncle's parlor.

When Louis the XVIII arrived in London to prepare for his return to France, a huge throng gathered not far from Hobhouse's apartments, and Lady Caroline braved the "[w]omen fainting & men swearing" to reach his door, only to be overcome by the "dread of appearing like another Miss Botherum exerting her energies before the beautiful Corsair if he were there." She begged Hobhouse to allow her to watch from his garrett window when Louis XVIII was escorted by the Prince Regent to Dover on 3 May 1814 to restore the Bourbons to power. A great mass of English visitors would trail not far behind the returning King, but all Caroline's thoughts were on her sad situation: "Every one is changed to me," she told Hobhouse, "*you* are."[100]

While she struggled to shore up support among her family, Lady Caroline gave way to the very compulsions she claimed to have transcended. She wanted "the worst of human Beings" to give her a sign that he still cared for her, and, strangely enough, Byron reciprocated. He met her and they exchanged locks of hair. He recorded the event in a poem: "This votive ringlet's tenderest hair / Will bind thy heart to that I gave thee."[101] Caroline ordered a locket with a frame of gold and small pearls on the outside, in which she planned to place the hair and the copy of the portrait of Byron upon which she had expended so much energy and money. She may have done so. However, she eventually put the portrait into a different locket, the one he had given her in August 1812, with his family inscription ("crede Byron") on it. Caroline later had the inscription altered to read "*ne* crede Byron," and on the verso of the locket, she had engraved the following: "san fedele alla mia Biondetta, non posso vivere senza te, August 14th, 1812," ("From your faithful [one] to my Biondetta [fair-haired one, or 'enamored spirit']; it is impossible to live without you.") The lock of her hair was on display at the Victoria and Albert Museum in 1974.[102]

Lady Melbourne was highly alarmed when she realized that Byron was again seeing Caroline, who walked or rode up from Whitehall to the Albany, gaining access to his residence through a doorway (still visible today from the vantage of Piccadilly) to the left of the front entrance. She had charmed him again, yet this temporary relapse of tenderness turned again to frustration and annoyance in May, then anger and vituperation in June. Byron wrote to Lady Melbourne on 26 June 1814: "You talked to me—about keeping her out—it is impossible—she comes at all times—at any time—& the moment the door is open in she walks—I can't throw her out of the window." Facing the specter of elopement once again, Byron vowed he would

> much sooner be with the dead in purgatory—than with her—*Caroline* (I put the name at length as I am not jesting) upon earth. . . . I would lose an hundred souls rather than be bound to C—if there is one human being whom I do utterly *detest* & *abhor*—it is she—& all things considered—I feel to myself justified in so doing—she has been an adder in my path ever since my return to this country—she has often belied—& sometimes betrayed me—she has crossed me every where—she has watched—& worried & *guessed*—& been a curse to me & mine.——You may shew *her* this if you please—or to anyone you please—if these were the last words I were to write upon earth—I would not revoke one letter—except to make it more legible.[103]

In his rage, Byron seems to strain at convincing Lady Melbourne of his determination never to be trapped into an elopement. After all, he had opened the door in the first place. Byron, whose texts are full of cross outs and erasures, and whose denials of authorship were legion, now found himself trapped—forced to watch, wait, and *fret:* "I am already almost a prisoner—she has no shame." What he precisely meant he does not tell Lady Melbourne, but we have a taste of it in her letter of this time, asking whether he would permit her to sit behind the curtain while he made love to his amour of the moment: "[B]etter listen to that—than see what I witnessed—if I had followed you—you would have made me make the Bed for your new favourites—you are just a Man to exact it & with all my violence you would have made me do it—I have done all but that already—have I not."[104]

Despite his savage words of 26 June, and a promise delivered more calmly two days later that "all bolts bars & silence" would be employed to "keep her away,"[105] Byron's heart was not entirely proof against Caroline's passion, which she poured out again to him:

[E]very feeling in me has been struggling for mastery till I have been mad & now that the little good left me has triumphed I must write—Farewell—not as you say so to your favourites or they to you—not as any Woman ever spoke that Word for they never mean it to be what I will make it—but as nuns & those who die . . . I lov'd you as no Woman ever could love because I am not like them—but more like a Beast who sees no crime in loving & following its Master—you became such to me—Master of my soul more than of anything else . . . oh between that first and that last kiss what volumes of contradictory feelings might be placed—all that love & passion can invent from the thoughts of Idolatry down to the cold torpor of indifference and pity on your part & regret & remorse on mine—. . . it would scarcely be a crime in me to go & offer myself to some other Man if by doing this I could unchain my soul from you but I cannot bear Men. I feel quite a loathing to them. Sometimes I try if I can talk in that Jargon I us'd to hear but I cannot endure it & the remembrance of what you said puts all they say out.[106]

Perhaps such a letter explains why he allowed himself to be inveigled into another intimate encounter with Caroline. On 1 July Hobhouse convinced Byron, despite his contempt for the Duke of Wellington, to go to a masked ball given in his honor by the members of Watier's at Burlington House.

It was the event of the season—a party to celebrate the glorious victory of Britain over Napoleon. Over 1,700 people sat down to dinner that night in dominoes and masks, with Byron dressed as a friar.[107] Hobhouse himself attended in the Albanian costume that was Byron's trademark, which was much admired, although one of Lord Kinnaird's sisters kept teasing him by asking if it was his electioneering dress.[108] Before dinner, Lady Caroline conversed with Hobhouse, who treated her with a deference that made her feel unexpectedly grateful.[109] She grasped his elbow and they turned to see Byron. "I was obliged to talk to her," Byron told Lady Melbourne. He found Caroline was in a mood, bursting into private rooms to see who was doing what with whom, flashing people glimpses of her green pantaloons, and badgering a guardsman into taking off his red coat. Although Byron told Lady Melbourne he was "anxious to appear as having done all that could be done to second your wishes in breaking off the connection," he actually stayed all night, leaving at 7:00 A.M. after having had "a long conversation with C."[110]

Byron could not perhaps help maintaining ties with someone who threatened to outstrip him in being mad, bad, and dangerous to know. He later said that he had often "wished for insanity—anything to quell memory, the never-dying worm."[111] Lady Caroline's craziness seems to have made him almost jealous. In a letter to Lady Melbourne of 10 June 1814 he wrote, "I am as mad as C[aroline] on a different topic and in a different way—for I never break out into scenes."[112] Thus Byron claimed that his madness was somehow *controlled,* in contrast to his lover's. However, the more he doubted her sanity, the less easy Byron felt about Caroline: "[S]he cannot be in her senses" he told Lady Melbourne on the day after the Watier's Club Ball.[113] Encouraged by his confidante, he renewed his suit for Annabella Milbanke's hand.

The game was about to get more complicated for Byron. That spring Lady Caroline had met music composer and vocal instructor Isaac Nathan, who would provide her a further means to emulate Byron. Nathan was a practicing Jew whose wife Rosetta had converted—an unusual act for a British gentile. In May 1813, Nathan had decided to take advantage of the popularity of national airs epitomized in Moore's *Irish Melodies* and similar publications of Scottish, Welsh, German, Portuguese and other songs. He had advertised that he was working on *Hebrew Melodies* in the *Gentleman's Magazine* of May 1813 and shopped for a premier lyricist, starting with Sir Walter Scott, who turned him down.

In spring of 1814, Lady Caroline wrote a duet that Nathan set to music and performed with the soprano Catherine Stephens at a party in honor of her brother Willy's engagement to Lady Barbara Ashley Cooper.[114] In mid-June, Nathan sent Byron a setting of some lines from the *Bride of Abydos* ("This rose to calm my brother's care"). Nathan's letter explains that he had set the lyrics to music "some time ago," but had only lately been encouraged by its "flattering reception" to send the song to Byron with "the greatest deference and respect." Receiving no reply, Nathan wrote again explaining what he had in mind, and describing the melodies as "very beautiful" and of "undoubted antiquity." He noted delicately that "several Ladies of literary fame and known genius" had encouraged him to write.[115] There was likely only one lady in question.

Lady Caroline hoped Byron would stay in London, and she was bent on cultivating friendships with anyone who had regular contacts with him, like John Murray. Even as Caroline assisted in the preparations for her brother's wedding in August she heard rumors of Byron's impending marriage to the statuesque Lady Adelaide Forbes. It became her habit to vent to Murray: "I think I shall live to see the day—when some beautiful & innocent Lady Byron shall drive to your door—& I picture to myself the delight with which you will receive her," she said.

> I really believe that when that day comes, I shall buy a pistol at Mantons & stand before the Giaour & his legal wife & shoot myself, saying as Billy Taylors Mistress did that as I must not live for him I will die . . . there is something so beautiful in virtue & innocence that it sets like a crown of glory round a Woman—& when she has cast it off—she is either contemptible or at best only worthy of pity—if you knew how good I was once how sorry you would be for me now.[116]

The popular ballad of "Billy Taylor" was a burlesque with a quite different ending. Billy's sweetheart went to sea with him dressed as a boy. When he took up with another woman, she shot the lovers, rather than herself, and received a promotion in rank from the captain, who "applauded what she had done." No matter to Lady Caroline; she always aimed the gun at herself.

As she worked on Murray to keep herself in his and Byron's thoughts, Lady Caroline also pressed young Nathan's cause, for he would provide another contact with Byron. But her promotion of Nathan would not have succeeded without Douglas Kinnaird, a banker who was on the managerial board of the Drury Lane Theatre. Nathan put music to lines from Byron's *Lara,*[117] and Kinnaird persuaded Byron to hear the composer perform them—not to assist Nathan, but to help John Braham (originally "Abraham"), the preeminent singer and vocal stylist of his period in London. Braham was collaborating with Nathan on the *Hebrew Melodies.* Byron agreed to supply a few lyrics, partly as a favor to Kinnaird, partly because he liked Nathan, and partly because he wanted to impress the religious and proper Annabella Milbanke, who had now agreed to marry him. By 20 October he had done nine or ten songs "on the sacred model." He couldn't resist adding: "Augusta says 'they will call me a *Jew* next.'"[118]

While Byron and Nathan worked on *Hebrew Melodies,* Lady Caroline also collaborated with Nathan in writing songs. An attractive man whose light, accurate tenor voice may have reminded Byron of John Edleston, the choirboy whom he had loved at Cambridge, Nathan had gained recognition as the music teacher for Princess Charlotte, to whom the *Hebrew Melodies* (1815-1816) were dedicated. He was a good performer. Leigh Hunt describes hearing Nathan play "Herod's Lament for Mariamne" at Byron's request: "[T]he noble Bard, who was then in the middle of that unpleasant business about his wife, asked him for one respecting Herod and Mariamne, which he listened to with an air of romantic regret." Hunt savors the irony of Byron's affectation of regret over Herod's having executed his beloved Mariamne, and he admired Nathan's performance: "Mr. Nathan had a fine head; and he made the grand pianoforte shake like a nut shell under the vehemence of his inspiration."[119]

Lady Caroline, who played the harpsichord and harp, loved music passionately—like Calantha of *Glenarvon:* "She feels it in her very soul—it awakens every sensibility."[120] Nathan offered Lady Caroline a chance to raise her own "master hand" and "strike the thrilling Lyre," as she said in one of her first letters to Byron.[121] She stole some of Byron's Promethean fire through collaboration with Nathan, who composed music "impromptu" for some of her poems and set no fewer than ten songs, holding exclusive copyright, by express permission—in contrast to Byron, who let Murray steal the words to *Hebrew Melodies* over Nathan's objections. As a Jew, Nathan had no legal recourse, despite Byron's acknowledged promise of copyright. "I therefore cannot grant what is not at my disposal[;] let me hear from you on the subject." But when Nathan demurred, Byron told Murray, "[y]ou may have them if you think them worth inserting."[122] The poems were important to Byron's ex-lover and his fiancée Annabella Milbanke, to whom he showed "Oh Snatch'd Away in Beauty's Bloom," saying "perhaps I was thinking of you when I wrote that." Annabella and Lady Caroline were both privy to manuscript copies of the lyrics for *Hebrew Melodies.*[123]

Caroline had other models than Byron, of course, yet even these fed into the erotic obsession of her composition. Women had published ballad-style song lyrics in periodicals at least as early as the 1790s. Songs written by women were also competitive in the sheet-music market in London. As the expressions of women's voices, they were only publishable, of course, so long as they conformed to conventions of feminine distress—generally the erotomaniacs whom Byron himself portrayed in such songs as "Francisca." A poem published in the *Scots Magazine* in 1795, for example, was titled "Ellen; or, the fair insane." Another, printed in the *Monthly Magazine and British Register* in 1797, was called "The Penitent Mother."[124] Caroline's Aunt Georgiana had published a song that Jane Austen chose for her personal songbook: "I have a Silent Sorrow Here." The titles typify the roles in which Lady Caroline was cast and the characters in her own sentimentalized fiction.

Quite aware of Caroline's penchant for such drama, Byron feared her reaction when his wedding announcement appeared, and he therefore arranged to meet her to deflate her fury. But, when they met he couldn't tell her directly. He joked about marrying someone else, then tried to kill her affection for him by admitting in euphemistic but obvious terms that he had slept with his half-sister and that he had engaged in homosexual acts. To drive home the nail, he showed her letters that left no doubt as to his relationship with Augusta and his "Greek" sexual experiences. Stunned, Caroline left.[125]

Still uneasy, Byron took the precaution of warning Annabella on 9 October that Lady Caroline's "whole disposition is a moral phenomenon (if she be not *mad*) it is not feminine—she has no real affection . . . but everything seems perverted in her— she is unlike every body—& not even like herself for a week together."[126] When his rumored engagement was oddly contradicted in the *Morning Chronicle,* he blamed Caroline immediately: "[I]t is not the first nor the fiftieth of these *monkey-tiger* tricks that she has played me—one in particular of *forging* a letter in my name so exactly that the person to whom it was addressed was completely deceived . . . she has crossed my every path—she has blighted or at least darkened my every prospect."[127] He also wrote disgustedly to Lady Melbourne that Caroline had "been at her cursed tricks again," but in a postscript added that he had discovered he had guessed wrongly: "It is *not* C—I beg her pardon."[128]

His assumption was disproved by a letter from Caroline herself, saying "you are to be married I am told I hear it on all sides & heard it jestingly as I concluded from you." She assured him, "you are safe—the means you took to frighten me from your door are not in vain."[129] She only asked that he send back "those rings & the drawings and Book all shameful witnesses of my misery & eternal disgrace— farewell for ever oh for ever—I will nor see nor write nor think of you again."[130]

Caroline's calm reaction to Byron's engagement undoubtedly pleased her friends and relatives. She told Murray she had finally regained her senses and asked him "to burn and to forget every memorial of what I now remember with deep contrition. I trust in God Byron will be happy. He has chosen one who is good and amiable and who deserves well of him. It is his last chance of keeping clear of what has too often led him astray." She described Annabella as "certainly handsomer than half the Biondettas and black and white ladies hitherto admired [by Byron]." And she said that Byron had written to her as if he were "a Lord Chief Justice during the Assizes—I assure you the style froze me—though it was superlatively kind and condescending. How has he disposed of the other unfortunates? I speak of them by dozens, you see." After portraying herself as one among the legions of the spurned, gnawed at by jealousy, she ended by begging Murray not to show the letter to Byron—probably expecting that he would do so anyway. She mocked her own melodrama by characterizing her letter as "the last page of my novel."[131]

Caroline's real reaction to Byron's engagement may be gauged by other letters she wrote to Murray. In one she said that Byron would never be able to live with "a woman who went to church punctually, understood statistics and had a bad figure."[132] At the moment she had no one other than Murray to whom she could express these feelings, for her mother had departed for Paris. To improve Harriet's fragile health, Lord Bessborough had taken her to winter in the south of France for seven months—their longest separation since Caroline's birth. Caroline sought escape from "resentment & that desperate feeling" by pouring energy into the novel. She now told Murray, "[m]y heart is set on the Publication of my novel," though she admitted it was "very unequal—I am going to recorrect it—answer me fairly as a Man & not in jest—is it your wish to undertake it?" Since she was definitely losing Byron to Annabella, she wished more than ever to be a writer: "Are you serious about my novel?" she asked Murray, for "I mistrust you."[133]

Playing Byron

1815–1816

Of all Bitches dead or alive a scribbling woman is the most canine.

—Byron[1]

B yron and Annabella were married on 2 January 1815. Two weeks later, he responded to one of Lady Caroline's letters. Receiving no reply, he told Lady Melbourne, "all is right."[2] But two weeks after that, he heard a disturbing rumor that William and Caroline might be about to separate. Lady Melbourne told him it wasn't true, but that Caroline continued manic: "I hope some day to see you undergo a Dinner, when she wishes to shew off."[3] When Lady Melbourne visited the Byrons at Piccadilly Terrace, she brought Caroline, who sat in subdued silence throughout the visit.[4]

Murray unwisely suggested to Caroline she would soon overcome her pain. "Do you know my heart so well?" she asked sardonically. But her view of Byron had really changed. Byron, she said, "has not a noble heart," and she predicted that his true character would emerge: "[T]here is a black speck in our divinity & like the most venomous of poisons though concealed from the eye it will shew itself at the hour appointed." She mocked his bride's stiffness, dishing out similar insults to the Whig circle that upheld him: "[I]f Fulvia [Annabella] Sporteth it must be like the dance of the Elephant that would vainly attempt to rival the Antelope. So sportive are all the Hobhouses Hollands Clarks Hertfords & Prince Regents."[5] She also mocked Augusta Leigh, whose home was in Six-Mile Bottom: "6 Miles Bottom??? How singular," she wrote, "Where ignorance is bliss—Tis madness to be wise."[6] But these feelings of anger at Byron's incestuous relationship with Augusta soon turned to guilt over having said nothing to Annabella before the marriage. "I would rather die than deceive her or play the hypocrite," she told Murray. But now it was too late. "What a melancholy year this is," she complained. Her mother was away, and her spirits dropped so low that she temporarily stopped writing.[7]

But when *Hebrew Melodies* appeared she found her pen again. She had earlier disdained the lyrics of Nathan's collaborator, John Braham.[8] Now, reading Byron's "It is the Hour" and "She Walks in Beauty," she pounced, taking special note that Byron claimed to have dashed them off thoughtlessly:

> It is a childish pride that our Poets now cherish to note the number of minutes and days in which they write a thing. They hurt themselves by these hasty and ill-digested performances. "She walks in beauty like the night," for example—if Mr. Twiss[9] had written it how we should have laughed! Now we can only weep to see how little just judgement there is on earth, for I make no doubt the name of Byron will give even these lines a grace. I who read his loftier lay with transport will not admire his flaws and nonsense. You will say it is only a song, yet a song should have sense.[10]

Lady Caroline felt growing confidence in her own judgment on Byron's or anyone's writing.

Despite her negative review, *Hebrew Melodies* influenced her own song lyrics. For example, Caroline's "Would I had seen the dead and cold" is cast in a common ballad rhythm and rhyme used by Byron in half a dozen of the *Hebrew Melodies*. Here is the first stanza of Caroline's poem:

> Would I had seen thee dead and cold,
> In thy lone grave asleep,
> Than live, thy falsehood to behold,
> And penitent to weep:
> For better, I thy grave could see,
> Than know that thou art false to me![11]

Compare this to the last stanza of Byron and Nathan's "The Wild Gazelle." The two are almost identical in rhythm and mood:

But we must wander witheringly
In other lands to die
And where our father's ashes be
Our own may never lie.
Our temple hath not left a stone
And mockery sits on Salem's throne.[12]

Caroline's literary judgment continued to sharpen as she drafted *Glenarvon*. Inevitably, she claimed she had dashed the novel off in a month—the very offence for which she had scathingly attacked Byron.[13] She sent Murray the first part and waited anxiously for his verdict: "[C]onsidering the agony which you know must arise from suspense—I am rather vex'd at your not writing to me—if it is execrable in your estimation you can say that it is not so happy as you expected—I shall not be offended." Fearing he had found it "stupid dull & bad," she waited for the blow.[14] Murray's response is lost, but he clearly thought *Glenarvon* needed work.

While she labored on revisions, Lady Caroline was distressed by the appearance of a novel, *The Baron of Falconberg; or, Childe Harolde in Prose,* by Mrs. Elizabeth Thomas, the wife of the Vicar of Tidenham, who wrote under the pen name of "Bridget Bluemantle." *The Baron of Falconberg* is long, but its plot is undemanding. After dropping several false lovers, including Arabella and Emmeline, the Baron chooses the angelic Caroline Dennison for her "purity of her heart." Mrs. Thomas describes Falconberg's salvation simply: "He is now good."[15] The novel's humorlessness comforted Caroline, but reminded her she was not the only one with an itch for scribbling.

The British forces under Wellington won their historic victory at Waterloo on 18 June 1815. Furious fighting engendered confusion among both hosts, and Caroline's brother Frederick had been wounded severely in both arms, knocked off his horse by a blow to the head, and stabbed in the back with a lance when he attempted to rise. Bleeding in a punctured lung, he was robbed of his belongings, then given a shot of brandy by a French officer who promised he would be removed from the field once the fighting stopped. But the French withdrew, and the Prussian cavalry followed. Frederick was trampled by the horses because the muddy field was so covered with bodies that they had no place left to step. He was still miraculously alive eighteen hours later when a member of his own regiment found him. Having been told positively Frederick had died on one day, the family got the news that he lived on the next.[16]

Caroline and William set off immediately for Brussels, arriving on 6 July. She wrote twice to her brother Willy on 7 July, the day that English troops entered

Paris and Louis XVIII was declared King: "I have just seen Frederick, & thank God he is said to be out of danger. I arrived here half an hour ago. Nothing you ever heard of is like the crowd." Mail service was terrible, and the Lambs received no letters while in Brussels. Frederick asked after Augustus, but Caroline had no news and felt "very low," William reported.[17] The gloom in the invalid hospital deepened with the news that Samuel Whitbread, the Whig politician, had committed suicide over his financial problems connected with Drury Lane Theatre. Whitbread had been a close acquaintance of William Lamb's.

Lady Bessborough had spent the winter and spring in France and Italy with her husband and Willy, and his wife Barbara (the former Lady Cooper). Now they all settled into the Place Royale in Brussels to await Frederick's recovery. From their apartments, they heard confusing accounts of Napoleon's surrender and transportation to England, and of Wellington's and Blücher's salute to the King of France. Angry Germans roamed the streets of Brussels looking for French citizens to molest. Harriet looked "far from well & most melancholy" to Caroline— "[m]y father too is grave."[18]

By the first week in August 1815, Frederick was well enough to travel home with his parents. William and Caroline went to Paris to join Hart. It was an extraordinary scene, with British troops in the Champs Élysées and encamped along the way from Paris to St. Cloud.[19] Longing to hear from family and friends, Caroline had been writing lengthy letters every day, and she now wrote in a magnanimous if not forgiving mood to Byron:

> Thanks for your goodness to me, which is fixed in my memory and heart never to be forgotten. Thanks too for your patience and forgiveness in many trying scenes. Even receive thanks for your cruelty as it has humbled a very proud and vain character whom none but you ever dared contend with before. . . . Could you but guess with such a character as mine, so like an untamed tigress, what I have suffered these three years you would judge me less harshly. If I go into the world, or if I stay with my family, and still more if I lie down in my bed, that horrid name I merit still pursues me.[20]

In this mood, she could feel and believe many contradictory things: It was her exclusive fault that she had betrayed William; yet it seems she felt neither repentance nor remorse.

According to her cousin Harryo, once in the city Caroline decided to make a conquest of the Duke of Wellington: "Nothing is *agissant* but Caroline William in a purple riding habit tormenting everybody, but I am convinced primed for an attack on the Duke of Wellington, and I have no doubt that she will to a certain extent succeed, as no dose of flattery is too strong for him to swallow or her to administer. Poor William hides in one small room, while she assembles lovers and tradespeople in another. He looks worn to the bone."[21] Caroline was in a manic mood—confused and short-tempered: "She arrived dying—by her own account—, having had French apothecaries at most of the towns through which she passed. She sent here immediately for a doctor, but by mistake they went for the Duke of Wellington." She did indeed see much of Wellington then and on occasions long after, including a soirée attended by Washington Irving, who observed the Duke dressed in black, with Star and Garter, exhibiting no inclination for conversation with the men because he was "quite engaged by Lady Caroline Lamb."[22] Wellington corresponded frequently with Lady Caroline, and Harryo heard him sing Caroline's praises: "I see she amuses him to the greatest degree, especially her *accidents,* which is the charitable term he gives to all her sorties."[23]

Byron had written to James Wedderburn Webster, who was in Paris with his wife Lady Frances, to warn him that Caroline was "mad & malignant . . . no human being but myself knows the thorough baseness of that wretched woman."[24] And yet, a poem he gave to Isaac Nathan at this time shows that Byron could feel quite differently. "When We Two Parted" addresses both Lady Frances (with whom Byron himself had had an affair late in 1813) and Lady Caroline. Byron had just heard that Lady Frances too had set her cap for the Duke of Wellington.[25] The poem laments broken lover's vows and public scandal: "I hear thy name spoken, / And share in its shame." The concluding stanza expresses regret and longing:

In secret we met—
In silence I grieve,
That thy heart could forget,
Thy spirit deceive.
If I should meet thee
After long years,
How should I greet thee!—
With silence and tears.[26]

Of the two women, Lady Caroline fared better in the fall of 1815, apparently winning her prize. She broke *two* busts of the Duke of Wellington because she said they didn't do him justice.[27] Nor was the Duke the only liaison Caroline pursued.

Byron's acquaintance Michael Bruce had just returned from the Near East, and Caroline was immediately drawn to him because he had met Byron in 1810, on the trip recorded in *Childe Harold's Pilgrimage*. As the traveling companion of Lady Hester Stanhope, Bruce had landed at Piraeus just in time to encounter Byron as he explored the terrain near Athens. Though Byron and Lady Hester disliked each other, Bruce warmed to the young man—so readily that he surprised him with an impromptu confession of friendship that Byron felt he had "done nothing to deserve."[28] As a fellow Byron-lover, Caroline now delighted in Bruce's company, calling him "He of the Desert." She may also have relished some rivalry with her mother-in-law, for Lady Melbourne seems to have competed for Bruce's attentions, much to the disgust of Caro George: "I am doomed to hear her's and [Lady Caroline Lamb's] mutual confidences of how the other makes up to him. [Lady Caroline Lamb] says the 'truth is he wants me, but I am not to be taken in, so he comforts himself with her.' This family is enough to make one sick."[29]

Preparing to leave Paris in October, Caroline wrote to Bruce: "Star of the East I go tomorrow & must entreat you to call on me tonight, till one you will find me at Home pray bring the Inconstant [Benjamin Constant, Madame de Staël's former lover] & any other you may find—how I regret the Bruce on quitting Paris—aye & all else in this delightful capital."[30] It had been a relief for her to keep out of London and attend the balls and fetes of post-Waterloo Paris. They had met many of the ministers of the new French government, including Talleyrand, and visited the battlefield to observe the souvenir-hunters. She had purchased a book that had belonged to Napoleon with an eagle on the cover, which she would later offer to Byron. She had even found time to write. Inspired by the theater they saw, including *Le Secret du Ménage* and *La Pie Voleuse,* she had herself written two plays.[31] And yet, she had continued to have fights with William.

Thus Lady Caroline failed to make herself less vulnerable to the attacks of William's family. A pariah to them, she was little more than a mild amusement to her cousins.[32] Her flirting had re-injured William's bruised sensibilities, and he became more withdrawn. She now sought to divert and involve him through the preparation of *Glenarvon* for publication. The highly sympathetic portrait of Lord Avondale (the William Lamb character in the book) and the penitence of Lady Calantha (one of the Caroline figures) pleased him.

Glenarvon had been mostly completed before news of Frederick's near-fatal injuries had diverted her attention and taken her abroad. She had written to John Murray before her departure for Brussels to say, "Miss Webster will send you my MSS—it is in a dreadful state I only had time to correct the 3rd vol.—which you read all the rest is merely copied from my Brouillon & terrible."[33] In the mean time, she passed her two play manuscripts to Annabella as potential scripts for the management of Drury Lane Theater, with which Byron was affiliated, asking Annabella to show them to her husband. "I know nothing of their Author except his having made me this request." She asked that the manuscripts be returned to Melbourne House "in case the Man should call whilst I am gone."[34] Caroline had become temporarily obsessed with the theater and often asked John Murray if he would like to share her mother's box.[35] She now had great hopes that he would publish her novel, through which she had relived her affair with Byron, expiating her guilt and creating a sympathetic portrait of William. Then, in Paris, her bad behavior had returned.

The Lambs pressed William harder to separate from Caroline. Ugly scenes took place that fall, and one weapon in the verbal war was the reminder of Caroline's and William's financial dependence upon the Melbournes, who were now actively encouraging friends to freeze Caroline out. They had their reasons. At a dinner party at Lady Holland's on 22 December, John Cam Hobhouse observed the reckless way in which Caroline was talking. Asked to define "truth," she responded that it is "what one thinks at the moment."[36]

During the first week of February 1816 temperatures dropped to twenty degrees below freezing, and it was then that Lady Caroline heard that Annabella had left Byron.[37] Lady Caroline wrote to Murray immediately: "[H]ave you heard the reports—is it really true & do you know why—they say it is certain—every thing is rumoured as cause of it even the worst possible—I have been litterally ill on account of it—pray write."[38] What she meant by "the worst" was undoubtedly the charge of incest.

Lady Caroline implored Byron to reconcile with Annabella so that he would not be exposed. She urged him to offer a generous separation agreement and seek an interview with his wife: "[L]et no pride—or resentment on your part prevent an immediate reconciliation."[39] The separation settlement would show him in the right light, and that would help him avoid public censure. "[A]ll the world will approve your conduct," she said, "which I know is not a consideration with you—but still should in some measure be thought of." Caroline knew Byron would suspect her of spreading rumors about him. There is no evidence that she did so, however. On the contrary, she was concerned for his position: "Lord Byron was at the House," she wrote Murray, "which I was glad of as it showed him calm."[40] If she observed him at Melbourne House (instead of merely hearing the report), this must have been the last time she saw Byron. Afterward, she wrote him to say that he was the subject of "odious reports," and urged him to act prudently. "I have disbelieved all the reports till now," she said, indicating that she was telling *others* not to believe them. He might not trust or believe her, but she warned him, "—could you know what some say—you would really be on your guard."[41]

As with the newspaper denial of his engagement, Byron was all too ready to believe that Lady Caroline was spreading gossip, but she was trying to bring the couple back together. At one point, she actually told Byron she would take the blame for any letters that might be produced to incriminate him with charges of incest or sodomy: "If letter or report or aught else has been malignantly placed in the hands of your wife to ruin you, I am ready to swear that I did it for the purpose of deceiving them. . . . If it is a mere letter I will swear I wrote it as a forgery."[42] Byron maintained silence. Aware that he had many advisors "wiser and better" to guide him, Caroline told Byron not to neglect the diplomatic abilities of Lady Melbourne, "your real & most affectionate & zealous friend . . . who loves you more sincerely than any one on Earth."[43] Though she mistrusted Lady Melbourne herself, she knew that in her mother-in-law's eyes Byron could do no wrong. She also believed that, even if Annabella knew the worst, she "cannot have the heart to betray you—if she has she is a Devil."[44]

All this was in the beginning. Caroline wrote Byron and Hobhouse to effect a reconciliation, and she complimented Hobhouse on standing "firm by a friend when he needs it even though he may be in the wrong."[45] But then Caroline talked to Murray and found out that Byron had been verbally and physically abusive, so violent and cruel that Lady Byron feared for her life and suspected he was mad. Suddenly, Caroline saw Annabella as—like herself—a victim. She was reminded that Annabella might lose her young child to its father. So Caroline changed her goal and sought to help Lady Byron negotiate a settlement that would protect her right to her daughter. She was motivated most of all by guilt that she had not warned Annabella of Byron's true character.

Having been too forgiving of Byron's faults, Caroline now became irrationally incensed. She wrote to Annabella begging to see her, and admitting that she had at first sympathized with Byron and even attacked the Milbankes for pressuring their daughter to separate. Now Caroline swore to have no more communication with Byron: "[N]ever till this hour did I feel disgust & indifference for him who deserves no other sentiments—so different is the feeling which arises from the blow given to ourselves when we feel that we deserve it from the hand of God— & the unmerited cruelty exercised on one—not only innocent—but by *his* own account exemplary & noble." Aware that she was no desirable ally, Caroline advised Annabella not to talk about their communication. Nevertheless, she promised, "I would stand by you not him were the whole world & every thing in it—in his favour—& if he has the cruelty to tear the child from you I will tell you that which if you merely menace him with the knowledge shall make him tremble." She had now broken her promise never even to hint at Byron's secrets. She was compelled, however, by her memories of 1812, when Lady Melbourne had betrayed her with Byron, "& her doing it added to the bitter agony I endured." Caroline had essentially turned "King's evidence."[46]

Caroline rationalized that she was trafficking only in the *threat* of exposure. She undoubtedly hoped that she could manage things so that Byron need never know who or what lay behind Lady Byron's strengthened bargaining position: "I would sooner die I think than reveal it—but if he thinks that you know it—if he feels he is in yr power he will not dare to push matters to extremity—he will not face a public trial [for divorce]—or if he does—he will yield to all demands as you must insist on." Lady Caroline now identified with Annabella as one who must assert herself against the Byron-Melbourne conspiracy. "[T]rust no one," she implored, for even Annabella's defenders " have a motive for their behavior . . . be cold to his friends & relatives—they are more *his* friends than yours."[47] This letter came at a moment when Annabella had grown angry at Lady Melbourne's silence, generally perceived as support for Byron. Gossip confirmed this assumption, and she wrote her mother that Lady Melbourne was as treacherous as a character out of *Les liaisons dangereux*. Her mother agreed: "I think it incumbent on You to break with her, that is cut her intirely."[48]

Lady Melbourne caught wind of Annabella's intentions and moved to neutralize the cut she was to receive. Protesting that she was being misrepresented, she wrote Annabella a letter on 20 March, denying that she clandestinely supported Byron. This communication caught Annabella completely off guard, and she was forced to respond rather awkwardly to her aunt's offensive.[49] Though Annabella backed down here, she moved ahead with her effort to guarantee a separation allowing her to keep her daughter. In this, she had several advisors, including Lord Byron's own lawyer, Samuel Romilly, who had managed to forget he was retained for Byron—a breach of legal etiquette Byron never forgave. Lady Byron had signed a statement on 14 March about Augusta and the charges of incest, and a few days later agreed to a legal separation.[50] Her advisors agreed that she should contact Lady Melbourne and Lord Holland. Additionally, she must find out what Lady Caroline knew. She wasted no time in holding a frosty interview with Lady Melbourne on 25 March 1816, wrote to Lord Holland the next day, and the day after that held an interview with Lady Caroline herself. The two women met at the house of Caro George, Lady Byron's ally. This was war, and Annabella looked for any advantage she could gain if the case went to court.

When Lady Caroline arrived, she first asked Annabella to burn her letters. Annabella promised to "seal them up, and write on them that in case of my death they should be returned," and then asked Caroline bluntly to explain what she knew that could be used against Byron. Having promised never to reveal his secrets, Caroline grew "greatly agitated," yet she felt so guilty at not having spoken up before Annabella's marriage that she began to talk with what Annabella described as "an unfeigned degree of agitation," describing how Byron had teased her with vague allusions to criminal behavior that finally became an explicit claim of incest with Augusta. Caroline said she had refused to accept the claim: "I could believe it of *you*—but not of *her*." Byron replied (according to Caroline) that the seduction of his half-sister had posed no challenge, and he produced letters from Augusta that proved they were lovers.

But this was not all. Caroline described "other & worse crimes"—"unnatural crimes"—that Byron had committed with his page, Robert Rushton, and others, including three "schoolfellows whom he had thus perverted."[51] Annabella now had confirmation of her own suspicions and ammunition to use against Byron, though it would be a delicate business, for if she fired she would destroy everyone and consequently lose her victory. She exulted quietly to Caro George that she had controlled her emotions so thoroughly that she had expressed neither belief nor disbelief in what Lady Caroline had said.

Caroline seems not to have noticed, and she began a letter to Annabella as soon as she returned to Whitehall, explaining that she had felt reluctant to speak up before Annabella's marriage because her statements would not have been believed. She promised William Lamb's support in Annabella's struggle with Byron and Lady Melbourne, "2 of the greatest Hypocrites & most corrupted Wretches that were ever suffered to Exist on this earth." "Make any use of what I have told & will stand by," she said, and "think of your own & your child's interest . . . I can feel & think of nothing on earth but you & your injuries."[52] Still apprehensive, she followed this lengthy letter with an even longer one warning Annabella not to risk attacking Lady Melbourne.

Caroline wanted to impress Annabella with the extraordinary loyalty of Byron's friends: "[R]ecollect my Dearest Lady Byron How artful *he* is & what a manner he has of turning things & pity sooner than hate those whom he deceives."[53] She advised Lady Byron to remember that "Lady Melbourne has a good & kind heart," despite the fact that she was "infatuated" with Byron.[54] Caroline reminded Annabella that Lady Melbourne was a key ally, and that she ought to avoid offending her, even if "it is perfectly useless to trust her . . . nothing can change her—but pray be kind should she call."[55] Lord Holland might be another ally, but he too must be disabused of his belief that Annabella had "only puerile charges." Caroline had already admitted that she wanted things settled amicably for Byron's sake, "provided your interest & dignity & child are left you."[56] Now she underscored the fact that "there is a difficult game to play & they are playing it skillfully." She and Annabella must be cautious not to divulge their communication: "[W]ere it but thought that I espous'd your cause—would it not hurt it—so she has joined with Lady C. L against him will be said—the cast off mistress & the Wife make common cause."[57]

Of course, the two women *were* fighting in a common cause. Caroline advised Annabella to let Lord Holland think she knew something "which nothing but dispair will tempt you to tell—but seem afraid of this . . . this is no letter of ceremony I write by stealth & in haste a thousand things crowd upon my mind that I think might be useful." She told Annabella to fire her maid because she was married to Byron's valet Fletcher. She also wanted another interview and offered to meet Annabella by stealth, begging that Caro George not be told. Annabella demurred, but she had been touched by Caroline's ferocious expressions of support: "[W]ere I to see your child taken from you," Caroline wrote to her, "I would appear myself against him in Justice & call on the humanity of strangers to prevent so wicked so barbarous an act."[58]

Despite the negative character she had given Caroline in 1812, Annabella now said "the language of sincerity has I believe been spoken on both sides."[59] For her part, Caroline even told Byron's friends she had wronged Annabella by not preventing her marriage. She also insisted she was not to blame for rumors of Byron's crimes—that it was "Lord Byron's own impudence" that betrayed him. "When you suspect me," she charged, "ask yourself if there are no others who had more interest than I had in causing this disunion, and whether my faults do not judge of a heart that has disdained every mean revenge and never will adopt that course but in one case, when by him that made me I will disclose all even upon oath and die the next moment."[60] Histrionic though it was, her stance appears sincere and consistent, once she knew of Byron's brutal behavior before the separation.

Lady Caroline identified so strongly with Lady Byron partly because she herself stood in danger of a legal separation in the spring of 1816. Lady Melbourne and Emily Cowper had called in a physician who was willing to declare Lady Caroline insane and commit her to an asylum. Caroline's Aunt Lavinia now colluded with Lady Cowper and Lady Melbourne to get Caroline declared mentally incompetent. Emily Cowper told Caroline's brothers their sister had suffered a breakdown, producing the written diagnosis, and made Caroline promise she would not fight a separation. Caroline later protested to her mother-in-law over these strong-arm tactics: "As to any promises I may have been forced to make when a straight waistcoat & a Mad Doctor are held forth to view—they cannot expect I should think them binding—I freely forgive my Relations but I will never speak to [Lavinia] again as long as I live . . . it is too sad to hear all this is for my own good."[61] Harriet protested her daughter's treatment, and for this both were told to leave Melbourne House: "I was ordered out of the house in no gentle language: my Mother was spoke to with the most barbarous roughness in my presence . . . I was *proved* mad."[62] It seems ironic, to say the least, that Caroline and Byron were both diagnosed as "mad" that spring.

Terrified, Lady Caroline wrote to Emily Cowper and Lady Melbourne, "[T]hank God I have friends to support me—& whatever measures are taken they shall be taken publickly—Wm Lamb has promised to agree to no private attempts to prove the mother of his child insane—& the Boys Parents & himself & every servant I have will stand by me." She condemned Lavinia "as my enemy & Lord Spencer as the weak instrument of her intrigues."[63] Lady Caroline felt the threat of incarceration strongly enough to send copies of her letter to several friends. Like Annabella, she feared losing her child.

Trying to fend off charges of madness, Caroline unfortunately weakened her position by losing her temper with one of her pages who loved tossing squibs (essentially tiny firecrackers) into the fire. When he did it once more, she threw a cricket ball, which hit him on the head, drawing blood. According to her own account, she panicked, running out into the street screaming, "Oh God, I have murdered the page!"[64] Such behavior validated the Lambs's claims. She was so mortified by this misadventure that, when, Lady Holland publicly downplayed the incident, Lady Caroline wrote her an effusive note of thanks. Lady Holland sent this stiff rejoinder:

> If an inclination to disbelieve what I heard & to suppress & soften the story I was at last compelled to believe is kindness I can with a good conscience accept your thanks but I do not know that on any other Score I deserve them on this occasion; Indeed I think that the less you express either gratitude or resentment for people's opinions on this unpleasant Subject or in plain english the less you talk or write about it, the more you will shew yourself sensible of the pain you must have inflicted upon those whom you ought to consider beyond all others.[65]

In addition to general madness, Lady Caroline was charged with feeding the boys from the stables at Brocket, and wantonly squandering money on servants while William was at the House of Commons. She defended herself, saying that they had no more of an "establishment" than when they were married and had little enough to squander. "If you think this too much," she told Lady Melbourne, "only arrange it as you like." Although Caroline's managerial abilities were not as great as her mother-in-law's, she was up to most domestic challenges. Her correspondence with Lady Melbourne of this time discusses the virtues of threshing machines, the dismissal of an obstreperous footman, and her proposal that they make their own butter at Brocket, based on the performance of a nearby estate's dairy, where "they have 7 cows in milk—& make 40£ of butter a week & have put by on that 1[£] 2[shillings] 6[pence] for salting tell me if this appears good to you."[66]

Regardless, the Melbournes intended to prove that Caroline had come unhinged and should be turned over to the care of two strong female "nurses"—"those brutes," as Lady Caroline described them, "who never would have allowed me freedom to claim even assistance."[67] They badgered William into agreeing to a separation, had the papers prepared, and forwarded them to Brocket. Lady Melbourne set out from London for Welwyn to make sure all went as planned. Upon her arrival at Brocket, however, "she found the happy couple at breakfast and Lady Caroline drawling out—'William, some more muffin?'—and everything made up."[68] The papers were put away, and Caroline had prevailed. Or so it seemed to George, Emily, and Lady Melbourne. In reality William had never desired the separation. To avoid confrontation and keep Caroline, he was willing to endure the scorn of his sister, who now openly called him a coward and lamented that Lady Caroline seemed "fixed to him for life."[69]

Lady Caroline's well-founded paranoia about the Melbournes set the tone for her correspondence with Annabella. From Lady Caroline's view, Byron was all-powerful and befriended by everyone, while she and Annabella stood alone. In early April 1816 Byron's poem "Fare Thee Well" was published. Murray had showed Lady Caroline an advance copy, and she begged Byron not to publish it because she knew it would be treated as an attack on Annabella.[70] At that time she had empathized with Byron—and even Augusta. The two had attended a reception for Benjamin Constant at Lady Jersey's only to be cut by Caro George and her friends.[71] There is a note of certainty in Lady Caroline's response to seeing "Fare Thee Well" in print that shows she had finally achieved the perspective on Byron she needed to finish her novel. She wrote to Murray, "It should be positive proof to you that I am no longer Lord Byron's friend and admirer—what I am now going to say to you—I think it a shame in you to shew those verses—to try & awaken feelings for him when his conduct I find has been too mean & too atrocious even for such as I am to tollerate." She called Byron a "Villain," and a "poor paltry Hypocrite a mean coward and a man without a heart that serpant his sister too."[72]

Byron's conflict with Annabella exemplified the double standard for wives and husbands. At Melbourne House, a not dissimilar drama played out, as Caroline was maneuvered toward the madhouse. And yet, she could not help trying to protect Byron from further harm. When Murray showed her Byron's "Stanzas to Augusta," in which he calls his sister "the solitary star" of his life, she wrote him imploring "for God sake not to publish these."[73] Byron ignored her good advice and scolded Murray: "Really you must not send any thing of mine to Lady C. L. I have often sufficiently warned you on this topic."[74]

It probably did not help that she received news during this period of the arrest of Michael Bruce in Paris. Bruce was tried and imprisoned for his role in the escape of Count Lavallette from France. The Duke of Wellington wrote spitefully to Caroline that "your dandy of the desert, or rather deserted dandy . . . is not hanged yet; but there are hopes he may be so if justice is done, by the end of the month."[75] It looked as though this new friend who had shared her love for Byron would die.

Murray had finally declined to publish *Glenarvon,* perhaps because he now foresaw a firestorm—though firestorms aren't bad for book sales. Perhaps Murray felt Byron would object to his publishing an ex-lover's kiss-and-tell novel—or that the powerful Melbournes, Devonshires, Spencers, and Bessboroughs would punish him. More likely he felt the work was inferior to the standard he wished to keep—he had only just purchased Jane Austen's *Emma* the previous fall. Turned down by Murray, Lady Caroline fixed upon Henry Colburn, who had a record of publishing women writers and in general for taking risks.

With a sense that the Lambs were preparing a new assault, Caroline acted to save her literary offspring, even though it lacked a proper ending. Later, she justified her momentous decision in a letter to Granville Leveson-Gower, saying she had been cut by too many friends: "Indeed, indeed, Lord Granville, I could not stand it; these people, too, had all taken Lord Byron's part, had all stood by him, though cruelty and falsehood were heaped upon him." In a repeat of her disastrous flight from Whitehall in 1812, she got into a rage with Lord Melbourne: "That night I sent the novel."[76] Once she had sent the manuscript to Colburn, Caroline found herself filled with foreboding that she would die before completing the task: "[I]n such case I beg you to do justice to my little narrative—to have it published with my name its errors will then be examined at once. A short preface and my name would make the sale such as to enable you to perform my wishes." Caroline gamely tried to convince Colburn he should take the work: "You will easily see by the style of this book that it is written more from the feelings than the mind. However careless it may appear to a Critic's eye it has caused me much labour." Cautious Colburn showed the manuscript to readers whose opinions (now lost) both frightened and annoyed the author. She told Colburn to say to "Mr W" that she was "unwell," though she admitted she would like to know what "Mr T" had to say; nonetheless, "Ackermans objection is I think absurd." She suddenly wrote in a fright that she had no second copy of the manuscript and that if it were lost, she couldn't possibly reconstruct it.[77] All this was not particularly reassuring to the publisher.

Colburn took the book anyway. He advanced her £200 with the promise of £300 more after publication—an unusual payout for a first novel by an unknown.[78] Just that year, he had paid Lady Morgan, an experienced and successful writer, £550 for the copyright of *O'Donnel*.[79] Lady Caroline was delighted, though as an aristocrat she had to make a show of giving the money away. She allocated £200 for Miss Webster, to whom she had dictated much of the manuscript and a substantial portion of another. Delightful as the money was, Caroline was seeking something more. With this novel, she would be launched on a quasi-Byronic literary career.[80] It was exhilarating—and exhausting. Luckily, her antagonists had grown tired of pressuring William, and she was able to work uninterruptedly editing and revising, with his blessing.

A welter of correspondence ensued between Caroline and Colburn. As the first volume was being set in type, she went over the proofs.[81] As was common, accidental alterations were introduced into the text as the errors were corrected, and the new author responded angrily: "I prefer abiding by my own errors whatever they are than any other persons. I shall be seriously angry if any alteration is made whatever either in punctuation or orthography & I entreat you to send me the proof sheets. Remember and send the remainder of the 1st vol.— for I have been obliged to alter it all back again—pray be cautious in future."[82] Colburn had been through it all many times before. He wished to publish as soon as possible, and Lady Caroline found it hard to keep up. She begged him to delay going ahead with the printing until she could finish completely re-correcting volume two. This necessitated her having the proofs and manuscript back for the first volume. "We shall get into a serious scrape," she warned him, "if you do not let me have the first two vols. to look over." Errors "hurt the sense" of the book, she said.[83]

Distracted by the editing of *Glenarvon*, Caroline was unprepared when Byron hastily left England on 23 April. Frustration and grief fueled her anger, and she resolved more firmly than ever to intervene on Lady Byron's side. Yet she still loved Byron, and the help she offered Annabella was always tempered by her desire to re-engage Byron's affections. She knew that Byron had been forced to liquidate his personal library to raise funds for his trip. He had departed just minutes ahead of the bailiffs, who seized everything they could find in lieu of the £500 that Byron owed the Dowager Duchess of Devonshire for his extended residency at No. 13 Piccadilly Terrace and many other long standing debts. Caroline wrote to Hobhouse offering to sell some "trinkets & things" worth about £300 if it would redeem some of his trunks. At the same time she stated definitively that in the quarrel between husband and wife, "I differ from you & take her part not his."[84]

On 27 April, as publication neared, she was filled with nervous dread. Hobhouse was visiting Lady Melbourne on that day, and he observed that Caroline seemed "ready to sink."[85] She worried that the novel might embarrass her, and she expected it might be published with little fanfare. Yet she wanted the recognition of her authorship. She wrote to Colburn shortly before publication that she had thought of "an expedient which without vexing my family may excite some attention—when you put this day is published Glenarvon a novel in 3 vols. ? ? ? add some such mark as this ! ! ! will that not attract—or will you like to put in a popular Irish air." The idea that three exclamation marks would sell the book must have amused Colburn, but he grudgingly agreed to print two songs in settings by Isaac Nathan. A last-minute uproar occurred when she discovered that the songs had been left out: "I am quite vex'd at seeing the songs without the music—will you not add the notes—they must positively write 'Farewell' again— it is very incorrectly written. . . . I am disappointed about the songs—those 2 are not pretty without music.[86] No doubt feeling somewhat vexed himself, Colburn quickly printed the music so that it could be inserted in the second volume.

Lady Caroline may have felt that Nathan's music was a selling point for the novel, because the second and final volume of Byron and Nathan's *Hebrew Melodies* had just been published on 18 April. The music was popular already (the first volume had sold well the year before), and Byron's well-publicized departure made sales even better. Nathan spent a great deal of time with Byron in the days just prior to his departure, and Byron gave him £50—an extravagance he could ill afford—and received in turn a package of matzos. Nathan's friendship with Byron was, of course, a factor in Lady Caroline's decision to include his music in her novel.[87]

When *Glenarvon* was published on 9 May 1816 and she held it in her hands, she hardly knew what she felt: "[I]t looks beautiful but made my heart beat!"[88] It had been a bit of a rush job. The epigraph from Dante had been dropped from the third volume.[89] The numbering of the chapters in the third volume was confused.[90] No matter. Caroline was very very proud. She sent advance copies to friends, including the prickly Madame de Staël, for whom she enclosed a letter. Other recipients of complimentary copies included booksellers like Hookham and Coombes, Bess, her copyist Thomasina Webster, the Duke of Wellington, her mother, Hart, John Murray, Lord Henry Brougham, and the Reverend Sydney Smith.

Obviously, Lady Caroline was unprepared for the negative reaction to *Glenarvon.* The day after it was published, messages of outrage began to arrive. Henry Webster called to berate her for unflattering portraits of his brother and mother.[91] Hobhouse threatened to publish some damning letters Caroline had written to Byron. When this message was delivered, "it was received calmly, and great astonishment expressed," according to Lady Melbourne.[92] Caroline's surprise was genuine. She never expected that the novel would reignite the family civil war, but it did. George and Emily again demanded that William separate from his wife. Lady Caroline suspected the Hollands of encouraging the separation and wrote them savagely, "it is my wish that the utmost severity may be shown me by every body."[93]

What was it that so enraged the first readers of *Glenarvon?* To start, it was a kiss-and-tell, or as Byron indelicately put it, a "— and publish" novel.[94] But there was more than that. The story is actually a sort of bildungsroman set in Ireland. It thus involved descriptions of controversial social and political events as factors in the education—meaning, as Byron scholar Peter Graham has noted, the *ruin*— of its main character, Lady Calantha Delaval, daughter of the Duke and Duchess of Altamonte.[95]

Lady Calantha is intended to marry her cousin William, who lives with her at Castle Delaval in Ireland. William, the handsome son of Calantha's widowed aunt, Lady Margaret Buchanan, grows up with Calantha while his mother lives a dissipated life in Naples. Lady Margaret expects William to inherit the Altamonte title and estates by marrying Calantha. However, the Duchess of Altamonte unexpectedly conceives again. A distressed Lady Margaret hurries back from Italy, accompanied by her friend Count Gondimar and lover Count Viviani. The Duchess produces a male heir, Sidney Albert, the Marquis of Delaval, and William's expectations are dashed.

Unable to accept this turn of events, Lady Margaret prods Count Viviani to arrange for the murder of the infant Marquis. The child is strangled in its crib by the assassin La Crusca. The Duchess of Altamonte succumbs to grief and dies. Viviani now becomes a hated reminder of the murder, and Lady Margaret sends him away. William then rebels against his mother and announces he will go to university and not marry. Lady Margaret sends him to England, hoping he will change his mind.

Calantha is cared for by her mother's sister, Mrs. Seymour, who shows "too much indulgence."[96] Impulsive and innocent, Calantha contrasts with Mrs. Seymour's daughters, who are "paragons of propriety."[97] Calantha, whose "motives appeared the very best, but the actions which resulted from them were absurd and exaggerated," soon falls in love with Henry Mowbrey, the Earl of Avondale, a handsome but nonreligious man who is the commander of a regiment of English forces in Ireland.[98] Though she hates "the name of wife," Calantha adores her husband, whose previous amorous conquests make him a man of the world.[99] She goes with him to live at Monteith, the family seat, where she is instantly at odds with her in-laws: "The refinement, the romance, the sentiment she had imbibed, appeared in their eyes assumed and unnatural; her strict opinions, perfectly ridiculous; her enthusiasm, absolute insanity; and the violence of her temper, if contradicted or opposed, the pettishness of a spoiled and wayward child."[100]

Unable to restrain his wife, Lord Avondale unintentionally corrupts her by mocking her naiveté and prudish reserve and encouraging her to read and socialize. She encounters ideas and people she cannot handle, and falls into the clutches of Glenarvon, a brilliant Irish rebel leader whose ancestors include a hero of the battle of Culloden. Glenarvon's family estate has been forfeited to Lord Clarence de Ruthven, who has mysteriously disappeared. Clarence is in fact the charismatic Glenarvon, unrecognized heir to the abbey at Belfont and the priory of St. Alvin. He is a singer and talker of prodigious talent, but he regards his abilities as negligible, preferring to spend his time mesmerizing and then ruining women. Vampirically, he induces erotomania in his victims, who include (beside Calantha) the Italian Fiorabella, who is murdered by her husband after he discovers her affair with Glenarvon, and the Irish maidens Elinor St. Clare and Alice Mac Allain, both of whom die after falling hard for Glenarvon's political radicalism and smoldering, gloomy good looks. (Glenarvon's name, "Clarence de Ruthven," may allude to Lord Grey de Ruthyn, or Ruthin, eight years Byron's senior, who had leased Newstead Abbey while Byron's mother was living elsewhere to economize. Byron spent time with the tenant, shooting and carousing. Sometime in early January 1804, Lord Grey apparently made a sexual advance that disgusted Byron, who returned to Harrow, though he had been very reluctant to go beforehand.[101])

Though he adores Calantha, Glenarvon abandons her, like all his previous lovers, but not before many plans of elopement, expressions of regret, guilty confrontations, and declarations of undying love. If we see *Glenarvon* as the expression of a common childhood fantasy of dying in order to teach everyone else a lesson, then Lady Caroline rehearses the fantasy thrice: Alice's death is a classic case of erotomania, told in a set-piece in the second volume.[102] Elinor St. Clare dies heroically, riding her horse off a cliff in the cause of Irish independence. Lady Calantha lingers and lingers, suffering from neglect because she will not heed Lady Margaret's warning that Glenarvon "unites the malice and petty vices of a woman, to the perfidy and villainy of a man."[103] When Calantha finally dies, Avondale challenges Glenarvon to a duel. Glenarvon refuses, but is provoked into shooting and wounding Avondale.[104] Viviani suddenly reappears to confront Lady Margaret with her guilt for the homicide, and we learn that Glenarvon/Clarence and Viviani are one and the same—and that the heir to the Altamonte estates was not murdered after all; another child, Billy Kendall, was put to death in its place. Zerbellini, a little page boy, turns out to be the lost heir of Altamonte. Glenarvon perversely tries to kill the child at the very moment he is returning him to his rightful place beside the astonished Duke of Altamonte—but fails. La Crusca is sentenced to death for the murder of Billy Kendall. Avondale himself then dies of a broken heart.

That same evening, Glenarvon joins the British squadron off the coast of Holland.[105] He is tormented by spectral visions of those he has destroyed, including Fiorabella, Alice Mac Allain, Lord Avondale, Lady Calantha, and a monstrous hooded monk who draws back his robe to reveal a "bosom gored with deadly wounds" whose black blood pours into the ocean and who chants: "Cursed be the murderer in his last hour!—Hell awaits its victim."[106] Glenarvon goes mad and flings himself into the water. His shipmates pull him out, but he expires on the deck, sinking "with horrid precipitance from gulf to gulf" into the darkness of the pit to which his perfidious actions have condemned him.[107]

In general, Glenarvon appears as a man whose practice and principle always differ. While the Irish rebels work under his leadership toward community ownership, he claims his ancestral lands.[108] He has not only betrayed Calantha, but his country as well, for he abdicates his role as leader of the Independence movement and receives a commission on a British ship of the line. This portrait of Byron is contradictory: beautiful assassin, heroic coward, political leader of no lasting convictions, passionate lover and cold-hearted seducer.

Glenarvon upset people not because of its gothic excesses, but because it appeared to be a *roman à clef*. Still, the handling of the gothic elements probably seemed strange for a woman writer, and their omnipresence made contemporary readers uneasy. Caroline herself told Murray after the publication of *Glenarvon*, "if you knew how sick I am of 'Moments of Gloom'—mysterious personages—care worn brows—marble hearts—and the whole of that which deceived me & many others."[109] But all the real offenses in the novel arise in the scenes describing London society at the end of volume one and throughout volume two, scenes which satirized the houses of Caroline's friends, including Lady Holland, who appeared vividly as the Princess Madagascar, accompanied by a cadaverous sycophant Tremore ("Fremore" after the second edition appeared), who was unmistakably Samuel Rogers.[110] Many readers noticed resemblances between Lady Melbourne and the cruel Lady Margaret, as well as Lady Monteith, although they tastefully avoided stating the obvious. As Byron scholar John Clubbe says, *Glenarvon* captured the "wit and artificial bonhomie" of Whig culture so perfectly that twenty years after *Glenarvon* appeared, friends still called Lady Holland the "Princess Madagascar" behind her back.[111]

Annabella's first reaction to *Glenarvon* was largely positive, though of course she condemned its tendency to blame circumstances for the bad behavior of its heroine. She sat down a week after the novel had appeared and wrote out comments on the character of Calantha, whose creed she described as, "I am thought of—therefore I am." More tellingly, she conceded that the reader might involuntarily give in to Calantha's self-justifications, and that this could lead to adopting her view that Glenarvon embodied the ideals of love and poetry. Without the cosmetic treatment of Calantha's homage, Lady Caroline's villain seemed pitiless, a man whose "rage was impotent in proportion to its impiety."[112] Perhaps it was Caroline's grasp of Byron's character that most impressed Annabella—in any case, she recommended the novel to others, including Lady Melbourne and Mrs. George Lamb. The latter was flabbergasted: "Your opinion of *Glenarvon* is very indulgent," wrote the normally timid Caro George. She ventured to say that in London the book was "more blamed than admired" and tried gently to turn Annabella along the right interpretational path: "I agree with you in the tendency of the moral and the cleverness of many parts," she conceded, "but I cannot forgive her, for the ridicule that she throws at William, by the publishing all their private secrets." She continued, "[h]e is abused for having allowed her to publish it, tho' I believe he was unconscious both of her doing so, and of what the book contained."[113] The party line was that William had been duped. But while others may have perceived him as an object of ridicule in *Glenarvon*, William apparently disagreed.

Not that Lord Avondale escapes censure entirely, for he exhibits an over-indulgent attitude and is described as a ladies' man: "Strong passion, opportunity, and entire liberty of conduct, had, at an early period, thrown him into [beauty's] power." He is charged with a "general laxity of morals" that blinded him to the fact that his bride was pained to hear "she was not the first who had subdued his affections," even when he assured her "that she should be the last."[114] Lady Calantha tells us that the worldly Avondale quickly transforms from "lover" to "master" (another parallel to Calantha's relation with her seducer, Glenarvon) and that he laughs at every "artless or shrewd remark" of his childish pupil.[115] These barbs directed at William, however blunted, glinted clearly for readers like Lady Holland, who interpreted the novel as a "*plaidoyer* against her husband . . . accusing him of having overset her religious and moral (!) principles by teaching her doctrines of impiety." William did not apparently share Lady Holland's belief that the facts stood against Avondale.[116]

No doubt he also realized that Avondale shared certain characteristics with Glenarvon, and vice versa—that the book was, in the end, *fiction*. Indeed, all the characters in the novel are drawn from multiple sources. Mrs. Seymour, for example, is Calantha's aunt, and she has two daughters, like Georgiana, Duchess of Devonshire. But other aspects of Mrs. Seymour's character are drawn from a different aunt—the prickly Lavinia, wife of Caroline's uncle George John Spencer—and from the hated Bess who usurped Georgiana's place. Another character, Lady Elizabeth Mowbrey, stands in relation to her brother Lord Avondale as Emily Lamb to her brother William. And yet the name "Elizabeth" recalls both the hated Bess Foster and Lady Melbourne—whose maiden name was Elizabeth Milbanke, and whose grandmother had been named "Delavel."

Many originals may constitute one character, and several characters may stem from one original. Glenarvon is both de Ruthven and Viviani. Zerbellini is also Sidney Albert. The novel's heroine, Calantha, is only one of several characters with whom Lady Caroline identified. Named after the protagonist of John Ford's *The Broken Heart* (1633), Calantha is no simple self-portrait, for she is never violent. Rather, she reflects Caroline's fear of failing to fulfill her potential.[117] Other reflections of Caroline are found in Alice Mac Allain, who becomes pregnant by Glenarvon and begs in vain for his help, and in the little page-boy, Zerbellini. Lady Caroline's breeches-roles often featured a page's outfit of hussar jacket, feathered cap and silver buttons, and she was sometimes called "Cherubina." Elinor St. Clare, with her penchant for playing the harp, writing songs, and dressing like a man, also embodies aspects of Caroline.

Such complex understanding of fictional resources missed most readers. Sitting in drawing rooms with the novel before them, they shook their heads and laughed or cringed, depending upon who was implicated in the feminine whirl of what Byron dubbed the "gynocracy." In Calantha's words we may read the prophecy of Caroline's fall: "She heard folly censured till she took it to be criminal; but crime she saw tolerated if well concealed."[118] Many times, the novel dramatizes her refusal to learn "to comprehend the language of hypocrisy and deceit."[119] A highly unflattering mirror had been held up to this English aristocracy.

Glenarvon was purchased as a *roman à clef,* and most readers wrote "keys" to the novel on its endpapers. Lady Holland identified Caroline's cousin Harryo as Mrs. Seymour's daughter Sophia because she exhibited "a passion for working fine embroidery." The traitorous Lady Oxford, who had encouraged Byron to write so cruelly to Caroline was fictionalized (according to Lady Holland) as the character Lady Mandeville. Lady Holland also believed that a character named William Buchanan was based upon her own son, Sir Godfrey Vassal Webster, presumably because of the physical description: "His hands were decorated with rings, and a gold chain and half-concealed picture hung round his neck: his height, his mustachios, the hussar trappings of his horse, the high colour in his cheek, and his dark flowing locks, gave an air of savage wildness to his countenance and figure, which much delighted Calantha."[120] Naturally, Lady Holland hated the Princess Madagascar, because "every ridicule, folly and infirmity (my not being able from malady to move about much) is portrayed." No doubt upset, she commented temperately, "The work is a strange *farrago,"* and confined herself to sympathizing with the *real* victims: "I am sorry to see the Melbourne family so miserable about it. Lady Cowper is really frightened and depressed far beyond what is necessary."[121] It does seem at times as though *Glenarvon* evoked a sort of hysteria among those who believed they had glimpsed their own caricatures.

Robert Wilmot was an acquaintance of Lady Byron's, and he wrote to her on 17 May 1816 with his own attributions:

> Of course Lady C & W L you will easily recognise. Miss Monmouth perhaps *you do not know*, but I do, & can assure you that she is a most delightful person [he means Lady Byron herself]. Lady Mandeville is Lady Oxford—P of Madagascar, Lady H . . . as to the other characters, I much question their being portraits, but rather compounds . . . there are traits in Lady Margaret meant for your dear Aunt [Lady Melbourne]. Some say that Buchanan is Sir G Webster, others that Lady Augusta is Lady Jersey, others that Lady Margaret is the present D[uchess] of D[evonshire]. Mrs. Seymour is I should think compounded of parts of the character of the late Duchess & Lady Bessborough.[122]

As we have seen, however, confidence about the identities behind the characters is quickly undermined. Mrs. Seymour is often described as a version of the sisters,

Georgiana and Harriet. Yet Mabell, Countess of Airlie, tells us that Lady Melbourne is "probably represented under the name of Mrs. Seymour."[123] Marjorie Villiers tells us, at the same time, that Lady Margaret is the Duchess of Devonshire.[124] And Paston and Quennell are confident that Lady Melbourne is represented in the novel by the character of Lady Monteith.[125] Often, readers were led to conclude they knew who a particular character must be when they believed they recognized some element in the plot connected with that person. As we shall see, the story of Zerbellini was read later as corroboration of the story that Hartington had really been Lady Elizabeth Foster's child. This naturally meant equating the devious Lady Margaret with Georgiana, Duchess of Devonshire—though that makes little sense.[126]

If she had hoped that the novel would provide relief from social ostracism, Lady Caroline had totally miscalculated. Hobhouse wrote Byron two weeks after *Glenarvon*'s publication to say, "this time she has knocked herself up—the Greys the Jerseys the Lansdownes and of course the Princess of Madagascar have done with her."[127] And shortly thereafter Hobhouse commented again: "*Glenarvon* has done nothing but render the little vicious author more odious if possible than ever."[128] Of course, Hobhouse was also upset because *Glenarvon* had completely eclipsed the publication of his own *Letters,* which had hardly sold a dozen copies when Caroline's novel had sold out.[129] Without intending to, she had inflicted damage on others, like Lady Holland, whose connection to the Greys, Jerseys, and Lansdownes suffered because she was presumed to have approved Caroline's fictionalization of their lives, even though she herself was lampooned in the novel.[130]

Lady Caroline's interference in the designs of the reigning "gynocrats" had provoked their formidable ire. Even Annabella—who appreciated Caroline's dissection of Whig hypocrisy—shuddered at the consequence of putting it into print. In a letter to her mother, Lady Noel, dated within a few weeks of *Glenarvon*'s appearance, she wrote: "Lady C Lamb was at Anglesea house the other night, and nobody spoke to her. I cannot help pitying her, for She must See around & *near* her so many whose Hypocrisy only has Secured them from Similar Scorn."[131] In *Glenarvon,* Lady Caroline "shrewdly and accurately captures Byron's special blend of liberal politics and conservative social attitudes,"[132] as Peter Graham has said. Unambitious William found it entertaining, but *Glenarvon*'s politics outraged Lady Melbourne and Emily Cowper, who feared it would damage William's political career. It did him no good with the conservative elements of the British power structure, though his mother and sister eventually accomplished their ambitions for him, despite William's disinclination. His political views were not strongly held, and his contemporaries later expressed puzzlement when he agreed in 1834 to become Prime Minister. Political ambition lay elsewhere in the Lamb household.

Lady Melbourne acknowledged to Hobhouse how painful the novel was for her: "I was so disgusted with the spirit in which it was written that after reading the first 20 pages, I declared I would read no more, and tho' of course I have heard a great deal from others I am still very ignorant of its contents."[133] Lady Melbourne, the mistress of every situation, found herself frustrated. She supported Hobhouse's desire to punish Lady Caroline by publishing letters that would tend to exculpate Byron and incriminate her, but warned, "it is nearly impossible for anyone to resist her arts, and it has required 7 or 8 years to make *me* perfect in them. . . ."[134] This is the statement of a woman who has tried mightily to pry her son away from his wife and failed.

Acknowledgement of Caroline's intractable hold on William coincides with a serious decline in Lady Melbourne's health. The once-indomitable doyenne of the gynocracy now wrote to niece Annabella that she had no "courage" to read *Glenarvon* to its conclusion: "I never can excuse the falsehoods she tells about Willm & ye acct she gives of a society in which she had lived from her Childhood. She knew them perfectly, unfortunately they did not know her."[135] This was Lady Melbourne's society, of course, which relied upon secrecy and subterfuge. What exactly were the "falsehoods" about this society of which Lady Caroline's knowledge was "perfect," and in which Lady Melbourne had expected William to succeed by marrying Caroline? The problem was not the falseness of the portrait, but rather its truth. Pettiness rather than justice characterized the response to *Glenarvon.* For example, Lady Melbourne's dislike of Annabella became mixed up in the family reaction. Lady Byron had sent a letter to Lady Melbourne insensitively praising the book and talking of "disclosures" that it had made or might cause.[136] No doubt Lady Melbourne was extremely upset at the suggestion that her daughter-in-law's indiscreet novel might lead to discovery of certain skeletons in her own closet. Worse, when she accused Lady Caroline of having already started writing a second novel, her daughter-in-law became defiant: "You say I have written another novel—I will not deny it."[137]

Caroline's future depended once again upon whether William would stand by her. And after the initial shock, it appeared he would. As she wrote later to Granville Leveson-Gower: "You should see my husband, who knows everything . . . and who says that he could not in good honour give me up."[138] Indeed, attacks on his wife had the reverse effect from that intended by his sister and mother. "For four years Lady Cowper and Lady Melbourne have supported Lord Byron to the annoyance of William," Lady Caroline told Granville, "recollect that

Lady Holland behaved to William, as he thought, contemptibly."[139] This context makes Caroline's earlier avoidance of a separation less surprising. She and William were really much closer than anyone thought, and he partly shared her view of his family.

Still, there were times when she was terrified by what she had done and begged for mercy from her in-laws, especially the dangerous Emily, to whom she wrote abjectly: "My Dearest Emily all I ask you is to write to Lord & Lady M[elbourne] say to them I dare not ask them to forgive me—but bid them burn those horrid letters . . . send my Pages away do all you will only let them know my heart is not quite hardened & I am miserable at having been so wicked—pray obtain their pardon & God Bless you."[140] William's support, however, made such moments less frequent.

On 5 June 1816, almost a month after *Glenarvon*'s publication, Hobhouse visited Lady Melbourne and observed William defending his wife. Hobhouse knew the Lamb family desired a separation, but Caroline, he said, "talks big of the rights of English women and swears she will not go."[141] George Lamb had tried to force her out by saying he would not enter Melbourne House so long as she was there, nor would he permit Caro George to do so. Confident in her support from William, Caroline responded sharply that since George "is a favourite I am not settle it therefore as you will amongst you amicably or no—War or peace only do not let masks of kindness be worn while daggers are stuck in the back." She charged accurately that the Lambs seemed not to care about William's feelings: "[E]ven if you succeed as no doubt you will in making him decide to live away from me for the sake of quiet & yr company you can never Hope to enjoy peace yourself for you do not deserve it ."[142]

William's support allowed her to respond confidently to threats from all quarters. When Hobhouse hinted again that Byron might retaliate for *Glenarvon,* Lady Caroline fired one of her trademark salvos of pique: "[H]ad I chosen to be ill natured," she told him, "God knows without deviating from truth . . . I had plenty of means." She assured Hobhouse that *Glenarvon* "may be stupid may be unseemly for me to write may be any thing you please but is assuredly any thing but malevolent." She dared Byron to retort: "[L]et him—tell him to publish all my letters let him use all his perfidies all his misrepresentations to my ruin it is what I wish what I ask . . . & if I fall he at least shall fall with me." She even mocked Hobhouse for hypocritically laughing over her portrait of the Princess of Madagascar and then going to "fawn at Holland House."[143]

Hobhouse remained silent, but it did no good. He had provoked her, and, still confident of William's support, she threw daggers:

[L]et him but publish the tenth part of a single line in any letter I ever wrote him—
let him but write verses or books against me—or any of you—or Lady Holland—&
if I die for it I vow to God I will on the instant publish not only all his—but the whole
exact journal which I have kept of my acquaintance with him—& his conduct during
these four last years . . . I only wait even for a Review & if malice be in it or detraction
if any personal application be given, Lady Holland & her minions shall have reason
to rue the hour they get it done—truth must prevail at last—& though my novel may
have made me foes—I thank God I have friends & spirit left.[144]

Caroline's threat to publish Byron's letters was not idle. She had sent a note to
John Murray indicating that she was prepared, "to publish a work—250 letters
from a young Venetian nobleman—addrest to a very absurd English Lady—they
are beautiful & might serve all other noblemen."[145] Hobhouse responded tersely
that he was merely acting properly in his role as Lord Byron's associate.

After *Glenarvon*'s publication William excused himself from calling upon
Lord and Lady Holland, on the grounds of "embarrassment" over the "wanton
and unjustifiable" character assassination in *Glenarvon:* "I did not write, because
what could I say? I could only exculpate myself from any previous knowledge,
the effect of which must be to throw a heavier load upon the offending party."[146]
William hated to be noticed at all, much less pitied, and he also fundamentally
agreed with his wife's portrayal of the Hollands in the novel. He would never
apologize to people he disliked. He knew he must pretend to have known nothing
of the novel before its publication, but he could not emphasize this without
undermining his wife's position. Caroline tried to protect William by telling Lord
Holland that she had published *Glenarvon* "in utter defiance as a woman without
his knowing anything of it."[147]

But William knew *Glenarvon* existed long before it was published, and
undoubtedly encouraged his wife's writing career. Only for the sake of deflecting
family outrage did he profess ignorance—especially to his mother—while still
defending the author. In the chaos of the week following the initial publication of
the novel, he had written to Henry Colburn from Whitehall to say his wife had
published "without any consultation with her friends upon the subject" and that,
in view of the furor, "there shall be published no second edition." He counted on
Colburn's "knowledge of the world" to make him concur.[148] He never said that
he himself was ignorant of his wife's plans to publish—only that her *friends* were,
or that if confronted he would be forced to "exculpate" himself from previous
knowledge. By degrees, he softened his account to the family. Within two weeks

after the novel's publication he had admitted he knew of it, but said that Caroline had never shown him the offensive parts.[149]

William also quietly agreed to further editions, despite the outcry. Within days of his request to Colburn to print no more, Lady Caroline wrote to her publisher, "I am happy to say that I have obtained leave to publish a second Edition which will be greatly improved without delaying the Printer. I have also written a most beautiful preface." She wanted her name printed on the title page this time, and she asked for an immediate reply "by the Bearer," requesting that Colburn give her £50. She demanded to see the proofs of the next edition: "I will learn all the marks to which the Printers are used . . . I see so many errors I corrected last time." She sent the preface and said she would expect him that evening or the next day. She also told Colburn to "get rid of the 1st Edition as quick as possible that I may correct some very ridiculous mistakes in the second."[150] Perhaps William underestimated the scandal *Glenarvon* would cause. The publication of a second and then a third edition, however, he could have prevented. Whether he colluded directly in this venture, or only looked the other way as it developed, he was implicated.

The cries of *Glenarvon*'s Irish rebels for the "rights of man" certainly reflected William's views, but also hurt his political future, a future that now took another blow, for on 7 July Sheridan died. Lady Bessborough went to visit him on his deathbed. Samuel Rogers was there and overheard Sheridan tell her he would appear to her after death: "[M]y eyes will look up to the coffin-lid as brightly as ever."[151] "But why?" Harriet asked, bewildered, and Sheridan replied, echoing the ghost in *Hamlet:* "Because I am resolved you shall remember me."[152] Sheridan's end was a bad one that his friends could have ameliorated.

As Murray was preparing the third canto of Byron's *Childe Harold* for the press, he allowed Lady Caroline to read an advance copy: "Upon the whole it seemed full of the same beauties & faults as the first part. Beautiful writing—no story—some things in bad taste, and too much about himself."[153] But once she looked more closely, Lady Caroline realized that the poem was quite different—much more witty. She was jealous. "Be not dazzled by his success—be not thrown into wild delight because his genius has shone forth," she warned Murray, reminding him that "self is the sole inspirer of [Byron's] genius." And, as if the poem threatened a personal attack upon her, she warned that if Byron "ever rises more though I may die or ruin myself in the attempt, I will prove no contemptible enemy. Truth and fearlessness can stand even against genius unsupported by those qualities."[154]

So she told herself as she fought isolation. She went out in public, though she was shaken by the uproar her mere appearance caused when she tried to attend a production of *Don Giovanni*. She arrived at the Opera House dressed in white and was announced as "Lady Caroline Lamb," to which some footman said, "Sooner Lady Caroline *Wolf*." This brought rejoinders, and a half-hearted brawl got under way. Two competing rack-chair carriers then tried to get her to hire them to spirit her away from the mêlée. While she was explaining that she wished to go *into* not *away from* the Opera House, she saw that her dog had trailed her carriage all the way from Whitehall. Bedraggled and mud-caked, it looked like a rat. It was on the point of being attacked when she came to its defense and cancelled her visit to the opera.[155]

She wrote of all this in artificially high spirits to John Murray, who had now become one of her most important correspondents, a friend to whom she would pour out her emotions. Murray could give her news of Byron and show her advance copies of his work, and some day she hoped he would publish her work. Beyond this, she genuinely liked him: "Your room speaks of [Byron] in every part of it," she wrote, "& I never see you without pain—yet is it not strange it seems to me most unpleasant if I pass any length of time without seeing you." She admired his loyalty to Byron, and she knew that he was prodigiously patient with her: "I feel yr kindness with the utmost gratitude & never never shall forget to name you among my real friends."[156] This was one promise she kept, though so many others would be broken.

Nor did she seem to blame Murray for declining to publish *Glenarvon*. Perhaps she even recognized that he had made a good business decision. Lady Caroline had put Byron into fiction by means of a story too gothically dark and yet too socially engaged. It was a success, but not because of its qualities as fiction. This novel was an exorcism and an amusement, but it was also a down payment on what she hoped would be a writer's career.

The Music of Glenarvon

1816, continued

What—& who—the devil is "Glenarvon"?

—Lord Byron[1]

*T*he reviews arrived. The *New Monthly Magazine* printed a short positive notice that praised *Glenarvon* as a history "ably and vigorously drawn" of Byron's crimes, and therefore "a fearful beacon to warn the young and inexperienced against the danger of talents unsanctified by a sense of duty."[2] More typically, the *British Critic* called *Glenarvon* "one continuous series of vice and misery" that endangered innocent readers with "scenes of seduction and adultery." The reviewer found Glenarvon himself an appalling figure, especially since he was presented as "the idol of the female heart," and treated the book as representing the "morals of Paris and Vienna," terrible evidence of "an influx of foreign profligacy," written by an author who seemed "to glory in her guilt."[3] The *Theatrical Inquisitor* acknowledged Lady Caroline's "animated style, brilliance of imagery," and her "skillful delineation of gloomy and mysterious character," but concluded that reading *Glenarvon* was nonetheless a "tiresome and revolting task" because the author was intent on exacting revenge upon "the society from which she has been excluded." Pointing specifically at the Princess of Madagascar, the reviewer accused Caroline of assassinating Lady Holland's character, and concluded by rating *Glenarvon* as essentially a pornographic work, like John Cleland's *Fanny Hill* though without the "gross indecency."[4]

With similar exaggeration, the *British Lady's Magazine* claimed never to have encountered "a more senseless farrago of extravagance . . . than this wretched production," which it found "disgusting, immoral, and tawdry" and worse, "farcical." Hoping to damn the author with her own words, the reviewer printed a long extract from Glenarvon's death scene on shipboard, concluding rather lamely that the novel was "the silliest production in the world." Acknowledging that the song lyrics in *Glenarvon* possessed "both nature and feeling," the review described them as wasted effort: mere "embroidery upon a blanket."[5] The *Monthly Review* could not decide whether *Glenarvon* was romance or biography: "[I]t is of the *doubtful gender,* though a feminine production," and (of course) "wearisome."[6] The *Augustan Review* chimed in: "There is a constant straining at *effect,*" even though the novel showed "indications of genius" and "gleams of tenderness and fancy."[7] Caroline was so desperate to have her novel treated as fiction, not memoir, that she actually told Murray she was pleased by the notice in the *Augustan Review:* "I like it, because it takes the thing fairly, and not as real characters.[8] Trying hard to put a good face on bad reviews, Caroline wrote Colburn to buck up his spirits. No doubt he was placated by brisk sales and needed little encouragement to continue exposing his author to public humiliation.[9]

To anyone who would listen, Caroline pointed out that the novel clearly condemns "miserable, guilty Calantha."[10] But she also set about revising Glenarvon: "I am doing every thing I can to stop the further mischief," she told Lady Melbourne. "They have written to me today to say that the 1500 copies are sold & a new Edition is wanted—I will either refuse it or make every alteration suggested—at all events I will leave out any thing obnoxious. you say I have written another novel—I will not deny it—but I have burnt it are you satisfied or do you still accuse me of acting the part of a Grub Str[eet] Author."[11] Lady Melbourne's reply goes unrecorded, but Caroline's revisions grew extensive as she sought to refute her critics. She changed the characterizations of Glenarvon and Calantha, dropped passages that supporters of Lady Holland and Samuel Rogers had complained about, and reduced the gothic elements. Glenarvon grew less Satanic, while Calantha became a Catholic convert. Their relationship changed from searingly sexual to primarily Platonic. Lord Avondale was made more noble and courageous; he also more dramatically repents that he did not seize control of his wife. Lady Caroline also did a great deal of sentence-level revision to tighten and sharpen the prose.[12]

As she tried to pacify her critics, she also defended herself. She refuted the charge that *Glenarvon* was immoral or indecent. Perhaps some scenes were ill-drawn and risqué, "but I could find you many such in all those novels which are looked up to as models," she retorted, alluding to provocative episodes in *Clarissa, Pamela, Joseph Andrews,* and *Tom Jones,* as well as the works of Sidney Biddulph, Lady Morgan, Jean-Jacques Rousseau, and Madame de Staël.[13] She took her defense public in a preface composed for the second edition:

> When we cast a glance around us upon the frailty of human nature, and the errors and follies of the world, we must, it is to be feared, confess that malignity, had malignity guided the pen, might, without departing from truth, or in the slightest degree infringing the sacred confidence of friendship, have found it easy to expose foibles far more ridiculous, and to cast aspersions far more ill natured and injurious . . . nor, on the other hand, is the shaft of satire in any one instance directed against the weak, the fallen, or the defenceless.[14]

Caroline was right. Contemporary reviewers treated *Glenarvon* with excessive harshness because they felt irritated with the author—often on someone else's behalf. The irritation persisted, which explains many twentieth-century condemnations of the novel as "a deplorable production"[15] that is "outrageous" and "badly written."[16] But if she writes badly and her story is the "silliest production in the world," how did she manage to satirize so many people so hilariously?

A more tempered view ought to be taken of Caroline's novel—her first, lest we forget. As scholar and historian John Clubbe says, the good things about *Glenarvon*—its emotional intensity and enthusiasm—are also its failings: its sentimentality, melodrama, and tendency to "slide into bathos." The novel does indeed strain for effects, and the characters of *Glenarvon* are insufficiently motivated for their extravagant behavior, acting in a "postured manner."[17] But we should remember that *Glenarvon* was meant not to *reproduce life* but to *render emotion.* Indeed, Lady Caroline had criticized feminist and historical novelist pioneer Maria Edgeworth for painting her characters "like the Dutch school true to life" instead of showing some spark of "genius,"[18] by which she meant the literary style of Ann Radcliffe.

Little acknowledgement has been made of Caroline's debt to her literary foremothers, like gothic novelist Radcliffe. Another obvious influence was her friend Lady Morgan (then Sydney Owenson) who had published *St. Clair, or the Heiress of Desmond* (1803) and *The Wild Irish Girl* (1806), her most famous novel, which focused on music and national identity. Glorvina O'Melville, the heroine of *The Wild Irish Girl,* first appears in the castle chapel playing the harp for her father and the chaplain, while the male protagonist spies upon her. Lady Caroline introduces Elinor St. Clare in *Glenarvon* in the same manner. Like Lady Morgan's heroines, the women of *Glenarvon* are mysterious, intelligent, and passionate about politics. Caroline also emulated Lady Morgan by incorporating Irish myth and legend into the setting of her novel.

Yet Maria Edgeworth, too, influenced *Glenarvon.* For example, the first song that appears in the novel is the "Pillalu," a "song of sorrow" chanted by the "tenants and peasantry" over the body of what they believe is the son of the local laird, the Duke of Delaval:

Oh loudly sing the Pillalu,
    And many a tear of sorrow shed;
Och orro, orro, Olalu!
    Mourn, for the master's child is dead.[19]

Lady Caroline might have observed an Irish funeral procession herself, but Maria Edgeworth's *Castle Rackrent* (1800) is the most likely source, with its Irish lamentation over the dead—called "Whillaluh," "Ullaloo," or "Gol."[20]

Music plays a huge role in *Glenarvon.* In fact, the emergence of the so-called national airs fad heavily influenced its narrative. Here, again, one finds the influence of Lady Morgan, for *The Wild Irish Girl* was the first "national tale" of the period written in novel form. Lady Morgan had lived with a father who had been "hissed off the stage for his Gaelic 'howls'" and guttural chants.[21] Lady Morgan published two of her father's songs, then persuaded a London publisher named Preston to bring out a collection of Irish melodies in 1805. This important work influenced Thomas Moore in the composition of his own more famous *Irish Melodies,* which in turn stimulated the national song fad that led Isaac Nathan to compose, and Byron to write, the *Hebrew Melodies.*

Lady Caroline wrote fourteen lyrics for *Glenarvon,* two with actual musical arrangements. The first that appears with music (by Isaac Nathan) was "Waters of Elle," set to a traditional French folk song. Two years later he printed it as sheet music.[22] The other song that was printed with musical accompaniment was "Farewell," sung by Glenarvon as he is about to make Lady Calantha his next victim. Though she has been warned by Elinor, Calantha falls under Glenarvon's spell when she hears his beautiful voice singing "Farewell." As Caroline well knew, Byron was a master of "come-hither good-byes": "Farewell / Ah! frown not thus—nor turn from me / . . . I wish thee not to share my grief." The second and third stanzas repeat:

> "Farewell."
> Come give thy hand, what though we part,
> Thy name is fixed, within my heart;
> I shall not change, nor break the vow
> I made before and plight thee now;
> For since thou may'st not live for me,
> 'Tis sweeter far to die for thee.

> "Farewell."
> Thou'lt think of me when I am gone,
> None shall undo, what I have done;
> Yet even thy love I would resign
> To save thee from remorse like mine;
> Thy tears shall fall upon my grave.
> They still may bless—they cannot save.[23]

Once again, Caroline cribs from Byron. Her "Come give thy hand, what though we part, / Thy name is fixed, within my heart" echoes Byron's "Maid of Athens, ere we part, / Give oh give me back my heart." Byron writes, "Maid of Athens, I am gone; / Think of me, sweet! when alone," and Caroline echoes, "Thou'lt think of me when I am gone, / None shall undo, what I have done."[24]

Song follows song in *Glenarvon*. Immediately after hearing the "Farewell" song, Calantha "turned in haste, and from above beheld a young man. Ah no— it was St. Clara."[25] The cross-dressing Elinor St. Clare, Glenarvon's previous mistress and partner in the Irish rebellion, also sings for Calantha. It is a song Caroline had drafted in Ireland in 1812 and sent to John Murray in 1813,[26] and it too echoes Byron's "Maid of Athens."

> By that smile which made me blest
> And left me soon the wretch you see—
> By that heart I once possest,
> Which now, they say, is given to thee—
> By St. Clara's wrongs and woes—
> Trust not young Glenarvon's vows.
>
> . . . .

> Each brighter, kinder hope forsaking,
>
> Bereft of all that made life dear;
>
> My health impaired, my spirit breaking,
>
> Yet still too proud to shed one tear:
>
> O! lady, by my wrongs and woes,
>
> Trust not young Glenarvon's vows.[27]

Byron writes, "By Love's alternate joy and woe," and Caroline echoes, "O! lady, by my wrongs and woes." Perhaps these echoes of his own verse contributed to the opinion Byron expressed later that Lady Caroline "used to write pretty songs, and certainly has talent."[28] The songs of *Glenarvon* were widely acknowledged to have merit apart from the narrative. Henry Colburn would later print a slim volume titled *Verses from Glenarvon* (1819).[29]

    Glenarvon is, so far as I know, the only novel of this period printed with music. Not even Nathan's wife's novels have music in them.[30] Seven of the fourteen songs in *Glenarvon* are sung by Elinor St. Clare (also known as St. Clara), who accompanies herself on the harp, an instrument Caroline loved. Caroline identified strongly with St. Clara, the doomed rebel whose voice dominates the second half of the narrative. Elinor's masculine clothes and horsemanship mirror Lady Caroline's own predilections for riding and writing like a man. The last song of the novel is sung by St. Clara just before she plunges to her political martyrdom in the sea. Each stanza ends, "Erin go Brah!"[31]

    Initially mystified, Byron apparently read and enjoyed *Glenarvon* as a tribute to his power. He wrote on 29 July 1816 to Samuel Rogers mocking Caroline as "furious Sappho,"[32] but he was gratified as much as bothered by her *jejune* literary effort, and even suggested how it might have been improved: "It seems to me that, if the authoress had written the *truth,* and nothing but the truth—the whole truth—the romance would not only have been more *romantic,* but more entertaining."[33] Byron's verdict that the novel was insufficiently *true* did not prevent its recurring in his conversation and letters:

> I read the 'Christabel,'
>
> Very well:
>
> I read the 'Missionary';
>
> Pretty—very:
>
> . . . .
>
> I read 'Glenarvon,' too, by Caro. Lamb—
>
> God damn!"[34]

On reflection, however, Byron found the novel reminded him of Caroline's forgeries. She had printed one letter of Byron's in the novel,[35] and there are many other passages that belie his protest that "the picture can't be good—I did not sit long enough."[36] Claire Clairemont, Byron's spurned lover, told him: "Some of the speeches in [*Glenarvon*] are yours—I am sure they are; the very impertinent way of looking in a person's face who loves you, and telling them you are very tired and wish they'd go."[37] It is probable that many passages in *Glenarvon* are based upon Byron's conversation or upon his (subsequently destroyed) letters.

Lady Caroline's first novel had appropriated Byron in fiction, and done so in a unique and creative way. Proof of this came in that sincerest form of flattery, imitation. Elizabeth Thomas, the author of *Falconberg*, rushed into print with a satire of *Glenarvon* titled *Purity of Heart, or the Ancient Costume, a tale, in one Volume, addressed to the author of Glenarvon. By an old wife of twenty years*, in which the main character is named "Calantha Limb." Mrs. Thomas's preface justified her attack by noting *Glenarvon*'s "horrible tendency, its dangerous and perverting sophistry; its abominable indecency and profaneness."[38]

News of *Purity of Heart*'s publication reached Lady Caroline through Henry Colburn, and it gave her some moments of anxiety, which subsided as soon as Caroline had the book in hand in mid-October 1816.[39] She wrote Colburn: "I feel quite relieved. Before a person attempts to turn another into ridicule as is stated in the preface they ought to know how, & the Author of purity of heart has less idea even of common humour—& liveliness than any one I ever met with—. . . better to take no notice whatever of it." And she went on to say that attacks like this one were so "vulgar and illbred" that they had actually "done me good," though she admitted that the verses at the beginnings of the chapters of *Purity of Heart* were rather good and asked Colburn if he might find out who had written them: "The imitation of the Poets is very good but like all else in these times too long—wit & irony should be short and cutting."[40]

The publication of *Purity of Heart* was a culmination—almost an anti-climax—to the attacks that criticized her novel for its immorality and viciousness. She had learned some hard lessons and reflected upon her shortcomings:

> [I]nstead of attacking Lady Calantha Limb where she is vulnerable they try by making her vulgar & mad to raise a laugh—but before they make the attempt at ridiculing an adversary they should measure their own strength & his—to compare little to great, it is like burning Buonaparte on a pitchfork at Sadler's Wells—he lived to make them tremble—& they now only admire him too much—

. . . When you want to crush an enemy treat him with respect—be afraid the villifying him only raises him.[41]

Of course, it was not the journal reviews nor Mrs. Thomas's sanctimonious scoldings that interested Caroline ultimately.

It was Byron's review she most wanted—and feared: "Have you ever heard what *he* said to *Glenarvon*—I burn to know," she asked Murray.[42] And though Byron never told her directly, he did communicate with Murray a year later, after he saw a review of *Glenarvon,* embellished "with the account of her scratching attempt at *Canicide* (at Lady Heathcote's). . . ."[43] And in August 1817, he became aware that an Italian translation of *Glenarvon* was in press. The local censor refused to let it be printed without Byron's permission. Byron responded that he would "never prevent or oppose the publication of *any* book in *any* language—on my own private account." He encouraged the translator and publisher to proceed: "You may say this with my compliments to the Author," he told Murray.[44] If he had wished, as he claimed, to pay Lady Caroline back for her many offenses, this would have been the moment. Instead, he gave the Italian translation to Teresa Guiccioli, who was reading it in February of 1820. She appears to have written in some consternation over the behavior of Calantha. He replied, "Your little head is heated now by that damned novel—the author of which has been—in every country and at all times—my evil Genius."[45] Undoubtedly, the book gratified Byron's ego.

But *Glenarvon* also showed that Caroline could harm Byron, and when he heard that she had tried to speak with Augusta, he became upset and told his half-sister once again that Caroline was a "seventy times convicted liar."[46] He was the more upset because Annabella herself had come to London expressly to see Augusta. He rightly suspected female intrigue, for Annabella too was upset about *Glenarvon.* It seemed the novel had stirred some sentiments in Byron's favor. Nervously, Caroline tried to arrange a meeting, but Caro George's pronouncements on *Glenarvon* had resolved Annabella not to see Lady Caroline again. The effect upon the battered author's nerves was not positive. "I heard that you were in Town," she wrote Annabella, "and I would have called but that I fear'd you might not like to see me otherwise I think you would have written. . . . pray tell me if there is anything on Earth I can do would please you." Using Caro George to bargain for a meeting, Caroline alluded in this letter to the bad relationship between George Lamb and his wife, which had resulted in her leaving town in the company of Lord Brougham. She urged Annabella not to "believe any unkind report you may hear of Caro—but indeed I think you might be of some little use at this time and it is chiefly on that account I should like to see you." Annabella did not take this bait, but replied that a meeting at this time would be unwise.[47]

Caroline wrote Annabella the next day to reveal the deeper cause for her anxiety. She worried that Annabella had forgiven Augusta:

> William will call on you & I will not—but let me hope that at some future period you will of yourself see me—I shall never speak or allude to any subject that is past & indeed I think you may have confidence in me in this respect—Yet to you before whom I opened my whole heart so entirely & for whom I broke so solemn an engagement I must yet relieve myself from one painful doubt—they say you live almost wholly with Mrs Leigh—it astonished me & William—yet promise me—that even if your better judgment—kindness—or any further investigation have altered your opinion of her entirely—promise me to open my eyes also—to say to me "You were deceived—he deceived you—& I know it["]—for that secret rests on my heart & makes me miserable & I would give any thing never never to have heard or thought it. . . .[48]

Augusta had acted in a way that made Caroline suspect Annabella had talked. "Mrs Leigh's manner to me is that of hatred," Caroline fretted, and though she was quick to say she did not believe Annabella had unmasked her, she could think of no other reason that Byron's half-sister would "thus look on me no not if I were black with every sin—for how should she judge me. . . ." And beneath this layer of anxiety stirred another, buried deep in her childhood: that Caro George was working her wiles on naïve Annabella while Lady Caroline risked Byron's discovering she had allied herself with his wife. Byron sensed these machinations and feared his wife would prevent him from seeing his child, damage his reputation, and (incidentally) hurt his book sales. All this must be born in mind when we read Byron's expressions of hatred toward Caroline in his correspondence with Augusta after his departure in 1816. He dramatized that hatred to reinforce the wall of silence that he wished to maintain between his half-sister and his former mistress: "Such a monster as that *has no sex,* and should live no longer."[49]

Unable to do much else, Lady Caroline stayed in anxious contact with Murray: "Write to me, I entreat you . . . tell me all you know of him—& any news besides." She and William had sold Murray a horse that had gone lame, perhaps because of being ridden hard. Regardless, they offered to return Murray's £60, and Caroline assured him "it is going to be sold to a Lady who knows all about it & its lameness so Have no more regrets on that head."[50] During October and

November, she stayed at Brocket writing and tending to the household. She posted letters regularly to her mother-in-law, trying to rebuild their relationship with chatty missives about the wine cellars, servants, and the health of a friend who was recuperating at the estate. She told Lady Melbourne that some horses had gotten into the pastures when the gates were left open and chased nine-year-old Augustus's pony "round the Park twice," and she sent her a recipe for Irish-style potatoes: "take the tatoes & cleene the earth off of em & put them in cold not in hot water & let them simmer till ye've nothing in life to do—that is from early morning until noon." She also commiserated with her mother in law over Caro George, who had gone off with Lord Brougham (an accomplished lawyer and co-founder of the *Edinburgh Review*) out of pique, though the squall had passed.[51]

Still curious who the author of *Purity of Heart* was, she wrote Murray, sending him a copy and a critique: "The authoress, actuated by a holy zeal, says in her preface that she is resolved to turn me into ridicule. She chooses an easy task—too easy, I fear—yet fails, and makes a most blundering business. Wit's razor's edge she has not, but a most unkind tongue to make up for it."[52] She also wrote to the editor of the *New Monthly Magazine* asking him to quash an uncomplimentary "portrait . . . and memoir about her."[53] She was the subject of numerous newspaper articles, all pandering to the public's appetite for scandal: "The *Morning Chronicle* disgusts me."[54]

In late September, Augustus's problems took center stage. Caroline confessed she felt "almost heart broken about Augustus I really am so dispirited I scarce know what to do he has had 4 attacks today 2 very very severe ones—& it is only the 4th day—he is to take one of Evans powders tonight as Mr Lucas says he should at all events give him a cleaning dose—& the moment the 3 are taken he goes to Brighton & if Wm can spare me I shall go too.[55] Caroline gave to "Moome" the task of keeping an accurate record of Augustus's epileptic seizures.[56]

At this point of low spirits, Caroline was very pleasantly surprised when Michael Bruce appeared in London. Rather than being executed, he had been released from his French incarceration and had arrived in time to catch the *Glenarvon* fiasco. He apparently brought her memories of Paris, restored her sense of proportion, and enhanced the vivacity of the parties she attended at her mother's. One of her notes begins, "[d]oes he of the Desert care to know that every one here thought him very very agreeable—& that all generally unite in begging him to make his visits as frequent as possible . . .—if you thought me unamiable pray pardon it. I am not very feminine & gentle, something like Catherine the Shrew before she was tamed." She signed this letter, boldly, "Calantha."[57]

Bruce provided exactly what Lady Caroline most wanted at this time—an opportunity to talk about Byron with someone who knew him; an opportunity to unburden herself. To Bruce she apparently revealed some of Byron's deadly secrets: "[H]ow could I tell you those things which I ought sooner to have died than name—it is little comfort for me to feel that you are honourable—I ought to have been so too—nothing can excuse my breach of promise." But with Byronic flare she also wrote "Fare the Well—come here—remember that I am always at home & alone from nine till eleven and that you are most welcome to me for I like you . . . yrs *Lady Avondale!*"[58] Claiming that she wrote carelessly ("there is no method in my Madness as there was in Hamlets") she nonetheless pursued a quite definable thrill in her relationship with Bruce, whom she now called "Bertram," after Charles Maturin's successful play.[59]

Caroline was rehearsing the same scenes of eroticized death that had obsessed her in *Glenarvon*. Compulsively, she sought a renewal of the feeling through a repetition of her affair with Byron through Bruce, who was a lightning rod for her emotions: "My heart's in torture & my whole soul the same—it is as if there was a sword run through me—or a fire burning in my brain. . ." she told him.

> There is but one thing could soothe & calm me & that were Religion—but I know neither how to believe or how to doubt—my heart inclines me to kneel down & pray—& my pride also rejects it—you said you could calm me & advise me—but you have only made me much worse—There are such thoughts in me at times that if they continue I must go mad . . . human weakness cannot bear up against it and in the night 'tis dreadful—if this is what is called remorse how can people say there is no Hell.[60]

Lady Caroline now consciously merged with the women of *Glenarvon*. She sought permission to wallow in the reiteration of the Calantha story, and Bruce gave it to her: "People who have seen me so gay & apparently so hardened because pride & spirit kept me up in their presence need not fear—could they see me alone they would not say the moral to Calantha was bad—it's such that I cannot struggle with it long."[61] Caroline needed Bruce, and she maintained a correspondence with him even after he married the widow of Peter Parker in 1818.

As fall waned, Caro George undermined Lady Caroline's credibility with Lady Byron at every opportunity. She told Annabella not to see Caroline, because she had "ruined herself so completely in public opinion by her *impudence* that it does not work upon one's compassion to protect her."[62] While Annabella and Caroline could never have been friends, the presence of the other Caro ensured a continuing comparison of the one's docility to the other's impudence, and consequently a deepening isolation for the woman who had told Byron's secrets. Pointing also to Caroline's improperly public relationship with Bruce, Caro George reinforced the disapproval of Caroline's cousins, Harryo and G.

Grateful for the slightest attention, and still confident in William's love, Caroline's natural arrogance brought her harsher criticism. In a letter to her brother Hart, now well-established in his role as 6th Duke of Devonshire, Harryo wrote of her visit to Melbourne House in mid-December 1816:

> I was received with rapturous joy, embraces, and tremendous spirits. I expected [Caroline] would have put on appearance of something, but to do her justice she only displayed a total want of shame and consummate impudence, which, whatever they may be in themselves, are at least better or rather less disgusting than pretending or acting a more interesting part. I was dragged to the unresisting William, and dismissed with a repetition of embassades and professions. I looked, as I felt, stupefied. And this is the guilty, broken-hearted Calantha who could only expiate her crimes with her death. I mean my visits to be annual.[63]

Caroline knew what was happening, but she could not stop herself. The words of *Glenarvon*'s Elinor St. Clare ring too truly: "When they tell me I am base, I acknowledge it: pride leads me to confess what others dare not; but I think them more base who delight in telling me of my faults: and when I see around me hypocrisy and all the petty arts of fashionable vice, I too can blush for others, and smile in triumph at those who would trample on me. It is not before such things as these, such canting cowards, that I can feel disgrace."[64] Caroline's disgrace was real and consequential, however. And if she managed not to feel it at that moment, she would soon remember the numbness and desperation of the outcast.

TWELVE

Politics and Satire

1817–1820

T hrough the winter and into the spring of 1817, Lady Caroline waited for a sign from Annabella that her trust had not been broken—that Byron did not know she had betrayed him. Following Lady Caroline's own advice that the two women should not appear to be colluding, Annabella had maintained complete silence. Caroline was correct, however, in assuming that Lady Byron had been influenced by Caro George, who continued to point out the awkwardness created by *Glenarvon* and to bemoan Caroline's liaison with Michael Bruce. Knowing she had little chance, Caroline took up her pen and wrote with her patented emotionality: "[Y]ou have given me pain—I have thought you unkind—but I know you enough not to judge you by appearances—you may think the line of conduct you pursue towards me deserv'd & yet be assured you are wrong—for on Earth I do believe—I am one of those most sincere towards you—& you may perhaps some day believe this though now you do not. . . ."[1] To Caroline's request for a meeting Lady Byron responded three days later with her own patented brusque candor: "It was unintentionally be assured, if I have *given you pain*—but as there has not of late been any communication between us, I am unable to conjecture *what* I have to regret on this account." Acknowledging that she was "greatly obliged" by Caroline's timely aid in her struggle to retain custody of her child, Annabella insisted that "the conduct I may for various reasons have thought it right to pursue has not been actuated by any motives personally reckoned towards you—If however such has been the appearance, it forms a reason why I should not make a change *because* you speak of a power to serve me."[2] What could Caroline say in the face of this cool refusal, when her very offer of help was used as an argument that it should not be allowed?

On her wedding anniversary, 3 June 1817, Caroline was alone and in low spirits. A letter from Michael Bruce arrived, stirring up painful memories of Byron and his manipulations: "I cried for an hour upon reading your letter—but I believe it was chiefly because my mind & body are both weakened—I have so often been the dupe of what I call the meanest of all Arts—that of attempting to create a strong interest by affecting to be on the point of going away from your Country or in an allarming state of Health—that I unwillingly allow myself to feel again for him. . . ." From this mood she derived some more philosophical reflections on death and the failure to appreciate "real goodness & real Talent": "[T]hose who can feel appreciate & understand are more wanted in this World & as rare as those who are worthy to excite admiration, & this may be particularly noted in Books, music—fine pages of poetry—great & heroic actions—few understand them & when we find one who does though they be unlovely in all else we cherish them & like to be with them. "Bruce was cast in the unlovely role of witnessing Lady Caroline's heroic agonies, as she in turn "appreciated" the evil career of Byron. While Madame de Staël "had fine & generous qualities," Byron did not, Caroline felt, and for Bruce she revived her Calantha role as, "one who is grown wise by experience & [has] paid a Huge price for that invaluable gem."[3]

Caroline's reflections upon her hero, Madame de Staël, had been stimulated by that woman's death on 14 July 1817. But having lost one literary hero, she made the acquaintance of another, the Italian novelist Ugo Foscolo, who had arrived in London the year before. Foscolo had been engaged in revising *Le ultime lettere di Jacopo Ortis,* an epistolary work of fiction that some consider the first modern Italian novel. Samuel Carter Hall, his literary secretary, described him as small, wiry, and highly animated, with a sensuous mouth and hot temper.[4] After hearing him read Homer and some of the English translation of *Jacopo Ortis,* Caroline invited him to dine, hoping he would teach her more about Italian literature. She sent him letters containing her drawings and admiration: "[O]ne could not exchange two words with you without gaining a great deal," she wrote him. "Unfortunately, whilst I was profiting, you were wasting your time. Therefore I have not badgered you to visit me."[5] Foscolo responded politely to Lady Caroline's request for literary enlightenment; he would later become instrumental in the artistic choices she made.

In October of 1817, Sir Gilbert Blane, a physician attached to the Devonshire House circle examined Augustus and found—no surprise—the boy's weight, uncontrollable seizures, and rambunctious behavior highly dangerous to his mother and the women servants, upon whom Augustus would sometimes leap playfully, knocking them to the floor. Blane recommended a young doctor named Lee who could live with the family to care for and educate Augustus. William thought the idea a good one, but balked at the particular candidate, who seemed overqualified. "My means are somewhat limited," he reminded Blane, warning him not to mislead the young man about "the advantages which are likely to arise to him from this connexion."[6] Dr. Robert Lee joined the Lamb household that month. He would stay for the next five years.

Lady Melbourne's health declined. Rheumatism and stomach complaints had made her addicted to laudanum, which she took in such large doses that it caused hallucinations. William had depended upon her for advice and guidance all his life. Now, he had to do without.[7] As Lady Melbourne sank, another event touched the heartstrings of the Whiggery. The death of Princess Charlotte while delivering a stillborn child in November 1817 was a great shock. Caroline and William had felt close to the Princess, whose politics were enlightened. Hart had once even offered his hand in marriage, but now they read with a chill down the spine that Richard Croft—the same doctor who had delivered the 6th Duke of Devonshire— had presided over the Princess's fatal delivery. After the Princess's funeral, a guilt-ridden Croft committed suicide.[8]

The death of Croft stirred up the old rumors that Hartington was really Bess's child after all. The 6th Duke was forced to refute the rumor with a deposition from the mid-wife who had attended his birth.[9] Emily Cowper also reported to her brother Frederick with malicious pleasure that Caroline was upset about renewed discussion of the child-switch plot in *Glenarvon:* "[T]here was some paragraph about it in the papers which has annoyed Calantha a great deal. But one cannot pity her for any annoyance that comes to her thro' that infernal book, as it is so richly deserved."[10] Emily and the Lambs still smoldered at Lady Caroline's indiscretions and lost no chance to berate her. Emily anticipated that Christmas at Brocket "will all be soured by the Devil, 'Cherubina.'"[11]

In this climate, Lady Caroline must have felt both relief and puzzlement when she received a pleasant letter from Emily, prompted apparently by William's remonstrances. Caroline hastened to follow up the advantage by her usual strategy of apology: "Emily I am of too violent a temper—all is my fault it is none of yours [. . .] your merely writing me kindly has quite rendered me weak and foolish." She thanked her sister-in-law for her "forbearance," asking her to mollify

George Lamb and pleading the uncontrollable nature of her emotions: "[I]t is this it is feeling too keenly it is suspecting evil perhaps never intended that makes me so harsh so violent so odious forgive me Dearest Emily."[12] For William's sake, Emily got Caroline tickets for a party at Almack's, the club controlled by women, where Lady Jersey made the decisions.

Feeling encouraged, Caroline dined a few days later at Devonshire House, where she encountered John Cam Hobhouse, upon whom she bestowed a ticket for the party. Byron's "Beppo" had just been published anonymously, and Lady Caroline knew the author immediately. She told Hobhouse it was "as good as anything that Swift ever wrote," and that it had delighted her so much that the emetic she had taken failed to work: "Now though this is not a pretty illustration of what should be felt on reading poetry, believe me it is emphatic and expresses much more than fairer words."[13] It was indeed a bizarre compliment to Byron's power, and another example of her callowness.

That winter, M. G. Lewis died, leaving William his entire library, valued at £3,000. William liquidated it to pay bills, and the small inheritance therefore affected his situation not at all. Though he regretted his cousin's death, he had no time to mourn, for his mother had entered the last stages of her illness in mid-February and he spent virtually all his time with her.[14] Sitting beside her bed, he was forced to admit to the truth of a rumor Lady Melbourne had heard, that nineteen-year-old Harriet Caroline Spencer, daughter of Lady Bessborough's cousin, had been attending the parties at Devonshire House and gotten pregnant. Biographer Dorothy Howell-Thomas explains: "It wasn't so much that she had been seduced that created the scandal, for such events were always capable of being hushed up. It was that she had already acquired a bad reputation by hanging around with young unmarried men. In short, she had committed the unpardonable sin of being talked about."[15] This young woman, who appeared to be following in Lady Caroline's footsteps, had given birth in March of 1818 to a baby girl named Susan who was immediately adopted as a very late addition to the children of the mist. Lady Melbourne was reminded once again that she had miscalculated in encouraging William to marry into the Ponsonby family.[16]

For three days before she died, William's mother experienced almost continuous convulsive fits. Then, she grew calm and expired "tranquil & free from pain."[17] William grieved wordlessly. Caro George came closest, perhaps, to describing Lady Caroline's reaction: "It is impossible to see a person so loved and so regretted & not to feel that they must have had great merits to counteract their faults."[18] William's long dependency upon his mother officially ended with her interment at Hatfield Church on 14 April, and he bethought himself once again of his political career. But so long as his father held the purse strings, there seemed little he could do. William now relied on Emily to smooth things over, visiting her often at Panshanger.[19]

Left to her own devices, Caroline attended private parties such as the one held by Lord Duncannon (her eldest brother John), where races were held. At this particular party, a man was hurt, and Lady Caroline had him taken to her carriage. Edward Bulwer, future Lord Lytton, who lived not far away at Knebworth, heard about the event and sent her a letter and poem lauding her charity. Lady Caroline's generosity was no secret in the Welwyn district.[20] The poem began effusively, "Daughter of feeling, queen of love."[21] Lady Caroline's polite response was directed to Bulwer's parents "for your son." After this, Bulwer sent her more poetry, and she gave it careful attention. Writing in the third person, she complimented him on his taste and said he should not emulate "Lord Byron, Moore, Walter Scott or any of the living race," who all had the defect of "affectation," especially the use of epithets and tricks to "terrify and astonish" readers.[22]

Caroline now renewed her friendship with Isaac Nathan, who had written the music for Edmund Kean's revival of *The Jew of Malta*, which had opened at Drury Lane on 24 April 1818. He now undertook to publish settings of two more songs of Lady Caroline's: "My Heart's Fit to Break" and "Amidst the Flowers Rich and Gay." "These last verses," he wrote in *Fugitive Pieces*, "were written one morning at Melbourne House by Lady Caroline, and I composed the music impromptu in the presence of her Ladyship's mother, the Countess of Bes[s]borough, to whom the composition was afterwards dedicated."[23] Evidence of their intimacy lies in a letter Caroline sent Nathan: "I am, and have been very ill; it would perhaps cure me if you could come and sing to me, 'Oh Mariamne'—now will you? I entreat you, the moment you have this letter, come and see me, and I promise you that if I get well I will come to your Theatre—but I use no bribe, I merely ask—come and soothe one who ought to be happy, but is not.[24] "'Herod's Lament for Mariamne' was one of Byron's favorites among the *Hebrew Melodies*, and Caroline's choice reflected her desire to relive (through Herod's sacrifice of his Mariamne) the betrayal she had experienced at Byron's hands and the imagined effect upon him inflicted by the loss of herself: "She's gone, who shared my diadem; / She sunk, with her my joys entombing . . . / And mine's the guilt, and mine the hell, This bosom's desolation dooming."[25] The renewal of her relationship with Nathan coincides with Lady Caroline's re-entering the world of balls, plays, and concerts.

That fall brought Caroline a chance encounter with Scrope Davies, friend of Byron and Hobhouse since they had met at Cambridge.[26] Davies had a wicked tongue, and he may have told Lady Caroline that Byron had grown corpulent. Around the same time, she heard the news that barrister and legal reformer Sir Samuel Romilly, depressed over the death of his wife, had committed suicide. Caroline had recently seen Romilly, apparently contented. "Oh God what a world we live in!" she wrote Ugo Foscolo, "so happy one day and then so sad."[27] She decided to write Byron one more time:

> [Y]ou will see by the papers and by letters from England that Sir Samuel *Romilly* is dead—it was in a moment of phrenzy brought on by grief that he did this—his children they say feel it dreadfully—it is a cruel thing to do—but he had lost his mind I am sure at the time—never do you do this Lord Byron never whatever may happen it is a cruel thing remember it—if even a dog is left on earth who loves you—but I did not write to you to say this—I wrote because his death brought you to my mind—as every thing does. . . .[28]

Caroline reminded Byron of his promise that, "whatever might happen, whatever my conduct might be you would never cease to be my friend." She concluded with an entreaty to "forgive me before I die . . . poor Romilly it breaks my heart to think what he has suffered. . . ." Caroline could not have picked a worse subject for Byron, who detested Romilly for intervening on Lady Byron's side in 1816 when he was supposed to be on retainer for Byron. Byron made numerous acid remarks on Romilly after his death, even commenting that the "sexegenary suicide" of Romilly was "almost an anomaly."[29] Caroline's letter only accentuated his loathing: "I hate him still," he told Hobhouse, "as much as one can dislike dust."[30] Caroline's message brought no forgiveness, no commiseration, no reply at all from Byron.

Perhaps Caroline expected none. In any case, she seems to have been distracted from thoughts of death when Lady Jersey agreed she could be readmitted to Almack's. Emily had decided to help her sister-in-law because William had made it clear he would not leave his wife, and since "he *will* stick to her, I think it is better to give her any lift I can—for her disgrace only falls more or less on him. I have therefore fought a battle for her and put her name down to Almack's Balls in spite of Lady Jersey's Teeth—let people do as they like in their own *private* Society but I think it hard to exclude a person from a ball where six hundred people go if they really are received anywhere."[31] Emily had taken on Lady Melbourne's role as advisor and helpmeet to William, but though she fought for Caroline at Almack's she felt little sympathy. She crowed over Caroline's ineptitude in failing to bring off a large dinner party at Brocket:

The whole House was lighted up, there were several supper tables, a band of twenty-four musicians, and the company consisted of the [two children and a servant] I sent, Dr. Lee, Augustus, Miss Webster herself, W[illia]m, Master George who had come from London for the Ball, and four strangers. . . . [T]he expence of these failures is as great as if she succeeded and in a concern of this sort she don't mind what she throws away—but means to make up for it the next week by the most miserable stingyness. There never was such a Woman!!![32]

Publicly supporting Caroline's social resurrection, Emily undermined it privately. She encouraged Lord Melbourne to say he was so fed up with Caroline's temper tantrums and the threat of her "breaking some more Heads with Candlesticks" that he would increase William's allowance to £5,000 per annum just to get her and her pets out of the house.[33] It was quite a menagerie of dogs and cats now, whether in Whitehall or in Welwyn, where Caroline kept a cockatoo that liked to attack books.[34]

Grateful to Emily for her efforts, and not unaware that the Lambs still reviled her, Lady Caroline decided to help George Lamb in his struggle for election to the House of Commons in February and March 1819. George was running against Hobhouse for the seat in Westminster that had been vacated by Romilly's demise, and Caroline threw herself into the election, hoping to gain favor with Emily and attract Byron's attention by defeating his friend. She wrote to everyone she could think of, including the philosopher and publisher William Godwin.[35] This would be the beginning of a long friendship with Godwin, though she had no time as yet to cultivate it as she canvassed for her brother-in-law. Westminster was dominated by middle-class voters: artisans, printers, tailors and assorted shopkeepers, and it was unusual in its enfranchisement of all the approximately 17,000 rate-paying householders.[36] Caroline "freely entered taverns, drank heavily, and exchanged kisses for votes."[37] Hobhouse's supporters attacked her character, but they knew that she had delivered a message to local tradesmen. She made them see that they faced loss of "custom" if they abandoned the Whig party.

Hobhouse's side retaliated by taunting George Lamb as "A RED HAIRED LAMB, *Cross Bred, got by Regent* out of *Melbourne,* God-son to the great *Prince.*" Caroline responded by persuading forty voters from Shepherd Market that Hobhouse was a faux liberal and Lamb the "true Liberty candidate."[38] She also protested about dirty tactics. "I know that during Elections songs & squibs are fair on each side," she told Hobhouse, but

ask yourself what your feelings would be if you found the grossest insults & imputations sanctioned by any of our Party against yr Birth or yr relations—

perhaps you care the less as you may be exempt from every imputation—I assure you no personal fear of what you may say of me actuates this—I am I know in yr power in this respect . . . [F]ind means to stop it and do not tell me you cannot— because I am sure you can & will.[39]

In the event, George Lamb was elected, and Lady Caroline given some credit for the final tally. Byron, who had refused Hobhouse's direct requests for support earlier, now wrote from Venice on 6 April to make amends. "I had much at heart your gaining the Election," he said. "If I had guessed at your *opponent*—I would have made one among you Certes—and have f——d Caroline Lamb out of her 'two hundred votes' although at the expence of a testicle.——I think I could have neutralized her zeal with a little management."[40] Byron's bravado at sexually dominating Lady Caroline was spiced with contempt for her husband and the whole "Cuckoldy family." Though still unhappy with his sister-in-law, George exulted in his political success and acknowledged her role in it. His tenure in Parliament would be short-lived, but Caroline had shown loyalty. Nor did she stop there. In November, when George's position began to look tenuous, she wrote to Henry Colburn begging him to influence the newspapers to portray George positively.[41]

Byron's political support might not have been the best thing for Hobhouse after all, because on 15 July 1819 the first two cantos of *Don Juan* (pronounced "Joo-wan" to rhyme with "true one") created a scandal and were severely criticized, with some booksellers refusing to carry the work (which naturally increased sales).[42] Caroline joined in the negative reaction: "The Don Juan is neither witty, nor in very good taste," she said. Murray had apparently provided her an advance copy of the poem, and she pronounced the couplet about Romilly "infamous—there is not the Razor edge of satire to make it go down & the levity of the style ill accords with the subject." The lines were cut from the first edition. She said she found most of *Don Juan* frankly "weak." Yet she soon admitted, "You cannot think how clever I think 'Don Juan' is in my heart."[43] She was not alone. Harryo wrote in her journal that she adored *Don Juan,* parts of which were "more beautiful than anything he has written." "There is a description of love by moonlight," she said, "that beggars all praise."[44]

Though Caroline did not know it, Byron had a new lover whom he described as "a sort of Italian Caroline Lamb, except that she is much prettier, and not so savage.—But she has the same red-hot head—the same noble dis*dain* of public opinion—with the superstructure of all that Italy can add to such natural dispositions."[45] He had met the Countess Teresa Guiccioli in April 1819, just before *Don Juan* was published, and the comparison reveals that Byron's hostility toward his "evil Genius" was still balanced by attraction to her qualities. Caroline and Teresa were even alike in criticizing *Don Juan*. After reading the first two cantos, the Countess asked him repeatedly to stop writing it. Byron interpreted this request as arising "from the wish of all women to exalt the *sentiment* of the passions—& to keep up the illusion which is their empire.—Now D.J. strips off this illusion—and laughs at that & most other things."[46]

If so, then it seems natural that Caroline recognized in *Don Juan* a response to *Glenarvon*, which had been, in turn, a response to Byron's earlier work. For example, the novel had developed the theme of weeping from several of Byron's earlier poems, including one that described a masculine response to overpowering pain: "From my eye flows no tear, from my lips flow no curses."[47] Caroline had responded with a song for *Glenarvon* which begins, "[m]y heart's fit to break, yet no tear fills my eye."[48] In the first Canto of *Don Juan,* Donna Julia writes, "[m]y eyeballs burn and throb, but have no tears," and the narrator underscores it: "[S]he did not let one tear escape her."[49] For Byron, a woman's teardrop "melts," while a man's "half-sears" and must be forced from his heart. For Byron, women employ tears to gain their ends, and their target is his alter-ego, Don Juan, who dissolves "like snow before a woman crying."[50] Julia's dry eyes, however, link her to Caroline, the ungendered woman.

Such clues indicate that *Glenarvon* may have given Byron ideas about inverting gender stereotypes. In order to feminize Juan, Byron had to portray women differently; instead of silent inspirations, they had to become "potent, complex beings."[51] There can be no doubt that in *Don Juan* Byron achieved a perspective on the male hero that transcends—or at least transforms—what he had done to that point. His affair with Lady Caroline Lamb and his reading of *Glenarvon* may account for some elements of his masterpiece, from the dedication, in which Byron seems anxious to dissociate himself from any *Glenarvon*-like betrayal of Irish Patriots, to certain aphorisms on sex and marriage. When *Glenarvon*'s Lady Augusta Selwyn tutors Calantha in the rules of marriage, she explains that she is neither in nor out of love with her husband: "He never molests me, never intrudes his dear dull personage on my society. He is the best of his race, and only married me . . . because I let him cheat at cards whenever he pleased."[52] Similarly, in *Don Juan* the Duke and Duchess of Fitz-Fulke have "that best of unions, past all doubt, / Which never meets, and therefore can't fall out."[53] The "unobjectionable matches" Don Juan mockingly celebrates—the ones that "go on, if well wound up, like watches"—owe something to Byron's relationship with Lady Caroline and her novel.[54]

Byron's near elopement with Caroline in 1812—as revised and retold in *Glenarvon*—is reflected in Don Juan's "earliest scrape" with Julia in Canto 1.[55] From this perspective, Julia's letter from the convent to which she has retreated at the end of the Canto appears as a sort of *touché* for Caroline's inclusion of Byron's letters in the novel. Julia's letter begins with a seemingly regret-free benediction to Juan: "I have no further claim on your young heart, / Mine was the victim, and would be again." But it goes on to reproach Juan:

> I loved, I love you, for this love have lost
> State, station, heaven, mankind's, my own esteem,
> And yet cannot regret what it hath cost,
> So dear is still the memory of that dream;
> Yet, if I name my guilt, 'tis not to boast,
> None can deem harshlier of me than I deem:
> I trace this scrawl because I cannot rest—
> I've nothing to reproach or to request.[56]

Byron might have gotten such phrases from Caroline's own letters, but he also had the ones Calantha writes in *Glenarvon:* "Remember that you are all on earth to me; and if I lose that for which I have paid so terrible a price, what will be my fate!" Another letter says, "I forsook everything for you."[57] Calantha never tires of naming her guilt: "It is myself alone I blame, on me, on me be the crime." Yet she also cannot regret: "Think not that I wish to repine, or that I lament the past."[58] She repeats many times the sentiment that Julia expresses in the last line of the stanza just quoted above: "Glenarvon, I do not reproach you, I never will"; "Oh fear not, Glenarvon, that I shall intrude or reproach you"; "I will never learn to hate or reproach you."[59]

The next stanza of Julia's letter focuses upon the contrasting possibilities for men and women:

> Man's love is of his life a thing apart,
> 'Tis woman's whole existence; man may range
> The court, the camp, church, the vessel, and the mart,
> Sword, gown, gain, glory, offer in exchange
> Pride, fame, ambition, to fill up his heart,
> And few there are whom these cannot estrange;
> Man has all these resources, we but one,
> To love again, and be again undone.[60]

These ideas have been traced to other sources, like Madame de Staël's *De l'Influence des Passions* (1796) and *Corrine* (1807).[61] They occur also, however, in *Glenarvon,* for Calantha says, "You know not what a woman feels when remorse, despair, and the sudden loss of him she loves, assail her at once."[62] The narrator underscores this theme: "That which causes the tragic end of a woman's life, is often but a moment of amusement and folly in the history of a man. Women, like toys, are sought after, trifled with, and then thrown by with every varying caprice. Another and another still succeed; but to each thus cast away, the pang has been beyond thought, the stain indelible, and the wound mortal." The narrator subsequently comments that "Calantha saw Glenarvon triumphant and herself deserted."[63]

When we compare the conclusion of Julia's letter with passages from *Glenarvon* we find numerous parallels and repetitions. Julia writes,

> My breast has been all weakness, is so yet;
> I struggle, but cannot collect my mind;
> My blood still rushes where my spirit's set,
> As roll the waves before the settled wind;
> My brain is feminine, nor can forget—
> To all, except your image, madly blind;
> As turns the needle, trembling to the pole
> It ne'er can reach, so turns to you my soul.[64]

In *Glenarvon,* Calantha also complains that her lover has seduced her with his power of attraction: "I am nothing, a mere cypher: you might be all that is great and superior. Act rightly, then, my friend . . . I have followed you into a dark abyss; and now that you, my guide, my protector, have left my side, my former weakness returns, and all, that one smile of your's could make me forget, oppresses and confounds me."[65] Repeating the theme that the man will go on to glory, Julia writes, "And so farewell—forgive me, love me—No, / That word is idle now—but let it go." These lines echo Calantha's sentiments: "Generously save me: I ask you not to love me."[66] In the conclusion of her letter, Julia says: "My misery can scarce be more complete." Calantha's words are: "Glenarvon, my misery is at the utmost" and "I am as lonely, as miserable in your absence as you can wish."[67] These typical recriminations and rationalizations of the jilted might have come from many places, but the evidence argues that *Glenarvon* gave them their particular form in Byron's poem. When Juan comments that Julia's seal read "Elle vous suit partout [She follows you everywhere],"[68] the phrase seems to comment on Caroline's pursuit of Byron, a recurring theme of his letters.

Lady Caroline read Julia's letter as an allusion to herself. This, taken with the insult of the second Canto's dismissive "Some play the devil—and then write a novel,"[69] provoked her *riposte:* She wrote her own "New Canto" of *Don Juan,* and it was published in October 1819. At this time, scores of Byron knock-offs were still being generated based on *Childe Harold,* and even Byron's old friend from Cambridge, the Reverend Frances Hodgson, had published one, titled *Childe Harold's Monitor.*[70] The hack satirist William Hone hired a printer to deliver to the public his own *Don Juan: Canto the Third,* which consists of 114 stanzas of indifferent rhyme and verse conveying what now sounds like very stale satire. The anonymously published *Jack the Giant Queller, or Prince Juan,* offered thirty-eight stanzas of similar caliber.[71] *A New Canto* is far better than any of these.

The apex of Lady Caroline's career as a mimic, *A New Canto* was an act of artistic fulfillment, so that she might become, in scholar Peter Graham's words, "in art the 'little volcano' she was so notably capable of being in life."[72] The poem evokes a British apocalypse—a sort of fantasy-fulfillment of British nightmares of political upheaval:

> When doomsday comes, St Paul's will be on fire
> (I should not wonder if we live to see it);
> Of us, proof pickles, Heaven must rather tire
> And want a reckoning—if so, so be it:
> Only about the cupola, or higher,
> If there's a place unoccupied, give me it,
> To catch, before I touch my sinner's salary,
> The first grand crackle in the whispering gallery.[73]

The poet then imagines the ball on the dome of St. Paul's "tumbling with a lively crash," as "[t]eeth chatter, china dances," the Bank of England collapses, and a raving Regent "sends about for ministers in vain."

London has become a volcano, and crowds run frantically about, seeking salvation in the church where "the font is hot, and fizzing."[74] As the earth tremors increase, the waves shake even the Peak District, far north of London, an allusion intended to amuse Hart, for that was where the 6th Duke of Devonshire's country estate, Chatsworth, stands:

> The Peak of Derbyshire goes to and fro;
>
> Like drunken sot the Monument is reeling;
>
> Now fierce and fiercer comes the furious glow,
>
> The planets, like a juggler's ball, are wheeling!
>
> I am a graceless poet, as you know,
>
> Yet would not wish to wound a proper feeling,
>
> Nor hint you'd hear, from saints in agitation,
>
> The *lapsus linguae* of an execration.[75]

The inventiveness and power of this verse derive from the same desire for revenge that created *Glenarvon*, augmented by mastery of Byron's cleverest tricks in the just-published first two cantos of *Don Juan*. Lady Caroline plays the tune *prestissimo*, as St. Paul's collapse roils the murky bowels of the entire Continent:

> Death-watches now, in every baking wall, tick
>
> Faster and faster, till they tick no more,
>
> And Norway's copper-mines about the Baltic
>
> Swell, heave, and rumble with their boiling ore,
>
> Like some griped giant's motion peristaltic,
>
> Then burst, and to the sea vast gutters pour;
>
> And as the waters with the fire-stream curl,
>
> Zooks! what a whizzing, roaring, sweltering whirl![76]

Lady Caroline may have been mocking earlier poems of Byron's with this volcanic scene. In his "Translation from Horace," published in *Hours of Idleness*, Byron had described the "flames of an expiring world," its "vast promiscuous ruin" and wreckage a "glorious funeral pile."[77]

A New Canto also mocks Byron's prurient interest in woman's pathos: "Mark yon bright beauty in her tragic airs . . . / Delicious chaos, that such beauty bares!"[78] And subsequent lines condescend to her pain: "A woman then may rail, nor would I stint her; / Her griefs, poor soul, are past redress in law."[79] But most of all, Lady Caroline mocks Byron through cutting allusions to his worship of Napoleon, who never flinched at "massacre or murder." Ruthless Napoleon is contrasted with Don Juan, who "pitifully wince[s]" at the conflagration. Thus Byron's hero proves no "true one," but a "bloodhound spaniel-crossed." The epithet "spaniel-crossed" carried for Byron and Caroline (both dog-lovers, and both readers of Cazotte, as we have noted,) connotations of impure breeding and bargains with the Devil.[80]

At this point, Caroline mimics Byron's pose of pretending to lose track of the story, as the narrator's mind wanders off and devils visit the London red-light district: ". . .they shut their ears against my rhyme, / Yet sneak, rank elders, fearful of denials, / To pick Susannahs up in Seven Dials."[81] A weakly constructed catalog of the damned draws the narrator back to the destruction of Europe: "Return we to our heaven, our fire and smoke." But the next line completes the deflation: "Though now you may begin to take the joke!"[82]

The joke is that Byron has wasted his talents on light, titillating verse, and Lady Caroline slings scorn on its improbabilities, especially the episode at the end of Canto 2, which describes Juan and the "fair Haidee" holding hands and making love in the rocky openings left by the sea's waves.[83] *A New Canto* charges that reading such tripe is "worse than an emetic" and that its sole purpose is to perpetuate Byron's fame, "And keep [his] name in capitals, like Kean," an allusion to the career of actor Edmund Kean and Byron's long-time connection to Drury Lane Theater.[84]

The author of *A New Canto* had served a long apprenticeship, and by this time, Byron had been well-tutored in responding to her. About *A New Canto* he said nothing. The poem received one brief notice recommending it "to those who are fond of extravagance, and doggerel versification," then disappeared, to be forgotten for decades.[85] Scores of biographies and reminiscences inspired by Byron reveal no awareness that Lady Caroline ever wrote it. After Margot Strickland's *The Byron Women* (1974) drew fresh attention to it, some have doubted that *A New Canto* is Caroline's work at all, mainly because it is more dense with allusions than her other poems. However, there is no other viable claimant to *A New Canto;* and who but the author would have requested Murray to send her brother Frederick a copy of *A New Canto* along with another book of her own titled *Penruddock*?[86]

Of one thing we can be sure—there was a political barb in this satire. Just as *Glenarvon* had made its hero a failed revolutionary, so *A New Canto* faulted Byron for failing to fight Tory tyranny. At the time, there was much reason to bemoan the lack of a heroic "true one" rather than the pusillanimous Don Juan. On 16 August 1819, there had been a confrontation between government troops and a mob in Manchester, which came to be known euphemistically as "Peterloo." At least eleven people had died and the legions of the wounded were estimated at over four hundred and possibly twice that number.[87] A peaceful crowd had gathered in muggy, oppressive weather to hear speeches against the corn laws and in favor of parliamentary reform and women's suffrage. Frightened by its size—more than sixty thousand people had gathered—the Manchester magistrates had panicked and summoned the regional cavalry and the troops of the 15th Hussars, who were supposed to effect the arrest of Radical leaders. When this proved impossible, they attempted to disperse the crowd—with their swords. Hobhouse reacted with outrage and was arrested on 14 December after publishing an anonymous pamphlet deploring the use of force against the people. He sat in Newgate prison until the end of February 1820. Around the same time, Arthur Thistlewood, who had a £1,000 price on his head, had been entrapped, along with other "Physical Force" Radicals, by a government agent who had persuaded them to murder members of the Cabinet. Caught in a small room in Cato Street off Edgware Road, the men fought desperately, and a police officer was killed. The mood in London was dark indeed, and darker still at Whitehall, where Augustus continued to have severe seizures. Feeling that Dr. Lee had not been able to do much to improve things, Caroline asked William's permission to forward a description of the case to a Doctor Blake, who was an acquaintance of John Murray. Though Augustus was now about to turn thirteen, she still had hope.[88] The consultation produced no ideas, however.

The gloomy mood was official, for on 29 January, 1820, George III had died, and the Prince Regent became George IV. The funeral took place on 16 February with a cold fog blanketing the city. The new King had pleurisy, and for a short while it looked as though there might be a double royal funeral. "He cannot leave off drinking," William told Lady Bessborough candidly, "& if there is a tendency to attacks upon the chest, he cannot drink & live."[89] Death as well as divorce hovered over the new King, and the latter provided a hot topic in the drawing rooms of Melbourne House, Devonshire House, and the Bessborough's residence in Cavendish Square.[90] The Crown charged the Queen with adultery committed with menials, including her courier Bartolomeo Bergami. A trial was in preparation.

The King's death necessitated the dissolution of Parliament, and so George Lamb stood for reelection. Shamed by familial criticism of Caroline's canvassing on his behalf, he forbade her to help, but some of his supporters apparently tried to avoid defeat by impersonating her in letters soliciting votes.[91] When the polling ended in late March, the Radicals had pushed George Lamb out, and Hobhouse had finally won election as a junior member to Parliament. He wrote exultingly and vindictively: "As for the mad skeleton [Lady Caroline]—she rode her a—e bone off, kissed, canvassed, & cuckolded, but all in vain and the bit of fig leaf which half hid her nakedness was torn off and flung in her face."[92] On 1 May Thistlewood and the other "Cato Street Conspirators" were beheaded at the Old Bailey. And in that same month, another election brought defeat to William's party, as he told his wife in a fat, newsy letter dated 3 May, though he himself had been quietly re-elected.[93]

A report circulated in London in the newspapers in late August that Byron had returned to England incognito. Lady Caroline believed the rumor and wrote to Murray pumping him for news and pressuring him to come see her at Brocket, where she now kept a room especially for him. She was desperate to know how Byron "looks what he says, if he be grown fat if he is no uglier than he used to be if he is good-humoured or cross-grained putting his brows down—if his hair curls or is straight as somebody said if he has seen Hobhouse if he is going to stay long." She didn't want Murray to tell Byron she had asked after him, but she wanted the news posthaste—"pray come here immediately."[94] But Byron was not in England, and no opportunity to see him would ever arise again.

The rumor had aroused the sleeping imp in Caroline's breast, and Emily Cowper undoubtedly regretted getting her back onto the list for Almack's balls when she arrived at a masquerade there costumed as Don Juan and accompanied by several pages dressed as devils.[95] She had recruited extra pages from her contacts at Drury Lane: "I must have a Devil—could you come with me as such. I want a very dear Devil not in bad taste. . . ."[96] The devils, however, proved intractable, as the *Morning Chronicle* reported:

> Lady Caroline Lamb appeared, for the first time, in the character of *Don Giovanni,* but unfortunately there were too many *Devils* provided for the climax. There seemed to be a whole legion of them, principal and subordinate; and so little inclined were they "to do their spiriting gently," that (notwithstanding they had been repeatedly drilled by the *Don* in private), they appeared determined to carry the whole crowd off to Tartarus by a *coup de main.*[97]

On hearing of this event, Byron wrote Murray from Ravenna that he wasn't surprised: "I only wonder that she went so far as 'the *Theatre*' for '*the Devils*' having them so much more natural at home—or if they were busy—she might have borrowed the bitch her Mother's—Lady Bessborough to wit——The hack whore of the last half century."[98] Byron's insults reinforce, rather than alleviate the sense that Lady Caroline had found her role. As Susan Wolfson notes, the physical description of Juan as a "stripling of sixteen" invites such a comparison with the woman whose signature costume was that of a page boy.[99]

Scarcely had the Lambs recovered from this latest outrage, when the trial of Queen Caroline began in the House of Lords. It lasted from August to November. Sensational as the experience was, it couldn't keep all the members awake, and even the Queen was caught dozing. This occasioned Lady Caroline's writing the following epigram in her commonplace book: "Her conduct at present no censure affords / The sin's not with menials, she sleeps with the Lords."[100]

Though widely believed guilty, the Queen was acquitted when the House of Commons could not agree upon a bill of divorce. The Queen's Whig supporters threw raucous and uproarious celebrations with bonfires, street dancing, and public rallies punctuated by the firing of squibs.[101] A further confrontation between Whigs and Tories developed when the King proposed to give the Queen an allowance but prohibit her recognition in the liturgy of the Church of England. The Whigs and Radicals had geared up for this symbolic fight, but Queen Caroline took the wind from their sails by capitulating for an increase to her annuity of £50,000.[102]

Lady Caroline now began corresponding with more writers, including Thomas Malthus and William Godwin. She made the acquaintance of James Hogg, the "Ettrick Shepherd," and she sent an invitation to Mrs. Amelia Opie to come visit Brocket Hall and to show Lady Caroline some of her poetry in progress.[103] Earlier, at an evening "conversazione," she had renewed her intimacies with the Duke of Wellington and Ugo Foscolo, and made the acquaintance of Washington Irving, who had lived in England since just before the publication of *Glenarvon*. She tried to introduce Foscolo and Irving to William Blake and his wife, who were especially interested in Irving's recently published *Sketch Book.*[104] Foscolo had not forgotten Lady Caroline, and he invited her to visit him at Digamma Cottage, his residence in Regent's Park. To her queries about the composition of novels, he responded with the brisk advice to "write a book which will offend nobody— women cannot afford to shock."[105]

Foscolo's advice did not enlighten Lady Caroline much. She wished devoutly not to offend; but given her nature, the question was, "How?" She decided to ask him to read one of her manuscripts, which she arranged for Murray to have set in type and printed especially for the purpose.[106] Foscolo probably never read all the printed text as she requested, but he did give her advice that led to the fruition of her second and third novels. He told Caroline to make the plot as simple as possible, building it around "one character as I have done in my Jacopo Ortis," and allowing narrative events to accumulate spontaneously. "I said I would try," Caroline told Godwin, "but the feeling was like writing a letter upon ruled paper." To ease the strain, she began writing another novel in her old style, "which pleased me better but which I fear is nonsense."[107]

Before these manuscripts finally reached maturity, they would go through much reworking. In her desire to compete with the best, Lady Caroline now decided to approach those she felt could best help her, and she seized upon the name of one who had a stellar reputation as a critic: Thomas Malthus. They were scarcely acquainted. She had met him years earlier at a ball in London and formed the impression that he would be kind, so she now wrote to ask him to look at a manuscript she was preparing to be called "Principle & Passion," after the fashion set by Jane Austen's *Pride and Prejudice* and *Sense and Sensibility*. She told Malthus that she had set her heart on being a writer, and that she had started out with a novel because "considering the very bad ones daily appear it did not seem presumptuous to make the attempt—but having tried I find that it is far from as easy as I expected." Not content to let her one attempt (*Glenarvon*) be her last, she had drafted two stories to go hand in hand: "Principle, or the Brothers," and "Passion, or the Impulse of the Moment." She begged Malthus to read the latter "with an eye to what others would think & not to what you might from your nature say to a 'Woman'."[108] Nervously, she begged him not to say anything about her work-in-progress to anyone.

William Lamb had agreed to read and make suggestions about "Principle, or the Brothers," which she described as "full of events rather terrific and in Monk Lewis's style," while the part to be called "Passion" was to be more in the mold Foscolo had recommended, "quite without events or story," and therefore much more in need of excellence in "language & manner." Malthus turned her down, advising her to send the manuscript to "Lord John," apparently a mutual acquaintance. It was a bitter pill. "I am sorry," she wrote to him, "very disappointed." Nonetheless, she said, "I shall do what few do—follow advice."[109] Whether Lord John ever read the manuscript, we do not know.

While Lady Caroline sought connections with other writers, her in-laws stewed in the frustrations caused by William's unwillingness to give her up. Emily had dropped most pretenses now. She wrote from Panshanger in November 1820 that Caroline "wanted to come here, but I hope I have poked her off; it would be insupportable." Caroline's only use for the Lambs was now to entertain Lord Melbourne, for "it gives him an employment to abuse her and quarrel with her."[110] The Lambs feared that Caroline would publish one more novel. She would produce two.

A Book to Offend No One: Graham Hamilton

1821–1822

I n early March 1821, just before William's forty-second birthday, Lady Caroline got down the Bible she had given him for his twenty-eighth, when she had asked him "to value it for *her* sake." She reinscribed it: "Caroline Lamb now begs you not to value it for *her* sake but for its own."[1] Still unreconciled to the Lambs' worldly philosophy, she had found therapy in writing about her alienation.

But as Caroline brooded over her manuscripts and marriage, she was not without consolation, for the beauty of Brocket always beckoned. She stayed there through the entire Spring, "this most beautiful season of the year," as she told William Godwin, whom she invited to visit. She badgered Murray for news of Byron. She had now read his *Marino Faliero: The Doge of Venice,* a drama in verse based upon the life of a twelfth-century political leader whose desire for revenge leads him to conspire to overthrow the Venetian constitution and who is executed. Unauthorized performances of the play had taken place earlier in London, but Caroline had not gone. Her writing languished, for beautiful Brocket, she said, made her "too stupid and comfortable to think of anything new or witty."[2]

In June, she returned to Melbourne House to find little had changed. Emily Cowper continued to spread gossip of Caroline "breaking Crockery, fighting Dr. Lee & dragooning her people."[3] Emily now reported that Lord Melbourne "will hardly speak to Wm and Caroline. I don't know why this is, but I suppose, as it is particularly to her, that he has heard of her riding about in the Queen's mobs."[4] Supporters of the politically liberal Queen had taken to roaming the parks and roads near the palace on horseback, Caroline among them.

The coronation of George IV was set for 19 July 1821. Dr. Lee, Augustus's tutor, and William, Caroline, Lord Melbourne, Emily, and her husband, Lord Cowper, dined together with several other guests more than once in the week before the great event, and they talked of little else. Dr. Lee stayed over night at John Murray's residence, where he met the famous strongman and archaeologist Belzoni before going to the spectacle, which was both magnificent and dramatic. The spurned Queen showed up at Westminster Abbey to find the door literally shut in her face.[5] By 7 August, she was dead of a bowel obstruction. Even after death she continued to disrupt life in London. Her funeral procession almost became a debacle when troops and a mob confronted each other at Hyde Park corner.[6]

The day after the Queen died, the third, fourth, and fifth Cantos of Byron's *Don Juan* were published by Murray, whose wife had been seriously ill since the birth of their last child during the spring. He was in Cheltenham, where she was recuperating, and thus not in London to observe the reaction to the new exploits of Byron. Lady Caroline wrote to Murray in August 1821, "I have felt a great deal for you having heard that Mrs Murray continues ill." In another letter of the same time she urged him "do not give way to despondency and as I have often sought you when I have felt ill & miserable do come & see me to allow me to see you." She even offered to entertain his little girls at tea.[7] Murray's despondency may have had something to do with *Don Juan*, for Byron's social and political satires spelled danger for their publisher. Murray, a Tory, feared retaliation.

Lady Caroline shared some of Murray's misgivings, though her political reproaches came from the other direction. Byron's choice to continue with *Don Juan* prompted her to write *Gordon: A Tale, A Poetical Review of Don Juan,* divided into two cantos. Caroline described *Gordon* as "partly a burlesque parody in the style of *Don Juan;* partly a sacrifice of praise offered at the shrine of talent, and partly arguments proving its immoral tendency."[8] This mixture of motives makes the poem ineffective, for it is neither an attack nor a send-up in the manner of *A New Canto.* The poem opens with the narrator purchasing the first two cantos of *Don Juan* and praising Byron:

Who can like him describe a dreadful scene?

Who can like him bring forth a tender passion?

Who can like him give an unsound machine

Life, being, motion, harmony, and fashion?

Or who like him so gently raise your spleen?

Or who melt down your heart with soft compassion?

Who can like him set all your soul on fire

With all the violence of a strong desire?[9]

Byron has the power to warm "the empire of poetic ground" with his "vivifying heat," and the narrator opens the covers of the new cantos of *Don Juan* expecting to find "intellectual joys."[10]

But the narrator is left cold by the "power of [Byron's] persuasive song," and the fire symbolically dies in the grate. The narrator perseveres and finds some things to praise in *Don Juan* after all: "Of all his brother poets, in the race / For fame and glory," Byron can still "run the best." "But just as he is on the point of winning," notes the narrator disappointedly, "[h]e turns aside, sits down, and falls a grinning."[11] The narrator traces Byron's shortcomings to perversity: "His florid pen is dipped, alas! too deep / In vicious sentiments' o'erwhelming ocean." The narrator's lament is simply stated: "Would that he used his talents for our good!" Instead, Byron's genius is used "but to infect: / Its powers perverted, all its time mispent."[12]

In the second canto the narrator meets a tall, cadaverous visitor who agrees it is a pity that Byron deals in degraded subject matter. This "foul tale," the visitor complains, is "quite licentious."[13] Coming to Byron's defense, the narrator protests that the judgment is premature, for Byron has promised to render Don Juan's tale a moral one, and it is not yet finished: "I have no fear but he'll accomplish all / That he has promised, and conclude it well."[14] The argument then rages over whether Byron is immoral or has simply described nature without being aware of its harmful effect upon the morality of readers. To bolster her argument, Lady Caroline introduces in a footnote a lengthy quotation from a review of *Don Juan* that was published in the *Imperial Magazine* for May 1820 attacking Byron for treating adultery comically and complaining that "sacred things are treated with levity."[15] These were Lady Caroline's oft-repeated complaints: that Byron had seduced her away from her marriage and further undermined her faith in God and the immortality of the soul.

At this point, the tall visitor becomes plainly supernatural: "The stranger's countenance was constant changing, / From pale to red, from red to pale again." Concluding that the stranger is "a real ghost," the narrator is startled by terrified screaming, at which the stranger laughs. Through the keyhole, the narrator sees gleaming flashes and hears hideous shrieking. His servants are being tortured.[16] The narrator struggles to overcome his fears while the stranger argues that Byron intends in a future installment of *Don Juan* "to show, / The very place where wicked people go,"[17] but that this will turn hell itself into a sideshow. "Grant him there is no God," the stranger says, and that heaven and hell do not exist. Byron's position leads anyone who reads him sympathetically "To be eternal nothings—our condition / Will equal his, *unconscious inanition.*"[18]

Lady Caroline's talent for monologue warms, and her ghastly stranger speaks fluently and with power on Byron's religious and moral shortcomings. *Don Juan* is compared to "a destructive stream of filthy water," a burning desert, Adam's body before he received his soul, a whirlpool, and a poisoned apple.[19] In a rising fury, the stranger spits venom on Byron's work. The final point is identical to that of *A New Canto:* Byron has squandered his genius merely to show off. His reward "for such enormous pains / Is, '*Byron did it!*—is this all he gains?'"[20] The stranger's revulsion now transforms him into a "dreadful goblin" beneath whose feet the floor boards crack and shake as the earth beneath the narrator begins to squirm and twine like a snake.[21]

Standing on a tiny spot of ground, the goblin is joined by a host of phantoms peering directly into hell. A gargantuan globe-shaped piece of machinery with winches on its sides is trundled out, and this machine displays the whole history of doomed humanity, "from Adam to the present," showing who they had been on earth and their fate in hell.[22] Having heard the ticking of an immense clock, the narrator is suddenly set free, but the yelling and screaming continues:

> More dreadful than the roar of beasts of prey,
> Or than the most tremendous thunder's rattle,
> Or British armies charging into battle.[23]

The host of apparitions assembles beneath the narrator, then rises into the air, seen only by the blue and smoking light of sulphurous torches. They turn upon the narrator, who sees that all traces of his room have vanished, together with his copy of *Don Juan.* He closes his eyes for death. But silence pervades the room, where all has been restored.[24] The poem's last two stanzas return to a light mocking tone, stating that the author, like Byron, is prepared to go on with the tale if the public insists.

Lady Caroline's best work in *Gordon: A Tale* is her apocalypse, just as it was in *A New Canto*. The first canto is tediously worked out, but the second shows signs of literary life. She has thought carefully about the scriptural, theological, philosophical, and biological arguments that might be made for and against Byron's seemingly agnostic and potentially nihilistic vision. She has also emulated Byron's tendency to show off and seeks to establish her equality in the field of learning by introducing some Greek allusions.[25]

Caroline paid to have *Gordon* published, gave copies to friends, and sent some to the magazines. Two years later, the *Monthly Review* printed a notice expressing the hope that the author "will suffer many, many suns and moons to rise and set, to grow and wane, before he re-commits himself to the press."[26] The review came too late to daunt her growing confidence. She had dined in July with Walter Scott and his friend, the poet and translator William Stewart Rose.[27] She continued a true friendship with Lady Morgan, relying on their mutual publisher, Henry Colburn, to pass messages between them.[28] She also attended the "*esprit* parties," or intellectual soirées, of bluestocking hostesses Lady Spence, Miss Benger, the ailing Lydia White, and the strenuous Lady Davy.

As she worked on her literary projects, Caroline once again became "full of bother," as her sister-in-law Emily put it on 19 September 1821.[29] We find corroboration of her emotional irritability and rising confidence in the journal of Dr. Lee, who had now lived in the house for four years: "Lady Caroline talked a great deal of nonsense at dinner," he wrote on 23 July. She was "rather more agreeable than usual, a certain prelude to a violent storm."[30] During one after-dinner conversation, Lady Caroline Lamb surprised Lee by saying she "thought it would be an improvement if ladies lived in houses different from their husbands, and that they only simply called upon them." Tom Sheridan, Richard Brinsley Sheridan's son, remarked dryly "how delightful it would be to have a card left for you on the table by your husband." William, who had already that evening branded Robert Southey "untrustworthy" and Walter Scott "sneaking, flattering, sycophantish," responded gruffly that "those who are not rich ought not to marry at all. People who are forced to live much together, are confined to the same room, the same bed, &c., are like two pigeons put under a basket who must fight." In the silence following this assertion, the ladies all agreed that they wished they were men. Lee said he did not understand "what they proposed to attain by the change."[31] Lee's incomprehension—tongue-in-cheek or serious—illustrates the bemusement of this male world at female desires for freedom.

In November Caroline heard a rumor that Lord Byron would soon publish his memoirs, and that Murray had advanced Byron £2,000. She had read the memoirs, however, for Murray had loaned them to her while keeping them safe for Thomas Moore. Caroline said they "were of no value—a mere copy-book," though they contained Byron's "profligate amours," which were worse than Rousseau's, with passages that could not be published. She told Dr. Lee that before she and her friends took him up Byron had read few classical works. She also said her *own* memoirs would be worth £5,000, since she had known "all the great people of former times, &c., &c."[32] Her claim that Byron had been uneducated before he was taken up by a circle of lady writers is no doubt a gross exaggeration. But even if it contains only a slight element of truth, it is worth pondering. Byron was a quick study. How much classical learning did he acquire *after* leaving the university?

Byron had always expected Caroline to publish a memoir and worse; he had warned Murray to check any letters of his that Lady Caroline returned to be sure that she had not forged them.[33] He told acquaintances that Lady Caroline had "the power of imitating his hand to an alarming perfection, and still possesses many of his letters which she may alter very easily."[34] Although Caroline apparently never engaged in the kind of forgery Byron feared, she continued to use Byron's work to test her literary ability.

On the very evening that Lady Caroline spoke with Dr. Lee about Byron's memoirs, family events transpiring in Italy had come to a terrible conclusion. Earlier that summer, while his parents were attending the coronation of George IV, little Henry Ponsonby had stayed in Geneva with his grandparents. The boy had contracted a fever which gradually worsened. Lady Bessborough had taken him up into the mountains to escape the summer heat. When Willy and Barbara returned after the coronation, they all traveled south to Parma. Harriet told Granville, "Every thing has been tried, but to day they have again repeated what they said at first, that this horrible disorder—water in the head—is incurable."[35] In the last stages, the child struggled through recurring convulsions for two full weeks before he finally expired on 5 November: "William, Barbara, Sally & I scarcely ever left him, & to see them hanging over him & trying to warm his little cold hands in theirs made my heart ache almost to breaking."[36]

Lady Bessborough's sympathies and energies had been overtaxed. Heartbroken over their son's death, Willy, Barbara, and their remaining son, Charles, began the slow return to England, traveling first from Parma to Bologna, where they found a run-down inn. The November cold was brutal. Lady Bessborough was in such discomfort that she could not rest at all, and her son became alarmed. He had a bed made in a carriage and set off as fast as he dared go for Florence. They arrived in that city at 6:00 A.M. on the morning of 9 November, where Lady

Bessborough suffered stoically under the ministrations of two helpless physicians. She died on 11 November.

Lady Caroline received news of her mother's illness on 28 November. The delay in the post drove her to "a state of agitation beyond all bearing," and she began writing notes to everyone she knew in case a letter had gone astray somehow. "In mercy try and get me a few lines," she begged John Murray. "[I]f my mother is [well] I am so—& if not there is an end of this World for me."[37]

Anticipating this desperation in his sister, Willy had sat down the day after Lady Bessborough died to write a long letter of comfort, saying their mother had told him she "had lived the happiest portion of her existence, that she derived much of that happiness from her children, and that the only pang she felt was quitting them & [our] father, & little remained to her but increasing infirmities, pains & vexations."[38] Loving to the end, Lady Bessborough made sure that her son and husband would tell Caroline that one of the doctors attending her had been epileptic, but had stopped having seizures at age fourteen or fifteen and had been perfectly healthy ever since. Willy told Caroline that Harriet's departure was serene: "She sent you her kindest love & she begg'd me to take to you the Pink Diamond ring which belonged to my grandmother." Willy conjured Caroline to pull herself together for her father's sake: "You know how he loves you, & that no one can [comfort him] so effectually as you." Even poor exhausted Mrs. Peterson, Lady Bessborough's maid, wrote to calm Caroline.[39]

They were right to worry. The loss of her mother, who had lavished so much love on her only daughter, jolted Lady Caroline's frail psyche. She was unable even to feign interest in Harryo's proffered sympathy, and Harryo wrote in her journal for November that, "Caroline, to whom I went with every early feeling of interest and kindness awakened, contrived somehow or other to deaden both."[40] The bodies of the deceased made their slow way home, as ignominious and increasingly gruesome searches of the coffins were conducted at every custom-shouse along the way.[41] The funeral was set for New Year's Eve at Chatsworth. While the rest of the family headed north to Derby, Selina Trimmer stayed in London with Caroline, who underwent "cupping," and took draughts to calm her nerves. In a letter to Ugo Foscolo of that time, she confessed that her mother's death made her suicidal, and that only the presence of her husband sustained her—not religion.[42]

Selina accompanied Caroline to Brocket and from thence the two women traveled to Chatsworth for the funeral. Hart had generously arranged for the funeral and an interment in the Devonshire family vault. Caroline dreaded the service, and William discouraged his wife from actually attending the ceremonies.

Two days before the funeral, she was still struggling "to do all I ought," but begged Hart "to forgive me if after all I fail—& do not go."[43] On New Year's Day she wrote to her fellow writer, Amelia Opie: "You will be surprised and vexd when I tell you that after arriving at Derby I was not well and did not go—I remained in Bed a kind friend read the service to me I heard the Bell and even the organ." Her brothers and William Lamb went as mourners into the vault to say their goodbyes to Lady Bessborough, "but I did not feel equal to bearing any more than the loss and the painful journey. . . . I have lost such a friend—next to William I loved her better than anything in life—but if it please God to spare him & I can grow good enough to dare die—I shall not consider myself as unhappy besides which I have passed such a very happy life & enjoyed so many blessings & so much kindness that it is wrong to repine."[44] Harriet's death hurt Caroline permanently. For months after, she exhibited no flicker of the fire for which she was famous. Her physician at this time, Dr. Tupper, assured her that she was "only very nervous" and gave her medical draughts to calm her.[45] In all likelihood, her alcohol addiction dates from her mother's funeral in the Peak District.

Yet Caroline's letter to Mrs. Opie also shows that her grief did not stop her writing. "I wrote two stories lately. . . . [I]t was my wish you should have seen them—I think your judgment so good that if you were to say burn them they will do mischief or alter such passages I would do it—but I know it is a great torment looking over others writings." And in a postscript written in a tiny hand she goes on to say that the wilder of her stories "of course is my favourite," though she admitted it was not necessarily better just because more adventurous: "[A] Cast Horse may stumble out of the Beaten path and Tumble Ungracefully down in the mire as well as a spirited thoroughbred," she confessed. Also, "genius is not necessarily the companion of the disorderly & odd—& I fear my wild story is not in good taste."[46]

Nor were her passions permanently abated. In a letter to Michael Bruce, now a married man, she described the impact that J. G. Lockhart's *Adam Blair* (1822) had upon her:

[The book] astonished me—it is all the while upon the verge of being ridiculous— the singular phraseology—the excessive virtue of the young minister, the Ladies extreme want of it—the scenes which are bordering upon indelicacy and yet the moral hue preserved throughout all this rather disgusts me—and yet I was deeply affected—excessively interested and upon the whole I think it excellent in its way—the Person who wrote it must be very clever and must have felt very violently.[47]

Adam Blair is the slightly gothic tale of a man who becomes wise through bitter experience. He is a callow minister whose wife, Isobel, succumbs to grief after the deaths of three of their four children. Blair is living alone with his only remaining child, Sarah, when Charlotte Campbell, an attractive woman who once hoped to marry him, turns up in the village. After many complications, Blair travels to the estate of her husband, from whom she is alienated but not divorced. Weakened by wine and her sad story, Blair has sex with Charlotte and wakes up revolted. He runs off, but becomes seriously ill. Charlotte finds him, nurses him, catches the illness herself, and dies. After thirteen years of penance, Blair returns to his church a real minister.[48]

Like Adam Blair, Lady Caroline thought of herself as alienated from God. She identified also with Charlotte, whose brazenness, shame, and death echoed *Glenarvon*. Caroline drew a picture of a scene from *Adam Blair* showing a woman "who was so desperately wicked & in love that she sought her lover when he was ill of some dangerous illness & died thus." The watercolor and ink sketch, about four inches by six inches, exhibits one cherub holding another who has been shot in the heart with an arrow, and on the back is a poem:

> Love sing'd for her his surest dart
> And plunged it in her guilty heart
> Even while contained within his arms
> She gazed upon his matchless charms
> Even as she pressed his lips of rose
> And heard the music of his vows
> The subtle poison through her frame
> Burst like the wild insatiate flame
> Remorse, despair and agony
> Mingled with every extacy
> One kiss—one last fond kiss he cried
> She gave him what he wished—and died.[49]

She sent the picture and poem to Michael Bruce, saying that "wicked as it may be I should not so much mind errors of the wandering heart if I had been gentle and made William happy."[50] Her fascination with guilt and suicide is further illustrated in her Commonplace Book, into which she pasted a clipping at this time that describes how two elderly brothers completed a suicide pact.[51]

Rumors of sexual alienation between William and Caroline in this period come almost exclusively from Emily Cowper, who was only too glad to believe and spread gossip the servants were happy to provide: "Her servants say she has been quite drunk for a week," she wrote to her brother Frederick. "She heard on Friday that Mrs. Fox Lane was brought to bed, so she came home and strewed her ante-room with hay, at least desired the servants to do so. When William came home he began damning and swearing, upon which she came out and said 'Mrs. F. Lane is brought to bed, and why should not I?'"[52] Caroline clearly still longed for children, but if William rebuffed her it would seem more likely that he did so out of concern for her health. He made other accommodations that might have helped assuage Caroline's longing for family. Lady Bessborough's little ward, Susan Churchill, now three-and-a-half years old, had become Caroline's responsibility. William accepted this responsibility willingly. He also agreed that they would become godparents to Isaac Nathan's newest child, Louisa Caroline Nathan.[53]

Augustus had acquired a playmate in Susan, but he lost his caretaker, for Dr. Lee now left to travel with the widowed Lord Bessborough and Willy Ponsonby in France and Italy, in late January 1822, retracing their journey to the country in which Harriet and her grandson had expired scarcely two months before. Lady Caroline was left to arrange her mother's affairs. She corresponded with her father and convinced him to give Mrs. Peterson and her husband a perpetual annuity of £100. Lady Caroline also successfully lobbied her cousin Hart to give the Petersons an annuity.[54] In a letter dated 31 January, Lady Caroline enclosed a miniature she had drawn of a lamb resting on a plinth inscribed with the date of her mother's death: "I like it very much," her father told her, "but must always look on the plinth with pain."[55] In August, her father and Willy returned with Dr. Lee, whose first encounter with Lady Caroline was tense. Then she seemed to relax, and it was as if they had not been gone at all. "Her conduct is as strange as ever," Lee said, noting that Augustus "has grown much, particularly in the extremities, but his head is small and there is a lamentable appearance of vacancy in his looks. His attacks are the same, although Sir A. Carlisle promises great things from animal diet, &c."[56]

Death, once a recurring fear, now became an obsession. When Caroline heard that Hart had lost a long-time servant, she wrote him, "death has been unusually active this year. . . . I shall not live many months longer; ask those who really surround me if I shall."[57] This constant sense of doom may have stemmed from near-suicidal depressions and laudanum-induced hallucinations, many of them based on fears that Augustus would die before she did. The recipients of such letters grew tired of the theme. Lady Caroline seems to have realized this, and yet she could not stop dwelling on her own end. During this period she made a drawing which she sent to young Edward Bulwer, whose home at Knebworth was just a few miles from Brocket, and whom she probably had seen occasionally since he had sent her his poem in 1818. Titled "Seul sur la Terre" (Alone on the Earth), it depicts a child sitting alone on a rock, surrounded by water.[58]

Lady Caroline had now finished the manuscript she had written following Foscolo's advice, which she had titled *Graham Hamilton*. She gave it to William and turned her attention to writing a realistic novel of social life modeled on Jane Austen's or Fanny Burney's work. William approved, and the manuscript went to Colburn with the promise that William would help to edit it.[59] William also wrote privately to Colburn, begging him in advertising the novel not to mention *Glenarvon*.[60]

Caroline's dialogue with Colburn seems typical of author-publisher correspondences, full of maneuvering about money, promises of future (unwritten) manuscripts, and touchiness regarding the deals other authors have managed. She hoped to publish another story titled "Sir Eustace: A Wild Romance," and to put in two songs for which she asked an advance of £300. These were undoubtedly settings by Isaac Nathan, to whom she intended to give the money directly. In addition, she claimed to have another untitled work in progress and wanted to revise *Glenarvon* and "put my name to it."[61] Caroline wanted Colburn to believe that he had a literary dynamo on his hands. She wanted money advanced as token of her status, saying, "Mr Lamb would no doubt give me this but I have a pride in giving what I have earned." *Graham Hamilton* was scheduled to be published that fall under conditions of "inviolable secrecy," the opposite strategy to the one pursued with *Glenarvon*. Caroline told Colburn to let the novel "come out quite quietly without a blaze."[62] And yet, she yearned to be recognized for her work. On another occasion she expressed her wish "to put my name [to *Graham Hamilton*]—I had rather stand by what I write however bad."[63] Only for the sake of William did she agree to anonymous publication.

Colburn took her up on the offer of a novel to be titled "Rose and Mary" and sent her £100. She replied in a sloppy hand on 14 March, sending him "the few pages of Rose & Mary I have already done" and promising to "give up the next 3 weeks to writing."[64] However, suddenly confronted with finishing two novels while proofing a third, she changed her mind and sent back the £100: "I wish to be off my proposal," she wrote, and instead promised him the first right of refusal.[65] Soberly she told Colburn that if she died and he published "Rose & Mary" she wished the £100 advance to be given to an orphan child she had adopted.[66]

Her anticipations of death were now accentuated by her conviction that Augustus was dying. In June, Emily Lamb described Augustus as "in a state worse than ever; he was in fits all yesterday and they called in all the doctors in London. The critical time seems to be coming on and very awkwardly too. She is frightened about it." Reporting the servants' gossip from Brocket, she said Caroline was "always raging or fainting."[67] In July, Caroline became desperate to do something for her son. She may have been drinking heavily before she met with six physicians, including Augustus's private one, Doctor Roe, to beg them to perform a treatment she had heard about from France which involved the application of a smoldering blister to the skull. Emily once again reported the rumor that "to please her they agreed to try it, but with Caustic, upon which she turned them all out, flew into a rage, abused them all, and threw everything in the room at Dr. Roe."[68]

Summer waned, and so did Augustus's episodes of grand mal epilepsy. With the help of William, Caroline managed to see *Graham Hamilton* into print.[69] The novel consists of a dialogue between the title character and a Mr. M, physically repulsive and amoral. Graham Hamilton wants to confess his sins, but keeps being interrupted by deflating remarks from his interlocutor.[70] The main character is partly a reincarnation of the willful Calantha:

> Wild and indocile, I struggled against discipline, and rejected instruction, preferring ignorance and liberty to accomplishments, rewards, and praise. Even my mother's gentle admonitions could not control me; and my boyhood was passed away in idle musings, visionary projects, and entire neglect of useful study. Early, too, I learned to dazzle and confound my own understanding by indulging the wild wanderings of fancy and yielding to the impulse of passion. Not only did I not see things as they were—but I saw them as they were not.[71]

Lest we miss the point, Mr. Hamilton tells us frankly, "I was spoiled."[72]

Graham Hamilton reiterates themes from *Glenarvon,* in which "disturbed characters see not things as they are," and guileless, sincere people become "desperate and hardened."[73] As in *Glenarvon,* cousins who are meant to marry do not. Graham loves his cousin Gertrude, who reads a lot, is modest and not inventive. Graham doesn't like to read but is passionate and impulsive.[74] Graham will become an heir if he can endure living with his miserly uncle, Sir Malcolm. This Scotch uncle instructs Graham in how to protect his wallet and character, but the instruction proceeds in a most sarcastic and peculiar manner:

> I, Sir Malcolm, thus speak to my heir: "Take money in thy hand—open thy house— ha' the best of everything . . . acquire an easy, and something of an insolent

manner; look nae modest, nae sharp, Have eyes that see not, ears that hear not; and repress every voice that would utter the genuine feelings of human nature. Learn neither to laugh loud, nor weep; say little, learn discretion. . . . Affect to be weary of everything and in time you will grow so. . . . Hate no one,—it is too much trouble: envy no one. . . . Aspire to nothing, then nothing can greatly humiliate you. Never love: and whilst you assume power over every other, beware of putting yourself into the power of any one. . . . Form no intimate friendships . . . associate with the worthless . . . Call feeling hypocrisy. . . ."[75]

The young Graham fails to heed this ironically expressed advice, becomes entrapped in social hypocrisies, and sacrifices his true love, Gertrude, for a false one, Lady Oroville, with the result that the latter's reputation is ruined. Though Lady Oroville survives, Gertrude does not. After the death of Sir Malcolm, Graham departs penitentially for America. After confessing his sins to the ugly Mr. M, he is advised to buck up and make the best of things, and he promises to do so in hopes of completing his penance honorably.

When *Graham Hamilton* was published, Caroline had two copies specially bound for herself and William. Fretting that the novel "should not be liked," she felt that "publishing has more pain with it than pleasure—suppose it be reckoned stupid—bad—How can I bear it?"[76] This time, the reviews were better. *Blackwood's Edinburgh Magazine* praised it as "belonging to the class of proper and good novels," and Lady Caroline was patted on the head for having "learned to restrain her exuberant imagination within the bounds of good taste" and encouraged, "should she still labour under the *cacoethes scribendi,* to persevere in her present strain." Lady Caroline told Colburn, "I hope you are pleased about Graham for it is liked," though she privately lamented that the story seemed "a Tale without imagination, Dull as our dullest dinners are."[77] Although Lady Caroline had not written another farrago, the reviewer thought the book's "moral" was peculiar. To say that weakness and instability of character "occasion more misery, and are consequently more mischievous, than positive vice" needed "qualifying," the reviewer gently suggested.[78]

There was little in this novel to which the Lambs could object, and they noticed it but little, being more concerned with Caroline's drunk and disorderly behavior. Emily tried once again to talk William into separating from his wife, and got him to admit that he was unhappy

that he never has a day's peace, and that her violence increases so much that he is always afraid of her doing some serious mischief to some of her Servants, and that he has written to Wm Ponsonby to say something must be done. He says she is the greatest bore in the world, and that there never was such a temper, because her fits of passion instead of being succeed by calm are only changed for the most eternal crossness and ill humour. He is a *great* ass, for having borne her as he has done, but one cannot help feeling for him, just part[icularl]y when it appears that he is not blinded about her, and that he really sees her as she is. . . ."[79]

No doubt William was tired of Caroline's tantrums, but Lady Cowper failed to perceive that he also empathized.

The completion of *Graham Hamilton* had made William believe that writing really was good therapy for Caroline, and that she truly was blessed with talent. So while he once again deflected his sister's demands for a separation, he encouraged Caroline's next novel and approved of his wife's continuing correspondences with Lady Morgan and Lydia White, both of whom believed in her. That December Caroline told Colburn that "it is Lady Morgan's advice that I should write," and with William's encouragement, she confirmed, "I am now seemingly going to write and shall request you to be my publisher—if you like it."[80] As she reviewed her accomplishments, however, she fell into a depression. She couldn't complete "Rose & Mary," nor finish "Sir Eustace de Grey," and her attempt at a novel modeled on Lockhart's *Adam Blair* (she had titled the manuscript "Charles & Julia") William had judged a failure. The novel she had written as an escape from *Graham Hamilton* was all she had left, and she believed with good reason that no one would like it.

Another Farrago: Ada Reis

1823

> I fear nobody except the devil, who certainly has all along been very particular in
> his attentions to me.
>
> —Lady Caroline Lamb[1]

L ady Caroline still carried on a correspondence with William Godwin, the
author and publisher. She regularly invited him to stay at Brocket: "Your room
shall be always ready."[2] Now, as she faced deepening despair over her failed
career as writer, her relationship with Godwin became more important, for he
was a man who could understand her despondency: "I seem to have lived 500
years, and feel I am neither wiser, better nor worse than when I began." She
frankly asked for Godwin's help with her emptiness: "For what purpose, for
whom should I endeavour to grow wise? What is the use of anything?" She
admitted that she really had no unfulfilled needs—unless for self-control—but
that did not lighten the gloom of her failure as a wife and a writer.[3] She told
Lady Morgan she had lost her "juvenile ardour" completely, and in doggerel
verse lamented

> my gay unthinking days are gone
>
> And I am now a weary Crone
>
> sitting beside my fire sighing
>
> Living but with—The dread of Dying—
>
> My Early friends or dead or changed—
>
> My Health not good my mind deranged[4]

Yet though, as she told Hart, she had lost her "former Dream," she also said that she wished to dedicate to him a new novel, to be entitled "The Witch of Edmonton."[5] The last dream to die would be that of authorship.

Lady Caroline's relationship with Murray had survived and become more intimate. She often invited him to Brocket: "[I]f you could come here with yr son he would be delighted William could take him out to see some shooting & the whole river is covered with skaters like the Serpentine do however as you please."[6] Having discovered that Godwin was in financial distress, Caroline persuaded Murray and William to help the publisher financially. In July 1823 they undertook to raise £600 by "subscription"—essentially begging letters to friends—to stop creditors from bankrupting Godwin that fall. Unfortunately, the subscription stalled, and Godwin wrote in September to Caroline that the "judicial avalanche" looked unavoidable:

> My subscription has gone on unfortunately, or rather has stood still. Mr. Murray, unluckily for me, undertook to be my Chancellor of the Exchequer and Secretary of State, and has slept in his offices. He has issued a very small number of letters. I have always been of the opinion that a bare circular letter was of little efficacy: persons even well-disposed are inclined to wait until some special messenger comes to rouse their attention. Mr Murray has, however, baffled me there: he has no list, and cannot even guess who are the persons to whom his letters have been sent.

Despite previous protests against her coming to his aid, Godwin now asked Caroline to put in a good word for him with her Uncle John and William Blake, hoping she could "turn the index to a yes, instead of a no." Acknowledging that he would normally have addressed his plea to William, he explained that she had simply become his most important advocate.[7]

Caroline interceded on Godwin's behalf with the Bessboroughs and also with the Blakes, whom she had entertained at dinner more than once. William Blake's stylized engravings for *Songs of Innocence and Experience* had influenced Caroline's watercolor and sketch work, and it is interesting (though strange) to imagine conversation between the fey hostess and the visionary poet. Caroline also suggested to Godwin that he approach at least eight others for help, warning him not to name her in case it might worsen his chances. She also helped by ordering supplies she did not need: "a ream of that thick drawing paper, 100 more pens, and two dozen sticks of wax" and, more importantly, paying up her account. Only now did she learn that Mary Shelley, the author of *Frankenstein* (1818), was Godwin's daughter.

That fall, Caroline sent Godwin several volumes of her journals, saying that she wanted to edit them for publication. She invited him to Brocket and arranged for him to meet Edward Bulwer, now a student at Cambridge.[8] They had discussed the uselessness of anxiety many times, but she had been unable to stop her anxiety attacks. "Is it not strange," she asked him, "that I can suffer my mind to be so overpowered, and mostly about trifles? can you think of me with anything but contempt?" She considered herself "tormented with such a superabundance of activity" that she could not control her behavior, and she desperately wanted him to guide her away from her customary histrionic scenes: "It is all very well if one died at the end of a tragic scene, after playing a desperate part; but if one *lives,* and instead of growing wise remains the same victim of every folly and passion without the excuse of youth and inexperience—what then? Pray say a few wise words to me. There is no one more deeply sensible than myself of kindness from persons of high intellect, and at this period of my life I need it." Caroline's was an existential crisis, for she felt that there was "no particular reason why I should exist." She continued:

> My experience gives me no satisfaction; all my opinions and beliefs and feelings are shaken, as if suffering from frequent little shocks of earthquakes. I am like a boat in a calm, in an unknown, and to me unsought-for sea, without compass to guide or even knowledge whither I am destined. Now, this is probably the case of millions, but that does not mend the matter, and whilst a fly exists, it seeks to save itself. Therefore excuse me if I try to do the same.[9]

Throughout this period, she shared her most intimate worries with Godwin, asking his advice about Augustus's condition, about publishing her journal, and about her lamentable lack of self-control.

With characteristic generosity, Caroline did everything she could to help Godwin. To give him desperately needed business, she ordered not only paper and pens, but picture frames and copies of his educational works for children. Caroline read these, and admired their brevity, simplicity, and clarity. They appealed deeply to an adult mind of philosophical bent, though not to the average young person, as she quickly found out when she tried to interest Augustus, Susan (her ward), and the offspring of her youngest brother, to whom she sent Godwin's books on Roman and Greek history. No matter. She had found in Godwin the teacher that William might have become, had he felt an instinctive faith in people's goodness:

> I have been studying your little books with an ardour and a pleasure which would surprise you. . . . oh, that I were twelve! quite good and quite well, to be your pupil.
>> "I'd drudge like Selden day and night,
>> And in the endless labour die."
> After all, what is the use of anything here below, but to be enlightened, and to try to make others happy? From this day I will endeavour to conquer all my violence, all my passions; but you are destined to be my master.

Godwin must have felt flattered but wary. His "pupil" was volatile. Those endless questions that had worn out her mother and grandmother now promised to wear out the most patient of philosophers: "For what purpose, for whom should I endeavour to grow wise?" she asked. "What is the use of anything? What is the end of life? When we die, what difference is there here, between a black beetle and me?" Caroline had regressed to her childhood, and Godwin was in for a difficult job if he tried to ameliorate the fears she listed for him:

> A want of knowledge as to what is really true.
> A certainty that I am useless.
> A fear that I am worthless.
> A belief that all is vanity and vexation of spirit, and that there is nothing new under the sun.[10]

Caroline helped William Godwin stave off his creditors that fall, and he in turn managed to avoid the delicate problem of printing her journals. Thinking about Godwin's publishing business, Caroline had thought of a project that would give her some sense of worth. She decided to become a writer and publisher of ladies' pocket diaries.

Pocket diaries were purchased by the mistresses of households as a resource and a record of important engagements, recipes, and expenses. Common throughout the eighteenth and into the nineteenth centuries, pocket diaries became, along with a ring of keys, a symbolic of women's domestic preeminence. They contained blank ruled pages and a miscellany of advice, calendars, marketing and interest tables, poetry, and even descriptions of dance-steps. They also generally printed rates of coachmen (as a defense against being taken advantage of) and tables allowing women to calculate daily wages from annual salaries for servants.[11] If successful, it could be updated and republished annually.

She called her first effort "Penruddock," a title taken from Cumberland's popular sentimental drama, *The Wheel of Fortune,* first produced in 1795. As a Harrow student, Byron had played the main character of Roderick Penruddock, whose enemies come within his power when he receives a windfall inheritance from a successful gambler. Finally in a position to destroy the man who stole his beloved Arabella, he conquers his urge for vengeance.[12] The play was published in London in 1805 and revived numerous times over the next fifteen years. The internal struggle of Penruddock may have been a dim precursor of the tormented heroes of Byron's later *Manfred* or *Cain.* Lady Caroline apparently wished to poach on Byron's past and play a sort of practical joke by titling her book of household management after a man whose emotional ledgers were kept in order despite his lusts.

Penruddock was supposed to be a challenge to pocket diaries then in existence, "a work upon domestic oeconomy which nobody dares publish as it is against the present system of Great Houses & servants."[13] Almost certainly, *Penruddock* included an extensive list of charitable institutions that Caroline wished to promote. Nonetheless, Caroline persuaded John Murray to bring it out. When the first edition was, unfortunately, delayed by copyediting problems, Caroline asked Murray to "have Penruddock advertised to quiet me," and pacified herself further by rewriting her short introduction to "the new account Book." Though she was partly responsible for the delay, she became irrationally fearful that someone might steal her ideas, and that "the novelty will be gone." Pocket diaries were like calendars; women bought them around New Year's. As the weeks dragged on she told Murray she was "disappointed and disheartened besides which it makes a material difference to me." She demanded that Murray make his wife "use Penruddocks account Book this year" and got her brothers to purchase them in advance for their wives.[14] With the intermediary assistance of Murray, *Penruddock* was apparently not printed until sometime after April 1823.[15] It had come out far too late to sell, and no copies are known to have survived. Fortunately for Caroline, it had already been eclipsed by *Ada Reis,* the wild tale she had started writing in 1821 as a relief from the drudgery of composing that "proper and good novel," *Graham Hamilton.* She had offered it to Murray then, and was delighted that he now decided he was interested in this other manuscript.

Ada Reis was actually a work of scholarship as well as imagination. She had been inspired by the exploits of Michael Bruce in the Middle East, and of the muscleman Belzoni, who had become an Egyptian explorer. She was also inspired by William Bankes, another of Byron's friends, who had sailed up the Nile, explored Egyptian tombs, and copied hieroglyphs.[16] Caroline did a great deal of research for the novel, which includes sixty-one pages of footnotes alluding to works like Tully's *Tripoly,* Don Antonio de Ulloa's *Voyage to South America,* Edward Volney's *Egypt,* Herrera's *Voyage to America,* and Humboldt's *Tableau de la Nature.* The theme of the novel is the fruitlessness of human striving. The title page of each volume quotes Xenophon: "At the same time that he pursued these studies, he made sport of them."[17] Belzoni, for whom Lady Caroline had fifty extra copies of the title page of *Ada Reis* printed, is mentioned in its preface as one of those who have proved that the most astonishing human productions are in the end, nothing but vanity.[18]

The story of *Ada Reis* is wrapped in a hieroglyphic exercise. The book is (supposedly) the partial translation of a text interred in the grave of Ada Reis's daughter, on whose gravestone his name is also inscribed. Supposedly translated from the original, written in Arabic, Spanish, and Incan, the text tells the tale of Ada Reis, "the once-famous Corsair, the Don Juan of his day," who is born in Georgia near the Black Sea and sold into bondage by his parents. Luckily, Ada is purchased by Adamo Remolo, a kindly Genoese merchant who raises him as his son, educating him at Pisa and arranging for him to become a page in the court of the Duke of Tuscany. The young man grows up impulsive, impetuous, cunning, and an intemperate drinker. After having been dismissed by the Duke for repeated offenses, he joins a privateer's crew and murders the captain (whose title is "Reis"). He takes the captain's title, and declares himself a follower of Islam, a gesture Caroline's readers would have understood as indicating Ada's complete alienation from European culture.

Ada Reis accrues a record of brutality and cunning and attracts the attention of the Pasha of Tripoli, who employs him in various schemes that cause him to travel the Mediterranean. His love-conquests include many women, some of whom he marries: Zoë, Orrellana, Issaline, Aura, Zemyra, Orgylia, Mania (one of Lady Caroline's nicknames), and an Italian beauty named Bianca de Castamela, who gives birth to a daughter named Fiormonda (an echo of "Fiorabella" from *Glenarvon*). After traveling for three years, Ada Reis returns to Italy to finds Bianca has married. He falls into a rage, strangles and stabs her, taking Fiormonda with him.

His anger melts into remorse, and he resolves to raise Fiormonda under the watchful eye of Shaffou Paca, the former governess of the Pasha's harem. This old woman is appallingly ugly, corpulent, and wall-eyed, with one leg shorter than the other. Worse, she is the mother of a sorcerer called Kabkarra the Jew, whose powers derive from his pact with the evil spirit Zubanyánn. Kabkarra has prophesied that Ada Reis will wear a monarch's crown "in a land where diamonds and emeralds shall be strewn under thy feet, and where the blood of the innocent may flow, without fear of revenge." Another wizard, Kara Dengis, repeats that Reis "shall be king in another land" and that Fiormonda "shall wear an imperial crown."[19] The remainder of the novel presents the effectuation of these prophecies, though not in the manner expected by the novel's central character.

Kabkarra knows all Ada Reis's crimes, and he demands that Fiormonda be promised to him in marriage. Since the wizard is so powerful, and since he possesses, among other items, the famous sword of Damascus—said to have been the property of Melchior, one of the three Magi—Ada Reis is forced to agree, although he has in the meantime allowed Fiormonda to become engaged to the Pasha's son. Kabkarra gives Fiormonda a clockwork chessboard that seems magical, though we aren't told why.[20]

Though he has now retired from public view and engages in the study of science, Ada Reis is still haunted by his former misdeeds. When he discovers that Zevahir, a little page, has befriended Fiormonda, he dismisses the servant. But Zevahir is actually the spirit of Good, whose real names are Phaos or Zamohr. He appears to Fiormonda in a vision when she has temporarily conquered most of her "violence and vanity."[21] Zevahir intends to act as Fiormonda's guardian spirit. However, the sorcerer Kabkarra understands that he can foil the good spirit's intentions if Fiormonda's passions and temper are encouraged. Though she falls ill and seeks him desperately, Phaos appears less and less often to her, and finally tells her that she has been seduced by the world of vanity and deceit and that he can come to her no more. Zevahir appeals one last time directly to Ada Reis to help save Fiormonda, but he is again turned away.[22]

As Kabkarra predicts, Ada Reis's many crimes become$ known, and he falls out of favor with the Pasha. He opens the chessboard, which magically begins to enact a battle between good (the White pieces) and evil (the Black). White is checkmated, and the battle becomes real; Ada Reis and Fiormonda are forced to flee the house while bombs explode nearby. Kabkarra protects the two and sends them to the New World, promising that exactly five years later he will appear to claim Fiormonda. Sailing for Lima, they come across a wrecked ship and pull from the water a young Venetian count, with whom Fiormonda falls in love. Count Condulmar wins her affection partly by his ability to sing, and his world-weary attitude is strongly reminiscent of Byron. In Lima, Fiormonda is courted by many suitors, including the attractive and well-to-do Alphonso,

Duke of Montevallos. Ada Reis's vanity is stirred by the stature of his daughter's suitors and the respect paid to him because of his wealth. Condulmar's attentions, however, do not encourage Fiormonda's good qualities. He breaks her heart by taking other lovers, and when confronted by Alphonso for the aspersions he has cast upon Fiormonda's character, Condulmar knocks him to the ground and kills him. Alphonso's ghost then appears to Fiormonda, begging her to change her ways.[23]

Though she continues to be affected by Condulmar's lyric intensity, Fiormonda is no longer under any illusion about the blackness of his character. The way is now paved for a conclusion of dark humor reminiscent of *A New Canto,* whose verses are recalled by the description of an earthquake that levels the city of Lima:

> The concussion was repeated: sulphurous flames broke forth from the bosom of the earth; then at once were heard, on all sides, the screams of the dying, the roaring of thunder, the wild howling of animals, the crash of churches, palaces, buildings, toppling one upon another, all in a moment destroyed, and burying under them their miserable inhabitants. The fort of Callao sunk into ruins; the ocean, receding to a considerable distance, returned in mountainous waves, foaming with the violence of the convulsion, and the whole country became as a sea—the multitudinous waters covering all that had so lately been fair streets and stately buildings.[24]

Lady Caroline loved the apocalyptic scene, just as she had loved the revolutionary politics of *Glenarvon:* "The world was convulsed to give him liberty, and assist him to his revenge."[25]

Ada Reis is hurled to the ground in the earthquake and loses sight of Fiormonda. He escapes Lima in the company of an Indian named Papo Taguacan, who guides him through the rainforest. They wander through wild mountains until Papo reaches his native territory, where his tribe appears to revere Ada Reis. Papo Taguacan kills the tribal leader Ciulactly (his own cousin) so that Ada Reis can be crowned their new King and assume the role of a divinity. Ada Reis bitterly recognizes the fulfillment of Kabkarra's prophecy.

Sick and disgusted, Ada Reis secludes himself, which only causes his subjects to venerate him more. One night he is watching a spider dexterously drawing the threads of its web from a corner of the room to a spot near him. Suddenly the spider grows immensely large and throws its web around Ada Reis, who startles and tries to run, but finds himself transported to a mountainous desert. He sees

Papo Taguacan, torn to pieces, but as he approaches the Indian turns whole again and transforms into Count Condulmar, who laments his loneliness and guilt. Kabkarra now appears, and Ada Reis demands to see his "innocent child." Kabkarra laughs at the word "innocent," and reveals that he is identical with the spirit of evil, Zubanyánn, and that Zevahir is his half-brother. Kabkarra then delivers a long monologue on his origins and journey through a three-thousand year existence, ending by telling Ada Reis that Fiormonda has taken her place in the retinue of the devil and wears an imperial crown, and also that Condulmar is his son.

The two men go then into the Valley of Death to Zubanyánn's palace, in which there is chaos and a "confusion of tongues," and yet a punctilious observance of fashion.[26] Hell, as Lady Caroline describes it, exhibits little of the "sultry heat so often alluded to," but rather a climate "cold, raw, and unpleasant, such as is felt in the capital of England when an east wind brings with it a fog."[27] Ada Reis is introduced to the various social strata of hell, ending with his own daughter's. As in Dante's *Inferno* the punishments suffered by the sinners are all suited to their failings. For example, a musician of low character is forced to take the shape of a huge viola de gamba and to endure the insensitive performances of "mock artists."[28] There is one woman, however, who suffers only because she fell under the suspicion of having committed errors and "lost her character without any reason." An astonished Ada Reis asks what the logic can be for her punishment, since she only hurt herself, and is told self-injury is one of the greatest crimes one can commit.[29] Similarly, poverty is a crime leading to hell.

Ada Reis offers a cameo appearance of Caroline herself. She appears as a "thin woman" whom Ada Reis questions. She tells him her fate:

> My punishment is now to see shades of every one once dear to me pass by me with indifference; to feel intensely, but to know that none do feel for me; to hear from time-pieces, all day and all night long, not the hours, but all my thousand follies and faults repeated; and to be conscious that all my thoughts, wishes, and actions are misrepresented. Sir, can I say more? I was idolized—I am—ah! would I were only forgotten!—But it is well—I lost myself. I felt the harshness and unkindness of some too keenly—I seized a pen—and the pen which knew once but to write with the milk of human kindness I dipped in gall.[30]

Here, Lady Caroline gave her final fictional rendition of Byron as Satan. The world's response to her literary work is contained in Ada Reis's response: "No woman should ever write."

When Ada Reis and Kabkarra reach the royal apartment, they find Fiormonda and Condulmar "seated in awful majesty upon thrones." Condulmar is triumphant, while Fiormonda begs that the damned be given one last chance to repent. Condulmar agrees, confident that he will prevail. And in the end, no one but Fiormonda is able to seize the opportunity for redemption and resist the temptations that had brought them there to begin with. Fiormonda lives out the remainder of her days as a Christian penitent and is buried, with her secrets, under her father's name.

Murray liked *Ada Reis* and so did William, though he was aware that its apocalyptic ending would remind readers of *Glenarvon.* Like her first novel, *Ada Reis* included a number of lyrics, and once again she collaborated with Isaac Nathan, who set "Weep for what thou hast lost, love" to music for printing in the book. As much to protect Caroline from a reprise of the debacle of her first novel as himself from further family troubles, William tried to get Caroline to tone down the book's final scenes. The negotiations dragged on into the final stages of proofreading. As publication approached, Caroline stayed home to work instead of going to a ball. "My heart is in *Ada Reis,*" she wrote to John Murray; "spend therefore any thing you would spend on or in facilitating its being well corrected well brought out 'the sooner the better.'" William prevailed upon her and Murray, however, to consult William Gifford, the editor of the *Quarterly Review* regarding the ending. Caroline agreed reluctantly, saying that if Gifford—well known as an opinionated and intrusive editor—would approve of *Ada Reis,* she would insist on having her name printed on the title page.[31] She waited nervously for the irascible critic's verdict: "I am in great anxiety about yr not writing me what Gifford says, I think it is a civil way of giving me my Death Warrant."[32]

Gifford, however, approved, and William found himself overruled. "If Mr. Gifford thinks there is in the first two volumes anything of excellence sufficient to overbalance their manifest faults," he conceded,

> I still hope that he will impress upon Lady Caroline the absolute necessity of carefully reconsidering and revising the third volume, and particularly the conclusion of the novel. Mr. Gifford, I dare say, will agree with me that since the time of Lucian all the representations of the infernal regions, which have been attempted by satirical writers, such as "Fielding's Journey from this World to the Next," have been feeble and flat. The sketch in "Ada Reis" is commonplace in its observations and altogether insufficient, and it would not do now to come with a decisive failure in an attempt of considerable boldness. . . . I wish you would communicate these my hasty suggestions to Mr. Gifford, and he will see the

propriety of pressing Lady Caroline to take a little more time to this part of the novel. She will be guided by his authority, and her fault at present is to be too hasty and too impatient of the trouble of correcting and recasting what is faulty.[33]

William failed to win his case. The ending stood. But he succeeded on another point, for despite Caroline's desires, *Ada Reis* was published without fanfare and, more importantly, without her name. Having long feared the book would "fall like a lump of lead into a lake," she pestered her family to know whether they had seen it, and pelted Murray once again with demands that he advertise more effectively. "No one of my relations or friends have even heard of *Ada Reis*," Caroline lamented shortly after its publication in a run of 750 copies.[34] Her sister-in-law described her at this time as "more termagent than ever."[35]

Caroline's mood was influenced by her double-anxiety over her novel's reception. It was a work of fantasy that she knew might be savaged by reviewers. But it was also a bid to be re-admitted to the circles from which she had been banished. She had dedicated *Ada Reis* to Lydia White, the hostess of those "esprit parties" that were the closest thing in London to a French literary salon. Novelist Maria Edgeworth knew Lydia White and described her in 1822: "Her bead hat crowned with feathers her haggard face—rouged and dying!—her life hanging by a thread over the brink of the grave and she turning and clinging to the gay world!—that world which is forsaking and laughing at her." Whatever Lydia White's health problems were, she faced them with courage: "Poor creature," Maria Edgeworth said, "how she can go through it I cannot imagine. It is dreadful to look at her."[36]

Thus, Lady Caroline had dedicated her novel to one who refused to be banished by ill health from London society: "To you, who, without paying undue deference to what is termed the world, have succeeded in retaining around you, even when sickness has rendered you incapable of exertion, many who are distinguished by superiority of intellect and literary talents, to you I dedicate these pages."[37] Although she dedicated her book to a specific person, in deference to her family she called herself only "The Author." She left no ambiguity about her intention, however: "I have been struck too, in the midst of my undertaking, by affliction. . . . I, too, have left the world, yet my heart is with those I have left."[38] Perhaps, she hoped, the leaders of the gynocracy would take pity upon her.

Caroline was proud of *Ada Reis*. The book had been beautifully produced by John Murray. The care with which it was printed and bound—including the excellent paper—drew specific comment from *The British Magazine*. Flush with success, Caroline thanked Lady Morgan in a late-night letter "for yr kind reception of Adamo el Reis—you must tell Lady or Mrs Fletcher that Condulmar not Ada is Ld Byron that is if there be a Byron in the Tale and as to the Radicals in Hell they must be some where you know & where the Deuce in these Aristocratic days can they be." She admitted her pride: "I myself rather admire it just as old men Love a little child & its fancies."[39] Lady Dacre and Mrs Opie both sent complimentary notes about *Ada Reis* to the author, and so did Edward Bulwer, who knew that Caroline had used him as the model for Zevahir. Caroline told him, "I feel very much flattered by your letter."[40]

Though less than glowing, reviews of *Ada Reis* were not unappreciative. *The Literary Gazette* labeled the book "a wild, inconsistent medley" that defied analysis, but it spent five full columns summarizing the plot.[41] *The New Monthly Magazine* endorsed *Ada Reis* as the work of an author "acute, ingenious, imaginative, capable of quick and shrewd observation, with feelings as exalted as her fancy," but allowed that it treated the book "leniently" because it was the work of a woman "so far removed from the flat realities of life, that she scarcely sees any thing as it really is." Nonetheless, the reviewer thought the descriptions excellent, citing the powerful evocation of the earthquake in Lima.[42] The *British Magazine* also gave an extensive plot summary before dismissing the book as a weak imitation of other fantastic tales, like Beckford's *Vathek*. Isaac Nathan received a nasty slap as the only composer who would stoop to setting such indifferent lyrics.[43] *The Examiner* allowed that the story seemed "concocted by opium and a wayward imagination out of the whole series of Eastern Tales," but called it "the work of no common hand" and recommended readers buy or borrow it to satisfy their curiosity.[44] All the reviewers seemed mystified by the dedication to Lydia White.

Amid the turmoil created by *Ada Reis,* Caroline was pleased when Isaac Nathan printed another of the songs from the novel as sheet music.[45] She sent free copies to Murray, Colburn, and other acquaintances. "Thank you for my song," she wrote Nathan from Brocket. "I gave one copy to Lady Cork, who is here, and she has nieces who play and sing very well. The weather is too delightful. Believe me, when I tell you, if I can serve you at any time, or in any way, I shall be most happy. I mean to send Mrs. Nathan *Ada Reis,* in return for her remembering me. Tell my God-daughter to love me."[46]

The publication of her third novel reignited the family enmities that had been smoldering since *Glenarvon*. Once again, William was taken to task for not controlling his wife. Therefore, despite her excitement, Caroline told Lady Morgan she hoped the book would not attract too much attention: "All I have asked of Murray is a dull sale or a still birth. This may seem strange, and I assure you it is contrary to my own feelings of ambition; but what can I do? I am ordered peremptorily by my own family not to write." When Lady Morgan protested that the book deserved attention, Caroline threw up her hands: "I ask you if one descended in a right line from Spenser [Edmund Spenser, author of *The Faerie Queen*], not to speak of the Duke of Marlborough, with all the Cavendish and Ponsonby blood to boot, which you know were always rebellious, should feel a little strongly upon any occasion, and burst forth, and yet be told to hold one's tongue and not write, what is to happen?"[47]

Caroline desperately wanted Lady Morgan's approval, and she sent her three copies of *Ada Reis,* along with copies of complimentary letters from William Gifford and Lady Dacre. The support of an established writer and close friend like Lady Morgan meant so much to Caroline because it seemed as if everybody wanted to snuff her tiny but essential "spark of genius."[48] In a mood of temporary defiance, Caroline told Henry Colburn that if he ever republished *Glenarvon* or *Graham Hamilton* "you have my order to put my name to them as I never again mean to publish anything without." She promised him to return to work on her unfinished manuscripts: "I hope you received and liked Ada Reis—Rose & Mary shall be ready soon or if you prefer it Sir Eustace Grey."[49]

Lady Morgan gave Caroline the approval she desired and persuaded her husband to read *Ada Reis* and profess his admiration. She also enlisted Caroline's aid as a researcher, for she was at work on a biography of the Italian painter Salvator Rosa (1615-1673), some of whose works hung in Devonshire House. Rosa's work had been very popular with the British aristocracy of the previous two generations, and Frederick Ponsonby himself had once owned some of his steel-plate engravings.[50] "I will do all I can for Salvator Rosa," promised Caroline. But in return she asked Lady Morgan to help Augustus's physician, Dr. Roe, secure a place at Westminster Hospital when a vacancy arose. "[A]s we both love Ireland, let me speak it to the honour of that country, that [Dr. Roe] sprung from it. He has done everything he could for my dear and only child. I therefore have done and will do everything for him."[51]

Domestic matters now captured Caroline's attention. In August, she found that a young woman in her employ was concealing a man in her room who may have been her husband, though she had presented herself as a spinster. The servant was escorted to an inn, though she retaliated by telling a reporter she had been beaten and turned out of the house without any clothes. "I have been much annoyed to-day," Caroline told Lady Morgan, "by a paragraph in two papers about my turning a woman out of doors—pray if you see or hear of it, contradict it."[52] Former servants also required Caroline's attention, such as a Miss Bryan, whose application for a position as governess Caroline promoted by noting that she was "more dignified, tranquil, calm, gentle, and self-possessed than I am," though she was unsure of Miss Bryan's pedagogical skills, for "the power of instructing is almost a gift of nature [and] many of the best instructed themselves are deficient in it."[53] But when Miss Bryan fell ill and lost the position, Caroline wrote of these developments philosophically, for Miss Bryan had formed an unfortunate attachment to an aging Russian mathematician: "[S]he has a cold and cough, and is in love. I cannot help it; can you?"[54]

Caroline's own health came to a sudden crisis in December, when she took a bad fall from a horse. She languished for a week before the servants carried her outside in a blanket to get some fresh air. Upon her recovery, she announced to Lady Morgan that "a new Lady Caroline has arisen from this death. I seem to have buried my sins, griefs, melancholy, and to have come out like a new-born babe unable to walk, think, speak; but perfectly happy." It was actually the weeklong respite from her addictions that had restored her health temporarily:

> I have positively refused to take ally draughts, pills, laudanum, wine, brandy, or other stimulants. I live upon meal-porridge, soda water, milk, arrowroot, and all the farinaceous grains; My mind is calm—I am pleased to be alive—grateful for the kindness shown me; and never mean to answer any questions further back than the 15th of this month, that being the day of this new Lady Caroline's birth: and I hate the old one.

The new Caroline would be cheerful, not bitter; forward-looking, not re-living her past. The new Caroline would give up scribbling: "As to writing, assuredly, enough has been written, besides it is different writing when one's thoughts flow out before one's pen, and writing with one's pen waiting for thoughts."[55] The new Caroline would be happy and contented.

Byron's Death

1824

It makes me so nervous to write that I must stop—will it tire you too much if I
continue?

—Lady Caroline Lamb[1]

I saac Nathan had once consoled Caroline with music. Now she would console
her friend with poetry. When his wife, Rosetta, died in childbirth on 19 January
1824, Nathan was laid low, and he asked Lady Caroline to versify some lines he
had written in Hebrew as he struggled to accept his loss. He gave her a literal
translation, and she told him, "I was so struck with the simplicity and melancholy
of what you sent me, that I just wrote these very imperfect lines. Will you write
and explain to me how you wish them done, and I will make another attempt."
Nathan was satisfied with the first attempt, a three-stanza poem beginning, "(a)s
the flower early gathered, while fresh in its bloom. . . ."[2] Nathan would now have
to discover how to raise six children—including the baby, who had survived—
without his beloved wife.

It was a year of death. Bess, the dowager Duchess of Devonshire, died on 30
March 1824, in Rome, eighteen years to the day after Georgiana had passed away.
And on 19 April Byron died at Missolonghi. It would be almost a month before
news reached England. After Byron's friend Douglas Kinnaird received the report
on 14 May, word spread quickly.

Caroline was staggered. She had sustained her new health regimen through the winter, with some lapses, and was enjoying the spring weather at Brocket, when word of Byron's death reached her. Despite the improvement in her health, she had not left off complaining that she was ill and preparing to die. Her relatives and acquaintances had become inured to her fretting, but everyone realized that Byron's death would almost certainly produce a strong reaction. She later told Thomas Medwin that she received the news while she was "laughing at Brockett Hall," and that the receipt of a letter "or some other cause produced a fever from which I never yet have recovered—It was also singular that the first day I could go out in an open Carriage, as I was slowly driving up the hill here,—Lord Byron's Hearse was at that moment passing under these very walls, and rested at Welwyn."[3] Her description of her illness is laden with gothic elements, like a nightmare the previous March in which she had seen a pudgy, straight-haired Byron grinding his teeth at her. Her description of her encounter with the hearse allows that she did not until later know what she had seen. It seems odd that in all this reaching for the outlandish she should have admitted that it was either the letter "or some other cause" that produced her illness. It also seems unlikely that she *accidentally* encountered Byron's funeral cortege on 13 or 14 July as it passed through Welwyn on its way to Nottingham.

As with so much of Lady Caroline's late accounts of her life, these descriptions must be tempered by comparison with reports of independent observers. Hobhouse reports that, far from being bedridden, she had written almost immediately after receiving news of Byron's death to ask Hobhouse to visit her in Whitehall. Too impatient to wait, she then arrived at the gentleman's quarters on May 22 before he was even up and sent a note: "If you are up will you see me one minute I am on my way to Brockett & have been ill—should I not see you I wish merely to say to you that if my letters are in *yr* hands it is all I care about."[4] Hobhouse reported in his diary:

This morning I was called up to Lady C. Lamb, whom I found waiting for me in my room. She had written to me saying she was perfectly satisfied if her letters (to Byron) were in my hands; she now added that she could not give up Byron's letters to her (Caroline), but she would leave them under seal directed to me in case of her dying before me, and she *was* dying, she said. I found her in a sad state; but I could not consent to give up any of her letters, the only guarantee against her making a novel out of Byron's letters. I shall give the same answer about Lady Melbourne's letters, and all to whom I have spoken agree with me in the propriety of this measure."[5]

Like a number of other female correspondents of Byron, Caroline hoped Hobhouse would relent and return her letters to him. She even asked Lydia White to intervene and speak with Hobhouse.[6] At first, Hobhouse had been distracted by a furious argument over the disposition of Byron's memoirs, which were burnt (over the protestations of Thomas Moore, who had a financial and personal stake in the matter) in John Murray's offices on Albemarle Street on 17 May. After his visit with Lady Caroline on 22 May, Hobhouse received a disturbing letter disclosing that at some earlier date she had persuaded Murray to let her read the memoirs. The charge was undoubtedly true, based on Caroline's communications with Murray: "The Journal you mentioned, were you serious if indeed you will permit me to look at it I will call on you & read it . . . you confer on me the greatest favour you can."[7] Murray's failure to keep the manuscript under wraps left the grim prospect that someone, somewhere, had copied out portions of the memoirs and might eventually publish them. Aware that she had exposed Murray to recrimination, she wrote again to Hobhouse: "I told Murray to tell you that I read his journal with sorrow & perhaps anger but upon my honour & soul I took no copy of any part of it—*others have* I have not I swear."[8] Unpacified, Hobhouse confronted Murray with his transgression, which the publisher denied, though all the while "looking red as fire and turning away his head."[9]

Byron's death may not have prostrated Caroline for a month and a half, but there can be no doubt she was physically affected. She told Hobhouse that her sorrow caught her by surprise: "I am sorry to find myself so very much overpowered at an event which after 10 years of indifference or perhaps enmity on his part ought to have excited no feeling in me but a similar one—however, there is no accounting for our nature. I loved him dearly—I do so still." She asked Hobhouse to call on her and to send Byron's servant, Fletcher, to tell her the "melancholy particulars" of Byron's passing.[10] In petitioning for such favors, Caroline offered to send Hobhouse a copy of her brother Frederick's translation of the oration delivered at Byron's funeral in Athens.[11] She also repeated that she would trust him to burn or otherwise dispose of any correspondence between herself and Byron.

Though Caroline was willing to trust him, Hobhouse knew Caroline too well to expect such mild weather to last. Then, too, news of the destruction of Byron's memoirs was beginning to circulate in London, and Hobhouse was uneasy that his role in their burning might be condemned, as it seemed to be in *Bell's Life in London,* where the 30 May issue led on its first page with a satire in which Rousseau queries Byron about his "Confessions," and Byron replies that "they will show to posterity what the English social world, which boasts of its morality, is, if my friends will have the courage (which I now greatly doubt) to publish the revelations."[12] Lady Caroline wrote to Hobhouse again on 27 May saying that if it was necessary to burn even Byron's letters to her she could not oppose it, but she still had not surrendered the letters on 13 July.[13]

Isaac Nathan must have been disappointed that the godmother of his daughter was so distracted during this period, for he had suffered a challenge to his ownership of her song lyrics. The songs he had published now numbered at least a half a dozen. One of them ("If thou couldst know what 'tis to weep") had appeared in *Graham Hamilton,* but in May of 1824 the composer J. Close pirated it and attributed it the actress Mrs. Jordan, who was said to have written it on her deathbed.[14] Nathan was upset and anxious to clear up the confusion, for the poem had been in his possession long before *Graham Hamilton* had been published.[15] It reminds us that Isaac Nathan and Lady Caroline were both insomniacs:

> If thou could'st know what 'tis to weep,
> To weep unpitied and alone,
> The live-long night, whilst others sleep,
> Silent and mournful watch to keep,
> Thou wouldst not do what I have done.[16]

Nathan's proprietary interest in Lady Caroline is symbolized in the title of the song he set to music for *Ada Reis:* "Sing Not for Others But For Me." When Nathan discussed this song, he made sure to note that it, and indeed "most of her Ladyship's verses, which were expressly written for me, may be had separately, of Cramer, Addison, and Beale, Music Publishers."[17] He was undoubtedly anxious to preserve his relationship with his patroness, and he persuaded her to write him a letter giving him exclusive rights to the lyrics from her novels. He published a facsimile of this letter after her death, along with specific advertising information about the ten or twelve songs of Lady Caroline's he was still selling in 1828.[18]

It was during this difficult period that Lady Caroline invited guests to Brocket, among whom was Edward Bulwer, now preparing for his fourth year at Cambridge. Dutifully and excitedly, he turned up at Brocket in September, and for a few days lived out his fantasy of a liaison with Lady Caroline, who offered to let him wear the ring Byron had given her. But she was a distracted and probably drug-influenced paramour, and perversely (it seemed to Bulwer) turned her attentions to young Mr. Russell, an illegitimate son of the Duke of Bedford, who was also visiting at Brocket. Lady Caroline had known Russell since he was three, but Bulwer did not know this, and when he observed Russell wearing the ring he had declined to accept on the ground of its sentimental value, Bulwer threw himself on the couch and sank into self-pity while someone (could it have been Isaac Nathan?) played music in the ballroom. Lady Caroline came to him and asked him if he was upset. Observing the tears in his eyes she said, "Don't play this melancholy air. It affects Mr. Bulwer so that he is actually weeping!" Bulwer was so stung that he leapt up and made sure he was "the life of the company." However, the next morning he left Brocket very early, without seeing Caroline.[19] From Cambridge in October, he sent letters of reproach to which she made conciliatory replies. She had wounded him, and yet Bulwer defended her to his mother, whom he told that even with the strongest temptation and any number of opportunities, Caroline had resisted having sex with him.[20] He also wrote in his copy of *Glenarvon* that the novel had impressed him: "(H)ad its literary execution equalled the intense imagination which conceived it—I believe it would have ranked among the few fictions which produce a permanent effect upon youth in every period of the world."[21]

Byron's death had slowly taken its toll, and Caroline returned to drug and alcohol abuse. On 11 October 1824, Harryo wrote to her sister Georgiana that she had received intelligence from the ancient Reverend Preedy "that Caroline Lamb is in a much calmer state at Brocket and under the surveillance of two women, that William is with her *de temps en temps,* but lives chiefly with Lord Melbourne at Whitehall."[22] The two women were "nurses" who acted as wardens. When financial problems forced the Melbournes to rent Brocket Hall to Sir William Rumbold late in 1824, and Caroline was forced to forego her great pleasures of rambling on foot and horseback in the Hertfordshire countryside, the "nurses" went with her.[23]

Then came another shock. Thomas Medwin's *Conversations of Lord Byron* was published on 23 October. Though Medwin was attacked for being "careless, muddleheaded, dishonest, or insufficiently informed," his basic veracity shone through for Caroline.[24] Thus, it was especially painful for her to read that Byron had said she possessed "scarcely any personal attractions to recommend her," except her vivacity and first-rate connections. Medwin also quoted Byron as saying that he had sincerely *tried* to be in love, implying he had never really been so, but that he was "easily governed by women, and (Caroline) gained an ascendancy over me that I could not easily shake off." Out of "spite and jealousy," Caroline was supposed to have promised one of her admirers "her favours if he would call (Byron) out."[25]

All this was hurtful, but incomparably more painful was Byron's reaction to Lady Caroline's invasion of his apartments in 1812, when she had scribbled in his copy of *Vathek* the phrase "Remember me!" Since she had not seen the earlier version (see Chapter 8), she had no idea that he had changed his first response from anger over shared guilt to condemnation of her. The poem reads like a curse:

Remember thee, remember thee!
Till Lethe quench life's burning stream,
Remorse and shame shall cling to thee,
And haunt thee like a feverish dream!

Remember thee! Ay doubt it not.
Thy husband too shall think of thee!
By neither shalt though be forgot,
Thou *false* to him, thou *fiend* to me![26]

She thought that she had heard everything that might be said against her by anyone, including Byron, and now this. She wrote to William Godwin to say she had been "deeply & painfully humiliated."[27] She was stung into trying once more to see Annabella, to whom she wrote on 31 October requesting an appointment and the return, via Hobhouse or Augusta Leigh, of her letters, pictures, and memorabilia, in return for which Caroline would surrender Byron's.[28]

Lady Byron responded to Caroline's protestations of illness that she herself had been extremely unwell and

obliged to avoid every fatigue or excitation—Whilst under the necessity of observing these restrictions I regret that I must not see you—the very interest which I could not but take in feelings such as you describe would affect me unfavourably. Do not suspect me of making a false excuse—in the little intercourse which has passed between us, the language of sincerity has I believe been spoken on both sides—& if I had other reasons for declining to meet you, I should frankly acknowledge them.[29]

Annabella reassured Caroline that she had no reason for alarm respecting the letters that Hobhouse now controlled. She also attempted to calm Caroline's fears about Medwin, whose book she had not yet read, saying "I hope you will not allow them to prey upon your mind—dare to consider the worst as in one respect a relief," and she concluded by wishing "that you may experience the calmness peace & consolation which no one wishes you more sincerely than I." But peace was impossible and consolation unattainable, for the "new Caroline" had been overtaken by the old.

She felt she must strike back, and showed one of Byron's tenderest letters to her brother Willy. Seeing her distress, Willy could not help but agree that she might as well send it as a retort to Medwin. On 1 November Hobhouse was called to reassure her about her letters, but she spent the whole time fretting over Medwin's *Conversations*. She also showed Hobhouse the letter from Byron which she said she would publish with Willy's blessing, since "no imputation was so dreadful as that of not having been loved." Hobhouse wrote in his journal: "She is certainly mad."[30]

Mad or not, she was lucid enough to draft a long letter to Medwin which she sent through Henry Colburn—her publisher as well as Medwin's—to whom she also wished to voice her pain. She appealed to Medwin not to portray her as heartless, but to balance his account of her in a new edition. She admitted that so far as she could tell Medwin had told the truth, but Byron had lied; that he had truly loved her, a fact made more believable precisely because, "as he and you justly observe, I had few personal attractions."[31] This long, painful *apologia* emphasized two main points: first, that she had loved both her husband and Byron, and second, that they each had loved her. Along the way, she reiterated two other points. One was that Byron had alienated her by telling her despicable and unrepeatable things about himself. The other was that William's loyalty to her had saved her, and that she saw him as the finest man she had ever known. All this, together with passages copied from Byron's love letter, did have an effect on Medwin, who altered his narrative by omitting the general attack and verse diatribe against Lady Caroline. However, when Edward Bulwer wrote on her behalf, asking him to withdraw the passage in which *Glenarvon* is described as an act of vandalism on the very character of Lord Byron, Medwin refused.[32]

Whatever Medwin thought of Caroline did not matter now. Her dead lover had spoken from the grave. To Hart, she said simply, "Those bitter lines are a legacy which grieves me."[33] She proceeded with her plan to have facsimiles of Byron's letter printed to prove his devotion, and this too made her notorious— an internationally famous erotomaniac. When Balzac sought to give a flavor of decadence to Florine's dining room in *A Daughter of Eve* (1838-39), he hung a copy of Caroline's lithograph on the wall: "a dainty picture of Eugene Devaria; a somber picture of some Spanish alchemist by Louis Boulanger, an autograph of Lord Byron to Caroline, in an ebony frame. . . ."[34]

Having failed in appeals to Annabella and Hobhouse, Caroline asked Hart to arrange an exchange of letters and memorabilia: "To you & to you only I will give up my journals, Ld. Byron's verses, every thing to burn, & you must make Hobhouse give up mine—you are like a King in the family & I want the whole thing to be done *really*." Her letter concluded with a general declaration of forgiveness to all those who were angry with her, "knowing how much I have tried all your patiences out."[35] Hart may have felt exasperated himself, but he remained loyal and sympathetic, one of the few friends she had left.

Exile

1825–1826

I feel violently; is that madness?
—Lady Caroline Lamb[1]

I n Whitehall, Caroline continued under the care of "the Women," her two nurses, who monitored her drug and alcohol consumption: "A little ill—a little pill," she wrote mockingly to Lady Morgan.[2] But it was no joke, for when she became fractious they locked her up. During one of these periods of confinement, Caroline started to write a plea for help on the end-pages of a book in the Melbourne House library. She spilled ink over it, then scrawled on the opposite page: "The Slaughter House—not Melbourne House."[3] Dr. Goddard, her physician, monitored his patient through the nurses.

In her calmer moments, Caroline now saw the inevitability of a legal separation from William. It had become a matter simply of *when* and *how much*. Financial negotiations absorbed considerable energy on both the Lamb and Ponsonby sides. The 6th Duke undertook to arbitrate negotiations between Frederick and William Ponsonby, on one hand, with Lord Brougham lending his support, and Frederick Lamb and Lord Cowper on the other.[4] Like most of the major scenes of Lady Caroline's life, this one became turbid, emotional, and drawn out. As the campaign to evict her turned into a siege, William lost his appetite for it. On Thursday 7 April 1825 he wrote Caroline from Brighton, "It is dull & cold here, I have a good fire in my room—let us go to Brockett—I shall be sure to be with you Sunday." Sunday the tenth would be Easter. On the eighth, Emily and George gave William a talking to. He then wrote Caroline to say he had been urged to part with her, and that it was something she had often proposed, so they might as well settle the matter. William went to London to avoid Brocket and Caroline's persuasive powers.

Caroline appealed repeatedly to Hart to stop the separation: "[C]an you avert it—can you retard it?"[5] She insisted she was "no more mad than a March Hare only now & then rumbustial when misunderstood." "[R]iding & being amused & treated with kindness" had cured her. She signed herself "yours ah would it were as it used to be."[6] Caroline argued truthfully that William was "wretched at the step he is taking," and that he was bending to the will of his siblings. Hart finally agreed to visit with her, and told her she would always have his support, but that he would not act as a negotiator for her side.

Staying out of the fray proved difficult, however. "I cannot help writing you a few lines" George Lamb wrote to the 6th Duke on 15 April, "in consequence of the representation, which I find [Lady Caroline] has made of your interview with her." Caroline was not, it seemed, "the unhappy reasonable creature" the Duke had described. Instead, "she had resumed her natural character of violence and threats of all sorts, and now she says she is determined to agree to nothing unless William comes back." George Lamb defended his family's position on the deed of separation and complained that Willy Ponsonby had dragged his feet. "If we are at last forced to take forcible steps," he warned, "the blame will all be upon the heads of her own family."[7] Hart replied temperately that he had no responsibility for the negotiations. "Her brother is the proper person to do that," he asserted, though he hoped that George and Frederick would "act with as much indulgence *as possible.*"[8] Immediately after this skirmish, the Lamb family's lawyer Mr Cookney informed them that a legal separation could only be achieved with the consent of both parties.[9] To sue for divorce would be humiliating and expensive. Caroline had found some leverage.

A month later, Emily Cowper confirmed to an impatient Frederick Lamb that no progress had been made: "Everything goes on at Whitehall as when you left us, no tidings of Wm. Caroline has now turned again to the sickly mood and says she shall not live and has not eat for four days. However it is very easy to rouse all her energy's by merely disagreeing with her. . . . The night before last she went down to the Women and offered them a Guinea if they would show her the straight waistcoat, but they would not hear of it."[10] Caroline's demand to see her strait-jacket proves she intended to fight. Doctor Goddard had convened a group of physicians, including Sir Henry Halford, the King's doctor, to confirm Caroline's mental unfitness, but she still had the protection of two brothers and Hart. Since she couldn't be forced to consent, the separation could be kept indefinitely at bay. Yet the pressure was still too great for her frail condition. She wrote to the Duke in a scrawled hand asking him to forward a letter to Lord Cowper in which she promised to "do anything desired, provided Mr Lamb goes to her & sees her now." She signed herself "broken hearted and too too ill to write."[11]

William's resolve crumbled again, and he visited Caroline on more than one occasion in May. He wrote to his brother Fred that Lady Caroline "was not violent—she was cross & abusive at first but at length grew quite good-humoured." She had amused him so much he said, "I could not help laughing." Caroline had promised "she would do everything that I desired her, that she wished to go to Brocket for a few days to fetch her things, then to Brighton & then abroad."[12]

Emily Cowper had a solution to this intolerable situation, however. In late May she visited and aggressively attacked Caroline, threatening a public trial: "I have bullied the Bully and told her Wm is now prepared to go to court. This was sobering and Caro Lamb immediately agreed to negotiate."[13] If William was willing to go to trial, all Caroline could do would be to threaten revelations damaging to the Lambs, which would only hurt William. She wrote to Lady Morgan on 2 June 1825: "Oh, God, it is punishment severe enough; I never can recover it; it is fair by William Lamb to mention, that since I saw you he has written a kinder letter; but if I am sent to live by myself, let them dread the violence of my despair—better far go away. Every tree, every flower, will awaken bitter reflection." She even considered fleeing to Ireland for a few months, "yet what shall I do at Bessborough alone?"[14]

Not swiftly but steadily, arrangements resolved themselves. Caroline later found out that her eldest brother, Lord Duncannon, had supported the Lambs during the negotiations, saying that the wayward wife ought to be locked up.[15] One sticking point was that William would be liable for his separated wife's bills, unless specifically released from that responsibility in the deed of separation. A small group of Trustees was constituted and an initial agreement reached for payment to Caroline of £2500 per annum during Lord Melbourne's and William's lifetimes and £3000 thereafter, with "£2000 by way of outfit & all debts to be paid up to the moment of the arrangement taking effect."[16] Emily told her brother Frederick that the terms were too generous, but worth it if they could finally be shut of Caroline: "I really think this great work will at last be achieved, and probably without anything being published."[17]

Lady Cowper should have known better. That very week, Caroline passed her wedding anniversary at Brocket and dramatized her impending eviction by organizing a celebration not unlike the infamous bonfire of 1816 in which she had burned facsimiles of Byron's letters and gifts. It is hard to know how much of this event really came off. Isaac Nathan described it sketchily, printing a poem Caroline wrote at the time and read aloud, according to Nathan, while she was seated beneath her favorite tree, where Queen Elizabeth was reputed once to have enjoyed its shade:

> Little birds in yonder grove,
>
> Making nests, and making love,
>
> Come sing upon your favorite tree,
>
> Once more your sweetest songs to me:
>
> An exile from these scenes I go,
>
> Whither, I neither care nor know.[18]

The poem itemizes Brocket's endearments, including it's "gladsome hall," and the gardener Dawson's "fruitful wall." She also bid "Farewell to Hassard's cheering smile, / His hearty laugh, which cares no guile."[19] "Hassard" was actually "Haggard," the butler, who may have been sorry for Caroline's plight, as were some other servants, no doubt, though they had passed along so much gossip for so many years. If she read it out loud, Caroline's farewell to the "Welwyn band" certainly pulled no punches: "My friends are either chang'd or dead," she said, "Husband, nor child, to greet me come."[20] Instead, she had her servants, Isaac Nathan, and a penniless young poet named Wilmington Fleming.

In March of 1825 Fleming had sent Lady Caroline a poem on Byron's death titled "The Poet's Grave."[21] Fleming inscribed the poem to her, the wealthy and talented patroness of the arts, and begged for money. She sent him a few pounds: "I could not help writing rather a bitter answer requesting him to come and see the child of prosperity he envied so much." Seizing this opening, Fleming sent back a request for an interview, along with some flattering verses on Byron's ungrateful conduct toward Caroline.[22] Although she did not find the verses good, she wrote kindly to Fleming and as usual tried to help him out. She asked Murray to do her "the favour of printing this Poem and the dedication to me—it is I think very pretty and the Man is in considerable distress—would it sell?"[23] Murray had the poem printed, but he refused to go further. He had refused all poetry manuscripts after Lord Byron died.[24]

As her wedding anniversary approached, Caroline told Fleming she would do what she could for him, though "on Monday I leave everything I love on earth."[25] She later said she allowed him to see her because "my weak state of Health affected me so deeply that I was all but Dead." Alone at Brocket ("No soul was there of my own rank"), she welcomed Fleming, who "remained there, prowling about and writing verses to me of the most flattering kind." He asked for cash, and she "kept giving him p[oun]d after p[oun]d until the very little money I had was gone."[26] Then, in a typical act of indiscretion, she let Fleming take her journals to read. Immediately realizing her mistake, she asked for their return. Fleming reproached her for not doing more to help him, and Caroline replied, "I assure you you wrong me I saw Mr. Murray and will try to serve you in every way I can. . . . [C]all tomorrow bring me the journals I gave you—I hope to think of something for your advantage write & tell me frankly your History."[27] According to Lady Caroline, Fleming was paid 10 pounds five shillings "from my Brother's Solicitor upon his returning my Journal."[28] Though still without a publisher for his poetry, Fleming took the money and left.

Immediately after the painful scenes of that first week in June of 1825, Lady Caroline responded to an invitation addressed only to her husband for a social event. She poured out her frustration to the "friend" who had cut her. "Do me a favour," she said,

> ask of those you think great schollars the meaning of the word *amicable* separation after 20 years of mutual attachment resentment and much forebearance eagerness to part and making it up again—but no I will explain it. It is to Idolize to flatter to be entirely governed by a Woman who every day errs and is never restrained nor reproved whilst she is young in Health & accounted clever—it is to retain her by protestation of kindness and love when others wished to take her away—it is to laugh at her termigant humours independent ideas proud spirit—& encourage her in these and when perhaps by her own fault she becomes miserable—ill & lonely—to find out all her errors blaze them to the world & have straight waistcoats. Physicians with all the Aristocracy of the country to say she had better go—go where? will you find that out & do not as John Bull Frederic Lamb Lady Cowper & others would say answer to the D——l let them go there if they like—I will not if I can help it—excuse me for troubling you—& pray mark that in this truly *amicable* arrangement I am accused alone of being *passionate* (—when ill used)—did they never find that out before!
>
> "I however still love the hand upraised to shed my blood."[29]

The last was a line from Pope's *Essay on Man* that she had entered into her Commonplace Book in 1812, which Byron had often repeated to her.[30]

Caroline knew quite well that if she could speak to William she might still avoid banishment. She begged Lord and Lady Cowper to let her see him once more: "My dear Ld Cowper thank you—I am too ill to write tell Emily to tell William if he will only see me one instant I shall do whatever he pleases—tell him if he pleases he may bring a straight waistcoat I am on my bed perhaps my bed of death—I *will* not accept half this money. . . . I can agree to nothing until I see William."[31] Angry one moment, despairing the next, Lady Caroline was making her last stand, and even Emily was moved: "She is in a strange state, good-humoured, but always muddled either with Brandy or laudanum. She is very willing to go from Whitehall but cannot fix her plans or her thoughts. . . . In short it is melancholy to see anyone in such a state."[32]

What should Caroline do? Go abroad? Throw herself on the mercy of her brothers? Retire to cheap lodgings over a shop in Shoreditch? Give lectures for children? "Or," she mused half-seriously to Lady Morgan, "shall I write a kind of quiet, everyday sort of novel, full of wholesome truths, or shall I attempt to be poetical, and failing, beg my friends for a guinea apiece, and their name, to sell my work, upon the best foolscap paper; or shall I fret, fret, and die; or shall I be dignified and fancy myself, as Richard the Second did when he picked the nettle up—upon a thorn?" Her reversal of fortune did not stop her thinking about "that mis-guided and misguiding Byron, whom I adore, although he left that dreadful legacy on me—my memory. Remember thee. . . ."[33] She was reduced to counting her allies, living and dead, starting with the ones she loved most: William, her mother, then Byron, Augustus, Willy, her father, and so on until she got down to young Mr. Russell, who had displaced Bulwer in her affections the previous June.[34] Dr. Goddard tried to stem her drinking but found it difficult to keep her from gaining access to wine and brandy.

Caroline had not given up writing, but she could not concentrate. She still talked about publishing her journal and publishing fiction to pay her debts. She asked Lady Morgan to edit some of her unfinished manuscripts, but warned, "if any one calls about my affair *be out* & take as much pain in correcting my Tales as they were yr own."[35] As the siege dragged on, Caroline shifted her objective. Why could she not continue to live at Brocket? It was now early July, and still she remained. "She is irresolute, and changeable, and drunken," wrote Emily, "but I think there is method in these variations, she hopes to tire every body's patience to get hold of Wm and to remain where she is." When Lord Melbourne conveyed William's reluctant wish that she depart soon, Emily reported "a violent turmoil for two days, but nothing more (thanks to the Women)."[36] Harryo wrote from Paris that she was sorry to hear of Caroline's determination to stay at Brocket since "to Lady Cowper, Mrs. [George] Lamb, etc., she is a calamity." And yet, Harryo asked, if Caroline wanted to stay, "Why not?"[37]

July waned, and nothing had changed. Caroline made visits to London and wrote letters of advice to Augustus, who had been persuaded to give up snuff. "I hope," she said, "you will abstain from taking that vast Tower of Bread with that immense sea of Tea as I am convinced the mammoth and the Ostrich alone could digest anything like the quantity." Like all parents alienated from their spouses, she was defensive about her son's behavior, and asked him to tell William and the Lambs that he had been well supervised at Brocket:

I do sincerely Hope that you will not be ungrateful enough to lay your bad Tricks & attacks & bad words to our door, as I think I may with truth say that you were reminded in rather severe terms once or twice by me that such pinching people & dogs and such other Idle habits were neither agreeable to us at Brockett nor to your Father nor to Mr Stuart. Do try and seriously break yourself off from doing these things they can give *you* no pleasure and they give all living things upon whom you inflict them real pain—I shall send you some balls which will save many heads & windows. Your Father kindly sent me some—Miss Wheeler actually spit blood & is not yet well from the blow she received in her chest from your cricket ball.[38]

This will give some impression of the risks run by Augustus's caretakers. After promising to visit him in London, Caroline admonished her son not to go out in the hot weather, to keep his hair short, and to write.

She visited Augustus at Melbourne House in late July. Emaciated and weak, she was unable to pull herself together to come down to dinner, and she sent Augustus to tell Lord Melbourne he could not come without his mother. Emily reported that her father "was stout for once and said he was sorry, in that case he could not see him."[39] Such scenes were wearing down everyone in the household, though Emily was pushing hard to achieve the ultimate goal of separating Caroline from William.

The first of August arrived, and the agreement had still not been finalized. Blind as ever to William's love for Caroline, Emily complained: "Never did I see in my life so irresolute a person."[40] Lady Cowper was "obliged to mount guard" against her brother's weakness. There can be no doubt that Emily loved her eldest brother: "[W]hat an easy Man he is to live with, and what a foolish Caroline she is to have thrown away such Cards.[41] The ten years' push to pry Caroline out of their lives appeared to be won finally on Friday, 12 August, when, accompanied by a servant, Caroline departed for Paris. Emily declared victory:

> Conceive what luck! She marched out without beat of drum last Friday morn[in]g at 8 o'clock by the steam boat to Calais, so that I think there is little fear of her wheeling back now. She will, I trust, have been so sick as to feel little anxiety to cross the water again directly. Otherwise I should have expected to see her back next day. . . . She went off in better temper & in a better frame of mind than I have seen her for quite a while, and she behaved remarkably well when I took her down the last night before she went to wish Papa goodbye—she was quiet & said nothing to worry him. Wm is *aux anges,* as happy as possible, and went off yesterday to Melbourne, but even here I am afraid he will find a drawback to his comfort in Augustus his son whom he has taken with him.[42]

Emily wanted Augustus, who was fast approaching his eighteenth birthday, sent away to a caretaker. Their elderly nanny had to lock him in the Drawing room, she said, "or else he runs down half-dressed & tumbles her on the floor & sits upon her." When the Lambs attended a performance of the popular play based on *Frankenstein,* "the huge creature without sense put us all in mind of Augustus."[43] But William had a pact with Caroline and refused to lock up his son. Was he, as Emily said, "as happy as possible"? Not apparently: "[I]n the evening—it will not do to be alone," he confessed.[44]

A week after Caroline departed for Paris, Emily reviewed the event uneasily. It had gone almost too smoothly, "as she went off in peace and Christian Charity with us all."[45] It was indeed too soon to celebrate. William received a long letter from Calais dated 8 September insisting that he send over her horses, for "my Health depends upon riding," and her Blenheim spaniel bitch, Bell. William was also to pay bills to a wigmaker, a tailor, and several hotels. She thanked him for keeping Augustus with him, rather than "sending him to stupid places where he remains with women & children learns nothing and grows silly." But recrimination boiled up immediately after:

> I deserved more mercy at yr hands than you have shewn—yr cruelty will one day recur to your mind—& may my curse bitter and entire fall upon the rest, as for you I never will curse you but if it be permitted to me to return I will come and look at you even as Ld Byron did at me [i.e., as a ghost]—the more I think of the mean barbarous manner in which I have been sacrificed the less I can understand how *you* could bring yourself to sanction it.

Caroline charged that "the proceedings have been as illegal as they were cruel," and that they had all taken advantage of her illness to force her out: "Lady Cowper upon her bed of death and Frederick Lamb and that abhorred scoundrel Jack Milbanke *shall* remember me—and when my memories appear with all my faults even in this world some will pity me—the only alleviation you can now make to the agonising sufferings you have heaped upon yr victim is to write—do so then & send me my Horses."[46] Pathetically, Caroline wanted William to "remember me to my own sweet kind boy, no one wrote to me on his birthday."

In mid-October Caroline returned to England for the disquieting necessity of William's signing the deed of separation. Caroline was visited at Thomas's Hotel by a nervous Lady Cowper, anxious to interdict any unsupervised reunion. Caroline had trusted Dr. Goddard with her copy of the Sanders' portrait of Lord Byron, and she now promised to leave it to Lady Morgan, whom she counted on for assistance with Henry Colburn.[47] She had told Colburn, "I am writing my Memorial," presumably the an autobiography gleaned from the sixteen volumes of her journals.[48] She returned to Calais briefly, then came back to London to look for a residence.

The deed of separation allowed her to live in London, but William's family intended no such thing to befall. They rejected any house close to the city center. Caroline, they insisted, must reside on the Continent or in lodgings out of town, where a close eye could be kept on her.[49] Dr. Goddard had furnished a formal diagnosis of her condition to William. Goddard was obviously speaking under duress:

My Dear Sir:

Lady Caroline has a predisposition to the high form of insanity, which shows itself at certain times, and particularly so, when exposed to any excitement, whether mental or physical.—Such is my answer to your letter of enquiry which I had the honor to receive this morning I have hesitated in forming my decision, but her conduct lately has been very inconsistent, and certainly proclaims that many of her actions proceed from other causes than the mere impetuosity of passion.— Positive coercion is seldom justifiable in any case; with respect to Ly Caroline it is by no means requisite—I consider that her Ladyship with kind treatment and occasional restraint, might recover, or at any rate, become calm and rational. But there are friends who *must* be removed from her; measures *must* be taken to make her take less wine, and some situation *must* be chosen where she can be governed with every appearance of governing herself.

Lady Caroline is very suspicious, & therefore I have only had time to write these few lines; perhaps I may see you in Town in a day or two; when, if you wish it, I should be happy to talk with you further on the subject.[50]

From Emily Cowper and George and Frederick Lamb's view, such a diagnosis confirmed the wisdom of their advice that William stay as far from Lady Caroline as possible. But William undoubtedly felt the usual stirrings of pity mixed with guilt. And Caroline knew the doctor was concealing something. "I hate Goddard," she told Hart,

> he is a great flatterer & very contemptible. When he found I did not mean to retain him he went over to William, & has been trying to do me every possible mischief— I am to be pitied for I always mean well & only get into real scrapes by a detestation for shabbiness & Hypocrisy—after you left me Duncannon never even bowed to me, he has now written me a very kind letter requesting to see me. Oh my dearest cousin, for pities sake do not join with them against me.[51]

Caroline saw Augustus several times that fall and wrote to him frequently, telling him to study the Bible so he could be confirmed and become a "Religious and a good Boy." She persuaded William to hire another tutor, reawakening her husband's tender feelings, as he shared her goal of giving their son skills to survive in life after their deaths.[52] When Caroline wrote about her concerns for Augustus, she also alluded to her own financial dependency: "Dearest William, I am delighted with Augustus's looks he was in want of money & I gave him 5£ & Mrs Stewart will write to you about his Winter Cloathing." She had spent two very happy days with Augustus, but a letter from William had caused "such violent grief that it gave him 3 fits." After bestowing this guilt upon William, Caroline asked him once again to pay her bills, not forgetting that "you took *12£* from me by George's draft, so that you may take this into consideration." This brisk tone was lightened in a postscript: "the filly is too beautiful—how pretty."[53]

Inside, however, she was desperate. She believed Dr. Goddard was "looking out for some place in the country to put me away in." She told Hart yet again, "I am not mad, & never was, but am inexpressibly wretched, unless you get me off this once more; do my dearest cousin, & God reward you for it. I will in such case go & live at Brighton with Mrs Peterson."[54] Goddard was indeed William's agent, and she was certainly at his mercy. But she had poor relations with her eldest brother, Duncannon, and her protests rang hollow even to Hart, who could do little directly to "save" her. And if she were freed from this "weak, mercenary" doctor and her "common keeper," Mrs. Stubbs, what then?[55] She could not live alone.

The issue was resolved on 17 November 1825, when William agreed to lease 39 Conduit Street, in the newly fashionable district of Mayfair, for one year at the exorbitant tariff of £546.[56] Caroline now resided just yards away from the lending library of Henry Colburn, and only a short walk up St. George Street to his offices in Hanover Square.[57] She was also not far from John Murray's publishing house at 50 Albemarle Street. She felt proud enough of her residence that she wrote to invite Murray to visit and perhaps to accompany her on a fortnight's-long trip to Paris.[58]

The Paris trip was a fantasy, for her health was bad. Dr. Goddard hired a Mr. and Mrs. Crosby to help look after his difficult patient. "Mr Crosby, I *command* you to come to me instantly," she wrote to him.[59] Goddard had given Crosby control of the purse-strings.[60] Crosby became her last male admirer in the mold of Michael Bruce. In appreciation, she helped him find a position for his daughter, and wrote a poem filled with the usual self-pity and honesty:

Cold was the season of the year—
The sun half risen, the skies looked drear—
A youth returning to his Bride
With none to cheer him by his side
looked on the frozen water nigh—
then on the glorious sun on high
and thought as he was passing on
of Hopes now crushed of pleasures gone
of Life how strange a Dream it proved
until his very soul was moved
just as he chanced to turn his eye
upon the stream he then did spy—
a Rat—of animals created
the most by Man & Woman hated

. . . .

Yet Crosby who at fights could see
Men fairly strive for victory
Who with shock nor Bulldog feard
Who never was to Rats endeard
remembered him of one same Woman—
who like the rat was lov'd by no Man
So he did try Her life to save
of one though Rat was not a slave
& though the Rat could not recover
It died at least with friend & lover.[61]

Caroline was now showing strong signs of organ damage from alcoholism. She endured "tapping," a procedure in which needles were inserted deeply into her flesh in an effort to draw off liquid accumulating due to kidney failure. A nurse was hired on 29 November to serve her for a month, and expenses associated with her health problems that week alone exceeded £91.[62]

The treatments worked, and Lady Caroline soon began paying visits and took up a protégée by the name of Rosina Doyle Wheeler, a stunningly good-looking young woman who accompanied Caroline to the salons of various important bluestocking women. They may have met at a soirée in Quebec Street hosted by the formidable Miss Spence, who had made her reputation as a writer on the strength of a modest piece about the Highlands. Miss Spence was a woman whose leftist politics made her "decidedly *'blue,'* when *'blue'* was by no means so general a colour as it is at present." Miss Spence honored Lady Caroline "more for her *litry* abilities than for her rank,"[63] and this egalitarian ethos suited Rosina Wheeler as it did Caroline. Several memoirists, including Samuel Carter Hall and his wife, observed Lady Caroline at Miss Spence's, "accompanied by a young and singularly beautiful Lady."[64] Such figures as Letitia Elizabeth Landon also attended these gatherings of the *literati,* where tea would be brewed in the bedroom, and Caroline apparently found it less awkward to meet friends there than to pay formal visits to their residences. She made quite an impression when she arrived wrapped completely in an ermine cloak that she liked to call her "cat-skin." She talked of starting a periodical to be titled *The Tabby's Magazine,* perhaps with the help of the "exceedingly haughty, brilliant and beautiful" Rosina Wheeler.[65]

William and Caroline were both terrified in December, when the banking house of Sir Peter Poole collapsed and seven other banks followed suit.[66] She stopped attending parties, and her emotional health declined. Dr Goddard wrote to his patient in December: "[Y]ou say you continually cry, pray do not do so. . . . How mournful, my dear Lady Caroline, your letter made me." Able to do little more for her, Goddard advised her to resist her passions and even offered to help with her bills.[67] No doubt he was also prescribing laudanum for his patient.

Wounded in mind and body, Lady Caroline still engendered fear in the Lambs. When Emily Cowper caught wind of a new novel titled *Granby,* she leapt to the conclusion that it was Caroline's work.[68] The novel, published by Henry Colburn early in 1826, featured a character named Lady Harriet Duncan who seemed based on Caroline: "She is absolutely charming—quite a grown-up child, stopped short at the entertaining age."[69] The book was by Thomas Lister, not Caroline.

One can understand the Lamb family's paranoia, for Caroline had talked incessantly about publishing her journals, and the first volume of the kiss-and-tell *Memoirs* of Harriette Wilson, former lover of Frederick Lamb, had just been published in Paris. The book also contained a juicy passage featuring William and Caroline. Harriette Wilson had hired their former maid, Thérèse, who was quoted as saying that Lady Caroline had slept with Doctor Lee when he had served as Augustus's caretaker: "Lady Caroline is often to be found, after midnight, in the doctor's bedchamber. . . . the servants tell a story about a little silk stocking, very like Her Ladyship's, having been found, one morning, quite at the bottom of the doctor's bed."

Wilson complimented Caroline on her musicianship, the quality of her poetry ("equally good in French, in English, or in Italian"), and her talent with the watercolor brush, but she also described her as eating and drinking "enough for a porter" and worst, as having participated in the following scene with her husband:

> *Lady C.* I must and will come into your bed. I am your lawful wife. Why am I to sleep alone?
>
> *William.* I'll be hanged if you come into my bed, Caroline; so you may as well go quietly to your own.
>
> Lady Caroline persevered.
>
> 'Get along, you little drunken——,' said William Lamb.
>
> The gentle Caroline wept at this outrage.
>
> '*Mais où est, donc, ce petit coquin de docteur?*' [Where in the world is that little rascal of a doctor?] said William, in a conciliatory tone.
>
> '*Ah! il a du fond, ce docteur-la,*' [Ah! He is a deep one, this doctor.] answered Caroline with a sigh![70]

Doctor Lee is thus portrayed as "deep" in his employer's wife. Making no excuses for repeating this sordid gossip, Wilson goes on to dismiss *Glenarvon*'s significance while also scolding Lady Caroline for being "not quite mad enough to excuse her writing, in her husband's lifetime, while under his roof, the history of her love and intrigue with Lord Byron!!" and concludes with this: "I admire her talents, and wish she would make better use of them."[71] When Caroline saw Wilson's *Memoirs,* she wrote a response—or perhaps someone wrote it for her:

> Harriet Wilson, shall I tell thee where,
> Beside my being *cleverer,*

> We differ?—thou wert hired to hold thy tongue,
>
> Thou hast no right to do thy lovers wrong:
>
> But I, whom none could buy or gain,
>
> Who am as proud, girl, as thyself art vain,
>
> And like thyself, or sooner like the wind,
>
> Blow raging ever free and unconfin'd.
>
> What should withhold my tongue with pen of steel,
>
> The faults of those who have wrong'd me to reveal?[72]

The poem was published posthumously by Isaac Nathan in 1829, and it concludes by wishing Wilson's book would go to "the Devil." It seems doubtful that this is a production of Lady Caroline's pen. The sixth line, "Who am as proud, girl, as thyself art vain" has uncharacteristically poor rhythm, employs the atypical "girl," and ungrammatically substitutes "thyself" for "thou." The poem's blunt beginning is also aberrant. Possibly Nathan took an existing scribble and shaped it hastily for the press.

Harriet Wilson's *Memoirs* might have suggested a return to her own autobiography for Caroline. Certainly Emily Cowper, Frederick Lamb, and John Cam Hobhouse expected her to attempt it. What they did not expect was the sudden reappearance of Wilmington Fleming, the starving poet. He had since published *The Destroying Angel,* which included the poem he dedicated to Lady Caroline. While he had possession of her journals, Fleming had copied passages, edited them, and had some parts privately printed—though no copies are known to exist. In the Victoria and Albert Museum Forster Collection there is a letter ostensibly by Lady Caroline to a Mrs. Blacquiere of Great Marlborough Street, not in her hand (although it might have been dictated). The letter requests return of the "MS which was in the hands of Fleming and originally printed for Mr. Loyd." It states that it is of the utmost importance to Lady Caroline's future peace that the work should be withdrawn. If the letter is authentic, it appears Mr Colburn was to act as a go-between, for she promises to indemnify him for any expenses. However, this letter is the sort of thing that might be forged in order to make the threat of publication more credible.[73]

Realizing he could get little from Lady Caroline, Fleming now attempted to extort money from Hobhouse, Lady Byron, and Augusta Leigh. Letters signed by Fleming claimed possession of the journal of a "Lady of Rank" disclosing unpleasant things about Lord Byron. The letters contained a copied passage mentioning the visit Caroline had paid to Lady Byron in 1816, just before her separation. Although Lady Byron claimed that she was "averse, for myself, to all transactions of this nature," she wanted William to know Fleming's address immediately so he could pay the blackmail to stop publication of Caroline's journal.[74]

In his note, Fleming pleaded poverty: "I am now perishing—with a mother dependent upon me for support—without a friend in the world—and in the hourly expectation of being turned into the streets."[75] The scam seems common, but some have speculated that Fleming conspired with others or that someone adopted his name as a ruse. Since no principle figure other than Lady Caroline (and possibly Isaac Nathan) ever laid eyes on Fleming, the field of surmise is broad. Joan Pierson has suggested that Augusta Leigh herself might have been behind the scandal. She follows a theory promoted by Lady Wilmot Horton as far back as 1870.[76] Doris Langley Moore disagreed. She thought Fleming real enough, but that he was evicted and ended up in debtor's prison.[77]

John Murray met with Lady Caroline in March of 1826 to discuss the Fleming problem, and he subsequently described their conversation to Augusta Leigh: "He began by saying Ly Caroline had told him the man *'was the Greatest Scoundrel.'* She had given him her Papers & some (other) papers & he had Sold two of her works to Colburn for 10 pounds sterling—and Colburn being *Another Scoundrel!* won't now give them back."[78] The next day, Murray sought Fleming at his address on Great Andrew Street in Seven Dials, a red-light district of London, but without success. From these scant facts, Augusta concluded that Lady Caroline was colluding with Fleming. Because Lady Byron worried that Lady Caroline's memoirs might yet be published, Murray was asked to mollify the blackmailer.[79] But Murray's repeated attempts to contact Fleming at his residence failed. The correspondence stopped, and all that was left was a rumor—promulgated, Doris Langley Moore believes, by Lady Byron—that Augusta had paid to suppress ugly information about Lord Byron.

One question yet to be answered is whether Isaac Nathan played a role in this squalid affair. Nathan's *Fugitive Pieces* includes a poem, perhaps of his own composition, titled "The Brocket Festival: June 3rd 1825." The poem is attributed to a "rising poet, patronized by lady Caroline Lamb."[80] It is seventy-eight lines long, includes footnotes, and provides an enlarged picture of events at the wedding anniversary "celebration" through which Caroline suffered before being evicted from Brocket. The poem concludes,

That's he!—'tis the poet!—Ah, pity his care,
His heart can be grateful, though dark its despair;
Tho' eccentric—yet spare him—nor rashly condemning,
Yet plant a fresh sting in the bosom of Fleming.[81]

That is not all. Another verse in *Fugitive Pieces* is printed with a poem memorializing William Lamb's addiction to oaths. This poem, another joke on "Lamb" drawn from a "sheep's head dinner," is attributed to Wilmington Fleming:

> Still condescending Caroline,
> Her presence deigns to lend,
> Nor will refuse the boon to dine,
> And grace her humble friend.

> But to a strange reverse it led,
> Tho' meant the guest to cram,
> And thus you see a bak'd sheep's head,
> Is offered to a *Lamb*.

Was Nathan taunting the Lambs? The final poem of the volume was the one addressed to Harriette Wilson, which strongly implies that Caroline's ostracism is the Lambs' fault.

How could Nathan have known of Fleming? Did Fleming give Nathan the sheep's head poem, along with "The Brocket Festival"? Could they have been co-conspirators in the blackmail plot? It is impossible to answer these questions with certainty. Fleming probably made a miscalculated blackmail attempt, withdrew, and suffered the fate of most debtors: prison or voluntary emigration.[82] Nathan could have gotten his knowledge of the blackmail threat through his friendship with Lady Caroline, or through letters or journals she put in his possession along with some of her literary remains upon her death. Being a composer in need of cash, Nathan published the Fleming allusions in *Fugitive Pieces* for unknown reasons. Did he hope to create fear of further disclosures? Was he simply paying back the Lambs for what he regarded as their shameful treatment of Caroline? Was he somehow actually jealous of Fleming? We don't know.

William had relented and said he would permit Caroline to go to Brocket for the spring. As she prepared to leave Conduit Street, she scrawled a note to Edward Bulwer that she had taken yet another fall from a horse, her black mare.[83] Bulwer had forgiven her behavior two years earlier, and had seen Caroline at more than one of Miss Benger's soirées. At one of these, in April 1826, he met Rosina Wheeler, and suddenly a courtship was under way. Bulwer was keenly aware he had made a strange triangle, and his lengthy declaration of love to Rosina in April 1826 concludes, "I need not caution you to keep this from Lady Caroline Lamb."[84] Bulwer's caution was warranted. However, Lady Caroline learned soon of their liaison, and the result seems to have been that they were both invited to visit Brocket Hall.

Lady Caroline coveted the attention she got from admirers, whether female or male. Edward's attraction to Rosina made her jealous of them both. And yet she seems to have encouraged their engagement, which took place unofficially while they were visiting at Brocket. Lady Caroline wrote to him on 2 August 1826, in excruciatingly clear penmanship:

> I should have answered your letter long ago had I even one innate Idea—but I am convinced there is no such thing—how then can I write even imagination must have some materials upon which to work I have none the passions might produce sentiments of some sort but mine are all calm'd or extinct—memory—a waste with nothing in it worth recording—happy Healthy *quiet* contented I get up at 1/2 past 4 ride about with Haggard & see Harvest men at work in this pretty confined green Country—read a few old Books, see no one hear from no one and occasionally play at Chess with Dr Goddard or listen to the faint High warblings of Miss Richardson.
> . . .
> Pray write to me as you then did even although your opinion of me and affection boyish affection be utterly destroyed. . . . Fare well give my adoration to the Dear sea—whose every change I worship and whose blue waves I long to dip in—provided two old women take me out again safely—excuse this stupid letter and write me a long and amiable one.

She insisted she was well and thanked him for his "beautiful and soothing" letters, reminding him, "I drew my good spirit in Ada Reis from you as I imagined you pray do not turn into a bad one." She noted that William, who was about to pay a visit, had "pined for quiet yet if I mistake not he is less happy than when he was plagued by these *apendages* [his wife and son]—if there are two p's in that word imagine one & pray excuse my spelling—yours with sincere interest and disinterested attachment."[85] This is a strained, sad letter. Caroline was ill, and yet she could write with exquisite sarcasm that she was happy, healthy, and contented in her "confined green country" where she saw and heard from no one and longed to swim in the sea—so long as her nurses were nearby to pull her out!—and mused contentedly on her husband's feelings about having escaped the duties owed to a wife and son.

Bulwer's engagement to Rosina Wheeler, off in October, perhaps because Lady Caroline warned her not to marry him,[86] was back on in November, with Edward writing love letters beginning "My Dearest Angel Darling Poodle" and ending with his trademark signature: "Zoo's own, own idolatrous and fond Puppy."[87] Ten years later they would separate. Bulwer-Lytton never quite got over Lady Caroline. He later described her as possessing "a wild originality" that featured

> sudden contrasts from deep pathos to infantile drollery; now sentimental now shrewd. It sparkled with anecdotes of the great world, and of the eminent persons with whom she had been brought up, or been familiarly intimate; and, ten minutes after, it became gravely eloquent with religious enthusiasm, or shot off into metaphysical speculations—sometimes absurd, sometimes profound—generally suggestive and interesting. A creature of caprice, and impulse, and whim, her manner, her talk, and her character shifted their colours as rapidly as those of a chameleon.[88]

In 1829 Bulwer burned Caroline's letters—a very unusual step for a writer who kept everything. And in 1831 he was still trying to get John Murray's attention by mentioning her name.[89]

With Bulwer preoccupied, and Hart busy at Chatsworth, Lady Caroline counted more and more on her youngest brother Willy's support. She wrote to him frequently and sent him poetry. He visited her several times in fall of 1826 and wrote to her on 13 December to invite her to make the ten-hour journey to Canford and eat Christmas dinner with his family. He also gave her some brotherly advice: "Many thanks for your pretty verses, but fight against melancholy thoughts." Willy had always pictured his sister in a respectable household, surrounded by family. But this domestic vision was complemented by acknowledgement of her intellect: "Could it ever be intended that with such a mind as yours, you should occupy it merely in such a manner as bodily exercise or change of place would admit of? & the proof that such is not its destination is the restlessness under which you suffer."[90]

Alas, it was too late for reformations, regimens, and rejuvenation. Lady Caroline's problems were too deeply ingrained to allow her to concentrate on attending to the poor or visiting the schools, where her appearance and behavior would no doubt have frightened the teachers as well as the pupils. The "scrapes and difficulties, & bad company" her brother warned her against stemmed from her lack of tact. She would talk to anyone, give anyone money, if she had it, and feel intensely wronged if her doctor or "nurse" tried to restrict or remove her. Although she had many lucid moments, she was unable to sustain her writing, and she was certainly not up to the hundred-mile drive to Canford. She spent Christmas at Brocket, the place she still loved above all the rest, alone.

SEVENTEEN

Rational and Quiet

1827–1828

> I had three children; two died; my only child is afflicted; it is the will of God.
> —Lady Caroline Lamb to Lady Morgan[1]

On 17 February 1827, William Lamb's political future was suddenly altered when the Tory Prime Minister Liverpool suffered an incapacitating stroke. Canning was sent for, and though he was himself in poor health, he formed a government by negotiating Whig support, and one of his first acts was to find William Lamb a safe seat in Newport. Though he was now in the thick of things, William saw Caroline frequently that spring. Emily said he was a fool to do so: "[W]hen will that child have cut his wise teeth?" she asked.[2]

Augustus was about to turn twenty and his seizures continued, yet neither Caroline nor William had given up on him. Caroline was invited to present the end of the year awards at the dame school in Hans Place she had attended years before, and she was determined to take Augustus with her to recite the seven ages of man speech from *As You Like It*. She practiced with him rigorously, yet when the day came Augustus was stupefied by the crowd of children and could not perform. Margot Strickland has written eloquently of how Lady Caroline was blamed for needlessly embarrassing her son. But Caroline's intentions were good:

to give him encouragement and to make others more sympathetic to the plight of the mentally retarded.[3]

William assured Caroline he would take care of Augustus, no matter what. "[T]he only noble fellow I ever met with is William Lamb," she wrote to Lady Morgan. She was grateful, but unhappy.[4] Lord Bessborough, now almost seventy, continued to see his grandson and assist in the itineraries that took him from one parent to the other. Once again, Caroline seemed to regress to early married life, when William was her tutor. He recommended interesting people and edifying books, like *The Objects, Advantages and Pleasures of Science,* by Lord Brougham. She would enjoy this popularization of science, he thought: "Pray read it carefully, do not be terrified by the *arithmetic* at the beginning but go through it, understand of it as much as you can & write me word what you think of it." William still defended his early treatment of her callow worldview: "I know you have a notion, hastily taken up, that instruction & education dispose people to be turbulent, & render them difficult to be governed. I am quite of a contrary opinion."[5] This was certainly a scene of former days. William sincerely believed that his wife and son might somehow achieve "tranquillity & order" through reading about science. He was pleased that their old friend John Murray sent her a new edition of Byron's works and copies of the *Quarterly Review* whenever it came out.[6]

But if their affection survived, everything else had changed. William's political career was taking off at last, and in April Canning appointed him Chief Secretary to Ireland (a bizarre echo of Avondale in *Glenarvon*). Caroline's calmness was her tribute to him, but it came at a price: "Being unhappy today I have drunk a whole bottle of wine which I bought for myself all at once," she confessed to Dr. Goddard. "I did it upon hearing Mr Lamb wished to speak to me. I was still able to do every thing he wished."[7] She did everything she could to reassure William before his departure, and continued the effort after he had taken up his residence in Phoenix Park, Dublin. To Emily's amazement, William took Augustus to Ireland, largely because Caroline begged him to, though she knew she might never see her son again.[8] From Ireland, William wrote Caroline: "I never knew you more rational and quiet." Not that all was placid. She conceived a sudden desire to revisit Paris, and William responded cautiously that it "would do you good, provided you can avoid making scamps of acquaintance, which is your great fault & danger."[9]

In July, Canning suffered a collapse, and just as the 5th Duke had done for Fox, the 6th Duke of Devonshire offered the Prime Minister a refuge at his Palladian villa in Chiswick. Like Fox, Canning accepted, and like Fox, he died there. He passed away on 8 August, throwing British politics—and William's future—into doubt. Lady Caroline was shaken by the event. She wrote to Lady Morgan, "I have heard to my excessive horror that Mr. Canning is either dying or dead. I am coming to town in consequence to know the truth, and if I can, to see the Duke of Devonshire. . . . I have two or three notes from William, evidently not knowing this disastrous news."[10] Canning's middle-of-the-road politics had appealed deeply to William, and comforted his Whig supporters. His early demise upset everyone: "It is a calamity of so fearful a nature," wrote Harryo, "the loss so irreparable to his friends, to the world . . . that one feels bewildered as well as grieved."[11] William was prepared to resign, but he stayed on when the Viscount Goderich was thrust unwillingly into service. "Goody" Goderich was a kindly, methodical man without the aggressiveness to lead, but he got enough support to stabilize the situation temporarily.

That fall, as if anticipating the empty space in his life that Caroline would leave, William had his first extramarital affair. Lady Elizabeth Brandon was a hotheaded, demanding, passionate, bright young woman whose ailing husband ignored her indiscretions while soothing his gout at Buxton or in France.[12] William later admitted to his brother Fred that Lady Brandon "was very like in her ways" to his wife.[13] His correspondence with her in the fall and early winter of this year proves that he was devoted to her company and that she often found his phlegmatic demeanor exasperating.

Sometime in August, Augustus took a fall, injuring his thigh. He wrote on the thirty-first to say he was better, while his mother was simultaneously writing to him of plans to serve mutton, beef, and beer at Brocket to 125 local workers on the thirtieth.[14] She had given up keeping her illness a secret from Augustus and admitted she was dictating most of her correspondence to Dr. Goddard because she was too "sick and ill to write to you with my own hand."[15] In September she asked Goddard to play a chess game with Augustus to be carried on by correspondence.[16]

Dr. Goddard and Dr. Lucas now agreed that Caroline must leave Brocket and go to London, where she could be cared for in one of the first-floor bedrooms at the back of Melbourne House. On 2 October Dr. Goddard warned William of the end:

My Dear Sir:

Lady Caroline has just desired me to let you learn how she is—some time ago I had wished to do so, but her ladyship prevented me, as she by no means would unnecessarily frighten or disturb you—

It has been with perhaps of the deepest regret that I have lately observed symptoms of water collecting about her—at present the case is too clearly manifest, and from the quantity of fluid contain'd & evidently felt in the abdomen, and from other visceral abstraction and disease I have apprehensions of the greatest danger . . . . Her conduct has been very amicable, indeed, her behavior of late has altered very much in every respect for the better—she appears convinced she cannot ultimately recover but with feelings of perfect resignation says she does not mind to die.

Though she had agreed to let Dr. Goddard tell William the truth, Caroline still tried to reassure her husband in a post script: "My Dearest William: I really feel better—the medicines agree with me and I have everything I possibly want." William was moved to write a letter telling his wife he loved and forgave her for everything. Anticipating the end, the Duke of Wellington dropped by Melbourne House. Even Frederick Lamb and Emily spent an hour at the invalid's bedside.[17]

The reports Goddard sent William over the next few weeks were accompanied by letters Caroline dictated. On 3 November she again made light of her illness: "I take my simple medicines and as Dr Goddard is writing for me he will probably tell you what they are (Blue Pill, squills and sweet sp. of wine with an infusion of cascara bark)... everything at Brocket is going quite well."[18] "Blue pill" was cyanide or perhaps mercury, given most often for syphilis, but also as a general prophylactic for the severely ill. Cascara bark, a licorice-flavored root that acted as a laxative, was given to her in a glass of sherry. The decline in her health had required a repeat of the dreaded "tapping" procedure she had undergone two years earlier to reduce water accumulation. The operation left her exhausted. "Tapping is by no means an agreeable sensation," she told William. "It does not give pain like a tooth drawn, but it turns you deadly cold and sick. The operation was more troublesome than usual; this is the first day I feel easy."[19]

Lady Morgan happened to be in Ireland that fall. She dined with William on 27 November, and William forwarded the note about tapping to her, trying to convince himself that it showed "how strong [Caroline] is both in mind and body." But Lady Morgan had received independent news of the operation from a friend who said that Lady Caroline's symptoms gave no hope for recovery.[20] Caroline wrote to her sister-in-law Maria Duncannon on 7 December, using a pencil because she could not yet sit up in bed, "I feel return'd to my God & my duty & my dearest husband, & my heart which was so proud & insensible is quite overcome with the great kindness I receive." It was the calm of the condemned: "I am quite resigned to die—I do not myself think there is a chance for me."[21]

Five days later, on 12 December, Goddard wrote William that Caroline "could speak only with difficulty and seemed not to know what was going on around her."[22] Bad as she was, Caroline still received visits from Emily, Willy, Caro George, and Edward Bulwer, who found her "dreadfully altered."[23] She dictated a note to Lady Holland expressing her "deep regret for the past—it makes me most unhappy now—I trust I may see you if not believe me with every affectionate and grateful feeling Yours, Caroline Lamb."[24] Lady Holland visited her old friend.

Though the end was nigh, William did not return immediately. Goderich had found the Prime Minister's job hateful, and rumors circulated that he would resign. At the end of the year he did so, becoming the only Prime Minister never to have met Parliament. William wrote to his dying wife on 6 January 1828: "My heart is almost broken that I cannot come over directly. . . . How unfortunate and melancholy that you should be so ill now & that it should be at a time when I, who have had so many years of idleness, am so fixed & chained down by circumstances."[25] At the King's request, the Duke of Wellington wrote to William on 12 January 1828 to request that he continue in his post.[26] William had no desire to serve a right-leaning, hard-line government, but he agreed to defer his decision until he could return to London. He packed hastily and made the crossing in bitter weather against a heavy gale. The trip lasted over fifteen hours and seemed to him like a punishment for "any harshness which I may have been guilty of."[27] Caroline's condition was now common knowledge, and one of Lady Morgan's correspondents, unidentified, wrote what many felt: that it would be "better her poor heart ceased to beat than stand in the way of what the good [William] may do."[28]

That heart did indeed cease to beat on 25 January 1828, but not before William and Augustus arrived. In one of those moments of lucidity that sometimes opens for the dying, she had been coherent enough to "converse with him and enjoy his society" before she closed her eyes around nine o'clock and "expired without a struggle."[29] Emily Cowper told Frederick Lamb:

> Poor Caroline died on Friday evening—she went off without any pain and from complete exhaustion. . . . She only fetched one sigh and she was gone. . . . Wm was not there at the time but he had been with her a few hours before. He was hurt at the time and rather low next day, but he is now just as usual, and his mind filled with Politicks. Augustus looked a little grave when he saw her, and when he heard [of] her death, but nothing makes an impression upon him.[30]

The evidence suggests, however, that Augustus and William did not recover from Caroline's death within forty-eight hours. William wrote to Lady Brandon that he felt "in a manner which I have often heard others describe, but in which I have never felt before myself, and did not think I could feel, a sort of impossibility of believing that I shall never see her countenance or hear her voice again, and a sort of sense of desolation, solitude and carelessness about everything, when I forced myself to remember that she was really gone."[31] These are not the words of a man who has suffered a minor loss, and since they were written to his mistress, they are likely to have muted his actual emotion.

Caroline's body was removed from Melbourne House on 4 February and conveyed in a hearse drawn by six horses to Hatfield. On 7 February 1828, Lady Caroline Lamb was interred in the Lamb crypt beneath the lectern at St. Ethelreda's church. Her coffin was placed alongside the small ones of her infant children. Its brass plate read simply: "The Right Honourable Lady Caroline Lamb. Died 25 January 1828. Aged 42 years." Lady Caroline had been infamous to many, but to the working-class of Welwyn she had been as well-known for her generosity as for her mercurial disposition. Add to this the natural desire of local citizens to curry favor with the powerful landowners of their locale and it will not seem strange that a number of mourners walked from Brocket, St. Albans and other small villages nearby to pay their last respects to the deceased Lady. Her favorites in the world she had left, William Lamb and Willy Ponsonby, led the mourners on foot.

Obituaries ran in the *New Commercial Telegraph* in Dublin, as well as the Paris and London newspapers. The *Literary Gazette* printed an anonymous, sympathetic "Biography" of Caroline which may well have been written by William. "Her character very early developed itself," noted the writer. "Wild and impatient of restraint, rapid in impulses, generous and kind of heart,—these were the first traits of her nature; and they continued to the last." Whoever wrote the obituary, he (or she) did not flinch to acknowledge that Caroline had loved Byron adulterously and publicly, for which she was excused, because such love arises "from imagination, not depravity."[32] The obituary was later augmented for a long entry in the *Annual Biography and Obituary* for 1829, in which the anonymous editor added simply, "Lady Caroline's literary pursuits were congenial with those of her husband. . . . "[33]

As Lady Morgan saw it, Caroline's inability to imagine an existence without footmen and servants was a major failing in her life and art: "[N]ever having lived out of the habits of her own class, yet sometimes mixing with people of inferior rank, notable only by their genius, she constantly applied her own sumptuous habits to them."[34] And yet, Lady Morgan felt deep respect for her unfortunate friend, who had been handicapped by her pampered upbringing: "I am sick of the jargon about the idleness of genius. All the greatest geniuses have worked hard at everything—energetic, persevering, and laborious. Who has worked so much and so well as Bacon, Kepler, Milton, Newton? it is the energy that gives what we call "genius;" Nothing but mediocrity is slothful and idle."[35] This was her tribute to Lady Caroline, whose energy was undeniable, but whose genius seethed, smoldered, and finally guttered out. "To write," she had told Lady Morgan, "was once my resource and pleasure."[36] But that had long since ceased to be.

In her will, Lady Caroline bequeathed Lady Morgan the picture of Byron that she had coveted since the days of her first stormy separation from the poet who had inspired her to become that anomalous thing: a lady writer.[37]

Epilogue

$\mathcal{A}$ fter Lady Caroline's death, her ward Susan Churchill was sent to boarding school. William complained about the money, but he sent her to Geneva to finish her education, even though he might easily have boarded her with a family, expecting she would become a governess. We may attribute his generosity to a genuine affection for Susan but also to his commitment to fulfill the responsibility his wife had inherited from her mother in 1821. He gave his consent to Susan's marriage in 1837, and lived to see her become a prosperous wife to an honest husband. Her biographer, Dorothy Howell-Thomas, observes that "[t]he very fact that William and Caroline, to whom tradition attributes so tormented a family life, so little consistency, responsibility, and generosity, brought her up and set her on her way to adulthood, and watched over her with affection to the end of their lives, speaks as only facts can."[1]

Five months after Lady Caroline died, Lord Melbourne passed away at age eighty three. William assumed the family title and his place in the House of Lords. Hobhouse sat beside William at a dinner around this time, and remarked that his "loud abrupt breaker of a laugh and attention to his plate and glass do not bespeak him the clever able man that he certainly is."[2] William was nursing his pain, and continuing his affair with Lady Brandon by correspondence. Lord Brandon had ignored his wife's affair while William was secretary for Ireland. Now, however, Lady Brandon decided to join her husband in London and resumed seeing William. Lord Brandon then brought an action for "criminal conversation." The action was brought in May 1828, and it would appear that Brandon had a fairly good case—

if not proof of adultery, at least of gross indiscretion. But when the day of the trial came, the suit was dismissed for lack of evidence, to the surprise of everyone connected. It is now proven that William bought off his attacker, who resurfaced two years later hinting that he might renew the suit.[3] William paid Lady Brandon 1,000 pounds a year. He ended the affair for good in 1832, and Lady Brandon reproached him pathetically: "I have suffered enough in various ways, God knows! I have nothing to look back to with *pleasure* or to look forward to with *hope.*"[4] Out of loyalty, or guilt, William continued to pay her annual allowance, and the practice was continued by his brother Frederick after William died.

Not long after his problems with Lady Brandon, William became involved with the novelist Caroline Norton. Her husband George, whom William had helped (for his lover's sake) to a position as magistrate in the metropolitan police courts, was making a grab for money rather than acting out of genuine spousal outrage when he brought criminal conversation charges against William in 1836. Once again, William escaped. Frederick Lamb wrote to Emily Cowper in relief after the verdict of 23 June 1836 against George Norton: "*Quel triomphe!,*" but he also warned: "Don't let Wm think himself invulnerable for having got off again this time; no man's luck can go further."[5]

In November 1836, William was engaged in paperwork at his desk while twenty-nine-year-old Augustus lay upon the sofa nearby:

> I thought he had dropped asleep. Suddenly he said to me in a quiet and reflective tone: "I wish you would give me some franks that I may write and thank people who have been kind in their inquiries." The pen dropt from my hand as if I had been struck; for the words and the manner were as clear and thoughtful as if no cloud had ever hung heavily over him. I cannot give any notion of what I felt; for I felt it to be, as it proved, the summons they call lightning before death. In a few hours he was gone.[6]

It is another tribute to the parental love of Caroline and William that Augustus lived so long and enjoyed such rafts of toast and oceans of tea and the company of so many friends and servants, however terrorized.

An autopsy was performed, on Augustus, and Dr. Copeland headed the team of three doctors that presented this report:

> a most unusual thickness of the bones of the skull, particularly of the bones of the forehead and temples. There were marks of former attacks of inflammation on the membranes and the substance of the brain was unusually dense, so much so

as to resist the knife in an uncommon manner. There was a larger portion of fluid at the back of the brain than is common, probably of recent origin, the ventricles also contained more water than usual. With this evidence of great disease within the Brain we did not think further examination of the viscera necessary & did not open the chest or abdomen.[7]

The doctors' findings are ambiguous. It has been guessed that Augustus suffered from neurosyphilis from birth. The description of the brain indicates extensive presence of gumma, a fibrous growth produced when the body attempts to fend off infection, possibly stemming from syphilis. However, the same effect could have been produced by years of seizures.

While William contemplated his juridical exoneration, Caroline Norton suffered the usual fate of the woman in "crim-con" cases: she was socially ostracized and lost visitation rights with her children. This drove her to wage a successful campaign for passage of an Infant Custody Bill, upon which Parliament acted in 1839. However, her husband removed her own children to Scotland and out of British jurisdiction.

Deeply embittered, Mrs. Norton wrote anguished letters to William Lamb after the trial reproaching him for his coldness, "the shrinking from me & my burdensome & embarrassing distress. God forgive you." She was fully aware she was a link in a chain. William told her about his liaisons, just as he had told his wife when they were married. The effect was just as negative: "I have a full recollection of Lady Brandon & the small space her supposed discomforts occupied in yr. mind. I wish I had never known that *experience by proxy.* . . . You will drive me mad and for my madness you may thank yourself. . . . You have made two or three unhappy destinies—look to mine and let yr women look to it."[8]

William's brother Frederick also caused some consternation in 1841 by marrying Alexandrina Julie Theresa Wilhelmina Sophie, Countess von Maltzahn, the daughter of the Prussian envoy to the Court of Vienna. Though Emily (now Lady Palmerston) herself threw the party, she was not happy. She had counted on her children inheriting the Melbourne estate. George Lamb had died childless in 1834. But now, at age fifty-nine, Frederick threatened to disrupt the peaceful flow of power and wealth to Lady Palmerston by bringing home a young woman who might bear him an heir. In the event, however, Frederick had no children.

William passed away in 1848, after having served as Prime Minister to the young Queen Victoria. Upon his death, Lady Byron wrote an elegy: "A heartless

Public saw the light grow dim."[9] It was the testimony of one who had relied upon William for advice and support over many years.

Isaac Nathan, who had been a catalyst for Lady Caroline's discovery of the power in Byron's pen, stuck by her at the end. He published a defense of her character and Byron's in *Fugitive Pieces* just after she died, reproducing her poetry right along with Byron's in a single volume. He told how he had composed music "impromptu" for Byron's poems; and how he had done the same for hers. He set and published her lyrics as sheet music and advertised them alongside Byron's. Nathan gave them billing on the same marquee, and his loyalty to both his collaborators was unfailing. He contributed to his patroness's doom by encouraging her to believe she had power, too, to strike the "thrilling lyre." Like Caroline, Nathan went into exile. He had been the friend of William IV and George IV, and had engaged in a little espionage and a lot of expense on their behalf— or so he asserted when he appealed to the government for relief of his debts in 1839. He was denied and emigrated to Australia. The Prime Minister was William Lamb, now Lord Melbourne.

Caroline's beloved Brocket Hall has been transformed by a Hong Kong-based developer into a hotel and conference center. There are rumored sightings of her ghost in the halls, at which, of course, one scoffs. Yet, walking the road from the train stop in Welwyn to the Hertfordshire Records Office one grey January morning, I still found it hard to believe she is entirely gone.

Lady Caroline Lamb and her Circle

Who's Who

Bessborough, Lord (3rd Earl). Frederick Ponsonby. Father of Lady Caroline Lamb. Held title of Lord Duncannon until his father, the 2nd Earl, died in 1793.

Bessborough, Lady (Countess). Henrietta Frances Spencer Ponsonby. Mother of Lady Caroline and her three brothers, John, Frederick, and William. With her lover, Granville Leveson-Gower, she also had two other children.

Bruce, Michael. Acquaintance of Byron's who had an affair with Lady Caroline after meeting her in Paris in 1816.

Bulwer-Lytton, Edward. Novelist and poet, he developed a youthful crush on Lady Caroline and almost became her lover late in her life.

Byron, Lord (6th Baron). George Gordon. Poet and political activist, he had many love affairs, including one with Lady Caroline Lamb in 1812, and died helping the Greek revolutionary movement.

Byron, Lady. Anne Isabella ("Annabella") Milbanke. Wife of Lord Byron and cousin of Lady Caroline's husband, William Lamb.

Canis. (*see 5th Duke of Devonshire*)

Cavendish, Georgiana. (Little G, or G) Lady Caroline Lamb's cousin, the elder daughter of Georgiana, Duchess of Devonshire. Later Lady Morpeth.

Cavendish, Harriet Elizabeth. (Harryo) Lady Caroline Lamb's cousin, the younger daughter of Georgiana, Duchess of Devonshire. Later Lady Granville.

Churchill, Susan Spencer. Illegitimate daughter of Harriet Caroline Spencer, a relative of Lady Caroline's, who became the ward of William and Lady Caroline Lamb.

Colburn, Henry. Publisher of Lady Caroline's most famous novel, Glenarvon (1816). Colburn ran a very active business that published a great quantity of British women's fiction of the early nineteenth century.

Cooper, Lady Barbara Ashley. Married Willy Ponsonby, Lady Caroline's favorite brother.

Cowper, Lady. née Emily Lamb. Later, Lady Palmerston. Sister of William Lamb. Upon Cowper's death, she married a future Prime Minister of England, Lord Palmerston.

Devonshire, Duchess of. Georgiana Spencer Cavendish. Aunt of Lady Caroline.

Devonshire, Duchess of (*see Lady Elizabeth Foster*).

Devonshire, 5th Duke of. William Cavendish (nicknamed "Canis"). Uncle of Lady Caroline.

Devonshire, 6th Duke of. (Hart) William Spencer George Cavendish. Cousin of Lady Caroline. Nicknamed "Hart," because he held the honorific title of "The Marquis of Hartington" until the 5th Duke died in 1811.

Duncannon, Lord John Ponsonby. Lady Caroline's eldest brother.

Duncannon, Lady Maria. John's Wife, formerly Maria Fane.

Fane, Maria (*see Lady Duncannon*)

Fleming, J. Wilmington. Obscure poet to whom Lady Caroline gave her journals to read and who later tried to use them for blackmail.

Foscolo, Ugo. Italian novelist. Advised Lady Caroline on her writing.

Foster, Lady Elizabeth. Lived with the 5th Duke and Georgiana, the Duchess, bearing the Duke two children, then married the 5th Duke after Georgiana's death.

Goddard, Dr. B. Lady Caroline's personal physician through the last years of her life.

Godwin, William. Author, publisher, and social philosopher, husband of Mary Wollstonecraft and father to their daughter, Mary Shelley (author of *Frankenstein*). He became Lady Caroline's close friend and mentor after they began corresponding in 1819.

Granville, Viscount. Granville Leveson Gower. Lover of Caroline's mother, with whom he had two children before he married Caroline's cousin, Harryo.

Grey, Lord Charles. Famous tea maker and lover of Georgiana, Duchess of Devonshire, who bore him a child, almost ruining herself when her husband discovered she was pregnant. Formerly Lord Howick.

Harryo (*see Harriet Cavendish*)

Hobhouse, John Cam. Political liberal and close friend of Byron as well as longtime acquaintance and correspondent of Lady Caroline Lamb, witnessing many scenes during and after Caroline's affair with Byron in 1812.

Holland, Lady. One of Lady Caroline's closest bluestocking (or liberal-feminist) friends. Caroline had an affair with her son, Godfrey, and later satirized Lady Holland as "The Princess Madagascar" in her novel *Glenarvon*.

Howick, Lord (*see Lord Charles Grey*)

Lamb, Augustus. Only child of William and Lady Caroline Lamb, born epileptic and retarded.

Lamb, Caroline Rosalie Adelaide St. Jules. Exact contemporary of Lady Caroline Lamb and illegitimate child of Lady Elizabeth Foster and the 5th Duke of Devonshire, she married William Lamb's brother, George and was nicknamed "Caro George" to distinguish her from Lady Caroline Lamb.

Lamb, Lady Caroline. Born Caroline Ponsonby. Attained the title of "Lady" when her father became 3rd Earl Bessborough. Also called "Caro William" to distinguish her from George Lamb's wife, the former Caroline St. Jules.

Lamb, Emily (*see Lady Cowper*)

Lamb, George. William's younger brother and a hack journalist and amateur playwright.

Lamb, William. Lady Caroline's husband. Later Lord Melbourne, Prime Minister of England under Queen Victoria.

Lee, Dr. Robert. Augustus Lamb's personal physician and tutor from 1817 to 1822.

Leveson Gower, Granville (*see Lord Granville*)

Leigh, Augusta. Lord Byron's half-sister, with whom he was accused of having an incestuous affair that resulted in the birth of an illegitimate daughter.

Little G (*see Georgiana Cavendish*)

Melbourne, Lady. Elizabeth Milbanke Lamb. William Lamb's mother. A dynamic and cunning mistress of Whig society. Through affairs with powerful men, like Lord Egremont and the Prince of Wales, by whom she had children, she advanced her family. By the time she realized William's marriage to Lady Caroline was a mistake, it was too late.

Melbourne, Lord. Peniston Lamb. William Lamb's father, who lived until after Caroline died, so that she never became "Lady Melbourne" and so that during her lifetime William never achieved financial independence.

Milbanke, Anne Isabella (*see Lady Byron*).

Morgan, Lady. Formerly Sydney Owenson. Novelist, feminist, and friend of Lady Caroline.

Morpeth, Lady (*See Georgiana Cavendish*)

Morpeth, Lord. Married Caroline's cousin, Georgiana Cavendish.

Murray, John II. Byron's and Lady Caroline's publisher. He was Caroline's close and dependable friend throughout her life, keeping her informed of Byron's activities and lending her manuscripts before publication. She often visited him at his offices in 50 Albermarle Street.

Nathan, Isaac. Jewish tenor, composer, and publisher who collaborated with Lord Byron on *A Selection of Hebrew Melodies* (1815-1816) and with Lady Caroline Lamb on almost a dozen songs, including music printed in two of her novels. Lady Caroline became godmother to his daughter.

Ossulston, Lady. Corisande de Grammont, a French émigrée who grew up in the Devonshire household with Lady Caroline.

Oxford, Lady. Jane Elizabeth Harley. Lady Caroline's friend and tutor, who betrayed her trust by having an affair with Byron after he had dropped Caroline.

Palmerston, Lady Emily (*see Lady Cowper*)

Ponsonby, Caroline (*see Lady Caroline Lamb*)

Ponsonby, Frederick Cavendish. Lady Caroline's older brother, a war hero at the battles of Talavera and Waterloo.

Ponsonby, John William. Lady Caroline's eldest brother, became Lord Duncannon and married Lady Maria Fane.

Ponsonby, William ("Willy") Francis Spencer. Lady Caroline's younger, favorite brother, who married Lady Barbara Ashley Cooper.

Preedy, Rev. James . Performed the marriages of William to Lady Caroline and of Lady Elizabeth Foster to the 5th Duke.

St. Jules, Caroline (*see Caroline St. Jules Lamb*)

Sheridan, Esther Jane Ogle. Nicknamed "Hecca," Richard Brinsley Sheridan's second wife, who participated in a bizarre scene on the night Lady Caroline gave birth to her son Augustus.

Sheridan, Richard Brinsley. Playwright, politician, and lover of Caroline's mother, Lady Bessborough.

Spencer, George John, 2nd Earl Spencer. Lady Caroline's Uncle.

Spencer, Lady Georgiana. Lady Caroline's grandmother.

Trimmer, Selina. Governess for the Devonshire and Bessborough households.

Webster, Sir Godfrey Vassal. Son of Lady Holland by her first marriage and lover of Lady Caroline in the two years before she met Byron.

Wellington, Arthur Wellesley, 1st Duke. Hero of Waterloo (1815), who had a liaison with Lady Caroline in Paris after his great victory.

Wheeler, Rosina Doyle. In the last years of Lady Caroline's life, her protégée who married Edward Bulwer-Lytton, the novelist.

Chronology

1779	March 15	William Lamb born.
1781		Caroline's brother John William Ponsonby (later Lord Duncannon) born.
1783	July 6	Caroline's brother Frederick Cavendish Ponsonby born.
1785	August 16	Caroline Rosalie St. Jules (later "Caro George") born.
	August 29	Harriet Elizabeth Cavendish ("Harryo") born.
	November 13	Caroline Ponsonby (later Lady Caroline Lamb) born.
1788	January 22	George Gordon, 6th Lord Byron born.
1787		Caroline's brother William ("Willy") Francis Spencer Ponsonby (her favorite) born.
1790		William Spencer Cavendish, Marquis of Hartington ("Hart," later the 6th Duke of Devonshire) born.
1791	November	Caroline leaves for Europe with her mother and aunt Georgiana, the Duchess of Devonshire, who has been banished by the Duke ("Canis") for becoming pregnant by her lover, Earl Grey.
1793	January	Louis XVI of France guillotined.
	March 11	Lord Bessborough dies, making her father the 3rd Earl Bessborough and Caroline officially "Lady Caroline."
	May	Caroline's Aunt Georgiana and Lady Elizabeth Foster are permitted by the Duke of Devonshire to return to England, but her mother, Harriet, is too ill to travel.
	October	Marie Antoinette guillotined.
1793-1794		Caroline suffers a life-threatening illness in Italy, and her mother, Harriet, falls in love with Granville Leveson Gower.
1794	August	Caroline's mother is well enough to travel home to England.
1799		William Lamb takes his degree at Cambridge and goes to Glasgow to study.
1802	March	The ill-fated Treaty of Amiens signed, negotiated by Pitt the Younger.
	August	Caroline and William Lamb meet and are infatuated.
1803	May 18	Britain declares war on France.

1805	June 3	Caroline and William Lamb are married.
1806	February 1	Caroline delivers a girl, who dies shortly after.
		William elected Member of Parliament for Leominster.
	March 30	Caroline's Aunt Georgiana, Duchess of Devonshire, dies.
	November	William opens Parliament and Caroline sneaks in dressed as a man to watch proudly.
1807	August 29	Caroline's son Augustus born.
1809	October 19	Lady Elizabeth Foster marries 5th Duke of Devonshire.
	May 17	George Lamb marries Caroline Rosalie Adelaide St. Jules.
	December 24	Granville marries "Harryo" (Lady Harriet Elizabeth Cavendish).
1811	February 5	Regency bill becomes law, and "Prinny" (the Prince of Wales) assumes the royal duties because George III is incapacitated by porphyria.
	March/April	Caroline has an affair with Sir Godfrey Vassal Webster.
	July 29	Frederick Cavendish, 5th Duke of Devonshire, dies, making "Hart" the 6th Duke.
1812	March 10	*Childe Harold's Pilgrimage* officially published.
	March 25	Byron attends a waltzing party at Lady Caroline Lamb's. Their affair begins.
	August 12	Caroline runs away and Byron manages to bring her home.
	September	Caroline is taken to Ireland by her family.
	November	Byron delivers the blow: Caroline is no longer his lover.
	December	Caroline burns Byron in effigy.
1813	January	Caroline forges Byron's handwriting to obtain a painting from John Murray.
	July 5	Caroline cuts herself in a chaotic scene at Lady Heathcote's ball.
	August 10	Austria declares war on France.
1814		Caroline's brother Willy marries Lady Barbara Ashley Cooper.
	March 18	Caroline's grandmother Lady Spencer dies.
	March 28	Byron moves into the Albany.
	Spring	Caroline meets Isaac Nathan, who arranges music in honor of her brother Willy's engagement.
	May 4	Napoleon exiled; arrives on Elba.

	July 1	Caroline attends a masked ball at Burlington House held by Watier's Club to Honor the Duke of Wellington's victory over Napoleon.
1815	January 2	Byron is married at Seaham to Annabella Milbanke
	March 20	Napoleon returns to power in France.
	March 28	The Byrons settle at 13 Piccadilly Terrace (house of the Duchess of Devonshire).
	April	Nathan and Byron's *Hebrew Melodies* volume 1 published.
	June 18	Napoleon defeated at Waterloo.
	August 11	Viscount Melbourne created Lord Melbourne in the peerage of the UK.
	August 12	Granville Leveson-Gower created Viscount Granville.
		William and Caroline visit Brussels and Paris.
	October 16	Napoleon exiled to Saint Helena.
1816	April 18	Nathan and Byron's *Hebrew Melodies* volume 2 published.
	April 21	Byron signs deed of separation from his wife.
	April 24	Byron leaves London for the Continent.
	May 9	Lady Caroline's first novel, *Glenarvon,* published by Henry Colburn.
	July 7	Richard Brinsley Sheridan dies; afterward, William is elected Member of Parliament for Northampton.
	November 18	Canto III of Byron's *Childe Harold* published in London.
1817	July 14	Madame de Staël dies.
1818	March	Susan Spencer Churchill born to Harriet Caroline Spencer; the illegitimate child becomes Lady Bessborough's ward.
	April 6	Lady Melbourne dies.
	Spring	Emily Cowper (William's sister) fights to get Lady Caroline admitted to Almack's Club.
1819	February/ March	Lady Caroline canvasses for William's brother George Lamb's election, in which he defeats John Cam Hobhouse.
	July 15	Byron's *Don Juan* Cantos 1 and 2 published.
	October	Lady Caroline's *A New Canto* (satire of *Don Juan*) published.
1820	January 29	George III dies.
	February 16	George III buried.
	April 27	George IV opens Parliament.
	Summer	Lady Caroline appears at Almack's dressed as Don Juan with attendant devils.

	August	Queen Caroline's trial for adultery with her courier, Bartolomeo Bergami, begins and will last through November. She is acquitted.
1821	July 19	George IV's coronation at Westminster Abbey.
	August 7	Queen Caroline (George IV's estranged wife) dies.
	August 8	Byron's *Don Juan* Cantos 3-5 published.
	Fall	Caroline's *Gordon: A Tale* (another satire of *Don Juan*) published.
	November 5	The infant son of Lady Caroline's brother William and Lady Barbara dies in Parma.
	November 11	Lady Bessborough dies in Florence.
1822	January 28	Annabella's mother dies (Lady Noel) and Lord and Lady Byron assume the additional name of Noel.
	April 19	Byron's daughter Allegra dies.
	Fall	Caroline's *Graham Hamilton* published by Henry Colburn.
1823	March	Caroline's *Ada Reis* published by John Murray.
1824	March 30	Lady Elizabeth Foster, Duchess of Devonshire, dies.
	April 19	Lord Byron dies in Greece, the victim of doctors who dehydrate him through bleeding.
	May 17	Byron's memoirs are burned at John Murray's offices in Albemarle Street, and it is disclosed that Murray let Caroline read them.
	June 29	The *Florida* arrives in England with Byron's remains.
	July 12	Byron's funeral cortege leaves London and passes through Welwyn, Hertfordshire, where Caroline encounters it.
	July 16	Byron's funeral.
	October 23	Medwin's *Conversations of Lord Byron* published and Caroline reads his vitriolic "Remember Thee" for the first time.
1825	Summer	William finally succumbs to family pressure to separate from Caroline, who signs separation agreement, meets Wilmington Fleming, and departs for Paris.
	October	Lady Caroline back in London; Doctor Goddard makes diagnosis of insanity.
1826	January	Lady Caroline returns to Brocket.
1827	April	William appointed Chief Secretary to the Lord Lieutenant for Ireland, takes Augustus with him.
	September	Caroline becomes severely ill with "dropsy."

x 1830 Earl Grey = Prime Minister

1828	January 15	William notified Caroline likely to die.
	January 25	Lady Caroline dies, William having arrived just in time to speak with her.
X 1834	July 22	William's father finally dies at age 83, and William becomes Lord Melbourne. *L M becomes Prime Minister*
1836		Caroline and William's son, Augustus, dies.
1837		George IV dies.
		Lord Cowper dies, leaving William's sister Emily free to marry Lord Palmerston, future Prime Minister.
1838		Victoria crowned Queen.
1848		William Lamb dies.
1853		Frederick Lamb dies.
1858		"Hart," the 6th Duke of Devonshire, dies.
1860		Lady Byron dies.
1862		Caroline St. Jules Lamb ("Caro George") dies.
		Harryo dies.
1864		Isaac Nathan dies in Sydney, Australia.
1869		Emily Palmerston (formerly Lamb, then Cowper) dies.

Abbreviations

Bessborough and Aspinall:	Bessborough, Earl, and Arthur Aspinall. *Lady Bessborough and Her Family Circle.* London: John Murray, 1940.
British Library:	The Althorp, Lamb, and Melbourne Papers of the British Library.
Byron's Letters and Journals:	Byron, George Gordon Lord. *Byron's Letters and Journals.* Ed. Leslie Marchand. 12 vols. Cambridge: Belknap Press of Harvard University Press, 1973-1995.
Devonshire MSS:	Letters and other papers of the 5th and 6th Dukes of Devonshire held in the archive at Chatsworth, Derbyshire.
Forster Collection:	Letters of Lady Caroline Lamb in the Victoria and Albert Museum Forster Collection MSS vol. 28 (Pressmark 48.E.22).
Granville:	Granville Leveson-Gower, Earl. *Private Correspondence of Earl Granville: 1781-1821.* 2 vols. Ed. Castalia, Countess Granville. London: John Murray, 1916.
Hary-O:	Gower, Henrietta Elizabeth Leveson. *Hary-O: The Letters of Lady Harriet Cavendish, 1796-1809.* Ed. Sir George Leveson-Gower and Iris Palmer. London: John Murray, 1940.
Hertfordshire Archives:	Papers of the Lamb [Melbourne] family held in the Hertfordshire Archives and Local Studies Office, County Hall, Hertfordshire.
John Murray Archive:	Letters and other papers of Lady Caroline Lamb, Lord and Lady Byron, and John Murray, held in the John Murray Archive in London.

Notes

Preface

1. *Byron's Letters and Journals*, 2:170-71.
2. Blyth, *Caro: The Fatal Passion*, 2, 7.
3. Marshall, *Lord Melbourne*, 43.
4. Blyth, *Caro: The Fatal Passion*, 231.
5. Morgan, *Lady Morgan's Memoirs*, 2:210-11.

Chapter 1

1. Journal of Lady Spencer for 1785. Devonshire MSS. 5th Duke's Group f. 2014.155 and following.
2. *Byron's Letters and Journals*, 2:170.
3. Journal of Lady Spencer for 1785. Devonshire MSS. 5th Duke's Group f. 2014.155 and following.
4. Lady Spencer to her daughter Harriet, 26 April 1786, British Library Add. MS 7560, unfoliated; and Lady Spencer to her daughter Harriet, 2 May 1786 and 22 December 1788, British Library Add. MS 75608, f.495 and unfoliated:
5. Bessborough and Aspinall, 166.
6. Ibid., 59.
7. Letter of Lady Spencer. British Library Add. MS 75608, unfoliated.
8. Bessborough and Aspinall, 15, 56, 70, 99.
9. Lady Spencer to her daughter Harriet, 20 June 1789. British Library Add. MS 75608, unfoliated.
10. Eden, *Miss Eden's Letters*, 79.
11. Morgan, *Lady Morgan's Memoirs*, 2:198ff.
12. See Mayne, *Byron*, 147ff.; Wallace, *The Nympho and Other Maniacs*, 88; Blyth, *Caro: The Fatal Passion*, 18, 25-26; and Grebanier, *The Uninhibited Byron*, 103-5. Each of these writers takes Lady Caroline's fabrications about her childhood at face value.
13. Lady Spencer had reassured Harriet just the year before that she need not worry about her sons' fates: "John has beautiful Eyes my Dearest Harriet & with a little Care will have good teeth—Nothing else is of consequence with regard to a Man's beauty." Lady Spencer to her daughter Harriet, 21 August 1784. British Library Add. MS 75607, f. 347.
14. Lady Spencer to her daughter Harriet, 2 December 1785 and 13 June 1786. British Library Add. MS 75608, f. 465 and f. 505.
15. Bessborough and Aspinall, 57, 59, 146.
16. The Osborne collection of Yale University's Special Collections.
17. Foreman, *Georgiana: Duchess of Devonshire*, 95.
18. Gower, *The Face Without a Frown*, 68-69.
19. I use the spelling "Harryo" preferred by Georgiana and by Lady Spencer in her journal for 1793, Devonshire MSS. 5th Duke's Group, f. 2014.185-252.
20. Calder-Marshall, *The Two Duchesses*, 76-77.
21. Foreman, *Georgiana: Duchess of Devonshire*, 87-88.

22. Calder-Marshall, *The Two Duchesses*, 26. The "Jerusalem Chamber" is an allusion both to the Jewish moneylenders who thrived in this system and to the illusory place of termination that is the setting for Act 4, Scene 4 of Shakespeare's *Henry IV, Part 2*.

23. Granville, *Private Correspondence*, 1:117.

24. Foreman, *Georgiana: Duchess of Devonshire*, 196.

25. Bessborough and Aspinall, 56, 59-60.

26. Calder-Marshall, *The Two Duchesses*, 27.

27. Lady Spencer to her daughter Harriet, 26 December 1783. British Library Add. MS 75606, f. 225.

28. Jenkins, *Lady Caroline Lamb*, 19. Macao and Faro were two of the most popular card games of the era.

29. Lady Spencer to her daughter Harriet, 28 February 1786. British Library Add. MS 75608, f. 476.

30. Sheridan had tried in 1779 to conciliate Lady Spencer by dedicating to her his elegy on the death of actor David Garrick. Years later, according to Byron, Sheridan became nearly apoplectic at the mere sight of the dedication he had offered to that "damned canting bitch" (*Byron's Letters and Journals*, 9:15).

31. Foreman, *Georgiana: Duchess of Devonshire*, 232.

32. Bessborough and Aspinall, 47-52.

33. Sheridan, *The Letters of Richard Brinsley Sheridan*, 1:207-8.

34. Foreman, *Georgiana: Duchess of Devonshire*, 232.

35. Lady Caroline Lamb to Lady Holland, 29 May 1811. British Library Add. MS 51560 f. 177.

36. Bessborough, *Georgiana, Duchess of Devonshire*, 149.

37. See Foreman, *Georgiana: Duchess of Devonshire*, 233; and Sheridan, *The Letters of Richard Brinsley Sheridan*, 1:208n.

38. Calder-Marshall, *The Two Duchesses*, 107-8.

39. Foreman, *Georgiana: Duchess of Devonshire*, 247.

40. Ibid., 298; and see Devonshire MSS. 5th Duke's Group, 1392.

41. Burney, *The Journals and Letters*, 1:41-43.

42. Ibid., 1:45-46, 49, 51, 60.

43. Lady Bessborough to Lady Melbourne. British Library Add. MS 45911, f. 15.

44. 5th Duke of Devonshire to Lady Bessborough. British Library Add. MS 45548, f. 44.

Chapter 2

1. See Bessborough and Aspinall, 60-61.

2. The letters were later censored by her descendants. See Foreman, *Georgiana: Duchess of Devonshire*, 259.

3. Ibid., 263-64.

4. Bessborough and Aspinall, 69-70.

5. Calder-Marshall, *The Two Duchesses*, 116.

6. Duke of Devonshire to Lady Spencer, 3 April 1792. Devonshire MSS. 5th Duke's Group, f. 1124.

7. Calder-Marshall, *The Two Duchesses*, 118.

8. Quoted in Foreman, *Georgiana: Duchess of Devonshire*, 268.

9. Sichel, *Sheridan*, 2:219.

10. Lady Spencer to Selina Trimmer from Florence, 18 February 1793. Devonshire MSS. 5th Duke's Group, f. 1151.

11. Calder-Marshall, *The Two Duchesses*, 121.

12. Bessborough and Aspinall, 93.

13. Lady Spencer to Duchess of Devonshire, 30 June 1793. Devonshire MSS. 5th Duke's Group, f. 1155.

14. Bessborough and Aspinall, 96.

15. Lady Spencer's journal for 1793. Devonshire MSS. 5th Duke's Group, f.2014.185-252.
16. Bessborough and Aspinall, 99.
17. Ibid., 101.
18. Calder-Marshall, *The Two Duchesses,* 81; Bessborough and Aspinall, 56, 59.
19. Lady Spencer to Selina Trimmer from Florence, 18 February 1793. Devonshire MSS. 5th Duke's Group, f. 1151.
20. Lady Spencer to Selina Trimmer, 4 September 1793. Devonshire MSS. 5th Duke's Papers 1174.
21. Lady Spencer's journal for 1793. Devonshire MSS. 5th Duke's Group, f. 2014.185-252.
22. Ibid.
23. Ibid.
24. Lady Spencer to the Duchess of Devonshire, 8 August 1793. Devonshire MSS. 5th Duke's Group, f. 1163.
25. Lady Spencer's journal for 1793. Devonshire MSS. 5th Duke's Group, f. 2014.185-252. Italics added.
26. Lady Spencer to Selina Trimmer, 4 September 1793. Devonshire MSS. 5th Duke's Papers 1174.
27. Lamb, *Ada Reis,* 1:51.
28. Ibid., 3:62-63.
29. Undated letter from Lady Caroline Lamb to Lady Morgan. *Lady Morgan's Memoirs* 2:211.
30. Lady Spencer's journal for 1793. Devonshire MSS. 5th Duke's Group, f. 2014.185-252.
31. Lady Spencer to Selina Trimmer, 4 September 1793. Devonshire MSS. 5th Duke's Papers 1174.
32. Lady Spencer's journal for 1793. Devonshire MSS. 5th Duke's Group, f. 2014.185-252.
33. Bessborough and Aspinall, 85-86, 95.
34. Ibid., 103.
35. Howell-Thomas, *Duncannon,* 23.
36. Lady Spencer's journal for 1793. Devonshire MSS. 5th Duke's Group, f. 2014.185-252.
37. Lady Spencer to the Duchess of Devonshire, 18 January 1794 and 18 February 1794. Devonshire MSS. 5th Duke's Group, ff. 1205, 1212.
38. Bessborough and Aspinall, 106.
39. Ibid., 106-7.
40. Devonshire MSS. 5th Duke's series f.1250, 1253.
41. Bessborough and Aspinall, 101.
42. Ibid., 108.
43. Calder-Marshall, *The Two Duchesses,* 125.
44. Bessborough and Aspinall, 112.
45. Lady Caroline Lamb, a book of poetry in the Hertfordshire Archives D/Elb F64.
46. Georgiana Cavendish ("little G") to Selina Trimmer, 1 April 1796. Devonshire MSS. 5th Duke's Group, f. 1328.1.
47. Selina Trimmer to the Duchess of Devonshire, 23 June 1796. Devonshire MSS. 5th Duke's Group, f. 1343.
48. Selina Trimmer to the Lady Spencer, 5 April 1796. Devonshire MSS. 5th Duke's Group, f. 1330.
49. Selina Trimmer to the Lady Spencer, 7 April 1796. Devonshire MSS. 5th Duke's Group, f. 1331. Lady Spencer to Selina Trimmer, 9 April 1796. Devonshire MSS. 5th Duke's Papers f. 1332.
50. Lady Spencer to Selina Trimmer, 3 June 1796. Devonshire MSS. 5th Duke's Papers f. 1338.

51. Lady Spencer to Selina Trimmer, 1 June 1796. Devonshire MSS. 5th Duke's Papers f. 1339.

52. Calder-Marshall names it "unilateral exophthalmos of endocrine origin" in *The Two Duchesses*, 126, 179.

53. Granville, *Private Correspondence*, 1:126, 134, 142.

54. Selina Trimmer to Lady Spencer, 6 September 1796. Devonshire MSS. 5th Duke's Papers 1369. Lady Spencer to Selina Trimmer, 16 September 1796. Devonshire MSS. 5th Duke's Papers f. 1371.

55. Morgan, *Lady Morgan's Memoirs*, 2:211.

56. Bessborough and Aspinall, 14.

57. Foreman, *Georgiana: Duchess of Devonshire*, 297-99. The Irish Rebellion of 1798, which was savagely put down, would form the historical context for Lady Caroline Lamb's first novel, *Glenarvon*.

58. Lady Spencer to her daughter Harriet, 1 February 1797. Quoted in Dorothy Howell-Thomas, *Duncannon: Reformer and Reconciler*, 12.

59. Bessborough and Aspinall, 113.

60. Granville, *Private Correspondence*, 1:197-98. Harryo wrote to Selina Trimmer on 21 January 1798, "I hear that Caro Ponsonby is a great deal better but that Willy has caught it of her." Devonshire MSS. 5th Duke's Group, f. 1423.

61. Granville, *Private Correspondence*, 1:195.

62. *Hary-O*, 11.

63. Calder-Marshall, *The Two Duchesses*, 127-28.

64. Bessborough and Aspinall, 115.

65. O'Toole, *A Traitor's Kiss*, 312.

66. Granville, *Private Correspondence*, 1:160, 162.

67. Ibid., 1:204.

68. Ibid., 1:216.

69. Bessborough and Aspinall, 115.

70. These nicknames are listed in her commonplace book; John Murray Archive.

71. Lady Caroline Lamb, a book of poems. Hertfordshire Archives D/Elb F64.

72. Ibid.

73. Lady Spencer to Selina Trimmer, 3 December 1797. Devonshire MSS. 5th Duke's Papers f. 1414.

74. Villiers, *The Grand Whiggery*, 144.

Chapter 3

1. Chapman and Dormer, *Elizabeth and Georgiana,*150.

2. Lady Caroline Lamb to Hartington, 14 November 1811 and 2 October 1810. Devonshire MSS. 5th Duke's Group, f. 1990 and 6th Duke's Group, f. 36.

3. Gower, *The Face Without a Frown*, 211.

4. Stuart, *Dearest Bess*, 84.

5. Granville, *Private Correspondence*, 1:205.

6. Bessborough and Aspinall, 116.

7. Calder-Marshall, *The Two Duchesses*, 131-32.

8. Bessborough and Aspinall, 117.

9. Granville, *Private Correspondence*, 1:317; Arthur Calder-Marshall, *The Two Duchesses* (London: Hutchinson, 1978) 135.

10. Granville, *Private Correspondence*, 1:314.

11. Ibid., 1:350-52.

12. Ibid., 1:366.

13. Washington Irving described her freckles in an undated letter. Washington Irving Collection (#6256-AJ), Clifton Waller Barrett Library, Special Collections, University of Virginia Library.

14. Morgan, *Lady Morgan's Memoirs*, 2:254-55.
15. *Hary-O*, 23.
16. Cecil, *Melbourne*, 57.
17. Bodleian Library, University of Oxford, Dep. Lovelace Byron 417. Extracts from the diary of Harriet, Countess Granville, 1810-1824.
18. Lamb, Lady Caroline. Letter to William Godwin. 18 April 1822. (Franked Welwyn 20 April 1822.) Bodleian Library, University of Oxford, [Abinger] Dep. c. 507.
19. Mitchell, *Lord Melbourne: 1779-1848*, 6.
20. Possibly Georgiana was trying to plug other leaks as well. She had secretly borrowed £6,000 from the Duke of Bedford at 5 percent interest, temporarily paying off the interest on her debts. See Foreman, *Georgiana: Duchess of Devonshire*, 317.
21. Howell-Thomas, *Duncannon*, 48.
22. Hertfordshire Archives D/Elb F64.
23. Granville, *Private Correspondence*, 1:382.
24. Bessborough and Aspinall, 121.
25. *Hary-O*, 44. Frederick Lamb's embarrassments initially formed part of Harriette Wilson's infamous *Memoirs of Herself and Others* (1825). Wilson had apparently demanded £200 from her former *amours* as "the price of omission" from the chronicle. Some paid; others concurred with the Duke of Wellington's reply: "publish and be damned." See David, *Prince of Pleasure*, 285.
26. Hertfordshire Archives D/Elb F64.
27. Granville, *Private Correspondence*, 1:379.
28. Bessborough and Aspinall, 121.
29. Granville, *Private Correspondence*, 1:380.
30. Ibid., 1:377.
31. I am indebted to Margot Strickland, who shared her unpublished research in this area. The translation of Sappho is by Paul Roche, *The Love Songs of Sappho* (New York: Signet, 1966), 59.
32. Hertfordshire Archives D/Elb F64.
33. Bessborough and Aspinall, 125-26.
34. O'Toole, *A Traitor's Kiss*, 371.
35. Ibid., 389-90.
36. Granville, *Private Correspondence*, 1:433.
37. Calder-Marshall, *The Two Duchesses*, 140-41.
38. Cecil, *Melbourne*, 68-69.
39. Askwith, *Piety and Wit*, 37.
40. Granville, *Private Correspondence*, 1:491.
41. Ibid., 1:491.
42. Victoria, *The Girlhood of Queen Victoria*, 2:64.
43. Cecil, *Melbourne*, 72.
44. Granville, *Private Correspondence*, 2:3.
45. Ibid., 2:3, 10.
46. O'Toole, *A Traitor's Kiss*, 390-91.
47. Granville, *Private Correspondence*, 2:5.
48. Ibid., 2:7-8.
49. Cecil, *Melbourne*, 69.
50. Granville, *Private Correspondence*, 2:17.
51. Ibid., 2:18.
52. Ibid., 2:32.
53. O'Toole, *A Traitor's Kiss*, 392.
54. Granville, *Private Correspondence*, 2:67.
55. Ibid., 2:68.
56. Ibid., 2:67.
57. Ibid., 2:67.
58. Victoria, *The Girlhood of Queen Victoria*, 2:158.

59. Granville, *Private Correspondence,* 2:67.
60. Ibid., 2:68.
61. Ibid., 2:21.
62. Ibid., 2:68-69.
63. Ibid., 2:67.
64. Devonshire MSS. 5th Duke's Group f. 1805.
65. Bessborough and Aspinall, 130-31.
66. Lady Spencer to Selina Trimmer, 8 May 1805. Devonshire MSS. 5th Duke's Group f. 1807.
67. Mitchell, *Lord Melbourne: 1779-1848,* 60.
68. Duchess of Devonshire to Lady Spencer, 16 May 1805. Devonshire MSS. 5th Duke's Group f. 1809.
69. Bessborough and Aspinall, 130-31.
70. Granville, *Private Correspondence,* 2:73.

Chapter 4

1. Duchess of Devonshire to Lady Spencer, 9 May 1805. Devonshire MSS. 5th Duke's Group f. 1808.
2. Melbourne, *Byron's "Corbeau Blanc,"* 70.
3. Stuart, *Dearest Bess,* 85.
4. Blyth, *Caro: The Fatal Passion,* 54.
5. Granville, *Private Correspondence,* 2:73. Description of the gown and veil is found in a letter of the Duchess of Devonshire to Lady Spencer, 4 June 1805. Devonshire MSS. 5th Duke's Group f. 1812.
6. The ball was given by Lady Kinnaird on 29 May 1805. Duchess of Devonshire to Lady Spencer, 8 May 1805. Devonshire MSS. 5th Duke's Group f. 1811.
7. Granville, *Private Correspondence,* 2:76.
8. Duchess of Devonshire to Lady Spencer, 4 June 1805. Devonshire MSS. 5th Duke's Group f. 1812.
9. Lady Caroline to her uncle Earl Spencer, 18 April 1814. British Library Add. MS 76113, unfoliated.
10. This tiara was exhibited in 2002 at the Victoria and Albert Museum. No name was attached to the piece, but Virginia Murray guesses that it may still be in the family.
11. Granville, *Private Correspondence,* 2:75-76.
12. Ibid., 2:75-76, 81. The Duchess of Devonshire's description of the wedding is in her letter to Lady Spencer of 4 June 1805. Devonshire MSS. 5th Duke's Group f. 1812.
13. Bessborough and Aspinall, 135.
14. Ibid., 133.
15. Granville, *Private Correspondence,* 2:76, 79.
16. Lady Spencer to the Duchess of Devonshire, 9 June 1805. Devonshire MSS. 5th Duke's Group, f. 1814.
17. Granville, *Private Correspondence,* 2:85. And see Foster, *The Two Duchesses,* 233.
18. Lady Caroline Lamb to the Marquis of Hartington, 23 June 1805. Devonshire MSS. 5th Duke's Group, f. 1814.1.
19. Bessborough and Aspinall, 133.
20. The scrapbook (one of two commonplace books) is in the John Murray Archive.
21. *Hary-O,* 117.
22. Mitchell, *Lord Melbourne: 1779-1848,* 61.
23. British Library Add. MS 38855. f. 225.
24. Dunckley, *Lord Melbourne,* 109-10.
25. British Library Add. MS 45549.
26. Granville, *Private Correspondence,* 2:86.
27. Ibid., 2:93.

28. Lamb, *Glenarvon,* 1:152.
29. Ibid., 1:285.
30. Mitchell, *Lord Melbourne: 1779-1848,* 65.
31. Cecil, *Melbourne,* 83.
32. Mitchell, *Lord Melbourne: 1779-1848,* 62.
33. Foster, *The Two Duchesses,* 242.
34. *Hary-O,* 118, 122.
35. Ibid., 125-26, 129.
36. Granville, *Private Correspondence,* 2:124.
37. Mitchell, *Lord Melbourne: 1779-1848,* 32.
38. G. W. E. Russell, *Collections and Recollections,* (New York: Harper, 1898), 64.
39. Hertfordshire Archives D/Elb F64.
40. Lady Caroline Lamb to Lady Morpeth, 1 August and 13 October 1807. Mitchell, *Lord Melbourne: 1779-1848,* 63.
41. Nathan, *Fugitive Pieces,* 177.
42. *Hary-O,* 137.
43. "GEORGE continues still to write, / Tho' now the name is veiled from public sight." Byron, *Complete Poetical Works,* 1:231.
44. *Hary-O,* 129.
45. Ibid., 141.
46. Bessborough and Aspinall, 141.
47. Ibid., 142.
48. *Hary-O,* 150.
49. Granville, *Private Correspondence,* 2:34, 41.
50. Foreman, *Georgiana: Duchess of Devonshire,* 370.
51. Hertfordshire Records Office, Panshanger Papers.
52. Masters, *Georgiana, Duchess of Devonshire,* 267-69.
53. Granville, *Private Correspondence,* 2:210.
54. Ibid., 2:186.
55. Calder-Marshall, *The Two Duchesses,* 151-52.
56. Foreman, *Georgiana: Duchess of Devonshire,* 374.
57. Bessborough and Aspinall, 146.
58. M. G. Lewis to Lady Melbourne. British Library Add. MS 45548.
59. Hertfordshire Archives D/Elb F64.
60. Mitchell, *Lord Melbourne: 1779-1848,* 78, 58-61.
61. Lady Caroline Lamb to Lady Bessborough, 15 January 1807. Ponsonby, *The Ponsonby Family,* 130.
62. Lady Theresa Lewis, *Extracts from the Journals and Correspondence of Miss Berry From the Year 1783 to 1852,* 3 vols. (London 1866), 3:524.
63. Bessborough and Aspinall, 149.
64. *Hary-O,* 159, 162.
65. Bessborough and Aspinall, 155.
66. *Hary-O,* 159-60.
67. Ibid., 166.
68. Bessborough and Aspinall, 155.
69. Hertfordshire Archives, Panshanger MSS D/Elb F12.
70. Lady Caroline Lamb to Lady Morpeth (November 1806). Quoted in Mitchell, *Lord Melbourne: 1779-1848,* 98.
71. Ziegler, *Melbourne,* 62.
72. Stuart, *Dearest Bess,* 155.
73. See Mitchell, *Lord Melbourne: 1779-1848,* 98-99.

Chapter 5

1. *Hary-O*, 182.
2. Granville, *Private Correspondence*, 1:215.
3. Ibid., 2:352.
4. Ibid., 2:236.
5. Lady Caroline Lamb to Lady Bessborough, 15 January 1807. Ponsonby, *The Ponsonby Family*, 130.
6. Hertfordshire Archives DELb F71.
7. *Hary-O*, 201.
8. Lady Caroline Lamb to John Allen, August 1807. British Library Add MS 52193, f.104,
9. Granville, *Private Correspondence*, 2:271.
10. Ibid., 2:274.
11. Ibid., 2:276.
12. British Library Add. MSS 51560, f. 7.
13. Granville, *Private Correspondence*, 2:289.
14. Ibid., 2:292.
15. Ibid., 2:293.
16. Ibid., 2:308-309.
17. Ibid., 2:309.
18. O'Toole, *A Traitor's Kiss*, 419.
19. Foss, *Here Lies Richard Brinsley Sheridan*, 287.
20. *Hary-O*, 229.
21. Bessborough and Aspinall, 165-66.
22. *Hary-O*, 242.
23. Ibid., 242-43.
24. Morgan, *Lady Morgan's Memoirs*, 2:200.
25. Ziegler, *Melbourne*, 106-7.
26. Hertfordshire Archives, Panshanger MSS Box 17.
27. Hertfordshire Archives, Panshanger MSS Box 37.
28. *Hary-O*, 242-43.
29. Ibid., 257.
30. Ibid., 255, 257.
31. Ibid., 261.
32. Granville, *Private Correspondence*, 317.
33. Ibid., 2:153, 234.
34. Mitchell, *Lord Melbourne: 1779-1848*, 67.
35. Bessborough and Aspinall, 167-169.
36. Villiers, *The Grand Whiggery*, 217.
37. *Hary-O*, 263.
38. Bessborough and Aspinall, 170.
39. Byron, *Childe Harold's Pilgrimage* 1:26. Byron, *Complete Poetical Works*, 2:30.
40. Bessborough and Aspinall, 181.
41. Ibid., 182-83.
42. *Hary-O*, 298.
43. *The Works of Lord Byron*, 2:114.
44. Lady Bessborough to her mother Lady Spencer, 26 April and 25 May 1809. British Library Add. MS 75608, unfoliated.
45. Lady Bessborough to her mother Lady Spencer, 17 May 1809. British Library Add. MS 75608, unfoliated.
46. Bessborough and Aspinall, 184-85.
47. Lady Bessborough to her mother Lady Spencer, 24 May and 5 June 1809. British Library Althorp Papers 75608, unfoliated.

Chapter 6

1. Lady Caroline Lamb to John Murray, n.d. (January-February 1814). John Murray Archive.
2. Bessborough and Aspinall, 185.
3. Lady Caroline Lamb to Marquis of Hartington, 31 July 1810. Devonshire MSS. 5th Duke's Group, f. 1983.
4. Lady Caroline Lamb to William Lamb, 27 May 1809. Hertfordshire Archives D/ELb F32/3.
5. Bessborough and Aspinall, 185.
6. Lady Caroline Lamb to Marquis of Hartington, 2 October 1810. Devonshire MSS. 5th Duke's Group, f. 1990.
7. Bessborough and Aspinall, 184.
8. The annuities are recorded in the ledgers of the 6th Duke of Devonshire, Devonshire MSS.
9. Granville, *Private Correspondence*, 2:345.
10. Bessborough and Aspinall, 191.
11. *Hary-O*, 334.
12. Chapman and Dormer, *Elizabeth and Georgiana*, 187.
13. Lady Caroline Lamb to Marquis of Hartington, 11 October 1809. Devonshire MSS. 5th Duke's Group, f. 1957.
14. Bessborough and Aspinall, 194.
15. Ibid., 195.
16. Stuart, *Dearest Bess*, 170.
17. Lady Spencer to Lady Bessborough, 22 March 1810. Bessborough and Aspinall, 204.
18. Bessborough and Aspinall, 186.
19. Ibid., 186.
20. John Murray Archive. Undated letter of Lady Caroline Lamb to an unnamed correspondent. By watermark and style, I have dated it to the 1809-1810 period.
21. Lady Caroline Lamb to Lady Holland, n.d. British Library Add. MS 51560 f. 124.
22. Wilson, *Memoirs of Herself and Others*, 588.
23. *Don Juan*, 15:65, 66, 72, 74. Byron, *Complete Poetical Works*, 5:607-10.
24. I am indebted here to the evocative descriptions of Arthur Bryant's *The Age of Elegance: 1812-1822* (New York: Harper & Brothers, 1950), 315ff.
25. Lady Caroline Lamb to Marquis of Hartington, 2 October 1810. Devonshire MSS. 5th Duke's Group, f. 1990.
26. Lady Caroline Lamb to Lady Holland, n.d., (9 or 10 August 1810). Holland House Papers British Library Add. MS 51560 f. 141.
27. Letter of Lady Caroline Lamb to her uncle George John, Lord Spencer, 10 August 1809. British Library Add. MS 76104.
28. Letter of Lady Caroline Lamb to her uncle George John, Lord Spencer, August/September 1809. British Library Add. MS 76104.
29. British Library Add. MS 51560, ff. 155, 166
30. British Library Add. MS 70951 f 434.
31. Bessborough and Aspinall, 187-88.
32. Hertfordshire Archives D/ELb F32/4.
33. Lady Caroline Lamb to John Allen, 9 October 1809. British Library Add. MS 52193, f. 171.
34. *Hary-O*, 327.
35. Lady Caroline Lamb to Marquis of Hartington, 29 September 1809. Devonshire MSS. 5th Duke's Group, f. 1954.
36. Lady Caroline Lamb to Lady Holland, n.d. (1810). British Library Add. MS 51560 f. 137.
37. Lady Caroline Lamb to Lady Holland, n.d. British Library Add. MS 51560 f. 141.

38. Lady Caroline Lamb to Marquis of Hartington, 9 November 1809. Devonshire MSS. 5th Duke's Group, f. 1962.
39. Ponsonby, *The Ponsonby Family*, 132.
40. Lady Caroline Lamb to her mother Harriet, 26 October 1809. Bessborough and Aspinall, 195-96.
41. Lady Caroline Lamb to Marquis of Hartington, 27 December 1809. Devonshire MSS. 5th Duke's Group, f. 1965.
42. Lady Caroline Lamb to her uncle George John, Lord Spencer, 19 November 1809. British Library Add. MS 76104.
43. Lady Caroline Lamb to Marquis of Hartington, 21 January 1810. Devonshire MSS. 5th Duke's Group, f. 1966.
44. Lady Caroline Lamb to Marquis of Hartington, 28 April 1809. Devonshire MSS. 5th Duke's Group, f. 1951.
45. Lady Caroline Lamb to Marquis of Hartington, 31 July 1810. Devonshire MSS. 5th Duke's Group, f. 1983.
46. Lady Caroline Lamb to Marquis of Hartington, 21 July 1810. Devonshire MSS. 5th Duke's Group, f. 1982.
47. Bessborough and Aspinall, 199, 207, 212, 213, 218-19. Also Lady Caroline Lamb to Marquis of Hartington, 31 July and 10 November 1810. Devonshire MSS. 5th Duke's Group, f. 1983 and f. 1993.
48. Lady Caroline Lamb to Marquis of Hartington, 2 October 1810. Devonshire MSS. 5th Duke's Group, f. 1990.
49. Bessborough and Aspinall, 204.
50. Grosskurth, *Byron: The Flawed Angel*, 157.
51. Cecil, *Melbourne*, 107.
52. Bessborough and Aspinall, 205.
53. I reiterate my great indebtedness to Margot Strickland, who shared her extensive research with me in the early stages of my writing. For her insights, such as the likelihood that Webster and Caroline had a sexual relationship, I am most grateful.
54. Lady Melbourne to Lady Caroline Lamb, 13 April 1810. Melbourne, *Byron's "Corbeau Blanc,"* 107.
55. Ibid.
56. Lady Caroline to Georgiana, Lady Morpeth, n.d. Quoted in Mitchell, *Lord Melbourne: 1779-1848,* 69.
57. Lady Caroline Lamb to Lady Melbourne, n.d. (1810). British Library Add. MS 45546, f. 21-22.
58. Lady Caroline Lamb to Lady Melbourne, n.d. (1810). British Library Add. MS 45546, f. 21-22.
59. Lady Caroline Lamb to Lady Melbourne, April 1810. British Library Add. MS 45546 f. 13-15.
60. Ibid.
61. Ibid.
62. Lady Caroline Lamb to Lady Melbourne, n.d. (1810). British Library Add. MS 45546 f. 20.
63. Lady Caroline Lamb to Lady Holland, 11 June and 31 May 1810. British Library Add. MS 45546 f. 23 and 51560 f. 131.
64. Lady Caroline Lamb to Lady Holland, n.d. (September 1810). British Library Add. MS 51560 f. 145. Lady Caroline Lamb to Lady Melbourne, 13 September 1810. British Library Add. MS 45546 f.25.
65. Lady Caroline Lamb to her uncle Lord Spencer, 2 October 1810. British Library Add. MS 76106. Lady Caroline Lamb to Lady Holland, n.d. (August 1810). British Library Add. MS 51560 f.141.
66. Harriet Granville, *A Second Self: The Letters of Harriet Granville 1810- 1845,* 18.
67. Bessborough and Aspinall, 211.

68. Lady Caroline Lamb to her uncle Lord Spencer, 23 August 1811. British Library Add. MS 76108.
69. Bessborough and Aspinall, 212.
70. Granville, *Private Correspondence,* 2:382.
71. *English Bards and Scotch Reviewers,* lines 1045-46. Byron, *Complete Poetical Works* 1:262.
72. Lady Caroline Lamb to Lady Holland, 29 May 1811. British Library Add. MS 51560 f.177.
73. Bessborough and Aspinall, 215.
74. Lady Caroline Lamb to Lady Holland (several letters), n.d. (April-May 1811). British Library Add. MS 51560 ff. 159, 162, 164, 166, 169, 171, 173, 175.
75. Lady Caroline Lamb to Lady Holland, 4 June 1811. British Library Add. MS 51560 f. 186.
76. Lady Caroline Lamb to Lady Holland, n.d. (4 June 1811). British Library Add. MS 51560, f. 184.
77. Lady Caroline Lamb to Lady Holland, n.d. (July 1811). British Library Add. MS 51560, f. 187.
78. Lady Caroline Lamb to Lady Holland, n.d. (July 1811). British Library Add. MS 51560, f. 190.
79. Lady Caroline Lamb to Lady Holland, n.d. (6 August 1811). British Library Add. MS 51560, f. 194.
80. Lady Caroline Lamb to Lord Holland, 27 June 1811. British Library Add. MSS 51558, f. 7
81. Lady Caroline Lamb to Lady Holland, 27 June 1811. British Library Add. MS 51560, f. 155.
82. Bodleian Library, University of Oxford, Dep. Lovelace Byron 417, Extracts from the diary of Harriet, Countess Granville, 1810-1824.
83. Lady Caroline Lamb to Lady Holland, n.d. (July 1810). British Library Add. MS 51560, f. 135.
84. Hertfordshire Archives D/ELb F64.
85. Lady Caroline Lamb to her uncle Lord Spencer, 23 August 1811. British Library Add. MS 76108.
86. Granville, *Private Correspondence,* 2:390.
87. Lady Caroline Lamb to the 6th Duke of Devonshire (formerly the Marquis of Hartington), 14 November 1811. Devonshire MSS. 6th Duke's Group, f. 36.
88. Bessborough and Aspinall, 218.
89. Lady Caroline Lamb to Lady Holland, 12 and 25 October, 1811. British Library Add. MS 51560, ff. 196, 198.
90. Lady Caroline Lamb to Lady Morgan, n.d. (April-May 1823). Houghton Library *43M-93. Quoted by permission of the Houghton Library, Harvard University.
91. Morgan, *Lady Morgan's Memoirs,* 1:440, 442.
92. Harryo to her sister Georgiana, Lady Morpeth, September 11, 1811. Gower, *Letters of Harriet, Countess Granville, 1810-1845,* 1:20.
93. Lady Caroline Lamb to Lady Holland, n.d. (May 1811). British Library Add. MS 51560 f. 164.
94. Lady Caroline Lamb to Lady Holland, n.d. (April 1811). British Library Add. MS 51560 f. 159.

Chapter 7

1. Joyce, *My Friend H,* 50.
2. Byron had proposed Hart for the Harrow Club in 1807. Marquis of Hartington to Lord Byron, 21 November 1807. Bodleian Library, University of Oxford, Dep. Lovelace Byron 155, f.44.

3. *Childe Harold* 1:9, 10, 13. Byron, *Complete Poetical Works,* 2:11-13.
4. Rogers, *Recollections of the Table-Talk of Samuel Rogers,* 190.
5. Morgan, *Lady Morgan's Memoirs,* 2:200.
6. Bodleian Library, University of Oxford, Dep. Lovelace Byron 155, f. 73.
7. *Childe Harold* 1:1. Byron, *Complete Poetical Works,* 2:8.
8. Elwin, *Lord Byron's Wife,* 141.
9. Moore, *Letters and Journals of Lord Byron,* 1:260.
10. Ibid., 1:255.
11. Dallas, *Recollections of the Life of Lord Byron,* 228, 246.
12. Moore, *Letters and Journals of Lord Byron,* 1:256.
13. Grosskurth, *Byron: The Flawed Angel,* 152.
14. Blyth, *Caro: The Fatal Passion,* 120-21.
15. Morgan, *Lady Morgan's Memoirs,* 2:200.
16. Marchand, *Byron: A Biography,* 324.
17. Ponsonby, *The Ponsonby Family,* 133. The scene Lady Caroline described in her letter is undoubtedly closer to the truth than the version she later gave to Lady Morgan, when she described rushing to clean herself up, drawing teasing comments from Rogers. See *Lady Morgan's Memoirs,* 2:200-1.
18. *The Works of Lord Byron,* 2:451.
19. "The Waltz," lines 147-48. Byron published the poem under the pseudonym of "Horace Hornem" in April 1813. Byron, *Complete Poetical Works,* 3:28.
20. *Byron's Letters and Journals,* 2:169-70.
21. Ibid., 2:194.
22. Bessborough and Aspinall, 223.
23. *The Works of Lord Byron,* 2:447, 451.
24. Marchand, *Byron: A Biography,* 339.
25. Lady Caroline Lamb to Lord Byron, 27 March 1812. John Murray Archive.
26. *The Works of Lord Byron,* 2:446-47.
27. Lady Caroline Lamb to Lord Byron. n.d. (June 1814). John Murray Archive.
28. Dallas, *Recollections of the Life of Lord Byron,* 246-47.
29. In October of 1813, Lady Caroline half-facetiously asked Murray to take for publication a collection of "250 letters from a young Venetian nobleman—addrest to a very absurd English Lady." Lady Caroline Lamb to John Murray, 7 October 1813. John Murray Archive.
30. Lady Caroline Lamb to Lord Byron, (1812). John Murray Archive.
31. Rogers, *Recollections of the Table-Talk of Samuel Rogers,* 191.
32. Harryo to her brother the Duke of Devonshire (Hart), 10 May 1812. Devonshire MSS. 6th Duke's Group, f. 58.
33. Quoted in Mayne, *The Life and Letters of Anne Isabella, Lady Noel Byron,* 44.
34. Ibid., 37.
35. Harryo to her brother Hart, the Duke of Devonshire, 10 May 1812. Devonshire MSS. 6th Duke's Group, f. 58.
36. Lady Melbourne to Lady Caroline Lamb, n.d. John Murray Archive.
37. *The Works of Lord Byron,* 2:116.
38. Dallas, *Recollections of the Life of Lord Byron,* 248-49.
39. Moore, *Letters and Journals of Lord Byron,* 1:147.
40. Rogers, *Recollections of the Table-Talk of Samuel Rogers,* 191.
41. Hobhouse, *Recollections of a Long Life,* 1:194.
42. *Don Juan,* 13.98. Byron, *Complete Poetical Works,* 5:553.
43. *Byron's Letters and Journals,* 2:170-71.
44. Marchand, *Byron: A Biography,* 344-45.
45. Moore, *Letters and Journals of Lord Byron,* 1:55.
46. Lady Caroline Lamb to Lord Byron, n.d. (a note in the hand of Doris Langley Moore suggests late 1814 or early 1815—she has known him "near 3 years"). John Murray Archive.

47. Lady Caroline Lamb to Byron, n.d. (June 1814). John Murray Archive. This is the only letter I have found that seems to corroborate Doris Langley Moore's extravagant claim that there are "letters, unpublished, which suggest that Byron, with his libertine's admiration for purity, may have been repelled by her [sexual] abandon." See Moore, *The Late Lord Byron*, 231.
48. *Byron's Letters and Journals*, 3:355.
49. Byron, *Complete Poetical Works*, 3:13, 392.
50. *Byron's Letters and Journals*, 2:175-76.
51. Marchand, *Byron: A Biography*, 338. And see Mayne, *The Life and Letters of Anne Isabella, Lady Noel Byron*, 42.
52. Lady Caroline Lamb to Lord Byron, May 1812. Bodleian Library, University of Oxford, Dep. Lovelace-Byron 155, f. 76.
53. Lady Caroline Lamb to Annabella Milbanke, 22 May 1812. Bodleian Library, University of Oxford, Dep. Lovelace Byron 359. This is a typescript. Marked as endorsed by A.I.M. (Anne Isabella Milbanke), "a letter of Lady Caroline Lamb to me—1812—very remarkable."
54. Lady Caroline Lamb to Lord Byron n.d. (1812). John Murray Archive.
55. Foster, *The Two Duchesses*, 364.
56. Stuart, *Dearest Bess*, 189.
57. Moore, *Letters and Journals of Lord Byron*, 1:262.
58. *Byron's Letters and Journals*, 2:177.
59. Lady Caroline Lamb to Lady Melbourne, n.d. (before 24 March 1813). British Library Add. MS 45546 f.56-60.
60. Lady Caroline Lamb to Lord Byron, n.d. (October-November 1818). John Murray Archive.
61. Lady Caroline Lamb to Lord Byron, 19 May 1812. *Byron's Letters and Journals*, 2:177.
62. Bessborough and Aspinall, 222.
63. Marchand, *Byron: A Biography*, 351.
64. Medwin, *Conversations of Lord Byron*, 216.
65. Grebanier, *The Uninhibited Byron*, 108.
66. Lady Caroline Lamb to Lord Byron. n.d. (1812). John Murray Archive.
67. Lady Bessborough to Lady Melbourne, British Library Add. MS 45548 ff.60, 58.
68. Cecil, *Melbourne*, 102-4.
69. Ziegler, *Melbourne: A Biography*, 365.
70. Marchand, *Byron: A Biography*, 355.
71. Hobhouse, *Recollections of a Long Life*, 1:44.
72. Bessborough and Aspinall, 223.
73. Marchand, *Byron: A Biography*, 356.
74. Lady Caroline Lamb to William Lamb, n.d. (1812). British Library Add. MS 45546.
75. Marchand, *Byron: A Biography*, 357-58.
76. Joyce, *My Friend H*, 39.
77. Marchand, *Byron: A Biography*, 358.
78. Lady Caroline Lamb to Lord Byron, 9 August 1812. Bodleian Library, University of Oxford, Dep. Lovelace-Byron 155, f. 79-81.
79. *Byron's Letters and Journals*, 2:184.
80. Bessborough and Aspinall, 223-24.

Chapter 8

1. The note wrapped around the hair starts with a rebus. Lady Caroline Lamb to Lord Byron, 9 August 1812. Bodleian Library, University of Oxford, Dep. Lovelace-Byron 155, f. 79-81. The John Murray Archive has many hair samples sent by adoring correspondents of Lord Byron, but no others from that region of the body.

2. Annette Peach identified the source for the name "Biondetta" in Jacques Cazotte's *Le diable amoureux*. Peach, "San Fedele," 285-95.

3. Lamb, Lady Caroline. Letter to Lord Byron, 9 August 1812. Bodleian Library, University of Oxford, Dep. Lovelace-Byron 155, f. 79-81.

4. Byron's remarks to Hobhouse and the account of their effect on Caroline are reported in letters of Lady Bessborough to Lady Melbourne in the Lamb Papers of the British Library, Add. MS 45911 f. 58, 62.

5. Blyth, *Caro: The Fatal Passion*, 127.

6. Granville, *Private Correspondence*, 2:447.

7. *Byron's Letters and Journals*, 2:187-88.

8. Granville, *Private Correspondence*, 2:448.

9. Byron's letter was reproduced as a lithographic facsimile, apparently by Lady Caroline for Medwin, after publication of his *Conversations with Lord Byron*. Leslie Marchand accepts the letter as undoubtedly Byron's handwriting, suggesting that it must have been composed on 12 August, just after Byron had convinced Caroline to rejoin her husband. *Byron's Letters and Journals*, 2:185.

10. *Byron's Letters and Journals*, 2:186.

11. *Byron's Letters and Journals*, 2:186.

12. Villiers, *The Grand Whiggery*, 256-57

13. Granville, *Private Correspondence*, 2:449-51.

14. Ibid., 2:452-54.

15. Lady Caroline Lamb to Lord Byron, n.d. (1812). John Murray Archive.

16. Lady Caroline Lamb to Lord Byron, n.d. (a different letter, 1812). John Murray Archive. The "flippant" letter has not been identified. It is one of the items that might help form the case for a diagnosis of manic depression for Lady Caroline.

17. Lady Caroline Lamb to Lord Byron. n.d. (1812). *The Works of Lord Byron*, 2:448.

18. *Byron's Letters and Journals*, 2:188-89.

19. Lady Caroline Lamb's commonplace book. John Murray Archive.

20. The character's name comes from Jacques Cazotte's novel. Peach, "San Fedele," 285-95.

21. Lady Caroline Lamb's commonplace book, John Murray Archive.

22. Ibid.

23. The first letter from Lady Bessborough sent to Granville from Ireland is dated 7 September 1812. Granville, *Private Correspondence*, 2:454. See also a letter of Hart to his grandmother dated 10 September 1812, Devonshire MSS. 6th Duke's Group, f. 74. There has been some confusion about the length of Caroline's stay in Ireland, possibly because of some misdated letters from her cousin, Harryo. See Gower, *Letters of Harriet, Countess Granville, 1810-1845*, 1:140-41.

24. Ponsonby, *The Ponsonby Family*, 192.

25. Granville, *Private Correspondence*, 2:456-57.

26. *Byron's Letters and Journals*, 2:192.

27. Ibid., 2:192-93.

28. Ibid., 2:193

29. Granville, *Private Correspondence*, 2:461-62.

30. Ibid., 2:462.

31. Ibid., 2:459.

32. *Byron's Letters and Journals*, 2:193-94.

33. Ibid., 2:194.

34. Ibid., 2:222.

35. Ibid., 2: 193-96.

36. Ibid., 2:222.

37. Ibid., 2:200.

38. Melbourne, *Byron's "Corbeau Blanc,"* 121; *Byron's Letters and Journals*, 2:198.

39. *Byron's Letters and Journals*, 2:199.

40. Ibid., 2:199-200, 202.

41. Ibid., 2:218.
42. Lady Melbourne to Lord Byron, 29 September 1812. Melbourne, *Byron's "Corbeau Blanc,"* 119.
43. *Byron's Letters and Journals,* 2:200.
44. Byron, *Complete Poetical Works,* 3:16-17. Christopher Fletcher points out a small but significant difference between the manuscript and the published poem indicating that when Byron originally wrote it, he wished to convey being still in a mood of missing Caroline. "Lord Byron—Unrecorded Autograph Poems," *Notes and Queries* 43.4 (Dec. 1996): 425ff.
45. Hertfordshire Archives D/ELb F64. The lines later appear in *Glenarvon,* 3:72-73.
46. *Byron's Letters and Journals,* 2:229, 241.
47. Ibid., 2:254.
48. Lady Melbourne's letters were probably culled for incriminating passages regarding her liaison with Byron. A number of her letters written in April 1813 are missing, according to Jonathan Gross, the editor of Lady Melbourne's letters, *Byron's "Corbeau Blanc,"* 116.
49. Ibid., 120-22.
50. *Byron's Letters and Journals,* 2:202.
51. Ibid., 2:203.
52. Ibid., 2:209.
53. Ibid., 2:217-18.
54. Granville, *Private Correspondence,* 463-67.
55. British Library Add MSS 45546.
56. *Byron's Letters and Journals* 9:44.
57. Ibid., 2:235.
58. Ibid., 2:230.
59. Melbourne, *Byron's "Corbeau Blanc,"* 121.
60. *Byron's Letters and Journals,* 2:233.
61. Ibid., 2:230.
62. Melbourne, *Byron's "Corbeau Blanc,"* 122.
63. British Library Add. MS 45548 f. 56.
64. Blyth, *Caro: The Fatal Passion,* 142.
65. *Byron's Letters and Journals* 2:236, 233.
66. Annabella Milbanke to her mother, 15 March 1812. Jenkins, *Lady Caroline Lamb,* 31. (This letter is supposed to be in the Lovelace Byron Deposit, but I have been unable to locate it.)
67. Bodleian Library, University of Oxford, Dep. Lovelace-Byron 118, ff. 5-6.
68. Bell, *Virginia Woolf: A Biography,* 1:171.
69. Bodleian Library, University of Oxford, Dep. Lovelace-Byron 118, ff. 9-10.
70. We do not have the complete original of Byron's letter, but we have three texts. One is a letter published in *Glenarvon.* The second is a letter Lady Caroline wrote to Lady Melbourne in fall 1812, now contained in the John Murray Archive. The third is a letter included in *Byron's Letters and Journals* which the editor Leslie Marchand guesses comprises part of what he wrote. I have used these three texts to recreate an approximation of the letter Lady Caroline received. *Byron's Letters and Journals,* 2:242.
71. *Byron's Letters and Journals,* 2:242. This part of the letter was printed by Lady Caroline in *Glenarvon* and has been accepted by Marchand as authentically Byron's text. A key phrase here echoes another from a probable earlier letter of Byron's. This fragment Marchand printed with the guess that it was composed in October 1812: "correct yr. vanity which is ridiculous & proverbial, exert yr. Caprices on your new conquests & leave me in peace, yrs. Byron." See *Byron's Letters and Journals,* 2:222.
72. Morgan, *Lady Morgan's Memoirs,* 2:201.
73. Caroline's actual departure probably occurred on 10 or 11 November 1812. The letter must have been sent at the very end of October, for Byron refers to it on 4 and

6 November in messages to Lady Melbourne, confidently predicting that he would visit Lady Melbourne at Melbourne House without regard to his former lover's presence or absence in the Lambs' apartments on the second floor. See *Byron's Letters and Journals*, 2:239, 240. In a letter of a year later, Lady Caroline told John Murray: "One year is passed since upon this very day I received the cruelest of letters." (John Murray Archive, with Murray's note that he received it on 13 November 1813, a Saturday.)

74. Lady Bessborough to Lady Melbourne, 31 October 1812. British Library Add. MS 45548 f.69.

75. Blyth, *Caro: The Fatal Passion*, 143. Blyth does not give his source.

76. *Byron's Letters and Journals*, 2:242.

77. Ibid., 2:243, 2:246.

78. Ibid., 2: 244.

79. Gower, *Letters of Harriet, Countess Granville* 40-41. This letter is erroneously dated 12 September 1812.

80. Bessborough and Aspinall, 232.

81. *Byron's Letters and Journals*, 2:247.

82. Granville, *Private Correspondence*, 2:543.

83. Lady Caroline Lamb to Ugo Foscolo (1817). Vincent, *Ugo Foscolo: An Italian in Regency England*, 74.

84. Hobhouse, *Byron's Bulldog*, 106.

85. *Byron's Letters and Journals*, 2:245-247.

86. Ibid., 2:248.

87. Ibid., 2:251.

88. Ibid., 2:255.

89. Ibid., 256.

90. Ibid., 2:259.

91. Leslie Marchand notes that the items cast into the bonfire were undoubtedly fake. *Byron's Letters and Journals*, 2:260n.

92. Quoted in Blyth, *Caro: The Fatal Passion*, 146.

93. Villiers, *The Grand Whiggery*, 271.

94. Small, *Love's Madness*, 14.

95. Lewis, *Poems*, 24-25.

96. *Childe Harold*, 1:6; 1:9; 1:82. Byron, *Complete Poetical Works*, 2:10, 11, 38.

97. Ibid., 1:84. Byron, *Complete Poetical Works*, 2:39.

98. Ibid., 2:61. Byron, *Complete Poetical Works*, 2:63.

99. Ibid., 2:72-73. Byron, *Complete Poetical Works*, 2:66-68.

100. Hobhouse, *Byron's Bulldog*, 112.

101. *Byron's Letters and Journals*, 2:260.

102. Melbourne, *Byron's "Corbeau Blanc,"* 132, 134.

103. *Byron's Letters and Journals*, 2:260.

Chapter 9

1. Lord Byron to Lady Melbourne, 10 November 1812. *Byron's Letters and Journals*, 2:244.

2. Doherty, "An Unpublished Letter of Lady Caroline Lamb to Clare," 297-99.

3. *Byron's Letters and Journals*, 2:224, 234.

4. The "Newstead Miniature" refers to a portrait by George Sanders. Peach, "San Fedele," 285-95.

5. *Byron's Letters and Journals*, 3:12.

6. *The Works of Lord Byron*, 3:60.

7. No original exists. The text we have from E. H. Coleridge is dated 22 February 1813. For a thorough explanation of the case (saving only the identification of "Bd." as "Biondetta"), see Stauffer, "Byron, Medwin, and the False Fiend," 265-76.
8. *Byron's Letters and Journals,* 3:12.
9. Ibid., 3:13-14.
10. Lamb, Lady Caroline. Letter to Lord Byron. n.d. (1814). John Murray Archive.
11. *Byron's Letters and Journals,* 3:15.
12. Lady Caroline Lamb's common place book. John Murray Archive.
13. Hertfordshire Archives D/ELb F64, 9.
14. *Byron's Letters and Journals,* 3:16.
15. Bessborough and Aspinall, 232.
16. *Byron's Letters and Journals,* 3:17.
17. Lady Caroline Lamb to John Murray, fragment of a letter, n.d. (1814). John Murray Archive.
18. Hertfordshire Archives D/Elb F69.
19. *Byron's Letters and Journals,* 3:21.
20. Ibid., 3:26.
21. Melbourne, *Byron's "Corbeau Blanc,"* 136-138.
22. Bessborough and Aspinall 233.
23. *Byron's Letters and Journals,* 3:23, 25.
24. Lady Melbourne to Lord Byron, 25 March 1813. Melbourne, *Byron's "Corbeau Blanc,"* 140.
25. Ibid., 140.
26. *Byron's Letters and Journals,* 3:37, 40.
27. Ibid., 3:40.
28. Ibid., 3:53.
29. Ibid., 3:43.
30. Ibid., 3:43-44.
31. By 7 May 1813 he was writing to Lady Melbourne in "protest against C's meeting me at all," and demanding that "you must be present." On 9 May he acknowledged the final arrangements for a visit, probably to take place the next day: "At nine be it then." *Byron's Letters and Journals,* 3:45-46.
32. Melbourne, *Byron's "Corbeau Blanc,"* 141.
33. *Byron's Letters and Journals,* 3:52, 59.
34. Lady Caroline Lamb to John Murray, 28 October 1813 and n.d. (1813). John Murray Archive.
35. Letter to John Murray, 1813. John Murray Archive.
36. Quoted in Blyth, *Caro: The Fatal Passion,* 135-36.
37. *Byron's Letters and Journals,* 3:40.
38. *The Giaour,* lines 999ff. Byron, *Complete Poetical Works,* 3:71.
39. Ibid., 1114-30. Byron, *Complete Poetical Works,* 3:75.
40. Lady Caroline Lamb to John Murray, n.d. John Murray Archive.
41. Lady Caroline Lamb to John Murray, no date (1814—but before she learned of Byron's engagement to Annabella in September-October 1814. Watermarked "1814.")
42. Lady Caroline Lamb to John Murray, 1813. John Murray Archive.
43. *Byron's Letters and Journals,* 3:65.
44. Ibid., 3:66-67.
45. Ibid., 3:69.
46. Melbourne, *Byron's "Corbeau Blanc,"* 143.
47. *The Works of Lord Byron,* 2:453.
48. *Byron's Letters and Journals,* 3:72.
49. Paston and Quennell, *"To Lord Byron,"* 50.
50. *Byron's Letters and Journals,* 3:71.
51. Melbourne, *Byron's "Corbeau Blanc,"* 143.

52. Grebanier, *The Uninhibited Byron,* 129.

53. Airlie, *In Whig Society: 1775-1818,* 154.

54. Melbourne, *Byron's "Corbeau Blanc,"* 142.

55. *Byron's Letters and Journals,* 3:74.

56. Lady Caroline Lamb to John Murray, 17 July 1813. John Murray Archive. Lady Caroline Lamb to Lady Holland, n.d. (sometime after 5 July 1813). British Library Add. MS 51560 f. 201.

57. *Byron's Letters and Journals,* 3:85.

58. Granville, *Private Correspondence,* 2:477-78. See also Melbourne, *Byron's "Corbeau Blanc,"* 144.

59. Lady Caroline Lamb to John Murray, n.d. (1813). John Murray Archive.

60. Lady Caroline Lamb to John Murray, n.d. (January-February 1814). John Murray Archive.

61. Lady Caroline Lamb to John Murray, n.d. (1814). John Murray Archive.

62. Lady Caroline Lamb to John Murray, 17 and 19 October 1813, and n.d. (October 1813). John Murray Archive.

63. Bessborough and Aspinall, 236.

64. Lady Caroline Lamb to John Murray, n.d. (January-February 1814). John Murray Archive.

65. Lady Caroline Lamb to John Murray, 7 October 1813. John Murray Archive.

66. Ibid.

67. Paston and Quennell, *"To Lord Byron,"* 52.

68. Lady Caroline Lamb to Lord Byron, 1813. John Murray Archive.

69. Lord Byron to Lady Melbourne, 22 November 1813. *Byron's Letters and Journals* 3:170.

70. Lady Caroline Lamb to John Murray, n.d. (1814). John Murray Archive.

71. Lady Caroline Lamb to John Murray, 9 November 1813. John Murray Archive.

72. Lady Caroline Lamb to Lady Spencer, 15 December 1813. British Library Add. MS 75609.

73. Lady Caroline Lamb to John Murray, n.d. (1814). John Murray Archive.

74. Lady Caroline Lamb to John Murray, 28 December 1813. John Murray Archive.

75. Lady Bessborough to her mother Lady Spencer, 21 December 1813. British Library Add. MS 75608, unfoliated.

76. Paston and Quennell, *"To Lord Byron,"* 55.

77. Lady Caroline Lamb to John Murray, January 1814. John Murray Archive.

78. Melbourne, *Byron's "Corbeau Blanc,"* 160.

79. Lady Caroline Lamb to Lady Holland, n.d. (February 1814—not, as the archivist has guessed, February 1813). British Library Add. MS 51560, f. 199.

80. Lamb, Lady Caroline. Two letters to John Murray, both 24 January 1814, with the second marked "rec'd 26 January 1814." John Murray Archive.

81. Lady Caroline Lamb to John Murray, n.d. (Feb. 1814). John Murray Archive.

82. Lady Caroline Lamb to John Murray, n.d. (January 1814). John Murray Archive. The artist was Miss Emma Eleanora Kendrick. I am indebted for my account of the circumstances surrounding the copying of the Sanders portrait to Peach, *Portraits of Byron.*

83. Lady Caroline Lamb to John Murray, 23 January 1814. British Library Add. MS 75609.

84. Lady Caroline Lamb to John Murray, n.d. (1814). John Murray Archive.

85. Lady Caroline Lamb to John Murray, n.d. (a different letter, 1814). John Murray Archive.

86. Lady Caroline Lamb to John Murray, n.d. (January-February 1814). John Murray Archive.

87. Lady Caroline Lamb to John Murray, n.d. (after 1 February 1814). John Murray Archive.

88. Lady Caroline Lamb to Lord Byron, n.d. (before 5 July 1813). British Library Add MS 45548 f. 132-35.

89. Lady Caroline Lamb to Lord Byron at the Albany, n.d. (1812?). John Murray Archive.

90. Lady Caroline Lamb to Lord Byron, 3 June 1814. John Murray Archive.

91. Lord Glenbervie, *The Diaries of Sylvester Douglas*, ed. Francis Bickley, 2 vols. (London, 1928), 302.

92. British Library Add. MS 45546 f.70-71.

93. British Library Add. MS 45548 f. 132-135.

94. Lady Caroline Lamb to her uncle Lord Spencer, 13 May 1814. British Library Add. MS 76113, unfoliated.

95. Lady Caroline Lamb to her uncle Lord Spencer, 18 April 1814. British Library Add. MS 76113, unfoliated.

96. Lady Caroline to John Murray, 15 April 1814. John Murray Archive.

97. Lady Caroline Lamb to John Murray, n.d. (early 1814). John Murray Archive.

98. Lady Caroline to her uncle Lord Spencer, 13 May 1814. British Library Add. MS 76113, unfoliated.

99. Lady Caroline to her Aunt Lavinia, Lady Spencer, n.d., (almost certainly May or June 1814, no watermark). British Library Add. MS 76113, unfoliated.

100. Lady Caroline Lamb to John Cam Hobhouse, 1814. John Murray Archive.

101. "To One Who Promised on a Lock of Hair," Byron, *Complete Poetical Works*, 3:268.

102. The order for the gold and pearl locket is in the John Murray Archive. The locket containing the copied portrait is now in the Bodleian Library at Oxford University, MS Eng. misc. g. 181. The exact significance of the date (14 August 1812) is not clear. It probably marks the approximate moment at which Byron agreed not to see Caroline alone. Jerome McGann provides information about the lock of hair being on display in Byron's *Complete Poetical Works* 3:459.

103. *Byron's Letters and Journals*, 4:132-33.

104. Lady Caroline Lamb to Lord Byron, n.d. (June 1814). John Murray Archive.

105. *Byron's Letters and Journals*, 4:134.

106. Lady Caroline Lamb to Lord Byron. n.d. (July 1814). John Murray Archive.

107. Marchand, *Byron: A Biography*, 459.

108. Joyce, *My Friend H*, 58.

109. Lady Caroline Lamb wrote to John Cam Hobhouse on 2 July 1814 to thank him for his "goodnatured manner." John Murray Archive.

110. *Byron's Letters and Journals*, 4:135-37.

111. Blessington, *Conversations of Lord Byron*, 178-79.

112. *Byron's Letters and Journals*, 4: 123.

113. Ibid., 4:135.

114. Nathan, *Fugitive Pieces*, 171-72.

115. Phillips, *Isaac Nathan: Friend of Byron*, 38-40.

116. Lady Caroline Lamb to John Murray, n.d. (1814—but before she learned of Byron's engagement to Annabella in September-October 1814. Watermarked "1814"). John Murray Archive.

117. The lines from *Lara* begin "Night wanes . . ." *Lara* 2.1; Byron's Poetical Works 3:236.

118. *Byron's Letters and Journals*, 4:220.

119. Hunt, *Lord Byron and Some of His Contemporaries*, 1:187-88.

120. *Glenarvon*, 1:184.

121. Elwin, *Lord Byron's Wife*, 141.

122. *Byron's Letters and Journals*, 4:249-50.

123. Elwin, *Lord Byron's Wife*, 284.

124. Martin, *Mad Women in Romantic Writing*, 23-24.

125. *The Works of Lord Byron*, 3:453.

126. *Byron's Letters and Journals*, 4:203-4.

127. Ibid., 4:193.

128. Ibid., 4:194.

129. Lady Caroline Lamb to Lord Byron, n.d. (1814). John Murray Archive.
130. Lady Caroline Lamb to Lord Byron, n.d. (a different letter, 1814). John Murray Archive.
131. Lady Caroline Lamb to John Murray, Friday 18 November 1814. John Murray Archive.
132. Lady Caroline Lamb to John Murray, n.d. (1814). John Murray Archive.
133. Lady Caroline Lamb to John Murray, n.d. (August 1814) and 19 August 1814 (franked 22 August). John Murray Archive.

Chapter 10

1. *Byron's Letters and Journals*, 2:132.
2. Ibid., 4:253. Byron continued to conspire with Lady Melbourne after his marriage: "Lady Byron sends her love—but has not seen this epistle—recollect—we are to keep our secrets—& correspondence as heretofore—mind that." *Byron's Letters and Journals*, 4:252.
3. Melbourne, Byron's "Corbeau Blanc," 284.
4. Grosskurth, *Byron: The Flawed Angel*, 236.
5. Lady Caroline Lamb to John Murray, 1815. John Murray Archive.
6. Lady Caroline Lamb to John Murray, n.d. (1815). John Murray Archive.
7. Two letters of Lady Caroline Lamb to John Murray, n.d. (between October 1814 and May 1815). John Murray Archive.
8. "[T]he words of Braham's best song were enough to make a mulatto sick." Letter of Lady Caroline Lamb (1807). Ponsonby, *The Ponsonby Family*, 130.
9. Probably Horace Twiss (1787 - 1849).
10. Lady Caroline Lamb to John Murray. n.d. (1815). John Murray Archive.
11. Nathan *Fugitive Pieces*, 178.
12. Nathan and Byron, *A Selection of Hebrew Melodies*, 68-69.
13. John Clubbe, "*Glenarvon* Revised—and Revisited," 205-6.
14. Lady Caroline Lamb to John Murray, n.d. (1814 - 1815). John Murray Archive.
15. Thomas, *The Baron of Falconberg; or, Childe Harold in Prose* 3: 181, 176. Pious and prolific, Mrs. Thomas had recently published *The Prison House; or, the World We Live In* (1814). "Purity of Heart" became the title of her later satire of *Glenarvon*.
16. Bessborough and Aspinall, 242-43.
17. Ibid., 244, 247.
18. Ibid., 252-53.
19. The 6th Duke of Devonshire to his uncle Earl Spencer, from Paris, 5 August 1815. British Library Add MS 76116.
20. Paston and Quennell, "*To Lord Byron*," 61.
21. Hary-O, 1:74.
22. Letter of Washington Irving, n.d. Washington Irving Collection (#6256-AJ), Clifton Waller Barrett Library, Special Collections, University of Virginia Library.
23. Bodleian Library, University of Oxford, Dep. Lovelace Byron 417, Extracts from the Diary of Harriet, Countess Granville, 1819-1824. My italics.
24. *Byron's Letters and Journals*, 4:310.
25. In 1823 Byron claimed that there was a stanza he had left out of the poem that made it clear the reference was to Lady Frances. However the stanza in question is actually the fourth one of a poem written in 1812 and titled "To Caroline Lamb." Byron, Complete Poetical Works, 3:16-17. Editor Jerome McGann does not doubt that "When We Two Parted" was written in 1815 and that it refers doubly to Lady Frances and Lady Caroline. Ibid., 3:475-76. Isaac Nathan published it for the first time as sheet music (date uncertain).
26. "When We Two Parted," Byron, Complete Poetical Works, 3:319-20. I have accepted McGann's dating of this poem, although there is a doubt in my mind created by a

letter of Lady Caroline's in the Chatsworth Archive (Devonshire MSS. 6th Duke's Group, f. 1130) that dates to late 1824 or early 1825, in which she tells her cousin the 6th Duke of Devonshire that she wants to send him a "[c]opy of the last letter written to me by Ld Byron 'When we two parted in silence & tears' it was written the very week after we supped at Devonshire House & my Mother was ill." If we accept Lady Caroline's statement, the poem was drafted in 1812, and Byron gave it to Isaac Nathan in 1815 to be set to music without disclosing its origins.

27. Letter of Harryo, 23 September 1815. Gower, *A Second Self,* 87.
28. Lord Byron to John Cam Hobhouse, 19 June 1811. *Byron's Letters and Journals,* 2:49.
29. Letter of Mrs. George Lamb, 9 August 1815. Mitchell, *Lord Melbourne: 1779-1848,* 74.
30. Lady Caroline Lamb to Michael Bruce, n.d. Bruce Papers, Bodleian Library, University of Oxford, MS Eng. C.5753, f. 121.
31. Lady Caroline Lamb to Lady Byron. Bodleian Library, University of Oxford, Dep. Lovelace Byron 78 ff.147. This letter offers the Napoleonic book to Byron through Annabella. It also mentions the play manuscripts, now apparently lost.
32. Harryo wrote in her journal in London, 1816 that Benjamin Constant had brought over his novel to read in Cavendish Square. "I mean to be present and I have begged C.W. Lamb may, to cry and make a sensation for us." Bodleian Library, University of Oxford, Dep. Lovelace Byron 417. Extracts from the Diary of Harriet, Countess Granville, 1810-1824.
33. Lady Caroline Lamb to John Murray, n.d. (June 1815). John Murray Archive.
34. Lady Caroline Lamb to Lady Byron. Bodleian Library, University of Oxford, Dep. Lovelace Byron 78 f.147. The conclusion that Lady Caroline wrote the two plays is my speculation, but the context makes it seem more than plausible. She says she thinks they "are not likely to answer" but also that she hasn't read them. The contradictions in the subterfuge seem classically, chaotically Caroline's.
35. Lady Caroline Lamb to John Murray, 1816. John Murray Archive.
36. Hobhouse, *Recollections of a Long Life,* 1:325.
37. The most likely source of this intelligence was Lady Melbourne herself. See Marchand, *Byron: A Biography,* 585n.
38. Lady Caroline Lamb to John Murray, n.d. (1816). John Murray Archive. Also printed in Paston and Quennell, *"To Lord Byron,"* 70.
39. Lady Caroline Lamb to Lord Byron, 1816. John Murray Archive.
40. Lady Caroline Lamb to John Murray, 1816. John Murray Archive.
41. Lady Caroline Lamb to Lord Byron, n.d. (1816) John Murray Archive.
42. Lady Caroline Lamb to Lord Byron, n.d. (a different letter, 1816) John Murray Archive.
43. Lady Caroline Lamb to Lord Byron, n.d. (a different letter, 1816.). John Murray Archive.
44. Lady Caroline Lamb to Lord Byron, n.d. (a different letter, 1816). John Murray Archive.
45. Lady Caroline Lamb to John Cam Hobhouse n.d. (March-April 1816). John Murray Archive.
46. Lady Caroline Lamb to Lady Byron, 1816. Bodleian Library, University of Oxford, Dep. Lovelace Byron 78 ff.157-61.
47. Lady Caroline Lamb to Lady Byron, 1816. Bodleian Library, University of Oxford, Dep. Lovelace Byron 78, ff. 157-61.
48. Letters exchanged between Annabella Milbanke and her mother Judith, Lady Noel, March 1816. Melbourne, *Byron's "Corbeau Blanc,"* 319.
49. Ibid., 320ff.
50. Marchand, *Byron: A Biography,* 589, 590.
51. Minutes of conversation with Lady Caroline Lamb, by Annabella Byron, 27 March 1816: Bodleian Library, University of Oxford, Dep. Lovelace Byron, 129, ff. 86-87.

52. Lady Caroline Lamb to Annabella Milbanke, 27 March 1816. Bodleian Library, University of Oxford, Dep. Lovelace Byron 78, ff. 173-174, 168.
53. Lady Caroline Lamb to Lady Byron, 1816. Bodleian Library, University of Oxford, Dep. Lovelace Byron 78, ff. 162-67.
54. Ibid.
55. Lady Caroline Lamb to Annabella Milbanke, March/-April 1816 (probably after 27 March, the meeting at which Annabella took minutes). Bodleian Library, University of Oxford, Dep. Lovelace Byron 78, ff. 171-172.
56. Lady Caroline Lamb to Lady Byron, n.d. (1816). Bodleian Library, University of Oxford, Dep. Lovelace Byron 78 ff.169-170.
57. Lady Caroline Lamb to Lady Byron, 1816. Bodleian Library, University of Oxford, Dep. Lovelace Byron 78, ff.162-67.
58. Ibid.
59. Lady Byron to Lady Caroline Lamb, 31 October 1824. Bodleian Library, University of Oxford, Dep. Lovelace Byron 78, ff. 188-189.
60. Lady Caroline Lamb to John Cam Hobhouse. n.d. (June-July 1816). John Murray Archive.
61. Lady Caroline Lamb to Lady Melbourne, n.d. (April or May 1816). British Library Add MS 45546, f. 89-90.
62. Hary-O, 2:541.
63. British Library Add. MS 45548. f. 141.
64. Morgan, *Lady Morgan's Memoirs,* 2:201-2.
65. Lady Holland to Lady Caroline Lamb, n.d. (April-May 1816). British Library Add. MS 51560 f. 167.
66. Lady Caroline Lamb to Lady Melbourne, 1816. British Library Add MS 45546, f. 109-10 and f. 111-13.
67. Lady Caroline Lamb to Hobhouse, n.d. (June-July 1816). John Murray Archive.
68. Eden, *Miss Eden's Letters,* 3. Other versions of this story involve Lady Caroline's sitting on William's lap and feeding him tiny scraps of transparent bread and butter. They seem to be embellishments of Miss Eden's simple domestic scene, which, though none too reliable, is the only contemporary account we have.
69. Hertfordshire Archives D/Elb F75.
70. Letter of April 1816 in the John Murray Archive: "I do implore you for God sake not to publish these."
71. Bakewell, Augusta Leigh: Byron's Half-Sister, 207.
72. Lady Caroline Lamb to John Murray, 1816. John Murray Archive.
73. Lady Caroline Lamb to Lord Byron. n.d. (April 1816). John Murray Archive.
74. *Byron's Letters and Journals,* 5:67.
75. The Duke of Wellington to Lady Caroline Lamb, 19 April 1816. Bessborough and Aspinall, 257.
76. Hary-O, 2:542.
77. Forster Collection.
78. Colburn's final receipt for the copyright of Glenarvon includes a list showing £50 paid to M. Nathan, £200 cash immediately, and £250 by a draft good in three months. Forster Collection.
79. Erickson, The Economy of Literary Form, 156.
80. James Soderholm has called it "her own kind of proto-Byronic notoriety," in "Lady Caroline Lamb: Byron's Miniature Writ Large." *The Keats-Shelley Journal* 40 (1991) 26.
81. Forster Collection.
82. Ibid.
83. Ibid.
84. Lady Caroline Lamb to John Cam Hobhouse. n.d. (April 1816). John Murray Archive.
85. Hobhouse, *Recollections of a Long Life,* 1:337.
86. Forster Collection.

87. Marchand, *Byron: A Biography,* 608. *Byron's Letters and Journals,* 5:68-69.
88. Forster Collection.
89. *"Disperato dolor, che il cor mi preme / Gia pur pensando, pria che ne favelle"* ("I renew a hopeless woe which burthens my heart even at the very thought, before I tell thereof").
90. Volume one of *Glenarvon* numbered its chapters from one to thirty-three; volume two from one to thirty-eight; and volume three from seventy-two to one hundred six.
91. Hobhouse, *Recollections of a Long Life,* 1:338.
92. Paston and Quennell, *"To Lord Byron,"* 73.
93. Lady Caroline Lamb to Lord Holland, n.d. (May 1816). British Library Add. MS 51558 f. 21.
94. *Byron's Letters and Journals,* 5:85.
95. Graham, *Don Juan and Regency England,* 96.
96. *Glenarvon,* 1:75.
97. Ibid., 1:72.
98. Ibid., 1:75.
99. Ibid., 1:132.
100. Ibid., 1:152.
101. See Marchand, *Byron: A Biography,* 79-80.
102. *Glenarvon,* 2:336-51.
103. Ibid., 2:359.
104. In the second edition of the novel, Glenarvon viciously stabs Avondale in the heart, though the wound is not fatal.
105. *Glenarvon,* 3:306.
106. Ibid., 3:318-19.
107. Ibid., 3:320.
108. Ibid., 2:80ff.
109. Lady Caroline Lamb to John Murray, n.d. (1816 or after). John Murray Archive.
110. Rogers certainly impressed many of his contemporaries as ripe for satire. In a letter to Lady Buckingham dated June 4, 1819, Miss Emily Eden wrote: "We have had the most alarming visit from Rogers the Poet this morning, the very recollection of which would make my hair, black pins, combs and all, stand on end, if they ever subsided since his first appearance. I never saw such a satirical, odious wretch, and I was calculating the whole time, from what he was saying of other people, what he could find ill-natured enough to say of us. I had never seen him before, and trust I never shall again." Eden, *Miss Eden's Letters,* 35.
111. John Clubbe, *"Glenarvon* Revised—and Revisited," 209, 213.
112. Lady Byron, Comments on Calantha in *Glenarvon,* 17 May 1816. Bodleian Library, University of Oxford, Dep. Lovelace Byron 118, ff. 7-8.
113. Mrs. George Lamb to Lady Byron, 17 May 1816. Bodleian Library, University of Oxford, Dep. Lovelace Byron 78, f. 24.
114. *Glenarvon* 1:138-39.
115. Ibid., 1:143.
116. Creevey, *The Creevey Papers,* 254-55.
117. I am indebted to John Clubbe. See note 111, above.
118. *Glenarvon* 1:153.
119. Ibid., 1:200.
120. Ibid., 1:228.
121. Creevey, *The Creevey Papers,* 254-55.
122. Elwin, *Lord Byron's Family,* 32-33.
123. Airlie, *In Whig Society,* 184.
124. Villiers, *The Grand Whiggery,* 321.
125. Paston and Quennell, *"To Lord Byron,"* 72.
126. Villiers, *The Grand Whiggery,* 321.
127. Hobhouse, *Byron's Bulldog,* 222.

128. Ibid., 226.
129. Peter Cochran contributed the information about Hobhouse's jealousy over *Glenarvon* and his frustration about his own *Letters.*
130. Hobhouse, *Recollections of a Long Life,* 1:339.
131. Elwin, *Lord Byron's Family,* 51.
132. Graham, *Don Juan and Regency England,* 108-109.
133. Paston and Quennell, *"To Lord Byron,"* 73-74.
134. Ibid.
135. Melbourne, *Byron's "Corbeau Blanc",* 328.
136. Hobhouse, *Recollections of a Long Life,* 1:341.
137. Lady Caroline Lamb to Lady Melbourne, (after 9 May 1816). British Library Add. MS 45546 f.91-92
138. Granville, *Private Correspondence,* 2:543.
139. Ibid., 2:542.
140. British Library Add. MS 45548 f.149.
141. Hobhouse, *Recollections of a Long Life,* 1:341.
142. Lady Caroline Lamb to Emily Cowper, n.d. (1816?). British Library Add. MSS 45548 f.157-8
143. Lady Caroline Lamb to John Cam Hobhouse. n.d. (June-July 1816). John Murray Archive.
144. Lady Caroline Lamb to John Cam Hobhouse, 10 July 1816. John Murray Archive.
145. Marchand, *Byron: A Biography,* 615n.
146. British Library Add. MSS 51558 f.35.
147. Lady Caroline Lamb to Lord Holland, n.d. (May 1816). British Library Add. MS 51558 f. 21.
148. William Lamb to Henry Colburn, 17 May 1816. Forster Collection.
149. William Lamb to Lady Caroline Lamb, June 1816. John Murray Archive.
150. Lady Caroline Lamb to Henry Colburn, n.d. (1816). Forster Collection.
151. Rogers, *Recollections of the Table-Talk of Samuel Rogers,* 50.
152. Granville, *Private Correspondence,* 2:541.
153. British Library Add. MS 45547. f. 19.
154. Lady Caroline Lamb to John Murray, 15 October 1816. John Murray Archive.
155. Smiles, *A Publisher and His Friends,* 1:380.
156. Lady Caroline Lamb to John Murray, n.d. John Murray Archive.

Chapter 11

1. *Byron's Letters and Journals,* 5:81.
2. *New Monthly Magazine* 5 (June 1816): 443-44.
3. *The British Critic* 5 (June 1816): 627-31.
4. *Theatrical Inquisitor* 9 (August 1816): 122-25.
5. *British Lady's Magazine* 4 (August 1816): 101-3.
6. *Monthly Review* 80 (June 1816): 217-18.
7. *Augustan Review* 3 (October 1816): 350-54.
8. Lady Caroline Lamb to John Murray, n.d. (endorsed but not dated September 1816). John Murray Archive.
9. Forster Collection.
10. *Glenarvon,* 2:112.
11. Lady Caroline Lamb to Lady Melbourne, n.d. (after 9 May 1816). British Library Add. MS 45546 f.91-92.
12. See Clubbe, *"Glenarvon* Revised—and Revisited."
13. Forster Collection. Biddulph was a playwright of the mid-1700s who wrote under the pen name Frances Chamberlaine Sheridan.
14. *Glenarvon,* 1:v-vi.

15. Cecil, *Melbourne,* 70.

16. Blyth, *Caro: The Fatal Passion,* 196.

17. Clubbe, *"Glenarvon* Revised—and Revisited," 208, 210.

18. Lady Caroline Lamb to John Murray, n.d. (January-February 1814). John Murray Archive.

19. *Glenarvon,* 1:51-52.

20. Edgeworth, *Castle Rackrent,* 11, 99-103.

21. Campbell, *Lady Morgan: The Life and Times of Sydney Owenson,* 62.

22. "Waters of Elle" had a popularity "longer than most West-end ballads," according to W. M. Torrens, one of the earliest of the memoirists to write about William Lamb's career (*Memoirs of the Right Honourable William, 2nd Viscount Melbourne,* 1:131). Other English composers also set the words during the 1820s. See, in the British Library, "Waters of Elle, A Favorite Canzonet from the Popular Novel of Glenarvon," published in London and attributed to B. Hime. The Dublin music publisher E. McCullagh also printed an arrangement by tenor G. A. Hodson (H.1648.0.(3.)).

23. *Glenarvon,* 2:191-92.

24. Isaac Nathan also set "Maid of Athens" to music sometime during this period. I am indebted to Graham Pont, who has established that it had been reprinted three times by 1816. The song is also sometimes titled "My Life I Love You," but in Byron's collected works called simply "Song."

25. *Glenarvon,* 2:194.

26. Lady Caroline Lamb to John Murray, Saturday 13 November 1813. John Murray Archive.

27. *Glenarvon,* 2:194-95.

28. Blessington, *Conversations of Lord Byron,* 151.

29. A copy of *Verses from Glenarvon* is held in the Harvard special collections. The book contains three stipple engravings by Henry Meyer from designs by Lady Caroline herself—engravings that were introduced as frontispieces to the three volumes of the third edition of *Glenarvon* in 1816. Colburn did not advertise the book in his catalogue for December 1819, so it is probable that it was only intended for private distribution.

30. Rosetta Worthington Nathan published *Elvington* (1819) and *Langreath* (1822). Neither of the novels has printed music.

31. *Glenarvon,* 3:293.

32. *Byron's Letters and Journals,* 5:86.

33. Ibid., 5:131.

34. Ibid., 5:187.

35. Ibid., 2:242. The letter begins, "I am no longer your lover. . . ."

36. Ibid., 5:131.

37. Claire Clairemont to Lord Byron, October 1816. Byron, *His Very Self and Voice,* 192.

38. Unpaginated preface to Bluemantle [Thomas], *Purity of Heart.*

39. Lady Caroline Lamb to Lady Melbourne, 20 October 1816. British Library. Add. MS 45546, ff. 102-3.

40. Forster Collection.

41. Ibid.

42. Lady Caroline Lamb to John Murray (endorsed but not dated September 1816). John Murray Archive.

43. *Byron's Letters and Journals,* 5:204.

44. Ibid., 5:255.

45. Ibid., 7:37.

46. Ibid., 5:89.

47. Lady Caroline Lamb to Lady Byron, 7 September 1816. Bodleian Library, University of Oxford, Dep. Lovelace Byron # 78 ff.149.

48. Lady Caroline Lamb to Annabella Milbanke, Sunday 8 September 1816? (This is the date written on the typed transcript, although there appears to be a mark of Lady

Byron's indicating 1817 on the address page.) Bodleian Library, University of Oxford, Dep. Lovelace Byron 78 ff. 175-180. 359.

49. *Byron's Letters and Journals,* 5:93.
50. Lady Caroline Lamb to John Murray, n.d. (endorsed but not dated, September 1816). John Murray Archive.
51. Lady Caroline Lamb to Lady Melbourne, October and November 1816. British Library Add. MS 45546, ff. 95-106.
52. Lady Caroline Lamb to John Murray, 5 November 1816. John Murray Archive.
53. Forster Collection.
54. Lady Caroline Lamb to John Murray, 1816. John Murray Archive.
55. Lady Caroline Lamb to Lady Melbourne, 28 September 1816. British Library Add. MS 45546 f.93.
56. Lady Caroline Lamb to Lady Melbourne. 20 October 1816. British Library Add. MS 45546, f.102-3.
57. Bruce Papers, Bodleian Library, University of Oxford, MS Eng. C.5753, f. 123.
58. Ibid., f. 125. It seems likely, however, that Michael Bruce already knew something about Byron's homosexual life from rumors he had heard in the Mediterranean.
59. C. R. Maturin's *Bertram, or the Castle of St. Aldobrand, a Tragedy* was produced in London by Edmund Kean in 1816 to great success. It is described as an overwrought drama of madness, love, and suicide with a Byronic hero.
60. Bruce Papers, Bodleian Library, University of Oxford, MS Eng. C.5753, f. 133-34.
61. Ibid., f. 133-34.
62. Mrs. George Lamb to Lady Byron, 4 October 1816. Bodleian Library, University of Oxford, Dep. Lovelace Byron 78, f.32.
63. Bodleian Library, University of Oxford, Dep. Lovelace Byron 417, Extracts from the diary of Harriet, Countess Granville, 1810-1824.
64. *Glenarvon,* 3:197.

Chapter 12

1. Lady Caroline Lamb to Lady Byron, n.d. (5 May 1817, because it prompts Lady Byron's response of 8 May). Bodleian Library, University of Oxford, Dep. Lovelace Byron # 78 ff.153. (There is a typed transcription of this letter in Dep. Lovelace Byron 359.)
2. Annabella Milbanke, Lady Byron, to Lady Caroline Lamb, 8 May 1817. Bodleian Library, University of Oxford, Dep. Lovelace Byron 78, ff. 186-187. Marked as a "copy." A response to Lady Caroline's letter, Dep. Lovelace Byron 78, f. 153.
3. Bruce Papers, Bodleian Library, University of Oxford, MS Eng. C.5753, f. 135-37.
4. Samuel Carter Hall, who served as his literary secretary in 1822, describes Foscolo thus in *Retrospect of a Long Life,* 1:99-100.
5. Lady Caroline Lamb to Ugo Foscolo, 1817. Vincent, *Ugo Foscolo,* 71-73.
6. Lee, *Extracts from the Diary of the Late Dr. Robert Lee 1821-22,* 7, 14.
7. Ziegler, *Melbourne,* 78.
8. Interestingly, a "Hebrew Dirge" for Princess Charlotte was commissioned and chanted in the Great Synagogue in St. James's Place, Aldgate by the master of the Hebrew Academy in Highgate, Hyman Hurwitz, with the English translation provided by Samuel Taylor Coleridge and published by H. Barnett in 1817.
9. Calder-Marshall, *The Two Duchesses,* 176.
10. Airlie, *Lady Palmerston and Her Times,* 1:43.
11. Palmerston, *The Letters of Lady Palmerston,* 15.
12. British Library Add. MS 45548. f. 153-55.
13. Lady Caroline Lamb to John Cam Hobhouse, n.d. John Murray Archive.
14. Hertfordshire Archives D/Elb F85/1-5.
15. Howell-Thomas, *Lord Melbourne's Susan,* 26.

16. Ibid., 10.
17. Melbourne, *Byron's "Corbeau Blanc,"* 367-68.
18. Letter of Mrs. George Lamb to Lady Byron, 1 April 1818. Bodleian Library, University of Oxford, Dep. Lovelace Byron 78, f. 27.
19. Cecil, *Melbourne,* 154.
20. Just a few months earlier, on 20 March 1818, Caroline had appealed to her uncle Lord Spencer to help a man who had been lamed in another accident. British Library Add MS 76121.
21. Hertfordshire DE/K C 28/9. Bulwer returned to this scene at age forty (in 1843) in a fictionalized reminiscence titled *Lionel Hastings,* in which he imagined himself leaping to the side of the ministering angel (a character he named Lady Clara Manford) and driving off with her to take the injured man to a doctor.
22. Hertfordshire DE/K C 24/21/2 and 4. The paper on these two letters of Bulwer is watermarked 1811, which has led some to think that their encounter happened earlier, but the date of the races is fixed.
23. Nathan, *Fugitive Pieces,* 176.
24. Ibid., 150.
25. Nathan and Byron, *Hebrew Melodies,* 82.
26. Hobhouse, *Byron's Bulldog,* 250.
27. Vincent, *Ugo Foscolo,* 73.
28. Lady Caroline Lamb to Lord Byron, n.d. (October-November 1818). John Murray Archive.
29. *Don Juan* 1.15. Byron, *Complete Poetical Works,* 5:13.
30. *Byron's Letters and Journals,* 6:80-84, 90.
31. Airlie, *Lady Palmerston and Her Times,* 1:43.
32. Ibid., 1:44-45.
33. W. Huskisson to Mrs. Huskisson 19 January 1819. British Library Add MSS 39949, f. 17.
34. Lady Caroline Lamb to John Murray, 15 September 1819. John Murray Archive.
35. Bodleian Library, University of Oxford, [Abinger] Dep. b. 229.
36. Peter Cochran, *Hobby-O: The Diary of John Cam Hobhouse, http://hobby-o.com/ newgate.php.* Accessed 23 October 2003.
37. Mitchell, *Lord Melbourne: 1779-1848,* 80.
38. Joyce, *My Friend H,* 125-26.
39. Lady Caroline Lamb to John Cam Hobhouse, February-March 1819. John Murray Archive.
40. *Byron's Letters and Journals,* 6:107.
41. Forster Collection.
42. Smiles, *A Publisher and His Friends,* 404-5.
43. Lady Caroline Lamb to John Murray, July and 2 September 1819. John Murray Archive.
44. Bodleian Library, University of Oxford, Dep. Lovelace Byron 417. Extracts from the Diary of Harriet, Countess Granville, 1810-1824.
45. *Byron's Letters and Journals,* 6:114-15.
46. Ibid., 8:148.
47. The poem is titled, strangely, "To Caroline," and dates from 1805, well before he met Lady Caroline—but she had undoubtedly read it. Byron, *Complete Poetical Works,* 1:135.
48. *Glenarvon,* 3:15.
49. *Don Juan* 5.70, 5.72. All citations from Byron, *Complete Poetical Works,* vol. 5.
50. Ibid., 5.118 and 5.141.
51. Graham, *Don Juan and Regency England,* 90, 118.
52. *Glenarvon,* 1:211-12.
53. *Don Juan,* 14.45.
54. Ibid., 15.40.

55. Ibid., 1.199.
56. Ibid., 1.193.
57. *Glenarvon* 3:61, 78.
58. Ibid., 3:60, 61.
59. Ibid., 3:58, 59, 77.
60. *Don Juan,* 1.194.
61. Hobhouse thought of de Staël's *works.* Jerome McGann suggests a possible alternative in Jane Austen's *Persuasion.* See Byron, *Complete Poetical Works,* 5:680n.
62. *Glenarvon,* 3:79.
63. Ibid., 3:90-91, 119.
64. *Don Juan* 1.195. Byron wrote "boils" and "curdles" rather than "rushes" in canceled versions of line three, an echo of the volcanism he continued to identify with Lady Caroline (see note to line 1555 in Byron, *Complete Poetical Works* 5:71).
65. *Glenarvon,* 3:60-61.
66. *Don Juan,*1.196 and *Glenarvon,* 3:80.
67. *Don Juan,* 1.197 and *Glenarvon,* 3:76, 58.
68. *Don Juan,* 1.198.
69. Ibid., 2.201.
70. *Childe Harold's Monitor; or, Lines, occasioned by the last canto of Childe Harold, including hints to contemporaries* (London: 1818) consisted of sixty-two pages of couplets and thirty-two of notes. Henry Colburn published *Harold the Exile* in September 1819—at three volumes and 21 shillings it was longer than, and twice as expensive as *Don Juan.*
71. Hone, *Don Juan, Canto the Third.* Anon., *Jack the Giant Queller, or Prince Juan.*
72. Graham, *Don Juan and Regency England,* 121. Lady Caroline has often been traced to the character of Lady Adeline Amundeville in Canto 13 of *Don Juan,* in which Byron's original association of Caroline with a volcano appears condescendingly: "Poor thing. How frequently by me and others / It hath been stirred up till its smoke quite smothers" (*Don Juan,*13.36).
73. Lamb, *A New Canto,* stanza 3.
74. Ibid., stanza 4.
75. Ibid., stanza 5.
76. Ibid., stanza 12.
77. Byron, *Complete Poetical Works,* 1:156.
78. *New Canto,* stanza 7.
79. Ibid., stanza 9.
80. Ibid., stanza 11. See Chapter 8 for a discussion of Jacques Cazotte's *Biondetta* (trans. 1810).
81. *New Canto,* stanza 15.
82. Ibid., stanza 24.
83. See *Don Juan,* 2.184ff. Byron, *Complete Poetical Works,* 5:146ff.
84. *New Canto,* stanza 27.
85. *Monthly Review* , second series, 94 (1821): 329.
86. Lady Caroline Lamb wrote to John Murray requesting he send "the New Canto of Don Juan and Moor(e)s poem if you have one—& if not a quarterly review—& if Mr Parker could give it him a Penruddock as it would I think amuse him." n.d. (1823?). John Murray Archive.
87. See chapter 19 of Carolly Erickson's *Our Tempestuous Day: A History of Regency England* (New York: William Morrow, 1986), for a vivid account of the events of August 16, 1819.
88. Lady Caroline Lamb to John Murray, 14 February 1820. John Murray Archive.
89. Bessborough and Aspinall, 261.
90. On August 27, 1820, Harryo wrote in her journal: "A large rat came just behind Lady Harrowby's ear, as we were wrangling about the Queen last night." Bodleian Library,

University of Oxford, Dep. Lovelace Byron 417. Extracts from the diary of Harriet, Countess Granville, 1810-1824

91. Lady Caroline Lamb wrote to apologize to Hobhouse in February or March of 1820 because of these bogus letters signed ignorantly "Lady Lamb." Lady Caroline Lamb to John Cam Hobhouse, n.d. (February-March 1820). John Murray Archive.

92. Hobhouse, *Byron's Bulldog*, 287.

93. Hertfordshire Archives D/ELb F85/6-8.

94. Lady Caroline Lamb to John Murray, n.d. (August 1820). John Murray Archive. Byron heard the rumors and mentions them to Countess Guiccioli in a letter of 9 September 1820. See *Byron's Letters and Journals*, 7:173-74.

95. *Byron's Letters and Journals*, 7:169.

96. The note is attached to a letter in French from Lady Caroline to Ugo Foscolo, and it is endorsed by Francis Cohen, a scholar and translator, as "given to me by Ugo Foscolo, 24th Dec(ember) 1819." The Carl H. Pforzheimer Collection of Shelley and His Circle, the New York Public Library, Astor, Lenox and Tilden Foundations.

97. Quoted in *The Works of Lord Byron*, 5:69. It was probably on this occasion that Lady Caroline asked Madame Vestris, an actress, to go with her to the masquerade and, according to Hobhouse, became so excited that she "frightened" the actress "with certain testimonies of personal admiration, such as squeezing, etc.," British Library Add. MS 56541.

98. *Byron's Letters and Journals*, 7:169.

99. Wolfson alludes to the description in *Don Juan*, 1.83, in "Their She Condition," 592.

100. Lady Caroline Lamb's commonplace book. John Murray Archive.

101. Fraser, *The Unruly Queen*, 442-43, 445.

102. David, *The Prince of Pleasure*, 419.

103. The letter is marked by Amelia Opie as the "1st letter I ever received from Lady C Lamb." British Library Add. MS 50142.

104. Lady Caroline Lamb to John Murray, n.d. (1819 watermark). John Murray Archive.

105. Blyth, *Caro: The Fatal Passion*, 204.

106. Vincent, *Ugo Foscolo*, 75.

107. Lady Caroline to William Godwin, 18 April 1822. (Franked Welwyn 20 April 1822.) Bodleian Library, University of Oxford, [Abinger] Dep. c. 507. The first manuscript, which caused her to feel so constrained, undoubtedly turned out to be *Graham Hamilton*, published in 1822. *Ada Reis* would be published by John Murray in 1823.

108. Lady Caroline Lamb. Three letters to Thomas Malthus. British Library Add. MS R.P. 4687 (ii) Box 108, photocopies. Originals are in the Carl H. Pforzheimer Collection of Shelley and His Circle, the New York Public Library, Astor, Lenox and Tilden Foundations.

109. Ibid. From the descriptions, we may suspect (though we cannot be certain) that the two parts of this bifurcated novel were the stories that would later be published as *Graham Hamilton* and *Ada Reis*, though we know that William was editing *Ada Reis* no later than November 1821 because Caroline says so in a letter to John Murray dated 28 November 1821. John Murray Archive.

110. Palmerston, *The Letters of Lady Palmerston*, 62.

Chapter 13

1. Hertfordshire Archives DELb F71.

2. Paul, *William Godwin: His Friends and Contemporaries*, 2:266-67.

3. Airlie, *Lady Palmerston and Her Times*, 1:88.

4. Ibid., 1:91.

5. David, *Prince of Pleasure*, 419.

6. Fraser, *The Unruly Queen*, 456, 461.

7. Lady Caroline Lamb to John Murray, n.d. (August 1821). John Murray Archive. I am indebted to Andrew Nicholson for furnishing me the date of Mrs. Murray's illness.

8. Lamb, *Gordon: A Tale; A Poetical Review of Don Juan*, 5.

9. Ibid. Further references are by canto and stanza: 1.10.

10. Ibid., 1.13, 17.

11. Ibid., 1.36.

12. Ibid., 1.37, 39.

13. Ibid., 2.8, 10.

14. Ibid., 2.16.

15. Ibid., pages 73-75.

16. Ibid., 2.25-30.

17. Ibid., 2.36; see *Don Juan* 1.207.

18. *Gordon: A Tale*, 2.42.

19. Ibid., 2.47.

20. Ibid., 2.54.

21. Ibid., 2.57.

22. Ibid., 2.61.

23. Ibid., 2.63.

24. Ibid., 2.65-69.

25. The stranger's monologue, for example, includes this stanza:

> "He mentions '*νοῦς*,' to tell us he knows Greek:
>
> "'*Νοῦς*' he possesses *quantum sufficit*:
>
> "'*Εὐπείθης*' if he were then would I speak,
>
> "One other word the phrase would neatly fit;
>
> "Put '*μετα*' first: perhaps if he should wreak
>
> "His vengeance on me, he might chance to hit
>
> "My '*μετα*' by his '*νοῦς*.' There's many a word
>
> "Would not suit him like that, though so absurd." (2.55)

The Greek words here make a clever game. The first, "*νοῦς*," is more or less synonymous with the second, "*Νοῦς*," meaning "mind"—although this is a huge subject. In any case, this quality of Intellect Byron possesses "sufficiently." "*Εὐπείθης*" ("*eupeithes*") can mean "persuasive" or "obedient." The latter is probably intended: The spectre would speak if only Byron were governable. The next two Greek words seem to allude to the word "*metapeitho*," meaning to change a man's persuasion: "*μετα*" is a preposition ("*meta*") sometimes used (as in English) in compounds to show change, though more usually to indicate the meanings "over" and "beyond." This is probably what is meant by the collision of the speaker's "*μετα*" with Byron's "*νοῦς*," leading us out of (or beyond) his mind.

26. Review of *Gordon: A Tale, Monthly Review*, second series, 96 (1822?): 325-26.

27. Bessborough and Aspinall, 263. Poet and translator of French and Italian literary and historical works, William Stewart Rose was reading clerk of the House of Lords and in 1821 was working on a translation of Ariosto's *Orlando Furioso* for John Murray.

28. Forster Collection.

29. Palmerston, *The Letters of Lady Palmerston*, 92.

30. Lee, *Extracts from the Diary of the Late Dr. Robert Lee 1821-22*, 20-21. It is vexing and suspicious that only the last few months of Lee's long sojourn with the Lambs are represented in the "Diary." All entries from October 1817 to July 1821 are missing.

31. Ibid., 23-26.

32. Ibid., 38.

33. *Byron's Letters and Journals*, 8:227.

34. Byron, *His Very Self and Voice*, 353.

35. Granville, *Private Correspondence*, 2:553.

36. Bessborough and Aspinall, 265.
37. Lady Caroline Lamb to John Murray, 28 November 1821. John Murray Archive.
38. William Ponsonby to Lady Caroline Lamb, 12 November 1821. A copy of this letter in an unknown hand is held in the Devonshire MSS. 6th Duke's Group f.599. It is also quoted in full in Bessborough and Aspinall, 268.
39. William Ponsonby to Lady Caroline Lamb, 12 November 1821. Devonshire MSS, 6th Duke's Group f. 599. This is a handwritten copy of the original in the hand of Dr. Lee. See also Bessborough and Aspinall 270-71.
40. Bodleian Library, University of Oxford, Dep. Lovelace Byron 417. Extracts from the diary of Harriet, Countess Granville, 1810-1824.
41. Chapman and Dormer, *Elizabeth and Georgiana,* 261.
42. Vincent, *Ugo Foscolo,* 75.
43. Lady Caroline Lamb to the 6th Duke of Devonshire, 25 and 28 December 1821. Devonshire MSS. 6th Duke's Group, f.581 and f.583.
44. Lady Caroline Lamb to Amelia Opie, 1 January 1822. British Library Add. MS 50142
45. Bessborough and Aspinall, 274.
46. Lady Caroline Lamb to Amelia Opie, 1 January 1822. British Library Add. MS 5014.
47. Bodleian Library, University of Oxford, MS Eng. C.5753, f. 144-45.
48. Lockhart, *Some Passages in the Life of Mr. Adam Blair.*
49. Bodleian Library, University of Oxford, MS Eng. C.5753, f. 127-29.
50. Ibid., f. 144-45.
51. Lady Caroline Lamb's commonplace book. John Murray Archive.
52. Palmerston, *The Letters of Lady Palmerston,* 51.
53. Nathan, *Fugitive Pieces,* 153.
54. A letter of thanks is in the 6th Duke's papers, Devonshire MSS., unfoliated.
55. Bessborough and Aspinall 277-78.
56. Lee, *Extracts from the Diary of the Late Dr. Robert Lee 1821-22,* 40-41.
57. Bessborough and Aspinall, 280.
58. A facsimile of "Seul sur la Terre" is printed in Lytton, *The Life, Letters and Literary Remains of Edward Bulwer, Lord Lytton.*
59. Lady Caroline Lamb to Henry Colburn, n.d. (1822). Forster Collection.
60. William Lamb to Henry Colburn, n.d. Forster Collection.
61. Lady Caroline Lamb to Henry Colburn, n.d. (1822). Forster Collection.
62. Lady Caroline Lamb to Henry Colburn, n.d. (a different letter, 1822). Forster Collection.
63. Lady Caroline Lamb to Henry Colburn, n.d. (a different letter, 1822). Forster Collection.
64. Lady Caroline Lamb to Henry Colburn, 14 March 1822. Forster Collection.
65. Lady Caroline Lamb to Henry Colburn, n.d. (1822). Forster Collection.
66. Lady Caroline Lamb to Henry Colburn, n.d. (a different letter). Forster Collection. The orphan was named Ellinor Mowbray, but of her fate nothing is known.
67. Palmerston, *The Letters of Lady Palmerston,* 101.
68. Ibid., 102.
69. *Graham Hamilton* will remind some readers of the young Charles Brockden Brown, whose work Lady Caroline knew, especially *Wieland* (1798), with its portrayal of madness.
70. Lamb, *Graham Hamilton,* 1:26.
71. Ibid., 1:20-21.
72. Ibid., 1:33.
73. *Glenarvon,* 2:144-45.
74. *Graham Hamilton,* 1:26-30.
75. Ibid., 1:57-59.
76. Lady Caroline Lamb to Henry Colburn, n.d. (1822). Forster Collection.

77. Lady Caroline Lamb to Henry Colburn. Forster Collection. Lady Caroline Lamb to Lady Morgan, n.d. (April-May 1823). Houghton Library *43M-93. Quoted by permission of the Houghton Library, Harvard University.
78. Review of *Graham Hamilton* in *Blackwood's Edinburgh Magazine* 11 (1822): 731-33.
79. Palmerston, *The Letters of Lady Palmerston,* 111.
80. Lady Caroline Lamb to Henry Colburn, undated (1822) and 14 December 1822. Forster Collection.

Chapter 14

1. Morgan, *Lady Morgan's Memoirs,* 2:211.
2. Paul, *William Godwin,* 2:267.
3. Ibid., 2:267, 286, 303.
4. Lady Caroline Lamb to Lady Morgan, n.d. (April/May 1823). Harvard Library *43M-93.
5. Lady Caroline Lamb to the 6th Duke of Devonshire, 12 July 1823. Devonshire MSS. 6th Duke's Group, f. 817A.
6. Lady Caroline Lamb to John Murray, n.d. (1823?). John Murray Archive.
7. Paul, *William Godwin,* 2:283-84.
8. Ibid., 2:304-305.
9. Ibid., 285-86.
10. Ibid., 2:302-304.
11. Vickery, *The Gentleman's Daughter,* 127ff., 277, 321.
12. Cumberland. *The Wheel of Fortune.* Elledge, *Lord Byron at Harrow School,* 135.
13. Lady Caroline Lamb to Lady Morgan, n.d. (1823?). Houghton Library *43M-93. Quoted by permission of the Houghton Library, Harvard University.
14. Lady Caroline Lamb to John Murray, January 1823. John Murray Archive.
15. Lady Caroline Lamb wrote to John Murray in April 1823: "I entreat you—let Penruddock come out soon." John Murray Archive.
16. MacCarthy, *Byron: Life and Legend,* 372.
17. *Ada Reis,* title page, from Xenophon's *Memorabilia* ed. W. R. Connor (New York: Arno Press, 1979). See verse 1:3:7. I am indebted to Marianina Olcott for her assistance in identifying and translating this epigraph.
18. Lamb, *Ada Reis,* 1:xviii.
19. Ibid., 1:22, 25.
20. The chessboard may have been suggested to Lady Caroline by a contemporary hoax, a supposed chess-playing machine that probably contained a human being, though the effect was so convincing that it confounded most contemporary attempts to explain the phenomenon.
21. *Ada Reis,* 1:83.
22. Ibid., 1:106, 143.
23. Ibid., 2:102.
24. Ibid., 2:127.
25. Ibid., 2:132.
26. Ibid., 3:39-40.
27. Ibid., 3:46-47.
28. Ibid., 3:55.
29. Ibid., 3:80-81.
30. Ibid., 3:95-96.
31. Lady Caroline Lamb to John Murray, n.d. (1823). John Murray Archive.
32. Lady Caroline Lamb to John Murray, n.d. (1823?). John Murray Archive.
33. Smiles, *A Publisher and His Friends,* 2:144.
34. Lady Caroline Lamb to John Murray, 26 November 1821 and April 1823. John Murray Archive. The Murray ledgers show the print run of *Ada Reis* was 750.

35. Palmerston, *The Letters of Lady Palmerston,* 123.
36. Letters of Maria Edgeworth to her mother, 1 and 24 April 1822. *Maria Edgeworth: Letters from England 1813-1844,* ed. Christina Colvin (Oxford: Clarendon Press, 1971), 377-78, 397, 378n.
37. *Ada Reis,* 1:iii.
38. Ibid., 1:xi, xii-xiii. I am indebted to Catriona Mills for insights into Lady Caroline's composition of the preface to *Ada Reis.* See "The Disappearing Author in Lady Caroline Lamb's *Ada Reis,*" paper delivered at the Work in Progress Conference, University of Queensland, Australia, October 2002.
39. Lady Caroline Lamb to Lady Morgan, n.d. (April-May 1823). Houghton Library *43M-93
40. Lady Caroline Lamb to John Murray, n.d. (June 1823). Murray Archive. Lady Caroline Lamb to Edward Bulwer, 21 May 1823. Hertfordshire DE/K C 24/21/1.
41. *The Literary Gazette* 323 (1823): 198-200.
42. *The New Monthly Magazine* 8 (1823): 317-21.
43. *British Magazine* 1 (1823): 87-92.
44. *The Examiner* 796 (27 April 1823): 284.
45. The song was most likely "Sir Henry De Vaux" from *Ada Reis,* but it could be "Sing Not For others, but for me."
46. Nathan, *Fugitive Pieces,* 153.
47. Lady Caroline Lamb to Lady Morgan (1823). Torrens, *Memoirs of the Right Honourable William, 2nd Viscount Melbourne,* 1:130-31.
48. Morgan, *Lady Morgan's Memoirs,* 2:210-11.
49. Forster Collection.
50. Morgan, *Lady Morgan's Memoirs,* 2:161-64.
51. Lady Caroline to Lady Morgan soon after publication of *Ada Reis* in 1823. Torrens, *Memoirs of the Right Honourable William, 2nd Viscount Melbourne,* 1:130-31. Lady Morgan's *The Life and Times of Salvator Rosa* was published in two volumes by Henry Colburn in 1824.
52. Morgan, *Lady Morgan's Memoirs,* 2:176-78.
53. Ibid., 2:176-78.
54. Ibid., 2:179.
55. Lady Caroline Lamb, from Brocket, 18 December 18 1823. Torrens, *Memoirs of the Right Honourable William, 2nd Viscount Melbourne,* 1:132.

Chapter 15

1. Lady Caroline Lamb to Thomas Medwin, n.d. (1824). Forster Collection.
2. Nathan, *Fugitive Pieces,* 155-56.
3. Lady Caroline Lamb to Thomas Medwin, n.d. (1824). Forster Collection.
4. Lady Caroline Lamb to John Cam Hobhouse, 22 May 1824. John Murray Archive.
5. Hobhouse, *Recollections of a Long Life,* 3:43.
6. Lady Caroline Lamb to Lydia White, n.d. (May 1824). John Murray Archive.
7. Lady Caroline Lamb to John Murray, n.d. (May-June 1824). John Murray Archive.
8. Lady Caroline Lamb to John Cam Hobhouse, n.d. (May-June 1824). John Murray Archive.
9. Marchand, *Byron: A Biography,* 3:1253.
10. Lady Caroline Lamb to John Cam Hobhouse, n.d. (May-June 1824). John Murray Archive.
11. Lady Caroline Lamb to John Cam Hobhouse, n.d. British Library Add. MSS 36461, f. 359.
12. "Dialogues of the Dead." *Bell's Life in London and Sporting Chronicle.* 3:118 (Sunday 30 May 1824): 1.
13. Lady Caroline Lamb to John Murray, 13 July 1824. John Murray Archive.

14. Lady Caroline Lamb to John Murray, 12 May 1824: "(M)y prettiest song out of Graham Hamilton is published is it not rather odd—as if written on her death bed by Mrs Jordan. The words begin 'if thou couldst know.'" John Murray Archive.
15. See Nathan (*Fugitive Pieces,* 160), for his claim that he had the poem "years before" *Graham Hamilton* was published.
16. Nathan, *Fugitive Pieces,* 159; *Graham Hamilton* 1:196.
17. Nathan, *Fugitive Pieces,*166.
18. Ibid., 161-64. I am indebted to Graham Pont for informing me how actively Nathan promoted Lady Caroline's songs he set to music and published.
19. Lytton, *The Life, Letters and Literary Remains of Edward Bulwer, Lord Lytton,* 1:328.
20. Bulwer to his mother, 14 January 1825. Quoted in Sadleir, *Bulwer: A Panorama,* 58-59.
21. David Lytton-Cobbold, "Sir Edward Bulwer-Lytton's Remarks on Lady Caroline Lamb, written in his copy of *Glenarvon,*" *The Byron Journal* 6 (1978): 113.
22. Gower, *Letters of Harriet, Countess Granville, 1810-1845,* 1:307.
23. Mitchell, *Lord Melbourne: 1779-1848,* 65.
24. Medwin, *Conversations of Lord Byron,* viii.
25. Ibid., 216-18.
26. Byron, *Complete Poetical Works,* 3:84.
27. Lady Caroline Lamb to William Godwin, n.d. (Fall 1824—after Medwin). Bodleian Library, University of Oxford, (Abinger) Dep. b. 229.
28. Lady Caroline Lamb to Lady Byron, Sunday, 31 October 1824. Dep. Lovelace Byron 359. A typescript copy of the letter.
29. Lady Byron to Lady Caroline Lamb, 31 October 1824. Dep. Lovelace Byron 78, ff. 188-189.
30. Quoted in Moore, *The Late Lord Byron,* 105.
31. Forster Collection.
32. Lovell, *Captain Medwin: Friend of Byron,* 171, 183.
33. Lady Caroline Lamb to the 6th Duke of Devonshire. Devonshire MSS. 6th Duke's Group, f. 1130, 1824-1825.
34. *A Daughter of Eve* was serialized in *La Siècle* December 1838 to January 1839. See chapter 5 in volume 9 of *The Works of Honoré de Balzac,* Trans. R. S. Scott (New York: T.Y. Crowell, 1901), 50.
35. Lady Caroline Lamb to the 6th Duke of Devonshire. Devonshire MSS. 6th Duke's Group, f. 1130, 1824-1825.

Chapter 16

1. Lady Caroline Lamb to the Duke of Devonshire, April 1825. Devonshire MSS. 6th Duke's Group, f. 1130.
2. Lady Caroline Lamb to Lady Morgan, n.d. (April-May 1823). Houghton Library *43M-93. Quoted by permission of the Houghton Library, Harvard University.
3. The book is now in the Hertfordshire Archives.
4. Villiers, *The Grand Whiggery,* 366.
5. Lady Caroline Lamb to the Duke of Devonshire, 10 April 1825. Devonshire MSS. 6th Duke's Group, f. 1129.
6. Lady Caroline Lamb to the Duke of Devonshire, April 1825. Devonshire MSS. 6th Duke's Group, f. 1128.
7. George Lamb to the Duke of Devonshire, 15 April 1825. Devonshire MSS. 6th Duke's Group, f. 1131.
8. The Duke of Devonshire to George Lamb, 17 April 1825. Devonshire MSS. 6th Duke's Group, f. 1132.
9. Mitchell, *Lord Melbourne: 1779-1848,* 87.
10. Palmerston, *The Letters of Lady Palmerston,* 134.

11. Lady Caroline Lamb to the 6th Duke of Devonshire, n.d. (1825?). Hertfordshire Archives D/EP F427/14.
12. William Lamb to Frederick Lamb, 16 May 1825. Hertfordshire Archives D/ELb F85/17.
13. British Library Add MSS 45550, f. 165.
14. Morgan, *Lady Morgan's Memoirs*, 2:203.
15. Howell-Thomas, *Duncannon*, 107-108.
16. Hertfordshire Archives D/EP f427/16.
17. Emily Cowper to Frederick Lamb, 7 June 1825. Palmerston, *The Letters of Lady Palmerston*, 134-35.
18. Nathan, *Fugitive Pieces*, 183.
19. Ibid., 184.
20. Ibid., 185-86.
21. Wilmington Fleming, *The Destroying Angel, A Fragment; The Captive's Boy and Other Poems* (1825) 23.
22. Lady Caroline Lamb to Henry Colburn, n.d. (before 20 March 1826). Forster Collection.
23. Lady Caroline Lamb to John Murray, March 1825. John Murray Archive.
24. Erickson, *The Economy of Literary Form*, 26.
25. Lady Caroline Lamb to Wilmington Fleming, n.d. (1825). Forster Collection.
26. Lady Caroline Lamb to Henry Colburn, n.d. (before 20 March 1826 and probably after 1 January1826). Forster Collection.
27. Lady Caroline Lamb to Wilmington Fleming, n.d. (watermark 1825). British Library Add MSS 50142.
28. Lady Caroline Lamb to Henry Colburn, n.d. (before 20 March 1826 and probably after 1 January 1826). Forster Collection.
29. Lady Caroline Lamb to an unknown correspondent, n.d. (1825). British Library Add. MS 38855. f. 234.
30. Paston and Quennell, *"To Lord Byron,"* 53.
31. Hertfordshire Archives D/EP f427/15.
32. Palmerston, *The Letters of Lady Palmerston*, 136.
33. Morgan, *Lady Morgan's Memoirs*, 2:208-209.
34. Ibid., 2:206-208.
35. Lady Caroline Lamb to Lady Morgan, n.d. (1825). Forster Collection.
36. Palmerston, *The Letters of Lady Palmerston*, 137.
37. *Hary-O*, 1:352.
38. Hertfordshire Archives D/ELb F76/11.
39. Palmerston, *The Letters of Lady Palmerston*, 138.
40. Villiers, *The Grand Whiggery*, 369.
41. Palmerston, *The Letters of Lady Palmerston*, 138.
42. Emily Cowper to Frederick Lamb, 14 August 1825. British Library Add. MSS 45550, f. 187.
43. Ibid.
44. Mitchell, *Lord Melbourne: 1779-1848*, 89.
45. Palmerston, *The Letters of Lady Palmerston*, 139.
46. Lady Caroline Lamb to William Lamb, 8 September 1825. Hertfordshire Archives D/Elb F 32/5.
47. Morgan, *Lady Morgan's Memoirs*, 2:209.
48. Forster Collection.
49. Lady Caroline Lamb to 6th Duke of Devonshire, 26 October 1825. Devonshire MSS. 6th Duke's Group, f. 1217.
50. Dr. Goddard to William Lamb, 19 October 1825. Hertfordshire Archives D/ELb F33/1.
51. Lady Caroline Lamb to 6th Duke of Devonshire, 26 October 1825. Devonshire MSS. 6th Duke's Group, f. 1218.

52. Lady Caroline Lamb to William Lamb, n.d. (1825). Hertfordshire Archives D/ELb F76/10.

53. Lady Caroline Lamb to William Lamb, November 1825. Hertfordshire Archives D/ELb F32/6.

54. Lady Caroline Lamb to 6th Duke of Devonshire, 26 October 1825. Devonshire MSS. 6th Duke's Group, f. 1217.

55. Ibid.

56. The record of the lease of 39 Conduit Street is to be found in the archives of Coutts Bank, 440 Strand, London WC2R OQS.

57. Erickson, *The Economy of Literary Form*, 144.

58. Lady Caroline Lamb to John Murray, 1815. John Murray Archive has a photocopy of this letter, the original of which is in the private collection of Mr. Simon Finch.

59. Hertfordshire Archives D/ELb F62/9 and 1.

60. Hertfordshire Archives D/ELb F62/19 and 22.

61. Hertfordshire Archives D/ELb F62 /10 and 69.

62. Hertfordshire Archives D/ELb F62 /4.

63. Devey, *Life of Rosina, Lady Lytton*, 43-44.

64. Hall, *Retrospect of a Long Life*, 1:264.

65. Ibid., 213, 221, 268-69.

66. William Lamb to Frederick Lamb, 26 December 1825. British Library Add MS 45548 f. 161.

67. Dr. Goddard to Lady Caroline Lamb, 13 December 1825. Hertfordshire Archives D/ELb F62/6.

68. Palmerston, *The Letters of Lady Palmerston*, 142.

69. Lister, *Granby*, 1:114.

70. Wilson, *Memoirs of Herself and Others*, 304ff. I am grateful to Professor Dominique Van Hooff for help in translating Wilson's French.

71. Ibid., 306ff.

72. Nathan, *Fugitive Pieces*, 195-96.

73. Lady Caroline Lamb to Mrs. Blacquiere, n.d. (before 20 March 1826). Forster Collection.

74. Bodleian Library, University of Oxford, Dep. Lovelace-Byron 78, f. 68.

75. Bodleian Library, University of Oxford, Dep. Lovelace-Byron 78, f. 70. Also quoted in full in Moore, *The Late Lord Byron: Posthumous Dramas*, 227.

76. Pierson, *The Real Lady Byron*, 182-83. For Lady Wilmot Horton's argument, see Mayne, *The Life and Letters of Anne Isabella*, 309.

77. Moore, *The Late Lord Byron*, 260.

78. Ibid., 254.

79. Ibid., 256.

80. Nathan, *Fugitive Pieces*, 187.

81. Ibid., 192.

82. If Fleming landed in jail or left the country around 1825-1826, he seems to have been back seven years later. There are two verses by him in the University of Nottingham Library, contained in the papers of Henry Pelham-Clinton, 4th Duke of Newcastle under Lyne, in the Newcastle Collection: Miscellaneous Correspondence and Papers (1827-1850). The poetry is dated tentatively by "internal evidence" to 1833 and lists Fleming's address as "Nottingham Court, Castle Street, Nottingham, Nottinghamshire" (items Ne C 8087/1 and Ne C 8087/2).

83. Hertfordshire Archives DE/K C1/4.

84. Knebworth Archive, Letters of Edward Bulwer, Box 71. I am very grateful to Cindy Lawford for furnishing this information to me.

85. Hertfordshire DE/K C1/5.

86. Lytton, *Unpublished Letters of Lady Bulwer Lytton to A.E. Chalon*, 353-55.

87. Lytton, *Letters of the Late Edward Bulwer, Lord Lytton, to His Wife*, 54.

88. Lytton, *The Life of Edward Bulwer*, 1:118-120

89. Mitchell, *Bulwer Lytton,* 15.
90. William Ponsonby to Lady Caroline Lamb, 13 December 1826. Devonshire MSS. 6th Duke's Group.

Chapter 17

1. Morgan, *Lady Morgan's Memoirs,* 2:212.
2. Palmerston, *The Letters of Lady Palmerston,* 162.
3. Strickland, "An Early Pioneer," 22-23.
4. Morgan, *Lady Morgan's Memoirs,* 2:213. Caroline said that William "is to me what Shore was to Jane Shore. I saw it once; I am as grateful, but as unhappy." *Jane Shore* (1714), a tragedy by Nicholas Rowe, tells the story of the mistress of Edward IV and later of Thomas Grey. Richard III accused her of sorcery, imprisoned her, and made her do public penance in 1483.
5. Bessborough and Aspinall, 288.
6. Letter of Lady Caroline Lamb to Mrs. John Murray, n.d. John Murray Archive, photocopy.
7. Hertfordshire Archives D/ELb F62.
8. Strickland, "An Early Pioneer," 22-23.
9. Bessborough and Aspinall, 289.
10. Morgan, *Lady Morgan's Memoirs,* 2:240.
11. Villiers, *The Grand Whiggery,* 375.
12. Ziegler, *Melbourne,* 101.
13. William Lamb to Frederick Lamb, 12 June 1828. Hertfordshire Archives, Panshanger MSS, Box 17, William Lamb to Frederick Lamb, 12 June 1828.
14. Hertfordshire Archives D/ELb F76/16.
15. Hertfordshire Archives D/ELb F76/12.
16. Lady Caroline Lamb to Augustus, 20 September 1827. Hertfordshire Archives D/ELb F76/9.
17. Hertfordshire Archives D/ELb F33/2.
18. Hertfordshire Archives D/ELb F33/7.
19. Morgan, *Lady Morgan's Memoirs,* 2:241, 248. See also Torrens, *Memoirs of the Right Honourable William, 2nd Viscount Melbourne,* 1:297.
20. Morgan, *Lady Morgan's Memoirs,* 2:245.
21. Bessborough and Aspinall, 290.
22. Morgan, *Lady Morgan's Memoirs,* 2:249.
23. Edward Bulwer to his wife, Rosina, 10 January 1828. Knebworth Archive, Letters of Edward Bulwer, Box 71. I am grateful to Cindy Lawford for giving me this information.
24. Lady Caroline Lamb to Lady Holland, n.d. (1828). British Library Add. MS 51560 f. 213.
25. Bessborough and Aspinall, 290.
26. Ziegler, *Melbourne: A Biography,* 101.
27. Hertfordshire Archives, Panshanger MSS Box 18.
28. Morgan, *Lady Morgan's Memoirs,* 2:253.
29. Ibid., 2:253-54.
30. Airlie, *Lady Palmerston and Her Times,* 1:129.
31. Ziegler, *Melbourne: A Biography,* 105.
32. "Biography: Lady Caroline Lamb," *The Literary Gazette, and Journal of the Belles Lettres* (1828): 107-108.
33. "Lady Caroline Lamb," *Annual Biography and Obituary* (1829): 51-57.
34. Morgan, *Lady Morgan's Memoirs,* 2:254-55.
35. Ibid., 2:255.
36. Ibid., 2:211.

37. Ibid., 2:256. The copy of the Sanders portrait of Byron is now held in the Murray Archive.

Epilogue

1. Howell-Thomas, *Lord Melbourne's Susan,* 2.
2. Hobhouse, *Recollections of a Long Life,* 3:280.
3. Ziegler, *Melbourne: A Biography,* 108-109.
4. Ibid., 110.
5. Airlie, *Lady Palmerston and Her Times,* 190-91.
6. Dunckley, *Lord Melbourne,* 236-37.
7. Hertfordshire Archives D/Elb F79/1-2.
8. Caroline Norton, *The Letters of Caroline Norton to Lord Melbourne,* 75, 120-21.
9. Bodleian Library, Dep. Lovelace-Byron 78, f. 138.

References

Manuscript Sources

British Library:The Althorp, Lamb, and Melbourne Papers of the British Library, in Additional Manuscripts (Add. MS).

Devonshire Manuscripts:Letters and other papers of the 5th and 6th Dukes of Devonshire held in the archive at Chatsworth, Derbyshire.

Hertfordshire Archives:Papers of the Lamb [Melbourne] family held in the Hertfordshire Archives and Local Studies Office, County Hall, Hertfordshire.

John Murray Archive:Letters and other papers of Lady Caroline Lamb, Lord and Lady Byron, and John Murray, held in the John Murray Archive in London.

New York Public Library:The Carl H. Pforzheimer Collection of Shelley and His Circle, the New York Public Library, Astor, Lenox and Tilden Foundations.

Oxford UniversityAbinger Collection and Papers of the Lovelace/Byron family on deposit with the Bodleian Library of Oxford University.

University of Virginia:Washington Irving Collection, Clifton Waller Barrett Library, Special Collections, University of Virginia Library.

Victoria and Albert Museum:Letters of Lady Caroline Lamb in the Victoria and Albert Museum Forster Collection MSS vol. 28 (Pressmark 48.E.22).

Yale UniversityThe Osborne collection of Yale University's Special Collections.

Printed Sources

Airlie, Mabell, Countess of. *In Whig Society: 1775-1818*. London: Hodder and Stoughton, 1921.

———. *Lady Palmerston and Her Times*. 2 vols. London: Hodder and Stoughton, 1922.

Anonymous. *Jack the Giant Queller, or Prince Juan*. London: W. Horncastle, Sloane Street, Chelsea, 1819.

Askwith, Betty. *Piety and Wit: A Biography of Harriet, Countess Granville, 1785-1862*. London: Collins, 1982.

Bakewell, Michael, and Melissa Bakewell. *Augusta Leigh: Byron's Half-Sister*. London: Chatto & Windus, 2000.

Bell, Quentin. *Virginia Woolf: A Biography*, 2 vols. New York: Harcourt Brace Jovanovich, 1972.

Bessborough, Earl. *Georgiana, Duchess of Devonshire*. London: John Murray, 1955.

———, and Arthur Aspinall. *Lady Bessborough and Her Family Circle*. London: J. Murray, 1940.

Blessington, Marguerite, Countess of. *Conversations of Lord Byron*. (1834). Ed. Ernest J. Lovell, Jr. Princeton: Princeton University Press, 1969.

Bluemantle, Bridget. [*see Elizabeth Thomas*]

Blyth, Henry. *Caro: The Fatal Passion: The Life of Lady Caroline Lamb.* London: Rupert Hart-Davis, 1972.

Burney, Fanny. *The Journals and Letters of Fanny Burney (Madame d'Arblay).* Ed. Joyce Hemlow, with Curtis D. Cecil and Althea Douglas. 12 vols. Oxford: Clarendon Press, 1972-1984.

Byron, George Gordon, Lord. *Byron's Letters and Journals.* Ed. Leslie Marchand. 12 vols. Cambridge: Belknap Press of Harvard University Press, 1973-1995.

———. *The Complete Poetical Works.* Ed. Jerome McGann. 7 vols. Vol. 6 co-edited by Barry Weller. Oxford: Clarendon Press, 1980-1993.

———. *His Very Self and Voice: Collected Conversations of Lord Byron.* Ed. Ernest J. Lovell, Jr. New York: Macmillan, 1954.

———. *Lord Byron's Correspondence: Chiefly with Lady Melbourne, Mr. Hobhouse, the Hon. Douglas Kinnaird, and P. B. Shelley.* Ed. John Murray. 2 vols. London: John Murray, 1922.

———. *The Works of Lord Byron: A New, Revised, and Enlarged Edition, With Illustrations.* 13 vols. Ed. Rowland E. Prothero and Ernest Hartley Coleridge. London: John Murray; New York: C. Scribner's' Sons, 1898-1905.

Calder-Marshall, Arthur. *The Two Duchesses.* London: Hutchinson, 1978.

Campbell, Mary. *Lady Morgan: The Life and Times of Sydney Owenson.* London: Pandora, 1988.

Cecil, David. *Melbourne.* New York: Bobbs-Merrill, 1954.

Chapman, Caroline, and Jane Dormer. *Elizabeth and Georgiana: The Duke of Devonshire and His Two Duchesses.* London: John Murray, 2002.

Clubbe, John. "*Glenarvon* Revised—and Revisited." *Wordsworth Circle* 10 (1979):205-17.

Creevey, Thomas. *The Creevey Papers: A Selection from the Correspondence & Diaries of the Late Thomas Creevey.* 3d ed. Ed. Sir Herbert Maxwell. London: John Murray, 1905.

Cumberland, Richard. *The Wheel of Fortune: A Critical Edition.* Ed. Thomas Joseph Campbell. New York & London: Garland, 1987.

Dallas, Robert C. *Recollections of the Life of Lord Byron, From the Year 1808 to the End of 1814.* London: Charles Knight, 1824.

David, Saul. *Prince of Pleasure: The Prince of Wales and the Making of the Regency.* New York: Grove Press, 1998.

Devey, Louisa. *Life of Rosina, Lady Lytton, with numerous extracts from her MS Autobiography and Other Original Documents, Published in vindication of her memory.* London: Swan, Sonnenschein, Lowrey, 1887.

Doherty, Francis. "An Unpublished Letter of Lady Caroline Lamb to Clare." *Notes and Queries* (August 1967): 297-99.

Dunckley, Henry. *Lord Melbourne.* 2nd ed. From the series Prime Ministers of Queen Victoria. London: Sampson Low, Marston, Searle & Rivington, 1890.

Eden, Emily. *Miss Eden's Letters.* Ed. Violet Dickinson. London: Macmillan, 1919.

Edgeworth, Maria. *Castle Rackrent.* Boston: T. B. Wait, 1814.

Eisler, Benita. *Byron: Child of Passion, Fool of Fame.* New York: Knopf, 1999.

Elledge, Paul. *Lord Byron at Harrow School: Speaking Out, Talking Back, Acting Up.* Baltimore and London: The Johns Hopkins University Press, 2000.

Elwin, Malcolm. *Lord Byron's Family: Annabella, Ada, and Augusta 1816-1824.* Ed. Peter Thomson. London: J. Murray, 1975.

———. *Lord Byron's Wife.* London: Macdonald, 1962.

Erickson, Lee. *The Economy of Literary Form: English Literature and the Industrialization of Publishing, 1800-1850*. Baltimore & London: Johns Hopkins University Press, 1996.

Fleming, Wilmington. *The Destroying Angel, A Fragment; The Captive's Boy and Other Poems*. London, 1825.

Foreman, Amanda. *Georgiana: Duchess of Devonshire*. New York: Random House, 1998.

Foss, Kenelm. *Here Lies Richard Brinsley Sheridan*. London: Martin Secker, 1939.

Foster, Vere. *The Two Duchesses*. London: Blackie, 1898.

Fraser, Flora. *The Unruly Queen: The Life of Queen Caroline*. New York: Alfred A. Knopf, 1966.

Goodwin, Frederick K, and Kay Redfield Jamison. *Manic-Depressive Illness*. New York and Oxford: Oxford University Press, 1990.

Gower, Henrietta Elizabeth Leveson. *Hary-O: The Letters of Lady Harriet Cavendish, 1796-1809*. Ed. Sir George Leveson-Gower and Iris Palmer. London: John Murray, 1940.

———. *Letters of Harriet, Countess Granville, 1810-1845*. 2nd ed. Ed. Hon. F. Leveson Gower. 2 vols. London: Longmans, Green, and Company, 1894.

———. *A Second Self: The Letters of Harriet Granville 1810-1845*. Ed. Virginia Surtees. Wiltshire: Michael Russell, 1990.

Gower, Iris Leveson. *The Face without a Frown: Georgiana, Duchess of Devonshire*. London: Frederick Muller, 1944.

Graham, Peter. *Don Juan and Regency England*. Charlottesville: University Press of Virginia, 1990.

Granville, Leveson-Gower, First Earl. *Private Correspondence of Earl Granville: 1781-1821*. Ed. Castalia, Countess Granville. 2 vols. London: John Murray, 1916.

Grebanier, Bernard. *The Uninhibited Byron: An Account of his Sexual Confusion*. New York: Crown, 1970.

Grosskurth, Phyllis. *Byron: The Flawed Angel*. New York: Houghton Mifflin, 1997.

Guiccioli, Teresa, Countess. *My Recollections of Lord Byron and those of Eye Witnesses of His Life*. New York: Harper & Brothers, 1869.

Hall, Samuel Carter. *Retrospect of a Long Life: From 1815 to 1883*. 2 vols. London: Bentley & Son, 1883.

Hobhouse, John Cam (Lord Broughton). *Byron's Bulldog: The Letters of John Cam Hobhouse to Lord Byron*. Ed. Peter W. Graham. Columbus: Ohio State University Press, 1984.

———. *Recollections of a Long Life: With Additional Extracts from his Private Diaries*. Ed. by (his daughter) Lady Dorchester. 4 vols. London: John Murray, 1910. AMS 1968.

Hofkosh, Sonia. "The Writer's Ravishment: Women and the Romantic Author—The Example of Byron." *Romanticism and Feminism*. Ed. Anne K. Mellor. Bloomington: Indiana University Press, 1988. 93-114.

Hone, William. *Don Juan, Canto the Third*. London: William Hone, Ludgate Hill, 1819.

Howell-Thomas, Dorothy. *Duncannon: Reformer and Reconciler, 1781-1847*. Norwich: Michael Russell, 1992.

———. *Lord Melbourne's Susan*. Old Woking: Gresham Books, 1978.

Hunt, Leigh. *Lord Byron and Some of His Contemporaries*. 2 vols. London: Henry Colburn, 1828.

Jamison, Kay Redfield. *Touched With Fire: Manic-Depressive Illness and the Artistic Temperament*. New York: Simon and Schuster/Free Press Paperbacks, 1993.

Jenkins, Elizabeth. *Lady Caroline Lamb*. London: Victor Gollancz, 1932.

Joyce, Michael. *My Friend H: John Cam Hobhouse, Baron Broughton of Broughton de Gyfford*. London: John Murray, 1948.

Kelsall, Malcolm. "The Byronic Hero and Revolution in Ireland: The Politics of *Glenarvon*." *The Byron Journal* 9 (1981): 4-19.

Lady Caroline Lamb (a film). Dir. Robert Bolt. Perf. Sarah Miles, John Finch, Richard Chamberlain, Margaret Leighton, Laurence Olivier, Ralph Richardson, John Mills. Pulsar Productions, 1972.

Lamb, Lady Caroline. *Ada Reis*. 3 vols. London: J. Murray, 1823; Paris: Galignani, 1824.

———. *Glenarvon*. 3 vols. London: Henry Colburn, 1816. Facs. 1st ed. Jonathan Wordsworth. Oxford and New York: Woodstock Books, 1993. Facs. 3rd ed. New York: AMS Press, 1975.

———. *Gordon: A Tale; A Poetical Review of Don Juan*. London: T. and J. Allman, 1821.

———. *Graham Hamilton*. 2 vols. London: Henry Colburn, 1822.

———. *A New Canto*. London: William Wright, 1819.

———. *Verses from Glenarvon, to Which is Prefixed the Original Introduction Not Published With the Early Editions of that Work*. London: Henry Colburn, 1819.

Lee, Elizabeth. *Wives of the Prime Ministers, 1844-1906*. With contributions by Mrs. C. F. G. Masterman. London: Nisbet and Co., 1917.

Lee, Dr. Robert. *Extracts from the Diary of the Late Dr. Robert Lee 1821-22*. London: Hurst & Blackett, 1897(?).

Lewis, Matthew G. *Poems*. London, 1812.

Lister, Thomas H. *Granby: A Novel*. 2 vols. London: Henry Colburn, 1826.

Lockhart, John Gibson. *Some Passages in the Life of Mr. Adam Blair: Minister of the Gospel at Cross-Meikle*. Edinburgh: W. Blackwood, 1822.

Lovell, Ernest J., Jr. *Captain Medwin: Friend of Byron*. Austin: University of Texas Press, 1962.

Lytton, Edward Bulwer, Baron. *Letters of the Late Edward Bulwer, Lord Lytton to His Wife, With Extracts from her MS "Autobiography," and Other Documents, Published in Vindication of Her Memory*. Ed. Louisa Devey. London: W. Swan Sonnenschein, 1884.

———. *The Life, Letters, and Literary Remains of Edward Bulwer, Lord Lytton, by his Son, With Portraits and Illustrations*. London: K. Paul, Trench, 1883.

Lytton, Rosina. *Unpublished Letters of Lady Bulwer Lytton to A. E. Chalon*. Ed. S. M. Ellis. London: Eveleigh Nash, 1914.

Lytton, Victor Alexander George Robert Bulwer-Lytton, 2nd Earl. *The Life of Edward Bulwer, First Lord Lytton*. 2 vols. London: Macmillan, 1913.

MacCarthy, Fiona. *Byron: Life and Legend*. London: John Murray, 2002.

Marchand, Leslie. *Byron: A Biography*. New York: Knopf, 1957.

Marshall, Dorothy. *Lord Melbourne*. London: Weidenfeld and Nicolson, 1975.

Martin, Philip W. *Mad Women in Romantic Writing*. New York: St. Martin's Press, 1987.

Masters, Brian. *Georgiana, Duchess of Devonshire*. London: Hamish Hamilton, 1981.

Mayne, Ethel Colburn. *Byron*. New York: C. Scribner's Sons, 1924.

———. *The Life and Letters of Anne Isabella, Lady Noel Byron*. New York: C. Scribner's Sons, 1929.

Medwin, Thomas. *Conversations of Lord Byron. Revised with a New Preface by the Author for a New Edition, and annotated by Lady Byron . . . and others who Knew the Poet Personally*. Ed. Ernest J. Lovell, Jr. Princeton University Press, 1966.

Melbourne, Elizabeth Milbanke Lamb, Viscountess. *Byron's "Corbeau Blanc": The Life and Letters of Lady Melbourne.* Ed. Jonathan David Gross. Houston: Rice University Press, 1997.

Mitchell, Leslie G. *Lord Melbourne: 1779-1848.* Oxford: Oxford University Press, 1997.

———. *Bulwer Lytton: The Rise and Fall of a Victorian Man of Letters.* London and New York: Hambledon and London, 2003.

Moore, Doris Langley. *The Late Lord Byron: Posthumous Dramas.* Philadelphia and New York: J. B. Lippincott, 1961.

Moore, Thomas. *Letters and Journals of Lord Byron: With Notices of His Life.* 2 vols. New York: J. J. Harper, 1830.

Morgan, Sydney Owenson, Lady. *Lady Morgan's Memoirs: Autobiography, Diaries, and Correspondence.* 2nd ed. 2 vols. London: William H. Allen & Co., 1863.

Morison, Alexander. *Outlines of Lectures on Mental Diseases.* 3d ed. London, 1826.

———. *The Physiognomy of Mental Diseases.* London: Longman, 1843. Repr. New York: Arno, 1976.

Nathan, Isaac. *Fugitive Pieces and Reminiscences of Lord Byron: Containing and Entire New Edition of the Hebrew Melodies, With the Addition of Several Never Before Published; the Whole Illustrated with Critical, Historical, Theatrical, Political, and Theological Remarks, Notes, Anecdotes, Interesting Conversations and Observations, Made by that Illustrious Poet: Together with His Lordship's Autograph; also Some Original Poetry, Letter and Recollections of Lady Caroline Lamb.* London: Whittaker, Treacher and Co., 1829.

Nathan, Isaac, and Lord Byron. *A Selection of Hebrew Melodies, Ancient and Modern.* (1815-16). Ed. Frederick Burwick and Paul Douglass. Tuscaloosa and London: University of Alabama Press, 1988.

Normington, Susan. *Lady Caroline Lamb: This Infernal Woman.* London: House of Stratus, 2001.

Norton, Caroline. *The Letters of Caroline Norton to Lord Melbourne.* Ed. James O. Hoge and Clark Olney. Columbus: Ohio State University Press, 1974.

Olney, Clark. "*Glenarvon* Revisited." *University of Kansas City Review* 22 (1955): 271-76.

O'Toole, Fintan. *A Traitor's Kiss: The Life of Richard Brinsley Sheridan.* New York: Farrar, Straus, and Giroux, 1998.

Palmerston, Emily, Viscountess. [formerly Emily Cowper and Emily Lamb]. *The Letters of Lady Palmerston: Selected and Edited from the Originals at Broadlands and Elsewhere.* Ed. Tresham Lever. London: John Murray, 1957.

Paston, George [E. M. Symonds], and Peter Quennell. *"To Lord Byron": Feminine Profiles Based Upon Unpublished Letters 1807-1824.* London: John Murray, 1939.

Paul, C. Kegan. *William Godwin: His Friends and Contemporaries.* 2 vols. Boston: Roberts Bros., 1876.

Peach, Annette. *Portraits of Byron.* Reprinted from *The Walpole Society* 62 (2000).

———. "San fedele alla mia Biondetta': A Portrait of Byron Formerly Belonging to Lady Caroline Lamb." *Bodleian Library Record* 14.4 (April 1993): 285-95.

Pierson, Joan. *The Real Lady Byron.* London: Robert Hale, 1992.

Ponsonby, Sir John. *The Ponsonby Family.* London: The Medici Society, 1929.

Rogers, Samuel. *Recollections of the Table-Talk of Samuel Rogers.* Ed. Morchard Bishop. Lawrence: University of Kansas Press, 1953.

Sadleir, Michael. *Bulwer: A Panorama—Edward and Rosina, 1803-1836.* London: Constable, 1931.

Sheridan, Richard Brinsley. *The Letters of Richard Brinsley Sheridan*. Ed. Cecil Price. 3 vols. Oxford: Clarendon Press, 1966.

Sichel, Walter. *Sheridan*. 2 vols. Boston and New York: Houghton Mifflin, 1909.

Small, Helen. *Love's Madness: Medicine, the Novel, and Female Insanity, 1800-1865*. Oxford: Clarendon Press, 1996.

Smiles, Samuel. *A Publisher and His Friends: Memoir and Correspondence of the Late John Murray*. 2 vols. London: J. Murray, 1891.

Soderholm, James. *Fantasy, Forgery, and the Byron Legend*. Lexington: University Press of Kentucky, 1996.

———. "Lady Caroline Lamb: Byron's Miniature Writ Large." *The Keats-Shelley Journal*. 40 (1991): 24-46.

Stauffer, Andrew. "Byron, Medwin, and the False Fiend: Remembering 'Remember Thee.'" *Studies in Bibliography* 53 (2000): 265-76.

Strickland, Margot. *The Byron Women*. London: P. Owen, 1974.

———. "An Early Pioneer." *Parents Voice* (1985): 22-23.

Stuart, Dorothy Margaret. *Dearest Bess: The Life and Times of Lady Elizabeth Foster, Afterwards Duchess of Devonshire, from her Unpublished Journals and Correspondence*. London: Methuen, 1955.

Thomas, Elizabeth. [Bridget Bluemantle]. *The Baron of Falconberg; or, Childe Harold in Prose*. 3 vols. London: A. K. Newman, 1815.

———. *Purity of Heart, or the Ancient Costume, a tale, in on Volume, addressed to the author of Glenarvon. By an old wife of twenty years*. London: W. Simpkin and R. Marshall, 1816.

Thorslev, Peter. *The Byronic Hero: Types and Prototypes*. Minneapolis: University of Minnesota Press, 1962.

Torrens, W. M. *Memoirs of the Right Honourable William, 2nd Viscount Melbourne*. 2 vols. London: Macmillan and Company, 1878.

Trotter, Thomas. *A View of the Nervous Temperament*. 2nd ed. London, 1807.

Vickery, Amanda. *The Gentleman's Daughter: Women's Lives in Georgian England*. New Haven & London: Yale University Press, 1998.

Victoria, Queen. *The Girlhood of Queen Victoria: A Selection From Her Majesty's Diaries Between the Years 1832 and 1840*. Ed. Viscount Escher. 23 vols. London: John Murray, 1912.

Villiers, Marjorie. *The Grand Whiggery*. London: John Murray, 1939.

Vincent, E. R. *Ugo Foscolo: An Italian in Regency England*. Cambridge: Cambridge University Press, 1953.

Wallace, Irving. *The Nympho and Other Maniacs*. New York: Simon and Schuster, 1971.

Wilson, Frances, ed. *Byromania: Portraits of the Artist in Nineteenth- and Twentieth-Century Culture*. London and New York: Macmillan Press and St. Martin's Press, 1999.

Wilson, Harriette. *Memoirs of Herself and Others*. (1825). London: Peter Davies, 1929.

Wolfson, Susan. "'Their She Condition': Cross-Dressing and the Politics of Gender in *Don Juan*." *English Literary History* [*ELH*] 54 (1987): 585-617.

Woolf, Virginia. *A Room of One's Own*. New York: Harcourt Brace & World, 1957.

Wu, Duncan. "Appropriating Byron: Lady Caroline Lamb's *A New Canto*." *Wordsworth Circle* 26.3 (1995): 140-46.

Ziegler, Phillip. *Melbourne: A Biography of William Lamb, 2nd Viscount Melbourne*. New York: Knopf, 1976.

Index